the
MYTH of
"BLOODY MARY"

THE
MYTH of
"BLOODY MARY"

A Biography of
Queen Mary I of England

LINDA PORTER

ST. MARTIN'S GRIFFIN ❧ NEW YORK

www.stmartins.com

The Library of Congress has catalogued the hardcover edition as follows:

Porter, Linda, 1947–
    [Mary Tudor]
    The first queen of England : the myth of "Bloody Mary" / Linda Porter.—
1st U.S. ed.
        p. cm.
    "First published in Great Britain as Mary Tudor : the first queen by Portrait, an imprint of Piatkus Books Ltd"—T.p. verso.
    Includes bibliographical references and index.
    ISBN-13: 978-0-312-36837-1
    ISBN-10: 0-312-36837-2
    1. Mary I, Queen of England, 1516–1558.   2. Queens—England—Biography.
    3. Great Britain—Kings and rulers—Biography.   4. Great Britain—History—Mary I,
    1553–1558.   I. Title.

DA347.P65 2008
942.054092—dc22
                                                                            2008013396

ISBN-13: 978-0-312-56496-4 (pbk.)
ISBN-10: 0-312-56496-1 (pbk.)

First published in Great Britain as *Mary Tudor: The First Queen*
by Portrait, an imprint of Piatkus Books

First published in the United States by St. Martin's Press as
The First Queen of England

First St. Martin's Griffin Edition: August 2009

10   9   8   7   6   5   4   3   2   1

To the memory of my beloved parents,
Kenneth and Kathleen Ford

Contents

Truth, the daughter of time

Mary's motto as queen

Acknowledgements

When I first told friends and acquaintances that I was writing a new life of Mary I there was a mixed reaction. Some agreed it was high time that England's first queen regnant was portrayed in a more positive light. Others, however, were convinced that the legend of Bloody Mary was so firmly established in popular consciousness that it would be impossible to change opinions. Yet there continues to be a growing body of cross-disciplinary research on Mary's life and reign which is opening up new ways of looking at the neglected mid-Tudor years. At the moment this is largely restricted to the academic community but it is worthy of a much wider audience. In researching and writing the book, I am conscious of the debt owed to the scholars who have specialised in the field, particularly Professor David Loades, Professor Robert Tittler and the late Dr Jennifer Loach. I hope that my biography will be a first step in bridging the gap and that it will persuade the sceptics that a historical reputation that has stood largely unchallenged for 450 years should be reconsidered.

Many people have provided guidance and support. I should like to thank in particular Charles Spicer, my editor at St. Martin's, for his consistent enthusiasm and suggestions for improvement. My agent, Andrew Lownie, has been an inspiration through a number of quiet years, when I almost gave up the idea of writing altogether. His constant encouragement is a great gift to authors. My thanks, too, go to Henry Bedingfeld for letting me see the wonderful collection of documents at Oxburgh Hall and for the hospitality that he and his wife Mary offered on a stormy November day. I am especially grateful to Jessie Childs for alerting me to what was at Oxburgh and for discussions on the Tudor period. Similarly, thanks are owed to Dr Alice Hunt of Southampton University for sharing her views on the latest direction of scholarly research. Professor Hilary Critchley at the Centre for Reproductive Medicine in the Queen's Medical Research Institute in Edinburgh took time to provide me with an understanding of the possible causes of Mary's health problems and I am grateful for her insights. On a lighter but no less fascinating note, Tanya Elliott advised on Mary's wardrobe and was eloquent in her own positive views of Mary herself. The superb replica of Mary's wedding dress is evidence of Tanya's enthusiasm for her subject, as well as her skill as a needlewoman. I must also thank Viscount and Viscountess De L'Isle at Penshurst Place for letting me see the portrait said to be of Mary in their private collection.

My thanks are also due to the ever-helpful staff of the London Library, the British Library, the National Archives and the Westminster Abbey Library. Last, but certainly not least, I acknowledge the debt I owe to my husband, George, who has lived longer with Mary Tudor than her own husband ever did. This book would have been impossible without him.

A note on monetary equivalents

Modern equivalents of 16th-century monetary values are generally avoided by scholars of the period. Rampant inflation, frequent debasement of the coinage and information on wages and prices that is, inevitably, incomplete have deterred most writers. This is not, however, very satisfactory from the perspective of the general reader, who would like some idea of what Mary's allowance from her father and her gambling expenditure, for example, might amount to today. I have used the equivalents given on Measuringworth.com, which was founded by Professor Lawrence H. Officer of the University of Illinois at Chicago and Professor Samuel H. Williamson of the University of Miami.

Picture credits

Prologue

4 July 1553

It is past midnight at the royal manor of Hunsdon and the rolling countryside where Essex meets Hertfordshire is hidden by the brief darkness of a midsummer's night. Yet there is activity; quiet, unobtrusive, but deliberate. A knot of people is gathering, ready to mount the horses that have been taken with great care from the stables, so that their hoofs hardly make a sound. The party is a small one, perhaps no more than four or five. In their midst is a thin woman, not beautiful but with a commanding presence, whose distinctive red hair is hidden under the hood of her cloak. Despite the warmth of the night, she prefers, indeed requires, to be hidden by her garments. She and her advisers have thought of a plausible story to cover her departure. They have put it about that her doctor himself is ill with the plague. Still, they would prefer her to be well away from Hunsdon before her absence is noted. This rural corner of eastern England is both the source of her wealth and her support but, in these unpredictable times, no one is to be entirely trusted. The fewer people, even in her own household, who know what she is contemplating, the better.

Once astride her horse – and she has been a fine rider since early childhood – she does not immediately move. For a few seconds, she looks back over the events of her dramatic life. She has lost much and now stands to lose even more. Once she was a princess, carefully raised to be a queen. She had felt secure in the affection of both her parents and confident that she would be able, when the time came, to fulfil the role of monarch. Then her world, a tranquil place of learning and music and privilege, came crashing down. Her father could not rid himself of the desire for a son and, as his anxieties preyed on him, so did the wiles of that woman whose name she could scarcely speak: Anne Boleyn. After six years of belaboured argument and spirited opposition, her mother, Katherine of Aragon, was cast aside and she, the true heir of England, bastardised. In the ferment, her father cut his allegiance to the pope in Rome and let heresy into his kingdom. There followed three years of absolute misery, during which she had known very little but persecution, ill health and fear. It ended with her capitulation to her father's wishes, but her conscience could never accept what her pen had signed.

Over time, she had been rehabilitated, even restored to the succession, but her illegitimacy remained. Her father's death left her a wealthy and independent woman. She was still denied the title of princess but she was her brother Edward's heir, by statute law and their father's will. But then arguments over religion began to threaten her security once more. The young king's councillors, those men with long beards in London, dared to tell her that she could not hear mass in her own house. She defied them and, in so doing, became a figurehead for opposition. She had known the price, even considered fleeing the country to be with her Habsburg relatives, but she was, at heart, an Englishwoman. And so she stayed, not realising that her brother, too, would turn against her.

All of this darts through her mind as she contemplates her situation. It is clear that the young king is dying and that she faces a period of great danger. The succession has been changed illegally in favour of her cousin, Jane Grey, but, in reality, to serve the ends of the duke of Northumberland. She has known him for 15 years, sensed his frustrated ambition when he lost position at the time of her father's divorce from Anne of Cleves, and watched apprehensively as luck and cunning helped him manoeuvre his way to supreme power. They have clashed openly, in front of the privy council. She knows his true feelings. He will keep her away from the throne that is rightfully hers if he can. She accepts that her liberty – and probably her life – is forfeit if he captures her. Whatever the future holds, she must now shape it herself, with the help of her loyal servants and the people who make up her affinity. They are not the great dukes and nobles of England but men of the lesser aristocracy. Like her, they support the old religion, the one true faith in which she has lived and will die.

So she sits and prays for guidance, to the God her mother's family has worshipped for centuries, as England itself did only six short years ago. And then it comes to her with absolute certainty that she will prevail.

All the doubts and fears evaporate in that one moment of divine conviction. This time, at last, the Lord is with her. Besides, she has always loved a wager and there could be no greater gamble than the one she is now taking. She turns, smiling in the shadows, to the gentleman beside her and nods. Then she spurs her horse to the north.

PART ONE

The Tudor Rose
1516 – 1528

Chapter One

Daughter of England, Child of Spain

'God send and give good life and long ... unto the excellent Princess Mary'.

Proclamation at Mary's christening, 20 February 1516

She was the child who survived. The midwinter baby born in the small hours of Monday, 18 February 1516, was bonny enough to dispel any immediate fears for her survival. After a difficult labour, Katherine of Aragon, queen consort of England, must have dared to hope that her prayers for a healthy child had, at last, been answered. Katherine did not know that news of her father's death had arrived in London only two days earlier; it was deliberately kept from her so that she could approach her delivery calmly.

In the seven years preceding the arrival of this daughter, Katherine had not produced the heir that either her father, Ferdinand of Aragon, or her husband expected of her. She had endured four miscarriages, one stillbirth and the death of an infant son who was not quite two months old. Seven years was a long time for England, a country so notoriously plagued by political upheaval and civil war, to be without an heir. This catalogue of failure had hit hard at the pride of Henry VIII's Spanish wife. Her deep religious faith and the determination she inherited from her parents, Ferdinand and his formidable wife, Isabella of Castile, had taught Katherine how to endure. Nor was Henry her first husband; that had been the doomed Arthur, Prince of Wales, Henry VIII's elder brother, who had left her a young widow in 1502. But in 1516 all the suffering of the past evaporated, at least temporarily, in the joyful realisation that she and Henry were, at last, parents.

The king's undoubted relief was evident. And any regrets about the baby's sex were disguised as optimism for the future. 'We are still young,' Henry told the Venetian ambassador, whose mingled congratulations and commiserations on the birth of a daughter evidently pricked him.[1] He expressed his confidence that, with God's will, sons would follow. But, at 31, Katherine was nearly six years older than her husband, and her gynaecological history was discouraging. What she privately thought of her chances we do not know but it was evident from the outset that she saw her daughter as England's heir.

Katherine and Henry were well matched intellectually. They had both received the benefits of an education by the leading humanists of Europe, at a time when learning was considered an essential part of the preparation for leadership among royal families. Both were the children of royal houses that had teetered before establishing themselves and there was a distant bond of consanguinity, going back to the marriage of John of Gaunt with Constance of Castile. They had known each other since Henry was ten and Katherine 15, when he had escorted her down the aisle at her first wedding. But, in 1516, the fact that Katherine had been his dead brother's wife was never mentioned.

Physically and temperamentally, however, the couple were completely different. Katherine had been a personable young woman, petite and slim. But years of pregnancies had now given her a figure that could optimistically be described as matronly. Her husband's French rival, Francis I, ungallantly described her as old and deformed, by which he meant that she was fat. After the birth of her daughter, she grew even fatter. On state occasions, resplendent in cloth of gold or silver and weighed down by expensive stones, she certainly had all the trappings of a queen, even if she did resemble a stout jewellery chest. She had always been a pious woman and still kept Spanish priests in her household. No one minded. Londoners, in particular, loved Katherine and her devotion to religion in her daily life was greatly admired.

That Henry no longer found her attractive is not surprising. But he respected her and she was still a force in politics, especially foreign affairs. In the first years of his reign she guided him through the turbulent waters of international diplomacy, with the dual aim of supporting Spanish interests and shaping her young husband as a serious force in Europe. She was an effective and energetic regent during the

Franco-Scottish wars of 1513. Henry probably knew what he owed her, though he may not have acknowledged it. Yet apart from a commitment to their regal responsibilities, they never had much in common. Henry's main pastime was sport. A tall and imposing figure at this stage of his life, Henry was a prince in his prime, handsome, gallant, a king to admire and revere. Katherine adored him and would do so until the day she died. He gave every appearance (and the appearance may have been misleading) of preferring the field and the joust to government. His personal favourites were bear-like men of little brain, such as Charles Brandon, duke of Suffolk, who had daringly married Henry's sister, Mary, without royal permission. He got away with it, and they continued to wrestle and ride in the lists, to hunt and backslap and enjoy the physicality of life. And while Henry was pursuing boar and deer in southern England, Katherine visited shrines, made offerings and prayed. Religious tourism was common in the early 16th century and it was one of the queen's major recreations. It also made her visible and popular.

Henry was an extrovert who loved music and public display. Katherine dutifully sat beside him and looked gracious, but her mind was increasingly elsewhere. Until 1516 she had played the role of consort with great aplomb, but her body had let her down. She could conceive easily but not bear healthy children. If she thought God was displeased, she kept her fears to herself and she turned, more and more, to religion. On that winter's day in the red-brick palace of Greenwich, it seemed that her devotions had finally been rewarded. It is easy to imagine that she felt that, at last, she had succeeded.

The little princess was named Mary, after her aunt, the beautiful and feisty star of Henry's court. Katherine and her sister-in-law were on very good terms and would remain so, but the queen was no doubt pleased at the choice of name for religious as well as family reasons. The child, small but pretty, already showed signs that she had inherited the red-gold hair of both her parents and the clear Tudor complexion. Few royal children can have been so longed for and so privileged. Her grandparents had been the foremost monarchs in Europe and her father was the epitome of a Renaissance prince. At the very least, she could expect to make an impressive marriage in Europe. If no son was born to Henry and Katherine, her future would be even grander. She would rule as England's first sovereign queen.

This was a glorious prospect, but not necessarily an enviable one. Mary was born into a turbulent Europe, where even the great flowering of art, literature, music and thought that characterised the Renaissance could not disguise the harsh nature of political realities. The balance of power might change but warfare was not just endemic, it was a prized way of life for the aristocracy. Europeans faced an existence that, for most, was indeed brutal and short. Recurring bouts of pestilence swept over the continent, decimating populations often weakened by famine. In 1485, the year of the accession of Mary's grandfather, Henry VII, England suffered its first outbreak of the sweating sickness, a type of virulent influenza that tended to be more prevalent in the warmer months. It struck swiftly and with frightening effect, killing seemingly healthy people in the space of 24 hours. By the time of Mary's birth the sweat, as it was known, was well established as an annual hazard. Just as deadly as the spectre of disease were the vagaries of the weather. Drought and flood ruined harvests, bringing further misery, and even the rich and high born, with more mobility and better diets, could not be sure of survival. Henry VIII spent every summer evading sickness by moving around the south of England, keeping well clear of London. His success in this respect did not make him less of a hypochondriac.[2]

In a Europe where life was so uncertain, the needs of the dead naturally occupied the minds of those who survived. The existence of God and the survival of the soul coloured the daily lives of everyone, from king to poorest peasant. Prayer was the means by which the living could intercede for departed loved ones, shortening their time in purgatory and eventually freeing them, it was hoped, from the torments of hell. These abstractions were absolute certainties for 16th-century people, for whom religion was as much a part of everyday existence as breathing and sleeping. But by the second decade of the century, there were many concerns about the role of the religious establishment that governed the earthly structure of religion. One minor aspect that would shortly acquire an unexpected significance was irritation at the idea that the soul could be speeded to its repose by the purchase of indulgences. This appealed to the gullible or just the plain lazy – prayer and Church ceremonial took up a lot of time – and it appealed to the Church's accountants even more. Everywhere, the power of the Church was evident and resented. The early 16th-century popes ran an enormously wealthy – and equally worldly – business enterprise. The Vatican was a byword for double-dealing, promiscuity and greed. Even the most devout sadly recognised that Rome was full of bankers and whores. As war leaders, the popes stood shoulder to shoulder with the kings of Europe and were determined, wherever possible, to profit from the conflicts that they so happily embraced.

But these failings and uncertainties were nothing new and they did not dent the enthusiasm of the rich and powerful in Europe for the good things of the Renaissance. When Mary was born the early artists were beginning to pass. Botticelli had died in 1510 and Leonardo, a refugee from his native Tuscany, died in France when Mary was three. Michelangelo, on the other hand, was at the height of his powers, having completed the Sistine Chapel in 1512. Desiderius Erasmus, the greatest of the humanist thinkers, was thriving in northern Europe, patronised by Mary's father and his fellow-monarchs. In the year before Mary's birth, Thomas More wrote his discourse on the ideal political state, *Utopia*, ensuring that the credentials of the English as contributors to the new ideas would be taken seriously. Universities throughout the continent thrived. Yet amid this ferment, fundamental questions about the nature of the relationship between the Church and the state, as well as the Church and the individual, had yet to find an effective outlet. Their first serious expression came from an unlikely source, when Mary was just one year old. An Augustinian monk in Germany, besieged by self-doubt and irritated by a friar from a rival order who was flagrantly selling indulgences on his doorstep, decided to raise an academic debate about the obnoxious practice of buying one's way out of sin. His name was Martin Luther. He would change the world, and, with it, the course of Mary's life.

The country into which Mary was born was regarded with varying amounts of condescension by its mainland European neighbours. The barbarity, duplicity and sheer effrontery of the English were often remarked upon. 'Pink, white and quarrelsome' was the splendid description of one group of disgusted Spanish visitors. England was not generally liked or respected in Europe. Ferdinand and Isabella considered it suitable only for their youngest daughter; they were not entirely convinced by the new dynasty's hold on power. When Mary was born, the Tudors had been ruling for only 30 years and Henry VIII's perception that his inheritance was not stable was real and alarming. England throughout Mary's lifetime was a dangerous, violent place, its political life characterised by faction and intrigue. Ambition could as easily bring death as power, and in this heated atmosphere men seldom kept their feelings in check. Tudor England was emotionally raw. It was not uncommon for blows to be exchanged in council meetings and Henry VIII himself apparently subjected his ministers to physical abuse. Cardinal Wolsey was known for his bad language; on one occasion he harassed a papal delegation who had come to see him and threatened them physically. Grown men wept readily, sometimes, no doubt, out of fear for their own survival. Ambassadors from France and Spain resident in London agreed on very little, but they both knew that you could not trust an English politician, no matter how much you paid him – and both countries often paid generously. The principled English politician seemed to be a contradiction in terms. Even worse were the general populace, a load of xenophobic drunks who would cut your throat sooner than offer you board and lodging.

Mary's Spanish inheritance, on the other hand, though no less violent in some ways, placed her at the centre of the struggle for power in Europe. In understanding Mary herself, this part of her background is often misconstrued. Generations of English historians have been mightily displeased with the fact that Mary was half Spanish, as if this 'impurity' of blood, in contrast to the wholly English credentials of her half-sister, Elizabeth, was some sort of birth defect. Yet, in 16th-century Europe, where dynastic marriages were a vital part of the struggle for power, such a descent would have been viewed as an asset, not a liability. The English kings were unusual in marrying their own countrywomen. This 15th-century habit was a result of a combination of civil war and personal inclinations which had kept them out of the European marriage market, and out of European influence, during the long period between 1445, when Henry VI married Margaret of Anjou, and 1501, when Prince Arthur married Katherine of Aragon. In later life, Mary would find her Spanish ancestry a source of both solace and pride, and she would look to the power of her mother's family to give England a role in Europe that she believed would enhance, rather than detract from, its influence.

Ferdinand and Isabella, Mary's grandparents, were, it has been said, the first 'power couple' in early modern Europe.[3] Theirs was certainly an effective, if sometimes fraught, alliance. Isabella was a warrior queen, equally ruthless in the pursuit of power and of religious certainty. She saw off the stronger claims of her niece to the throne of Castile with as much single-mindedness as she undertook campaigning in the south of

Spain against the Moors. Her alliance with Ferdinand was politically expedient to both of them but does seem to have been characterised by passion, despite Ferdinand's infidelity. Isabella was a woman of great mental strength and physical determination. The inconvenience of successive pregnancies and a growing family did not stop her spending long months with her armies, much of the time on horseback. She was a woman untroubled by doubt and her narrowly focused vision did not permit her to recognise the damage done to Spanish culture by the destruction of its rich Moorish and Jewish heritage. In an intolerant age, Isabella was a true heir of the Crusaders, and fiercely proud of her achievements. Her portraits show a reserved but determined, almost ascetic woman. It is not hard to imagine her in a nun's habit, but Isabella's service to the Lord was offered outside the cloister, on the battlefields of Spain. Her calmness is evident in her face. She knew that God had given her victory.

Nor does she ever seem to have questioned the ability of herself, a mere woman, to rule. Why should she? Political reality meant that her husband's need of her was actually greater than her need of him. This does not mean, of course, that she would ever have considered ruling alone and unmarried. Marriage was the destiny ordained by the God she served for all women, even queens who ruled in their own right. Her example was not lost on her own family, even if it did not find much of an echo in other European countries. And the growth of that family allowed the achievements of Isabella and her husband to reach beyond Iberia, so that two generations later their descendants would be the masters not just of Europe, but of the new worlds opened up by explorers they had supported. When Isabella's eldest daughter, the lovely but mentally unstable Juana, married Philip the Fair of Burgundy, two of Europe's most powerful ruling houses were united. The Habsburg family ruled much of Europe from the Low Countries in the north to the tip of the Iberian peninsula, and laid claim to most of South America. Isabella's grandson, Charles V, invested with the ancient title of Charlemagne, Holy Roman Emperor, was hated by Rome and feared by the encircled French. He was Mary's first cousin and a powerful presence in her life.

The daughter of Henry VIII and Katherine of Aragon, was, nevertheless, brought up as an entirely English princess. This emphasis began with her christening at the church of the Observant Friars in Greenwich, just two days after her birth. Following tradition, neither Henry nor Katherine was present at the ceremony, but the flower of the English nobility certainly was. Not since the marriage of Katherine and her first husband had so many of the great names of the aristocracy gathered together for a public event. It was not, however, a family occasion, like a modern christening, but an affair of state. Henry wanted to display his own continuing power in an impressive setting, and he also wanted to remind any of his great lords who might feel disgruntled that he was the heir of both York and Lancaster. Acting as one of Mary's godmothers was her great-aunt, Princess Katherine of York, the only surviving child of Edward IV. At 37, she was a young great-aunt, though already a widow. She had married Sir William Courtenay and become countess of Devon, where she lived in considerable style near Tiverton. How dutiful a godmother she was we do not really know, though the 1517/18 accounts show that she gave her god-daughter a golden spoon.[4] Mary was 11 when Katherine died in 1527. But Katherine's grandson, Edward Courtenay, earl of Devon, was closely linked to Mary at several points of her life and was considered more than once as a possible husband.

The Howard family, who had fought alongside Richard III at Bosworth Field but who were thereafter to serve the Tudors in a relationship that became increasingly strained under Henry VIII, also figured prominently at Mary's christening. The duchess of Norfolk was another of Mary's godmothers and her daughter-in-law, the countess of Surrey, carried the baby into the church. The christening was immediately followed, as was the custom, by confirmation, and this required a third godmother. The lady chosen was Margaret Pole, countess of Salisbury, the daughter of George, duke of Clarence – Shakespeare's 'fast, fleeting, perjured Clarence', memorably drowned in a butt of malmsey according to the playwright – and, as Mary's future lady governess, she would play perhaps the most important role of any woman in Mary's early life.

So Mary was christened surrounded by the mightiest of her father's subjects, those whom she could expect to command directly as his heir. To reinforce the significance of her birth, her godfather was Henry's chief minister, the immensely capable and gifted Cardinal Wolsey. The French king Francis, who had recently inherited the throne, was pointedly not asked. No one could have failed to miss the point that Henry so effectively made in choosing his daughter's godparents.

Four knights of the realm held the canopy over the well-wrapped baby as she entered the church. One of them, in an irony that became apparent only with the passage of time, was Sir Thomas Boleyn, a career diplomat of talent and ambition, who had sent his own daughter, Anne, to learn how to be a great lady in the courts of Burgundy and France.

The way to the church had been cleaned, gravelled and covered with rushes and the ceremony was carried out with all the pomp and circumstance required. Sixteenth-century London was surprisingly capable of producing spectacle at very short notice and it did not let Mary down at her christening. Once the ceremony was complete, the little princess was returned to her mother in the Queen's Chamber at Greenwich Palace, Katherine presumably having made a sufficient recovery from the birth 48 hours earlier to be up and about, at least for a while. We do not know when Henry first saw his daughter, though both parents were undoubtedly pleased with her. Henry was reported to have boasted that she never cried. In his presence, she probably never did. Mary was an attractive baby, and there was genuine parental affection. But she did not stay with them long.

From these very early days, Mary would live close to, but separate from, her parents. As a baby she seems to have stayed very near to them, and to have passed Christmas with them at Greenwich, but babies and all their paraphernalia did not figure in the day-to-day lives of 16th-century monarchs. There is evidence that Henry and Katherine, in particular, took more interest than other monarchs might have done in Mary's development, but the notion that Katherine raised her daughter herself is at odds with the role of a queen consort, and Katherine had been a very diligent practitioner of this role during her years of childlessness.

So, in the first two years of her life, Mary was cared for by a wet-nurse, Katherine Pole (later Lady Brooke), wife of one of the king's gentlemen ushers, a team of four rockers, no doubt intended to soothe her when she was lying in her magnificent cradle, and the highly necessary person of a laundress, to deal with all the washing that a small child generates. In the feeding, changing and daily routine of her daughter's life, Katherine took no part. We can imagine that every effort was made by Mary's first lady governess, Elizabeth Denton, to have the baby as presentable and quiet as possible when Queen Katherine came to see her. By 1518, Elizabeth Denton's role had reverted to Lady Margaret Bryan, who subsequently fulfilled the same role for both of Henry's much younger children when they were in the early stages of infancy.

The princess's household seems to have been a functioning unit within days of her birth. As well as the nursery staff and the lady governess there was a treasurer to manage finances, a chaplain and a gentlewoman. Mary's expenses soon began to grow. In the six months between October 1517 and March 1518 they stood at £421.12s 1d. By 1519/20 they had risen to £1,100, about £400,000 today.[5] Not until her father's death in 1547 would Mary actually have any income of her own, but she grew up as the focus of a substantial business unit, whose members had considerable responsibilities as well as privileges.

But it was also something more than a royal institution in its own right. Mary's household was, in a very real sense, her family. Katherine of Aragon conceived once more after Mary's birth, in 1518, but the child was another girl and we do not even know whether it was born dead or succumbed shortly after birth. From this point onwards, it was an accepted fact that Mary was her father's only legitimate child, and, therefore, his heir. The chagrin Katherine must have felt when Henry's mistress, Elizabeth Blount, gave birth to a son in 1519 did not cause her to fear for her daughter. Later, young Henry Fitzroy's position in respect of his half-sister was less clear-cut, though never in Katherine's mind.

Mary grew up surrounded by a staff who may well have had some degree of self-interest in maintaining their employment but who seemed to have held her in genuine affection. This early ability to inspire loyalty and love in those who served her remained a constant throughout Mary's life and she was always solicitous of her servants' welfare. Although she was a little girl in an adult world, her life was not necessarily devoid of amusement. A later fixture in Mary's life was her fool, Jane Cooper, one of the few female examples we have of a role that was generally given to men. The two seem to have had a close relationship, with Mary meeting Jane's expenses for haircuts and illness. Fools were not just entertainers, they were something of an emotional safety valve. It is probable that as a child Mary enjoyed the antics of her father's court jesters, even if there was no fool officially attached to her household.

There are no records of Mary having contact with other children or being educated with them, unlike her siblings Elizabeth and Edward two decades later. This is not conclusive proof that she grew up in complete isolation, and it is possible that she knew the daughters of her aunt Mary. Her earliest relationship, if it can be called that, with another child came in 1517, when she was named as godmother for her cousin, Frances Brandon, daughter of Mary Tudor and Charles Brandon. As young women in their teens, the cousins spent considerable amounts of time in each other's company. It may be that they saw each other occasionally when younger. Fate would strain their relationship to the limits, but not, finally, undermine it.

Mary's life was always peripatetic; she had no fixed abode. From her earliest days she moved from palace to palace, more in the summer than the winter, frequently close to her parents but not often staying with them. Most of her summer residences as a very small child were in the western Home Counties, where her father loved to hunt. In general, things were arranged so that Katherine could visit easily whenever she chose. But it was not her mother who saw the baby Mary from early childhood into womanhood. That responsibility lay with the countess of Salisbury, who was the main direct influence on the princess in the formative years of her life. It was a close and affectionate relationship that Mary never forgot, even when anguish and then death parted her from the woman who had raised her.

The countess had assumed the role of lady governess by May 1520, when Mary was four years old. Her appointment seems to have been at the express wish of the queen, who counted Margaret Pole among her closest friends. Margaret's son, Reginald, a key figure in Mary's reign, claimed that Katherine had been so keen for Margaret to take on the role of lady governess that she had been willing to go to his mother's house in person with Henry to implore her to take on the burden.[6] This does not seem to have been necessary. Margaret Pole knew her duty and was devoted to the queen. They had known each other since Katherine first came to England. Margaret's late husband, Richard Pole, had been Prince Arthur's Lord Chamberlain, and she had accompanied him to Wales during the brief five-month marriage of Katherine and her first husband. There a bond seems to have been forged between the two women, despite the fact that Katherine spoke little English and was 12 years younger than Margaret. Arthur's premature death at Ludlow parted them, but they continued to correspond until Henry VIII's accession rescued Katherine from penurious widowhood and made her the queen consort she had always expected to be. Margaret had also known financial distress during this period (her husband died in 1504), but her loyalty and friendship were not forgotten. She came to court with her eldest son to attend Katherine's coronation and was soon appointed one of the queen's chief attendants. In 1512, possibly at his wife's behest, Henry VIII granted Margaret's petition for restoration of the earldom of Salisbury and she became a countess in her own right.[7] This made her one of the most influential and powerful women in England. Her estates covered 17 counties as well as land in Wales, the Isle of Wight and Calais. It has been estimated that this placed her among the top five wealthiest nobles in early 16th-century England. She had four main residences in the south of England, one of which, Bisham in Berkshire, was sometimes used as a summer residence for Mary when she was a baby. Margaret's London house, Le Herber, stood on the site of what is now Cannon Street station.

Mary's lady governess was one of the foremost women of the realm, an entirely fitting choice for a difficult task. But, as the daughter of the disgraced duke of Clarence, she had grown up in perilous times, well aware of the dangers of proximity to the throne. The countess had much experience, even if it was indirect, of violence and intrigue. Her father was murdered on the orders of his brother, Edward IV, in 1478. He had also fallen out with his younger brother, the future Richard III. His demise left the five-year-old Margaret and her younger brother, the earl of Warwick, as the orphaned children of a traitor. Edward IV made them his wards but their future hung in the balance when he died. They certainly presented a threat to Richard III, because they could not be declared illegitimate like Edward's own sons. The children may well have escaped a similar fate to that which befell the princes in the Tower of London. Instead, they were sent north to Yorkshire. Henry VII placed Margaret and her brother in his mother's household on his accession and they returned to court. Margaret was married probably the following year to Richard Pole. She was a very young bride but the marriage seems to have been happy and gave Margaret security and stability, both of which had been lacking in her life until then. Her approach to the job of bringing up Princess Mary demonstrated how much she valued those aspects of her life. She certainly fared better than her brother, who was put in the Tower of London and later executed when he tried to escape with the pretender Perkin Warbeck.

When the countess of Salisbury entered Mary's life she was 47 years old and still an imposing woman. 'Tall, thin and elegant, she boasted the auburn hair of the Plantagenets and the pale skin which accompanied such colouring.'[8] She had five children of her own, including one daughter, Ursula, and she was intelligent, virtuous and pious. No stain attached to her person or behaviour and she had the considerable advantage of knowing the court and its etiquette inside out. A better choice for Mary's welfare or role as a princess could not have been made.

Her influence appears to have been quickly established. On 13 June 1520, the Lords of the Council wrote to Henry, who was in France with Katherine to attend that ostentatious display of one-upmanship between himself and Francis I known as the Field of Cloth of Gold, that Mary was 'daily exercising herself in virtuous pastimes and occupations …'[9] This was, of course, to be expected. No parent, and certainly not a king, wants to hear that his child is misbehaving, and playtime was probably not a 16th-century concept. But this does not mean that Mary was always treated as a miniature adult. The pattern of her year changed with the seasons, but the main excitement came at Christmas. Then the countess of Salisbury and other members of the princess's entourage made sure that there was plenty to entertain a little girl.

The household accounts give us a glimpse of the type of Christmas that Mary experienced. It is a far cry from the Germanic Christmases that were introduced into Victorian England and seems closer to a medieval celebration. But it was lively and very visual. The content did not differ greatly over time, but Mary may well have found such familiarity enjoyable as she grew older. In 1521 there was a Lord of Misrule, a kind of master of ceremonies, to lead Mary's festive entertainment. He was one of Mary's valets, John Thurgoode. Three boars, 'furious and fell', were purchased for the proceedings and the highlight was the ceremonial introduction of the boar's head, 'crown'd with gay garlands and with rosemary, smoak'd on the Christmas board'. The boar's head was an impressive sight, and painters and decorators were brought in to gild and decorate it.

Thurgoode was paid 40 shillings (around £700) for the costumes and entertainments he devised that Christmas. These involved a considerable number of players and props and a lot of activity and noise. There were two tabourets, a man who played the Friar and one who played the Shipman, a stock of visors, coat-armour, gold foil and coney-skins and tails for mummers. It is not clear precisely how these were used but there appear to have been a succession of tableaux or short plays. As well as the Shipman and the Friar, Thurgoode ordered four dozen 'clattering staves', two dozen morris pikes, 12 crossbows, gunpowder, four gunners, ten dozen bells, a hobby horse and enough straw 'to cover twelve men in a disguising'. Finally, in what seems to a modern reader a distressingly heartless role, there was 'a man to kill a calf behind a cloth'.[10]

There is every reason to suppose that Mary liked these raucous interludes. She loved such entertainments when she grew up and they figured significantly at her own court. She probably found them, as did her contemporaries, amusing and diverting. Her father was an inveterate japester who loved the old chivalric tradition of surprise and disguise. It is not hard to imagine the young princess laughing out loud at the comic antics played before her. So much of her life as a child seems to the modern eye to have been serious and dutiful, but it was not without times of relief and pleasure. Music became an early and abiding pastime and her delight in it was something she shared with her father. It may have been the earliest part of her education, and her precocious enthusiasm was noted when she was just two years old. On one of her visits to court she heard the Venetian organist, Dionysius Memo, playing for her father's guests and ran after him calling, 'Priest, priest!', not because she was interested in his religious role but to encourage him to play more.[11] Henry was proudly indulgent of this slight lapse in his child's otherwise dignified behaviour. Her taste he could not fault, since it had been Henry himself who brought Memo, the organist of St Mark's, to England not long after Mary's birth. Memo would give concerts after dinner, sometimes lasting up to four hours, 'to the incredible admiration and pleasure of everybody'. It seems likely that he was Mary's first music teacher. No young princess could have had finer.

The combination of lighter pastimes with an orderly existence would not in any way have deflected the countess of Salisbury's prime objective, which was to prepare her charge for the life of an English princess and a European queen. For even if there were, in the future, to be a male heir to Henry VIII, Mary's potential on the European marriage market was scarcely diminished. Henry always wanted a son, but now he had a daughter he was determined to use her as a diplomatic tool, early and often. This was not heartless, it was just good international relations. Accustomed to command from the moment she acquired speech, Mary found out not long afterwards that there would always be a string of suitors for her hand and that her appearances at court would often coincide with some new marriage negotiation. By the time she became queen, there had been so many suitors and betrothals that it seems unlikely that she could have kept track of them all herself.

The first of these came before Margaret Pole was part of her life. At the age of two and a half, Mary was betrothed to the dauphin of France and went through a form of marriage ceremony at Greenwich with her future husband's proxy, the French admiral, Bonnivet. Wearing cloth of gold and a bejewelled black velvet cap, she behaved impeccably during a long ceremony in which the bishop of Durham preached about marriage for the edification of the adults present. Henry may have been serious at the time but the power games of mainland Europe made it improbable that his daughter would ever be delivered to France. She was not expected until the dauphin was 14 and could consummate the marriage. As shrewd a participant in the ebb and flow of diplomacy as Henry VIII would at least have suspected that the path ahead was not straight. But, for the time being, it looked like a glorious match, even if Katherine of Aragon privately preferred one of her own relatives as a husband for Mary.

The first sign that all was not well with this Anglo-French union came when Mary failed to accompany her parents to the Field of Cloth of Gold in 1520. The meeting had been postponed from 1519, when Mary was expected to attend, but when it finally took place, she was not there. Her absence may have been regretted by Francis I's plain but intelligent wife, Queen Claude. As Mary's prospective mother-in-law she had already sent a jewelled cross worth six thousand ducats and a portrait of her son, the dauphin, but she was not rewarded with a sight of his child bride. There could have been any number of reasons for this, of course. There was tension between Queen Katherine and Cardinal Wolsey, a deterioration of what was often a difficult relationship. Perhaps Katherine did not want her daughter, still so young, caught up in this, or maybe she and Henry felt that a camp, no matter how luxurious, was not the right place for their child to be introduced to her in-laws and the devious world of diplomacy. We shall never know whether Henry would have shown off a son, if there had been one. As it was, Mary was spared any awkwardness and Henry did not have to face any potentially difficult questions about the succession.

The king of France, however, was not to be so easily deterred. Before Henry had even returned to England, Francis sent three of his gentlemen to see the princess. No doubt he wanted to make sure that she was in good health and did not have some physical or mental defect that had been concealed. Their coming was unexpected and their reception demonstrates how much importance was attached to the occasion and how the political and social establishment rallied round the princess. 'Notwithstanding the short warning', they were banqueted by the mayor of London, shown the major sights of the capital and entertained by the duke of Norfolk.

The countess of Salisbury would have explained to Mary who the gentlemen were and what was expected of her during their visit, perhaps even rehearsing the princess in what to do and say. Mary handled the situation with great aplomb for one so young, surrounded as she was by all the great and the good of England who were not accompanying her father to France. 'There were with her divers lords spiritual and temporal; and, in the Presence chamber, besides the lady governess ... the duchess of Norfolk, her three daughters' and several other titled ladies. The princess was a credit to herself, her parents and the probably anxious Margaret Pole. Her behaviour and demeanour were completely appropriate to the occasion. She entertained her visitors graciously on 2 July at Richmond, 'with the most goodly countenance, proper communication and pleasant pastime in playing at the virginals'.[12] The French deputation left suitably impressed by their royal hostess, after further generous hospitality: 'goodly cheer was made unto them ... strawberries, wafers, wine and ypocras [a kind of cordial] in plenty'. Yet by the time the year 1520 was out Henry, concerned by the implications of French aggression against Katherine's nephew, the emperor Charles V, was already considering a new match for Mary. The prospective bridegroom was Charles himself.

Charles was 16 years older than Mary and would have to wait another six years before she could reside with him, and perhaps two beyond that before they could cohabit as man and wife. Still, it was a wonderful opportunity for the English princess. Her marriage prospects had become even grander, and no one remarked on the irony of her first suitor having been a toddler and her second a man old enough to be her father. Royal marriages had nothing to do with sentiment and only rarely with suitability. The negotiations, the hammering out of carefully considered clauses, the tactical advantages, however brief, that might accrue to the parties, these were the aspects that mattered. They certainly exercised the minds of Henry and Wolsey on the English side and Charles and his advisers across the Channel. But it was not just Henry's underlying doubts about relations with France which made him think about other options for his daughter. In his instructions for the treaty negotiations, Henry pointed out: 'it is to be considered that she [Mary] is now our sole heir; and may succeed to the crown'.[13] This made his daughter a very valuable bargaining tool: 'We ought to receive from the emperor as large a sum as we should give with her if she were not our heir.' It also shows that Henry did not baulk at an alliance that would surely have major dynastic implications for England if Mary did become queen in her own right. It was never suggested that Mary should marry an Englishman. She was only six years old but she already knew that her destiny was to marry a foreign prince.

Despite the age gap, Charles was not necessarily an unsuitable husband for Mary. After all, he was family. He was her first cousin and papal dispensation was necessary for marriages with such close relations, but that was no more than a minor bureaucratic hurdle. It was precisely because Charles was her nephew that Katherine of Aragon, quietly triumphant at the disappearance of the French match, wanted him also as her son-in-law.

Charles was a tall, lanky, rather serious young man, not at all prepossessing physically. He was no storybook prince in this respect. If Mary expected him to rival her father in appearance, she must have been very disappointed. The emperor's prominent chin was the precursor of the famous Habsburg jaw that came to disfigure his descendants by the end of the 18th century. His father and mother had brought together Spain and the Low Countries, a union that was to prove as unhappy as their own marriage. When Charles's father, the inveterate womaniser Philip of Burgundy, died young, he left the Spanish wife he had never loved a disconsolate widow. She lived on for another 30 years but never wanted to govern. They called her Juana la Loca (Juana the Mad), but her main problem seems to have been chronic depression. In 1519 Charles's grandfather, Maximilian I, died and the young prince inherited Austria and Germany, as well as the ancient title of Holy Roman Emperor. It was a heavy mantle to bear. The problems that came with these vast territories, so soon to be the prey of social and religious unrest, were innumerable and, ultimately, insoluble. Charles's life was already dedicated to ceaseless hard work and the merry-go-round of diplomacy and war. Henry VIII's task as king of part of a small island must have seemed easy in comparison.

In 1522, as any dutiful fiancé should, Charles came to visit England. The treaty of Bruges, in which he and Mary were affianced and Henry promised him support in his continental struggles, had been signed the year before. Charles may have wanted to reinforce Henry's commitment by putting in a personal appearance. Perhaps he was at least curious to see his young cousin, though neither he nor Henry privately thought that there was much likelihood of her ever becoming his wife. We do not know how Mary felt. The idea of marriage can mean little to a six-year-old, especially one brought up an atmosphere as rarefied as Mary experienced. She would have associated her parents' marriage with being at court for great occasions, with the reverence they received and the power they evidently enjoyed. But since she had known only privilege herself, this may all have seemed perfectly natural. No doubt the importance of what was being arranged for her would have been explained in general terms and emphasis laid on the way she was to behave when she met the emperor. It has been suggested that Katherine may have put romantic ideas into her head about Charles and fed childish fantasies about the thrilling prospects of the imperial bridegroom who awaited her. But who knows what Mary's fantasies were? The pony and goshawk she was given about the same time may well have been more attractive preoccupations. Katherine was not an excitable woman by nature and though she would have wished – expected, indeed – for Mary to behave with all the aplomb that a carefully prepared little princess could muster, reminding her daughter of her dignity and underlining her importance are not the same as encouraging the child to think she was in love.

The visit was a great success at the time and both Mary and Charles played their parts perfectly. He had already had favourable reports on Mary's musical and dancing skills from his ambassador, who was invited to inspect the prospective bride's abilities in these courtly pursuits. On this occasion, Mary played the spinet and performed a French dance, the galliard.[14] Perhaps when Charles arrived she wore some of the jewellery that had been specially made for her, an impressive brooch with the name *Charles* on it, or another with *The Emperour* picked out in lettering. We do not know whether she danced in person for her cousin, but it seems probable that her parents would not have missed the opportunity for Mary to impress.

Although she was never to see him again, Charles stayed in Mary's mind. He was a charming and gracious guest and his visit was one of the great state occasions of the early 16th century. On his arrival by boat at Greenwich Palace on 2 June 1522, he was greeted by Queen Katherine and her ladies and, of course, the Princess Mary. All her life she remembered his kindness to her, which seems to have been natural and not in any way forced. What else does a six-year-old princess expect in a husband? Admiration for the way she carries out the set-pieces expected of a great lady? Compliments leading to evident parental approval of her deportment? Later, she would see him as a father-figure, a constant in times of unpredictable and unwelcome change, beset by danger. They had met when she believed her future was to be his bride, and both her parents talked of her as the heir to the throne. It was a happy time.

England took to Charles as well. He was the first – and, as it turned out, last – Holy Roman Emperor ever to visit and Londoners, who always loved a spectacle, warmed to him when he entered their city with Henry, accompanied by great pageantry and rejoicing. The emperor himself reported that he was 'met with a magnificent reception from a great company of knights and gentlemen, with solemn and costly pageants, to the great joy of all the people'. Records of the preparations made for two days of jousting, on 4 and 5 June 1522, are further evidence of Tudor England's impressive ability to entertain lavishly. For the decorative backdrop to the jousts, 46 yards of cloth of gold of damask, 11 yards of cloth of silver and 26 yards of russet velvet were ordered. One William Mortimer was hired to embroider the russet velvet with 'knights on horseback, riding upon mountains of gold, with broken spears in their hands and ladies coming out of clouds, casting darts at the knights …'.[15] Charles was equally well received as he toured southern England on a month-long hunting trip. When he left on 6 July, Mary's thoughts may have turned to making the trip across the North Sea to Brussels herself in years to come, as Europe's empress and England's queen. But it was not to be. Both Charles and Henry knew the harsh realities of diplomacy; the benefits of the treaty of Bruges were tangible but temporary. Charles needed a bride nearer his own age and readily available. A man with his responsibilities could not wait for years and years, no matter how sweet his little cousin was. So he married the handsome Isabella of Portugal, and she soon produced the male heir that his aunt had so conspicuously failed to provide for England. There would be plenty of other suitors for Mary's hand.

Perhaps she was disappointed. Or perhaps she never viewed it as anything other than a play in which she was the leading actress for a while. During this period of raised expectations Mary was without Margaret Pole, temporarily removed as lady governess because her daughter's father-in-law, the duke of Buckingham, had crossed Wolsey and been accused of conspiring against Henry. He was executed and Margaret, through association, found herself, not for the first time, mistrusted.[16] The affair, the first in Henry's reign when he moved against a great subject, blew over without permanent damage to Margaret. By 1525 she was back in charge of Mary's daily life and ready to support her in the next phase of her preparation for queenship. Henry, with an eye to the future, thought it was time that his daughter got some practical experience of government. He had decided to send her off to the Welsh Marches, where generations of princes of Wales had gone before her to play their part in the royal family and to finish their education. If Mary's childhood was not yet over, it was definitely entering a different and more serious phase.

Chapter Two

The Education of a Princess

'She is very handsome and admirable by reason of
her great and uncommon mental endowments.'

The French envoy, Turenne, reports on Mary in February 1527

At an early age, Mary had already been given a lesson in the harsh
realities of English politics and one that had a direct bearing on her
own life. To be near to her father was as dangerous as it was glorious,
though it is unlikely that she realised this at such a young age. No doubt
any questions she may have raised about the replacement of her lady
governess would have been met with easy answers and, even if there
were new relationships to be forged, her world, the world of England's
heiress, continued as before. By the time the countess of Salisbury
returned, the formal approach to Mary's education was established. It did
not encourage idle speculation about over-mighty subjects, and
Margaret Pole herself could be relied upon to keep quiet about the real
reasons for her absence. Failure to do otherwise would have put her in
great peril.

The king's decision to send his daughter to Wales does not mean that
her education had been neglected or unstructured up to that point. Both
parents took an evident interest in how Mary would be moulded to
meet her destiny as a king's daughter. Henry liked to show her off and
his attitude was part parental affection but also prudent. It was making a
statement about his own power and ambitions. The greater the effect
Mary had on those who met her, the more it reflected well on him. To

say that Mary was brought up 'among the women' is to give a false impression of the learning she had already received. Like other European princesses, she was taught by men, following the precepts of the leading thinkers of the day. Her education was at the cutting edge of Renaissance theory, though there must have been a need to adapt it to her own abilities. But her unique situation as Henry's successor was enveloped in uncertainty. Here the theorists and tutors were in uncharted territory, for no one had ever formalised how a future queen regnant should be taught. Did her preparation need to be different from that of a male heir? The question was never directly raised, and Henry, who was privately ambivalent and touchy about the future, did not encourage such speculation. Neither did Katherine, who always believed with absolute firmness that her daughter must inherit the throne and did not want to open up a debate on the subject. She made sure that Mary would be appropriately trained for what lay ahead.

Information on Mary's early studies is fragmentary, but a considerable amount can be deduced, pieced together from reports of her official appearances and the accounts of her household. As she grows older, the picture becomes clearer and a polished humanist princess emerges from the schoolroom. Even as a very small girl, she was able to acquit herself superbly in public demonstration of her skills, and there were regular occasions of state that kept up the pressure on her to show what a king's daughter could do.

She clearly had an early aptitude for music and dancing and grew to be highly accomplished in both. At the age of four she could play the virginals and she later learned the lute and the regal.[1] Playing these instruments was one of her main sources of relaxation and entertainment as she grew up, and the comments on her ability seem to have been more than the studied politeness of official observers. Dancing was also a vital accomplishment for royal ladies, and Mary's enjoyment of it began early. She learned to dance at least as well as any lady at her father's court. After Henry's death, her brother Edward VI would criticise Mary for her unseemly devotion to this pastime at which she excelled.

Mary also became an accomplished linguist and had evidently learned some French by 1520, when she so impressed the French lords sent to inspect her. Again, this may have been, like the musicianship, a skill inherited from her father, who used it to communicate with the emperor's French-speaking diplomats throughout his reign. There would have been no need for such a young child to converse at any length, only to demonstrate that she could exchange pleasantries and formal greetings. As an adult she relied on her French for communication with the imperial ambassadors at a time when they were almost her sole support and, later, for speaking to her husband. She may have picked up some Spanish from those around her mother, overhearing the conversations of Katherine with people like her confessor and her ladies-in-waiting, but the numbers of those who had, long ago, accompanied Katherine from Spain were dwindling, and the queen did not regularly use her native tongue any more except with her priests. Mary could, though, read Spanish; in the 1530s, when their worlds changed so dramatically and Katherine needed to be very careful in her letters to her daughter, she wrote to Mary in Spanish. The princess, however, does not seem to have spoken it well, and she did not use it in public.

We do not know who taught Mary her first French, though there were French speakers at court and she may have received initial coaching from one of them. Nor is it possible to say with precision how she acquired basic literacy in English. The notion that Katherine of Aragon sat down and taught her daughter the alphabet is fanciful. It is appealing to think of the Spanish queen and her dutiful daughter bending their heads over Mary's first attempts to form letters, but they were apart too often for Katherine to have had a sustained role as a teacher.[2] Her oversight of the process of Mary's education was, though, close. She followed Mary's progress keenly, and there is no doubt that her influence would have started as soon as Mary could talk and be socialised.

There is not a separate line in the princess's accounts for a schoolmaster until she went off to Wales in 1525, when Dr Richard Fetherstone is first mentioned. Probably Mary learned the basics of literacy from her chaplain, Henry Rowle. General education as well as religious instruction was one of the services performed by chaplains for aristocratic households.[3] At the age of nine, Mary could already write in Latin, and her first steps in this language, the prerequisite of greater learning, may well have been guided by one of the foremost English humanist scholars of his day, the royal physician, Thomas Linacre.

Linacre was a distinguished Oxford scholar who, like many of his contemporaries, had travelled widely in Italy at the end of the 15th century. He combined an interest in Greek with medicine and his translation of the Greek physician, Galen, into Latin gave him a European reputation. He took his medical degree in Padua in 1496, and two years after Mary's birth, in 1518, he and five other physicians, supported by

Wolsey, petitioned the king to set up a College of Physicians in London. Katherine of Aragon had first met him during her time as princess of Wales, when he had been Prince Arthur's tutor. She seems to have supported his appointment as royal physician when Henry VIII came to the throne. His credentials as a scholar would have made him an ideal choice for introducing a princess to the study of classical and humanist Latin.

By the time Mary came to sit down with her first Latin textbooks, probably at the age of around seven, Linacre was more than 60 years old and greatly revered. He counted among his friends the three leading English humanists, More, Colet and Grocyn, and the towering European figure of Erasmus. He had already published, in English, two works on Latin grammar, and was shortly to bring out a more detailed one, in Latin, for students who had gone beyond the basics. Mary's ability in Latin was widely remarked upon by the time she was 12, so it seems that the elderly Linacre, who died in 1524, gave her a good grounding in its study.

Perhaps in his medical capacity he also advised on the importance for a child of a healthy lifestyle. Certainly, the physical side of Mary's early education was not neglected. Sixteenth-century England placed a great deal of emphasis on physical fitness, believing that it was good for moral fibre as well as warding off sickness. Despite the challenges of long clothing and the vagaries of the weather, Mary was expected to exercise regularly: '… at seasons convenient, [she is] to use moderate exercise for taking open air in gardens, sweet and wholesome places and walks which may confer unto her health, solace and comfort …'.[4] She would have been able to ride before she received the present of a horse from Lord Abergavenny in 1522, and she enjoyed horses and hunting throughout her life. Her accounts for that year show only one stable-boy, but her stables quickly grew, as was to be expected with an expanding household. She also kept a pack of hounds and liked coursing and hawking. Such blood sports were an essential part of aristocratic life. Mary was introduced to them early.

Though Queen Katherine's personal presence in Mary's schoolroom was irregular, she had considerable input into her curriculum. At about the same time that Linacre was putting the princess through her first

Latin primer, Katherine, looking to underline her credentials as a patron of new ideas, commissioned a work on female education. The writer was the Spanish humanist Juan Luis Vives, and his book, *The Education of a Christian Woman*, was considered radical. In his introductory letter to Katherine, Vives made a claim that ran counter to the still-prevailing negative attitude of the time towards women – he stated unequivocally that the proper education of a woman, as man's essential companion, was vital for the well-being of the state. It was an outlook shared by Katherine herself and it coloured her own attitude to the role of a queen consort. But what did it mean for Mary, when she came to succeed her father?

Many writers have seen Vives as a malign influence on Mary's entire life. In effect, he has been accused of taking an intelligent girl and denying her the chance, through his theories, of developing as an independent, confident woman. This fits well with the long-held view of Mary as a victim; at the point in time when she began the more serious part of her schooling, she was trussed into the straitjacket of Vives's ideas and emerged permanently damaged, believing that she was inferior to men and could not trust her own judgement. In this interpretation, she never stood a chance of being a successful ruler since her education had alienated her from the very qualities needed to become one. Nearly a generation later, her much younger half-sister, Elizabeth, benefiting from the new ideas that spread with the Reformation, was not so encumbered and was thus better equipped to take the reins of government.

This conveniently symmetrical explanation for one of the apparent differences between the daughters of Henry VIII has condemned Vives to be widely misunderstood and, more seriously, to be judged without reference to the context in which he produced *The Education of a Christian Woman*. Katherine of Aragon commissioned him to write the work in 1523, shortly before his arrival in England to take up a teaching post at Oxford. She may have been inclined to patronise him because he was Spanish (he was from Valencia), but it is more likely that she chose Vives because he was already a well-established writer and thinker. After studying in Paris, he was appointed professor of the humanities at Louvain, a leading centre of study in the Low Countries. While there, he wrote a general treatise on education, *On the right method of instruction for children*, and a commentary on St Augustine's *The City of God*, which he dedicated to Henry VIII. If not directly competing with her husband in her support for learning, Katherine certainly wanted to be identified

with Europe's prominent thinkers. In this ambition, she was typical of
most high-born women of her day. It was an outlet for their intellects
and interests in a world dominated by men, and it gave them influence
and, indirectly, power. But it does not necessarily follow that Katherine
intended Vives's work as a precise blueprint for Mary's tutors to follow.

In the unctuous introductory letter to his treatise, Vives made it clear
that he understood that the commission was more about Katherine than
it was about Mary:

> I dedicate this work to you, glorious Queen, just as a painter might
> represent your likeness with utmost skill. As you will see your physical
> likeness portrayed there, so in these books you will see the image of
> your mind, since you were both a virgin and a promised spouse and a
> widow and now wife (as please God you may long continue) and since
> you have so conducted yourself in all these various states of life that
> whatever you did is a model of an exemplary life to others. But you
> prefer that virtues be praised rather than yourself ...

Quite what Katherine made of these references to her early life in
England, as well as the strange aside about her marriage, is impossible to
know. It would have made uncomfortable reading in the years to come.
But then Vives turned to Katherine's daughter, the beneficiary, he hoped,
of his ideas: 'Your daughter Mary will read these recommendations and
will reproduce them as she models herself on the example of your goodness and wisdom to be found within her own home.' A touching idea,
but very much at odds with reality; Katherine and Mary had never lived
together in the kind of cosy domestic bliss that Vives described. He
would, of course, have known this very well, but it sounded good and
related to the philosophy he developed in the writing itself. So he
continued in confident vein: 'She will do this assuredly, and unless she
alone belie all human expectations, must of necessity be virtuous and
holy as the offspring of you and Henry VIII, such a noble and honoured
pair.' Clearly, it was important to remember Henry as well, and not just
for form's sake. Vives believed that the institution of marriage itself was
the foundation of society. He went on to conclude: 'Therefore all
women will have an example to follow in your life and actions ... and
precepts and rules for the conduct of their lives. Both of these they will
owe to your moral integrity'.[5] In these closing lines, Vives demonstrated
a shrewd understanding of his royal patron. Katherine's moral integrity

was the cornerstone of her being and the unwavering certainty it gave her she would pass on to Mary. The princess did not need Vives's prompting, as she grew older, to absorb its importance.

The Education of a Christian Woman has irritated many commentators in modern times, though the most recent edition is more generous in its editorial stance and acknowledges that Vives's insistence on the intellectual superiority of women is important. But social equality was not something that the Spaniard advocated. His emphasis on the domestic virtues desirable in women is very much in tune with his times – and, indeed, the prevailing attitudes of the next four hundred years. If this seems unrealistic as part of the education of a future queen, it is worth bearing in mind that Katherine of Aragon and her sisters had been taught to bake bread as children in Spain. Presumably they had little occasion to put their expertise into practice as adults. Mary herself told her brother's privy councillors that 'her parents had not taught her to bake and brew', but Vives would have considered this an omission; it was directly counter to his own ideas. He thought all girls should learn the art of cooking, though 'not the vulgar kind associated with low-class eating houses'. Vives envisaged something closer to a domestic goddess than an innkeeper's wife, a woman not afraid to work with her hands, fully equipped to manage a home. We should not sneer too much at his insistence on the attainment of such attributes. Running a large household in the 16th century was a formidable undertaking. The skills it called for were eminently transferable to the running of a country, even if this was not officially recognised by a patriarchal society.

Before the Renaissance, women had been seen not so much as second-class citizens as a subspecies. They were the living embodiment of the biblical Eve, an outgrowth of the male that was tainted by sin. Their weakness was explored in the French work *The Romance of the Rose*, which, despite its pretty medieval title, saw women as defiled. The suggestion that such creatures were scarcely fit to inhabit the same world as men was challenged, not surprisingly, by women themselves, notably Christine de Pisan, in her *Book of the Ladies*, written in 1405. Once the debate was opened, the general climate of questioning which characterised the Renaissance had led to the topic recurring and male as well as female writers taking up the pen.[6] Some even argued that women were superior to men.

Vives upheld this view, saying that women often exceeded men in their intellectual capacity. The problem, as he and many contemporaries saw it, was not their minds, but their bodies: 'In the education of a woman the principal and, I might say, the only concern should be the preservation of chastity.' There are seven pages in *The Education of a Christian Woman* on the virtues of virginity, and the overall assessment of the carnal weakness of the sex is highly pessimistic. Women were to be kept away from men at the onset of puberty: 'During that period they are more inclined to lust.' How to cope with these sudden, raging sexual appetites that consumed previously innocent girls? Vives's philosophy did not lend itself to sex education.[7] The best approach was through diet. Frequent fasts were beneficial and 'a light, plain and not highly seasoned diet' was recommended. One fears that girls brought up in this way, struggling with the hormonal changes of puberty, would have had little enjoyment of life, but it was not all deprivation. Water was the best drink, but a little wine or beer was permissible. The importance of sleep was also recognised: 'The sleep of a virgin should not be long but not less than what is good for her health.' It was an austere regimen and not to be relieved by the frivolity of nice clothes or any jewellery other than simple adornment. Silks and fine linens were too worldly and cosmetics vile – rouge and white lead had no place on a Christian face. But worse than all of these was idleness of mind and body because it could easily introduce a girl to completely unacceptable pastimes such as cards and dice. The mere thought of the gaming table appalled Vives: 'What will a woman be able to learn or think about, who gives herself to gambling?' he lamented.

The princess for whom these blandishments were intended clearly did not read the distinguished humanist's writings too closely. Or perhaps she did, but could not really see herself as Vives's prototype. In truth, not much of it was relevant to her. Mary was a great lady, a future queen, leading a life of luxury and complexity beyond the imagination of ordinary people. She was expected to dress superbly and wear gorgeous jewels, to symbolise power and magnificence in a way that all her father's subjects, from the highest to the lowest in the land, would understand. She might be a weak woman as far as the theory went, but the real princess was a person apart, for whom Vives's images of simplicity had no meaning. The moral precepts (and they were important) aside, she would not have recognised this colourless, idealised figure so diligently constructed in *The Education of a Christian Woman*. Her life was privileged, comfortable and predictable. Much was expected of her and she was carefully nurtured to meet these expectations, but austerity was not something she knew as a child. Attention was certainly paid to her diet, which was not as rich as an adult's, but she was spared the light-headedness of regular fasting recommended by Vives. As the head of her own court, she was served separately, with as many as 35 different dishes to choose from. This might make a fussy eater, and Mary does seem to have become difficult where food was concerned in her later teens, but that was partly through stress and ill health.

During her time in Wales, the array of offerings had more to do with etiquette than with choice. This was how a princess was served. But variety there was in plenty: seasonal fruit and all sorts of meat and game, desserts and cheese. The ambiance in which Mary ate was also carefully considered. Despite popular Hollywood myths of the Tudors, and especially Henry VIII, as gargantuan eaters with the table manners of swine, dining was intended to be a civilised experience for Mary. Her meals were to be taken with 'comfortable, joyous and merrier communication in all honourable and virtuous manner'. And, in an age when personal cleanliness was inhibited by the sheer weight of fancy and heavy clothing, not to mention the problems of bathing in draughty, poorly heated rooms, Mary's servants were to make sure that she achieved standards of hygiene that would have pleased Vives. Careful attention was to be given 'unto the cleanliness and well wearing of her garments and apparel, both of her chamber and body, so that everything about her be sweet, clean and wholesome ... as to so great a princess doth appertain, and all corruptions, evil airs and things noisome and displeasing to be forborne and eschewed'.[8]

It was in the area of her own amusements that Mary diverged most dramatically from the life of Vives's Christian woman. From her early teens, she adored the very pastime the Spanish educationist had so abhorred. She became an inveterate gambler. Her passion for cards and dice never faded. She was not, and never would be, the one-dimensional girl who could only be fulfilled through domesticity. A princess has the power to follow her own inclinations, and Mary preferred a wager to the embroidery needle. On the scale of priorities for equipping her for her adult life as the heir to the throne, it hardly seemed to matter.

In this situation without precedent, the content of the princess's syllabus was all important. Yet here, key issues were fudged. It was not in Vives's brief to address the political implications of Mary's status, and his writing implied that Mary would marry, an assumption that provided an inbuilt solution, or, at least, a deferment of difficult decisions about her role as head of state. Vives's work was as much moral as practical, but his suggestions for the substance of Mary's education, the actual reading and study, may well have been followed by her tutors. They certainly reflected the belief in a classically based education that characterised the teaching of royal offspring throughout the courts of Europe. The emphasis was on the great Latin writers, St Augustine, Boetius, Tertullian, Cicero and Seneca, and in reading Latin translations of the Greek philosophers such as Plato. The Bible was also a favourite source of reading matter. Lighter material did, of course, exist, in the form of chivalric romances, but Vives felt that these were unsuitable for girls, who might get carried away with ideas of courtly love. Licentious books, such as Boccaccio's *Decameron*, were definitely to be avoided. This all sounds very dry; Vives's syllabus, though not perhaps suppressing all imagination and enquiry, especially in a good intellect, was nevertheless unlikely to foster these qualities. Whether it was followed more or less closely, Mary developed as a girl with a sound knowledge of the great writers of antiquity, who could translate to and from Latin with considerable facility and who had an abiding love of books. Her study of French continued, under the guidance of Giles Duwes, who had been one of the gentlemen of her chamber but was now given accreditation as her French teacher. Apart from Mary, there was not much call for his services in Wales.

As she grew up, it was evident that Mary was a credit to her tutors. She expressed herself with clarity and elegance. Her hand was clean and legible, much easier to read because it is personal handwriting, rather than the stylised hands used for official 16th-century correspondence. If not truly precocious, she was certainly gifted and her progress seems to have satisfied both of her parents.

Mary's studies continued to occupy her mother's mind even after she had left for Wales and Katherine could no longer participate directly in her education. There was regret but also optimism. The appointment of Richard Fetherstone seems to have pleased the queen, who was confident that he could improve Mary's Latin: 'As for your writing in Latin, I am glad that ye shall change from me to Master Federston [*sic*], for that shall do you much good to learn by him to write aright.' But she would like to see some of Mary's work once the tutor had corrected it, 'for it shall be a great comfort to me to see you keep your Latin and fair writing and all'. This wistful undertone and references to her husband and daughter's 'long absence' as well as her own health, which she describes as only 'meetly' good, tell us that the queen was far from happy at the parting with her daughter.[9] The circumstances of Mary's move had made her angry at first, and regretful, but in the end the honour accorded her daughter must surely have given her satisfaction.

Not since Prince Arthur's sadly brief sojourn had there been a member of the royal family living in Wales. How comfortable Katherine was in discussing this with her daughter we can only guess. She had long been Henry VIII's wife, not Arthur's widow, but it seems unlikely she would have dwelt on the topic, and Mary, with the innate understanding that her upbringing had already given her, probably did not press her mother for information. Ludlow Castle, where Katherine and her first husband lived, was the traditional seat of princes of Wales, but it was in desperate need of repairs. Though these were undertaken and Mary's council was based at Ludlow, there is no evidence that Mary actually lived there during her time in the Marches. Tickenhill, in Worcestershire, was a palace that she used, as well as Hartlebury. But in the summer of 1525 she went first to Thornbury Castle, not far from Bristol.[10] On a clear day, taking one of the walks prescribed as beneficial to her health and overall contentment, the princess and the countess of Salisbury could have looked out over the lovely surrounding countryside and seen the Severn estuary and the hills of Wales, Mary's principality, in the distance. Margaret Pole may have had mixed feelings about her destination. Thornbury had been built by the executed duke of Buckingham, whose fatal clash with Henry VIII first parted the princess and herself four years earlier. On arrival, she was no doubt too busy to concern herself overmuch about the castle's builder, and she seems to have found her time in the Marches pleasant enough.

The official line on Mary's move was straightforward; Wales needed government: 'forasmuch as by reason of the long absence of any Prince making continual residence either in the Principality of Wales or in the marches of the same, the good order, quiet and tranquillity of the countries thereabout', it was claimed, had been 'greatly altered and subverted', and the administration of justice had suffered.[11] The statement overlooked the reasons for the long absence, the lack of any prince of Wales for a generation. And there was ambiguity in Mary's new responsibilities; the title of 'Princess of Wales' was never formally bestowed on her, though she was a Tudor and had more Welsh blood than any other prince sent to Wales, except for Prince Arthur himself. She was, though, often referred to as princess of Wales until 1533, and seems to have adopted that style herself. The move reinforced her position as Henry's only legitimate child and his presumptive heir, but it did not mean that Henry was comfortable with the inevitability of her succession.

The international situation in the momentous year of 1525 had changed the balance of European power decisively in favour of the emperor, and Henry had ample reason to reflect on what this meant for his kingdom. In February, on the plains of northern Italy, Francis I of France suffered a crippling defeat by the imperial forces at the battle of Pavia. His army of 28,000 men was all but annihilated, and Francis himself taken as a prisoner to Madrid. He managed to negotiate his release, at the price of giving up all claims to Italy and sending his two eldest sons into an honourable captivity for several years, as hostages. This level of personal misfortune was something that Henry, for all his difficulties, would never know. Yet while the outcome was a triumph for Charles V, it did not necessarily sit well with the king of England. The rivalry between Charles and Francis suited him, allowing him to act as mediator and ensuring that he was courted by both sides. Now Charles, all at once disturbingly powerful, did not need him. The impact this would have on England was uncertain. It brought the absence of a male heir into sharp perspective once again.

Troubled by what might lie ahead, Henry decided to give both his children, the legitimate Mary and her half-brother, Henry Fitzroy, places in the administration of the realm. Katherine was appalled at this elevation of the king's bastard son, who had been living quietly away from his now safely married young mother.[12] Uncharacteristically, for she knew her husband and his likely reaction very well, the queen lost control of her emotions and let her displeasure be known. This outspokenness did not sit well with Henry or with Cardinal Wolsey, who had been charged with the supervision of young Henry Fitzroy's upbringing. Disconcertingly, as far as Katherine was concerned, Wolsey was godfather to both Mary and young Henry. There was no love lost between the cardinal and the queen, who had spent much of Henry's reign warily circling one another. The role of Henry Fitzroy was another area of conflict between them and, on this occasion, Katherine saw herself as the loser. Her perception was not necessarily correct, but the insult mattered a great deal to her at the time.

Of course, a nine-year-old girl and a six-year-old boy were not expected to execute power themselves, but they represented the king as important figureheads. Their wider educations, through observation and the association of their names with the exercise of authority, would also benefit. So, as Mary prepared to turn west, Bessie Blount's son was given the double dukedom of Richmond and Somerset, created earl of Nottingham and Knight of the Garter and named as lord admiral of England. On 28 August 1525, with a larger retinue than Mary, he took up residence in Yorkshire as head of the Council of the North, an institution that had fallen into abeyance. Some may have seen in this an indication that Henry intended to make him his heir. They were reading too much into the situation, as it turned out. Henry put great stock in legitimacy. There was no precedent for an illegitimate son succeeding. It called into question the very institution of monarchy and Henry was a stickler for moral and legal principles when it came to the future of his throne and dynasty.

Mary was probably unaware of any of these developments. They had no direct impact on her own life or status as she knew it. She may not even have known of her younger brother's existence at this stage. But Katherine of Aragon saw the boy as a threat. It could even have been her outburst against the elevation of the duke of Richmond which sealed Henry's decision to separate her from Mary and let both of his children develop well away from the court. Mary does seem to have missed her mother initially, or, at least, to have been concerned about her welfare. She may have sensed the queen's reluctance when they parted, as she certainly wrote swiftly, enquiring about her mother's health and updating her on the progress with Richard Fetherstone. Her attentiveness gave Katherine some solace, as did the presence of Juan Luis Vives himself at court. But the queen's isolation was growing and the separation from Mary only underlined this. Katherine realised she would need to adjust; yet she was pensive rather than despairing and saw no reason why, if she continued to show the forbearance she had uncharacteristically abandoned in the summer of 1525, all would not continue as before.

Early in August 1525 Mary and her senior household officers and councillors were gathered together at The More, Wolsey's residence near Rickmansworth in Hertfordshire. Over lunch, their duties were outlined by the cardinal, rather as the board of a large business nowadays is briefed by its chief executive. Wolsey was responsible for all the arrangements and appointments for Mary's new role, and he was keen to ensure that everyone understood what was expected of them. This would have included Mary herself, the centre of all this attention. On 12 August the princess and her retinue began their journey westward. It must have been an exciting moment in Mary's life, as all the carts and provisions, the great servants and the humble ones – her affinity, as they were known – left Wolsey's elegant home for parts of England that many had not seen before. Clad in Mary's personal colours of blue and green, the princess's retinue moved by easy stages to Thornbury, where they arrived on 24 August.

Although many appointees to Mary's new household were already living in the Marches, her train was impressive. Certainly the household itself was greatly expanded, officially numbering 304 persons. Re-established at the same time to undertake the practical business of government in Wales was a separate Council of Wales and the Marches, the counterpart of the young duke of Richmond's Council of the North. Its president, John Veysey, bishop of Exeter, was already over 60 years old and better known for his courtliness than his spirituality.[13] Mary, however, seems to have viewed him with favour. His delightful manners and love of ceremony probably appealed to her. Like many people who were with her in her childhood, he was not forgotten by her, and she made sure that he was restored to the bishopric of Exeter, from which he resigned during her brother's reign, when she became queen. By that time he was approaching 90. As president of the council, Veysey had a substantial staff. He was supported by a chancellor, six lawyers and a secretary as well as the ceremonial posts of a herald, a pursuivant and two serjeants-at-arms. A suite of 41 personal servants was assigned to the council itself. In practice, there was a blurring of distinction between appointments; some of the leading members of Mary's household acted as councillors themselves if the need arose for greater membership to deal with specific aspects of administration.

How much Mary knew of the council's day-to-day activities is impossible to say. It was what she represented which mattered. The experience of ceremonial and the ability to behave appropriately, to begin to create an image – these were all deemed to be important for Mary's development. The many visitors who daily thronged her court in the Marches are testimony of the importance that local families attached to her presence among them. There were so many of these importuners that Veysey, only too well aware of Mary's place in national life, became

concerned by the potential threat to her health. Disease spread easily in
crowded places in the warm summer days. But Mary stayed healthy and
adapted well. If she missed her mother's visits and the familiarity of the
royal residences in the Home Counties, she did not show it. Nor would
it have been wise to report any misgivings back to the court in London.
Princesses were supposed to know their duty, and those who served
them would be blamed if they fell short of the high standards expected.
It was the countess of Salisbury's task to make sure that the transition
from London to the Marches was as smooth as possible. Mary's welfare
was the first consideration and Katherine of Aragon was comforted by
the knowledge that her old friend was at her daughter's side.

Initially, Mary would not have known the knights and minor nobleman of Wales who sought her favour, and most of the members of her
large establishment were new faces. The most remarkable of these, in
terms of a colourful past, was Mary's chief lady-in-waiting, Lady Katherine Craddock. This Scottish-born noblewoman had been the wife of
Perkin Warbeck, pretender to Henry VII's throne. She could have opened
Mary's eyes to the fleeting nature of happiness and the uncertainty of the
future but she had long since obliterated the memory of Perkin. Content
now as the wife of a knight with substantial lands in Glamorgan, it is
unlikely that she entertained the princess with her life story. She had once
been a great beauty, but there were no children to inherit her looks. She
and the countess of Salisbury had both known the fickleness of fortune
but their job was to provide Mary with stability, not to raise the spectre
that the course of her own life might not run smooth.

The most striking aspect of the three most senior members of Mary's
household in Wales is how old they were. Margaret Pole, Katherine
Craddock and John Veysey had a combined age of 173. They were
undoubtedly experienced and worthy but not, one would have thought,
the most stimulating of company for a girl of nine.

Of the rest of Mary's Welsh staff, only Katherine Pole, her former wet
nurse, Alice Baker, one of her ladies, and Richard Sydnor, promoted to
be treasurer of the chamber, had been with her since her birth. Her laundress, the Welshwoman Beatrice ap Rice, joined the household in 1519
and stayed with her throughout Mary's life. The others were newcom-
ers, about a quarter or more of them from Wales. Mary's arrival was a
godsend for these Marcher families, neglected for a generation, who had
reason to see the princess as a good employer, as well as their liege lady.
Within a year, the total expenses of Mary's household and council, plus

the upkeep of several palaces, ran to £4,500. Her presence in the Marches came at a high cost.

Mary's daily life as the head of a large household was structured and not too onerous, regardless of how many lords seeking redress or favour besieged her courtyards and Presence Chamber. The frequent moves from one residence to the next might seem unsettling, but they were an accepted part of court life, and Mary had never known anything else. She did not expect to live in one place for more than a few months and often for no more than a few weeks.[14] Location mattered far less than the familiar rhythm of day-to-day activity. Its focus was religious observance and her studies, as well as regular exercise, and relaxation, in the form of music or drawing. There was great emphasis on purity of body (in the form of attention to personal cleanliness) and spirit. The countess of Salisbury was explicitly directed that Mary must 'at due times, serve God'. This meant the observance of the forms of traditional religion, the hearing of mass at regular intervals during the day and time spent in prayer and reading of scripture. The mass and prayer were the outward forms of religious observance that Mary shared with all her countrymen. They were the markers of daily life that had endured for centuries. Probably most people did not think about them too deeply and were not encouraged to do so. There was comfort in the familiarity of the great religious festivals and the processions that accompanied them, a kind of free entertainment for the ordinary people. All these holy days were observed in Mary's household, which was untouched by any taint of religious controversy. There were undercurrents of discontent with the church in England, dismay at its power, wealth and worldliness and disgust at the ignorance and lax attitude of many parish priests. Mary knew little of this. Across the Channel, there was much more serious religious ferment, but it did not intrude into Mary's upbringing. The countess of Salisbury, a devout woman herself, did not need to be told her duty. The princess's spiritual development might be guided by her chaplains but behind them was Margaret Pole, the epitome of a Christian noblewoman, whose son Reginald, the future Cardinal Pole, had already committed his life to the Church. Mary did not really know this distant cousin then, but she would have heard about his progress from her lady governess, who was a proud mother.

Mary is so closely identified, even today, with Roman Catholicism that it is difficult to disentangle the woman from her faith. Popular history books still refer to her as 'the Catholic Queen', implying that this was an impediment, an underlying flaw that may explain, but cannot condone, who she was. Yet nobody thought of her, during her childhood, as 'a Catholic Princess'. What else would a princess of England be? Her own father had issued a learned broadside against the teachings of Martin Luther in 1521 and been awarded with the title of Defender of the Faith. In Mary's early childhood, there was no irony in that. As she knelt before the priests of her household at mass, Mary would not have recognised herself as the pious practitioner of an old-fashioned, beleaguered creed. The religion that she followed was so much a part of her life that she probably did not dwell on it at all. It was the ritual she grew to love; the familiar cadences of the Latin, the superb, uplifting music, the colour and richness of the textures of robes and ornaments. Religion was beauty to Mary, a beauty that daily gave hope of eternal life. For at its centre was the miracle of the translation of the bread and the wine into the body and blood of Christ, a mystery that promised salvation to every soul. But her personal beliefs were unremarkable. Her father loved his mass as well, even when he had long since parted company with the rule of Rome. Mary was no different from her parents, her cousin the emperor or, in 1525, all but a small number of Englishmen who were beginning to be influenced by ideas from the nearby Continent. The worship of God was at the core of her life and would always be there.

When she translated the Prayer of St Thomas Aquinas into English at the age of 11, while still in Wales, she saw it primarily as a school exercise, something to prove to her mother that the Latin was going well. The prayer may have been suggested by Fetherstone but it could have been her own choice. Given its sentiments, it is tempting to think that the princess may have thought, as her life unfolded, of the lines she had translated when the world revolved around her:

> Good Lord, make my way sure and straight to thee, that I fail not between prosperity and adversity, but that in prosperous things I may give thee thanks and in adversity be patient, so that I be not lifted up with the one, nor oppressed with the other … My most loving Lord and God, give me a waking heart, that no curious thought withdraw me from thee. Let it be so strong, that no unworthy affection draw me backward. So stable that no tribulation break it. And so free that no election by violence make any challenge to it.[15]

Religious practice was not confined to Church ceremony and Mary's establishment played its part in the giving of alms to the poor and the sick. When Mary was a very small child this was obviously done in her name, but as she grew older she took an interest in the recipients themselves. She was a regular, though not extravagant, benefactress. It was part of her duty as a Christian and a great lady.

Mary passed from childhood to the threshold of womanhood while she was based in the Marches. This was, in itself, part of the reason for sending her there. The 16th century had no concept of adolescence, and if 12 seems young to be considered as an adult, it was also viewed as old enough to marry and cohabit. The girl herself, the real Mary, is elusive, but not invisible. The infant princess, who had expressed so early a love for music, charmed visiting French diplomats and endeared herself (though nothing more) as the child-fiancée of the emperor Charles V, was becoming a young lady. She had poise and regal bearing and she loved her parents. Mary was solicitous for her mother's health but enjoyed her father's company, his *joie de vivre* (which she seems to have shared, for it was remarked that she was a joyful child) and the culture of his court. Her time in Wales was a progression in her training, not a banishment, and she returned to court for state occasions. The Christmas of her first year away she did not spend with her parents but the late summer of 1526 was passed with the king and queen in Oxfordshire and Gloucestershire. She journeyed with them west to Ampthill until 1 October, when she returned to Wales. Richard Sampson, diplomat and confidant of Wolsey, witnessed her arrival at Langley, near Woodstock. He was struck by her composure and bearing: 'My lady princess came hither on Saturday; surely, sir, of her age as goodly a child as ever I have seen, and of as good gesture and countenance.'[16] He was also impressed by Mary's substantial retinue, many of whom were apparently present when she and her father greeted each other.

Foreign commentators spoke highly of Mary as well, and it is from them that more can be discovered about her appearance. In the spring of 1527 the Venetian ambassador, Gasparo Spinelli, writing to his brother, was nearly breathless in his description of the princess and the magnificent pageant in which she had played a prominent part. This spectacle was part of the entertainment given by Henry VIII to honour the count of Turenne and other French dignitaries, as discussions continued about another French marriage for Mary. This time the prospective bridegroom was the second son of Francis I, the duke of Orléans, and Mary was very much on show.

After a joust marred by the spring rains, the company went back to the palace at Greenwich to witness the kind of spectacle for which the English court was renowned. Spinelli said he had never witnessed the like, anywhere. The decorations, the plate used at the sumptuous banquet, even the decorum and silence in which such public entertainments were given, all amazed him. Yet most stunning of all was the princess Mary herself. She was one of eight damsels 'of such rare beauty as to be supposed goddesses. They were arrayed in cloth of gold, their hair gathered into a net, with a very richly jewelled garland, surmounted by a velvet cap, the hanging sleeves of their surcoats being so long that they well nigh touched the ground.' In this company, Mary outshone all the others: 'Her beauty in this array produced such an effect on everybody that all other marvellous sights ... were forgotten and they gave themselves up solely to contemplation of so fair an angel. On her person were so many precious stones that their splendour and radiance dazzled the sight.' Mary and the ladies then performed a dance with great skill. And at the end, when Mary presented herself to her father, he 'took off her cap, and, the net being displaced, a profusion of silver tresses as beautiful as ever seen on human head fell over her shoulders'.[17]

It is a wonderful description, but Spinelli's Italian gallantry was perhaps overstated. Mary's hair was auburn, not silver, unless it had been specially dressed for the occasion. Nor was his rapturous description of the princess's appearance shared by the hard-headed Turenne. The Frenchman confined his compliments to Mary's intellectual achievements, but his primary concern was to find a bride who could be married without delay. In his judgement, Mary was 'too thin, spare and small' to be married for the next three years. She did not look like childbearing materrial for the House of Valois. The French king took Turenne's advice. He married his son, the future Henry II, to a plainer, podgier and very rich young Italian called Katherine de Medici. She failed, for many years, to produce children, but when she did, they came thick and fast. Her marriage was desperately unhappy and there is no reason to suppose that Mary would have fared any better, so perhaps it was a lucky escape.

So there were contrasting views of the princess, but they were not necessarily contradictory. Mary was described elsewhere as being small for her age, though before her teens her health does not seem to have been a problem. She was a small-framed person, which might explain

Turenne's comments about her weight. There were reports in 1528 that she was suffering from smallpox, but if she did it could not have been a serious bout of that often deadly and disfiguring ailment. One thing on which all observers would agree, throughout her life, was that she was blessed with a beautiful complexion. She seems also, as a girl, to have had a charming and endearing personality, not as extroverted as her father but less withdrawn than her mother, or, at least, as her mother had become. Her servants loved her devotedly and she frequently repaid them with lifelong support. She revered and loved her parents, and she was a dutiful god-daughter, writing to Wolsey in 1528 that she knew it was through his intercession that 'I have been allowed, for a month to enjoy, to my supreme delight, the society of the king and queen my parents.' The one thing that had vexed her, she told the cardinal, was that she had been unable to visit him and thank him personally for 'your frequent favours vouchsafed to me and mine'. It is the earliest of Mary's letters to survive, and it has about it an air of sincerity and warmth.[18] Mary was a princess full of grace, with the presence of royalty and a mind well suited to the duties that lay ahead.

Another Italian, Mario Savagnano, was not so effusive as Spinelli when he met Mary four years later, at the palace of Richmond, though he acknowledged that she was attractive and accomplished. Mary came out to greet Savagnano and other members of an Italian deputation, supported by the faithful countess of Salisbury and six maids of honour. He described her as 'not tall, [she] has a pretty face, and is well-proportioned [no longer, apparently so thin and spare], with a very beautiful complexion … she speaks Latin, French and Spanish, besides her own mother-English tongue and is well-grounded in Greek and understands Italian but does not venture to speak it'. This, if true, showed a formidable range of linguistic achievement. 'She sings excellently and plays on several musical instruments, so that she combines every accomplishment.' After the Italian visitors had left, Mary, ever the perfect English hostess, sent them a present of wine and ale and white bread.[19]

The princess Mary was 15 when she received this testimonial, though four years had passed since she was recalled from the Marches. At the time, her return may not have been intended as permanent – she had come and gone on several occasions during her residence there – and the Council of the Marches continued to function at Ludlow till 1534. Yet Henry chose to keep his daughter in the south-east of England and her public appearances became less frequent. The reasons for this are not clear. There were concerns about the size and expense of her establishment in the west, but this could always have been managed differently. Far less easy for Wolsey, or anyone else among the king's advisers, to soothe was their monarch's underlying doubts about the wisdom of having Mary, no matter how well trained, succeed him at all. The failure of yet another French marriage negotiation could have played on Henry's mind. The inescapable truth was that the future of the Tudors depended on a young girl and her ability to produce the male heirs that Henry himself did not have. Even if there was a realistic chance that she might do this by the age of 16, the interval in between would have been uncomfortable, given the state of European politics. And the personality of the king himself was hardly that of an indulgent grandfather.

There was no hint of tension or undercurrent of concern in the Italian account of the meeting with Mary, but by then both she and the countess of Salisbury knew that her life had lost the simple certainties of childhood. This unpalatable truth, complicated by the onset of menstruation, was made worse because it had been unspoken. The countess had seen it as her duty to protect Mary for as long as possible, rather than introduce her to emotional complexity or the harsh realities of power politics. This well-meaning reluctance only made the inevitable realisation of what was happening to her parents' marriage harder for Mary to bear. Even when she grasped it, when it became impossible to shield her any longer, she still refused to face the implications for her own situation.

Yet the disaster that would overturn her world had been creeping up on Mary for some time; its origins went as far back as 1522. In that year, the year of the princess's engagement to Charles V and the emperor's memorable visit to London, the daughter of an English knight and diplomat made a sensational debut at the English court. Her sophistication, wit and sexuality immediately made her the centre of attention. In Katherine of Aragon's rather staid circle of ladies and maids of honour, there was nothing like this newcomer at all. She had been educated as a European gentlewoman in the courts of Burgundy and France, but her charisma was all her own. Her name was Anne Boleyn, and when she eventually caught the king's eye, the course of English history, and of Mary's life, was changed.

PART TWO

The Rejected Princess
1528–1547

Chapter Three

The Queen and the Concubine

'I say I am his lawful wife, and to him lawfully
married.'

Queen Katherine to a delegation of the king's council, 31 May 1531

Anne Boleyn is English history's most famous 'other woman', and
before he became a wife-murderer, when he was still full of longing
and the romance of unfulfilled love, Henry VIII wrote her a series of
beautiful letters. No Renaissance monarch could have better expressed
the journey from the stylised amours of courtly love to the passion of
real emotion: 'The proofs of your affection are such,' he wrote at the
beginning of 1527, 'the fine poesies of the letters so warmly couched,
that they constrain me ever truly to honour, love and serve you, praying
that you will continue in the same firm and constant purpose, ensuring
you, for my part, that I will the rather go beyond than make reciproque,
if loyalty of heart, the desire to do you pleasure, even with my whole
heart root, may serve to advance it.'[1]

The extraordinary woman who prompted such proofs of her
monarch's devotion was a tall, dark-eyed brunette, attractive but not
really beautiful, with an oval, almost sculpted face and long, elegant
fingers. Henry's former mistress, Bessie Blount, despite a name which
conjures up the image of a plump housewife, was said to be considerably better looking. Anne's figure was trim rather than voluptuous and
contemporaries were critical of her lack of embonpoint, though it does
not seem to have bothered Henry. What she possessed in abundance was

presence, and she was well aware of the effect that she had on men. Today we would describe her as charismatic and sexy; she was the sort of person who stood out in a gathering because of her personality and social skills. The style of her dress, her deportment, her repartee, her sense of fun, all underpinned by a keen intelligence, gave her an edgy distinctiveness. This was no mean achievement in a fiercely competitive setting, where ladies who wanted to make good marriages vied with each other for attention. Henry's court was a difficult place for women who got it wrong. Though Katherine of Aragon might be increasingly devoted to things of the spirit, her husband's courtiers were largely pursuing personal power and fleshly pleasures, and who better to provide the latter than the young ladies paraded by anxious parents in court society. A daughter could be as much a key to worldly success as a son, but the pitfalls if she succumbed too soon to the temptations of the steamy atmosphere of court life were very evident to Anne Boleyn. Her elder sister Mary had a reputation, on both sides of the Channel, for sleeping with anyone. A brief period as Henry's mistress had seen Mary fade into obscurity and had not materially advanced her family's prospects. Widowed young, she settled down and married for love, without seeking permission. She was relieved to be away from court, with all its hypocrisy and intrigue. Only the passage of time would show that Mary was actually the more fortunate of the two sisters.

Anne continues to divide opinion, nearly five hundred years after the obscene charade of her downfall. To her enemies, she was nothing more than an upstart schemer, an alluring opportunist who seduced the king from the affections of his lawful wife, bastardised and ill treated his daughter and opened the floodgates for the tide of new religious ideas to sweep over England. She was characterised as an outspoken, self-serving shrew who failed to produce a male heir, could not hold the king's affections, and got her comeuppance. Many thought it richly deserved but others, who had known her well, thought of her as a highly intelligent woman with an enquiring mind, genuinely committed to religious debate and the study of the scriptures in English. They pointed to her interest in education and the poor and the higher standards of behaviour among the ladies of her court, a contrast to the decadence from which she had emerged.

Fascination with Anne Boleyn has never gone away, but the scholarship of the last two decades means that we know a great deal more about her tempestuous life and can make more balanced judgements about her role. In fact, Anne was of good birth and closely related to both the Howards, who, as dukes of Norfolk, were the premier aristocrats of England, and to the earls of Ormonde, the top echelon of the Anglo-Irish nobility. Born in Norfolk, she certainly spent some of her childhood at the Boleyn family's mansion at Hever in Kent, but she was no country girl with artificial airs and graces beyond her station. Her father, Sir Thomas Boleyn, was one of the most able diplomats of his day. A fluent French-speaker, he was highly regarded by Margaret of Austria, regent of the Low Countries, and by Francis I of France. It was Sir Thomas's standing with these rulers which enabled him to give his younger daughter an advantage over her potential rivals in England, by sending her to their courts to be educated and 'finished' as the perfect female courtier. So Anne began her notorious career as very much part of the establishment, though with the secret weapon of an exotic continental gloss.

Yet to her denigrators, she came to represent alienation – of a king from his queen, of a country and its Church from the rest of Christendom, of a father from his daughter. To the imperial ambassador, Eustace Chapuys, struggling to support his master's suffering, humiliated aunt and cousin, she had no redeeming features. Mostly, he refused even to name her, as if denying her identity might in some way minimise her power and the wrong she had done. To him she was merely 'the Concubine', a disgraceful appendage to Henry's life unworthy of individual recognition.

In Anne's path, some political careers stumbled and were lost while others prospered. The king's long-serving chief minister, Cardinal Thomas Wolsey, who had orchestrated Princess Mary's time in the Welsh Marches, could not persuade the pope to free his master from Katherine of Aragon, and was dismissed. Meanwhile, Anne's family and those who had supported her received honours and titles, and Thomas Cromwell, one of Wolsey's men, stepped out of the shadows to implement the dismantling of the English Church. Even at the time, Anne was seen as a catalyst for changes in English society. These might, indeed probably would, have happened without Anne, since they mirrored convulsions shaking Europe as a whole, but her own personality and interests influenced the direction that England took. For six long years this redoubtable woman was at Henry's side, as neither wife nor mistress, encouraging, cajoling, complaining, wheeling and dealing, but never, ever contemplating defeat. She had committed to him as wholeheartedly as he committed to her. She would be England's queen, not a royal mistress, whatever the cost. And the cost, in money, prestige and international uncertainty, was high indeed, even if the ultimate rewards of sole authority in religious matters in England and the financial subservience of the English Church to Henry were worth the battle. It was a struggle with one major winner – the king – and many losers. And chief among these losers were Katherine of Aragon and her daughter, the princess Mary, who was to become Anne's mortal enemy.

Nobody had a more lasting impact on Mary than Anne Boleyn. Like Chapuys, Mary would not even pronounce her name – 'that woman' was how she described her, and we can almost see the shudder when she uttered the words. Yet there was much more to their mutual enmity than mere personal hatred. Anne had a profound effect on Mary's relationships with her father and mother and on her own view of who she was. Her physical health and emotional well-being never fully recovered from the strain of the break-up of her parents' marriage and the anguish that followed. In exploring what happened through Mary's eyes, it is possible to learn a great deal about the woman she became.

In other circumstances, Mary and Anne might have respected each other and even been companions, at least in the sense that favoured ladies-in-waiting were part of the inner circle around queens and princesses, close enough to be a comforting presence in their daily lives. The two women shared a love of music and dancing and a taste for the latest fashions. Both liked display and creating an effect in public, though Mary would have expected to be noticed by virtue of who she was, while Anne needed to work harder, using her training and wits. Anne had to entertain while Mary expected to be entertained. They were well-educated ladies, but to different ends, and Anne Boleyn had a far wider frame of reference than Mary. Growing up in Margaret of Austria's court at Mechelen in the Low Countries, she had been developed under the direction of one of the most cultured women of the early 16th century. From there she went to join the entourage of Henry's sister, Mary, during her brief reign as queen consort of Louis XII of France. For reasons that are not clear, Anne stayed on in France after Louis's death and joined the household of Queen Claude, the 15-year-old wife of the new king, Francis I. For the better part of seven years she was one of Claude's ladies, supporting her through annual pregnancies in the pleasant surroundings of the Loire chateaux. Francis used the delicate Claude as breeding stock but otherwise largely ignored her. His behaviour could not have left Anne, who was the same age as the queen, in any doubts about the basic expectations of the queenly role, but this does not seem to have been a deterrent in her own life.

So Anne, unlike Mary, knew about other countries and their customs first hand. She spoke French because she had lived there, rather than having been taught it by a schoolmaster in a quiet room in an English palace. And she had a far better idea of the ebb and flow of influence at court, the shifting allegiances and factions in which friends could become foes in a very short space of time. Flexible and intuitive, a natural manipulator, she simply knew more about the world than Mary did. And she was 15 years older. Yet when it came to confrontation, Anne found Mary an implacable opponent.

Mary probably saw Anne for the first time during the pageants given in honour of the imperial ambassadors who had come to finalise the details of the treaty of marriage between herself and Charles V, in early March 1522. It is unlikely she took especial interest in her. Why should she have noticed one among many of the pretty ladies who entertained the diplomats, when she herself, a six-year-old princess gorgeously bejewelled and attired, was the centre of attention? Yet the occasion was important for Anne, her first public performance at Henry's court, and one for which she was well prepared. She was one of eight ladies, each representing a female virtue, who played in an entertainment known as the *Chateau Vert*. There is no modern equivalent of this piece of theatre, which was a spectacle without words, relying on lavish display and expenditure and evidently some degree of forward planning and rehearsal but not really calling for any acting ability. Anne would have known the plot, if it can be called that, already, since the *Chateau Vert* (a specially constructed wooden castle, painted green) was one of a number of standard masques involving imperilled ladies requiring rescue by chivalric forces, in this case led by the king himself. The performance took place after supper (which was eaten early, around five in the afternoon, in Tudor times) and the princess Mary would have watched as her aunt, known for ever after her few months in France as 'The French Queen', took a starring role representing Beauty, one of the eight qualities of the perfect mistress. Anne Boleyn was Perseverance, her sister Mary, Kindness, her future sister-in-law, Jane Parker, was Constancy

(peculiarly inapt, in view of the role she would play in the downfall of
two of Henry's wives, Anne herself and Katherine Howard), and
Gertrude, countess of Devonshire, a close friend of Katherine of Aragon,
appropriately took the part of Honour.

Anne was clearly in good company as Henry and his knights, at first
repulsed with a shower of sweets and rosewater, eventually overcame the
ladies' reluctance by a barrage of fruit. She and her companions emerged
from the castle and agreed to dance with their chivalrous pursuers before
the audience and performers went off to an expensive banquet, and the
young princess, perhaps, went off to bed. The occasion must have been
an exciting one for a little girl, but for Anne it was, despite the significance of the underlying international politics, very much a reflection of
her upbringing and its accompanying expectations. She was trained as a
court entertainer and knew her place. She must look decorative, perform
professionally in masques, dance well and hold her own in social conversation. Flirtatious behaviour with admiring gentlemen was perfectly in
order, so long as the bounds of decency were not exceeded. After all, the
idea was that one might become her husband. A princess had different
standards and Mary's husband, it was believed, would be grand indeed.
Sexual attractiveness, even a pleasing personality, was not required by
either party, despite the ritual exchange of portraits. It was all about power.

It is not possible to say when Henry VIII first noticed Anne Boleyn,
though she evidently did not make an immediate conquest of him by
her performance in the *Chateau Vert*. Her father he knew well and her
sister he preferred to forget. In the years between Anne's court debut and
Princess Mary's departure for the Welsh Marches, Henry had many other
things on his mind. Chief of these, the one that would not go away –
indeed, got worse with every passing year – was the succession. For
although Mary never acknowledged it, and probably did not realise it at
the time, her father had decided to end his marriage to Katherine of
Aragon before he fell in love with Anne Boleyn. If it had not been Anne,
it would have been someone else. Henry's growing affection for Anne
explains the timing of his moves to have his marriage to Katherine
formally annulled, but it was not the prime motive. That motive had to
do with power and security, just as in the marriage negotiations with
Charles V, which never came to anything. Indeed, it could have been the

realisation of just how difficult it was proving to find a match for Mary, young as she still was, which brought home to Henry the realities of a situation that he regarded with growing desperation.

In 1525 he was only 34 but his wife was 40 and it was obvious she would never have any more children. The future of his dynasty, and of England, lay with a girl of nine, unlikely to produce children before her mid-teens at the earliest. Who was to say they would be sons, even when they came? And if they were, would they be true heirs of England, or, more probably, foreign princes brought up outside the realm? Though he had himself acknowledged that Mary was England's heir, Henry never fully convinced himself that she could succeed him as queen in her own right. There were too many uncertainties, and these concerns themselves weakened Henry's own position. Eventually, there came a point when he told himself that matters must be addressed, that sending his illegitimate son off to the north of England and his daughter to the west was not the solution. Like all men of his time, Henry looked to God for explanations of his predicament and guidance for the way forward. Disquietingly, the Bible seemed to provide an answer that was not regarded as an impediment at the time of his accession. He had married his brother's wife and the book of Leviticus said that this was unlawful. No wonder he and Katherine were never blessed with sons who lived. They had flagrantly disregarded God's will and lived in sin all these years.

Once the light dawned, Henry saw a way out of his wider dilemma. It was not unheard of for monarchs to put aside their wives and in his case there was no alternative, as he had sinned. A papal dispensation would be needed and he still held Katherine personally in great esteem (in fact, he seems to have been rather cowed by her and was often left tongue-tied by her defiance in the face of his attempts to put her aside), but they were no longer having sexual relations and their different interests and outlooks meant that they had little in common. Now he must settle his account with God, his conscience and his country. He had every intention that Katherine would be well served and generously treated, but his priority was to find a new wife and beget male heirs. What this would mean for Mary was left studiously vague. The indications are that he evaded directly addressing the issue for as long as he could, as did those around him. A child born in what was, at the time, believed to be lawful wedlock was not necessarily illegitimate if the marriage was later found to be invalid. But his doubts about Mary's viability as his heir were only too apparent.

At first, Henry's reasons for ending his marriage were mostly negative. He was tired of Katherine, who could have no more children; his dynasty hung on the slim thread of a young girl's life, and though she had been well prepared he could not bring himself to accept that Mary, alone, was his future. He had erred and God had shown his disfavour. Yet by the time that Henry and his daughter met in Oxfordshire in the late summer of 1526, Henry had a much more positive reason to turn from shifting anxieties to positive action. He had fallen for Anne Boleyn.

At first he seems to have noticed Anne because she was the object of courtly pursuit by the poet, Sir Thomas Wyatt the elder, one of Henry's diplomats and companions. Perhaps it began as curiosity and a regal flexing of muscle, the desire to remind Wyatt that all those near to the king were there because he wanted their society but that it was all a game played by his rules. Wyatt must stand aside and make way for his monarch, an expert in the etiquette of courtly love and its progression to sexual surrender. The lady would surely succumb, just as her sister had done.

But the lady did not succumb, either to chivalric gestures and protestations, or to the less subtle signals that Henry would like to sleep with her. Anne was in her mid-twenties and still without a husband, despite various suitors being mentioned. She had seen what happened to her sister as the king's mistress, married off to a cuckold of a husband to give her an air of respectability. Anne was not impressed. At first she rejected Henry, which only enflamed his ardour. Deciding that she must be worried about security and status, and also yearning for her lively, feisty company, Henry made it clear that he wanted Anne as *maîtresse en titre*. He envisioned this as a permanent arrangement, like the relationship between the king of France and his Françoise de Foix.[2] It would have been an impressive success for Anne Boleyn and her family, but she remained unpersuaded, preferring to absent herself from temptation and pressure at home in Hever. We do not know at what point she began to reciprocate Henry's feelings, or which of them first thought of marriage as the only way their relationship could develop, but by the spring of 1527, not long after Mary's marriage plans with the duke of Orléans had been deferred, Henry began to consult about an annulment of his own marriage. By the summer of that year, convinced at last that she could be Henry's wife, Anne apparently agreed to marry him. From that point, events moved swiftly. At the end of August, Henry, having consulted with a number of advisers during an extended stay at the palace of New Hall in Essex (where, ironically, his daughter Mary later lived), decided to send an envoy to Rome to seek a papal dispensation for the annulment of his marriage to Katherine of Aragon. His mind was made up. He would put aside Katherine, his wife of 18 years, who was really no wife at all, and marry Anne Boleyn. With Anne, he could realistically hope to have male heirs. And he did not expect to have to wait long.

Seldom can hopes have been so comprehensively crushed, or with such momentous results. Convinced of the legal and theological strength of his case, Henry proceeded on the basis that Wolsey would establish a court to try the validity of his marriage. The court finding that Henry had, indeed, been unlawfully wedded to his brother's widow all these years, the door would be opened for an annulment from the pope. Thus Rome would rubber-stamp a decision already made in England and Katherine, sidelined and not even officially informed of what was going on, would become the victim of a classic fait accompli. By the autumn it might all be over.

This scenario, however, was far too good to be true. It may have had an elegant simplicity but it overlooked the personality of the queen and the international context in which she was still a player. More crucially, it supposed that the Medici pope, Clement VII, would share Henry's interpretation of canonical law. Events were soon to prove that whether he did or did not was largely irrelevant. Henry had also failed to appreciate the impact of continued instability in continental Europe. On 6 May 1527, before Wolsey's court was even assembled, a mutinous and unpaid imperial army attacked Rome, pillaging and murdering in a manner reminiscent of barbarian hordes. The pope became the prisoner of the emperor. Charles V was a good Catholic and rather embarrassed by the orgy of looting and rape carried out by troops in his employ, but he did not much care for Italian popes. Now he had one under his control. In England his aunt, though no doubt suitably shocked by what had happened to the Holy City, knew that she had been given a breathing space and an opportunity to challenge her husband. Wolsey, meanwhile, could turn the information coming from Europe to his own advantage, since it seems likely that, privately, he was never fully persuaded of the arguments that the king wanted him to make. On the last day of May he pronounced that he could not proceed to judgement and referred matters to a learned group of churchmen and lawyers. Henry's straightforward annulment was stopped in its tracks.

Katherine would have fought, in any case, but her opposition would have been muffled and far less effective. Excluded from the first steps to have her marriage annulled, she was not officially informed of Henry's intentions until 22 June. The confrontation was painful, apparently for both of them. Henry confirmed his wife's worst fears when he told her 'they had been in mortal sin all the years they had lived together'. His conscience could abide it no longer. They must separate. He asked her to give thought to where she might like to retire. He must have hoped that she would see the futility of opposition, presenting his case with a ' terse finality that signified that he would not change his mind. He was her sovereign, and she must obey him. He could hardly have expected her to obey him as his wife, since he had just informed her that she was no such thing. Did he seriously believe that she would meekly disappear from the scene or that she would not challenge his arguments? Despite the strength of his personal beliefs, Henry's interpretation of what the book of Leviticus had to say about marrying his brother's widow was selective. Childlessness was the biblical penalty for a sinful union and Mary was clearly proof that, while the marriage had not been blessed with sons, it had produced one healthy offspring.

Katherine burst into tears on hearing her husband's intentions, though she had known for a while that he was contemplating putting her aside. The realisation that he had already chosen a replacement may have been more of a shock, though of course Henry was careful not to mention Anne Boleyn to Katherine, but it was hard to keep such things secret in court circles. The queen's distress alarmed Henry and he attempted to console her, assuring her that it would all turn out for the best. Probably they both knew it would not. The queen denied vehemently, as she was to do at every future stage of proceedings, that her marriage to Arthur had been consummated. It was so long ago that there was only the evidence of a few men who had been Arthur's companions in Wales, and their memories were inconclusive, though they remembered the young prince's boasts about his prowess and what a pleasant thing it was to have a wife. Only Katherine herself knew the truth. Modern writers have tended to take the view that she could have been lying, that it was a convenient blank in her memory of a sad interlude in her life. Might she have overcome her powerful religious convictions and compromised with her conscience in this way? Perhaps. But surely equally significant in trying to judge her veracity is the fact that she never conceived by Arthur, whereas she became pregnant shortly after marrying Henry.

At this stage, there is no record that Katherine mentioned Mary and her future. That might have been a step too far, since the queen was well aware that it was the lack of a male heir which preyed at the back of Henry's mind. But she had invested so much of her youth in discomfort, uncertainty and penury, as she struggled to become queen of England, that she would not contemplate conceding her throne. Her pride and conscience would not let her and her intellect told her that she could make a strong case. She must defend herself because it was not just her crown which was at stake, but Mary's too. She wanted legal advice and she desired to seek opinions from learned men outside England, rather than rely on those who would essentially do Henry's bidding. In introducing this international dimension, she immediately raised the stakes. She was giving notice that her struggle with the king of England would be conducted at European level and was bound to involve her nephew, Charles V. Shortly after her interview with the king, she sent one of her Spanish servants with a message seeking the emperor's help. It would be a protracted dispute but she could not now be easily outmanoeuvred by a husband who wanted to shut her up in a rural retreat. Winning the legal case did not ensure reconciliation with the king, though Katherine seems to have clung to the belief for at least four years that she was going to win Henry back, but it would save her pride and her soul. It would also safeguard Mary.

Only six weeks before Henry told Katherine that their marriage was built on a lie and his conscience could not permit him to live that lie any more, Mary had danced with the French ambassador and taken part in the lavish spectacle that so impressed Spinelli the Venetian. The queen's presence at this event was the last time she and Henry appeared together before the king went public on his decision to obtain an annulment. There is no information as to when Mary herself first learned of what was happening between her parents, or when she realised that she could not avoid taking sides. The surviving evidence, fragmentary and indirect, suggests that she was shielded from the truth for some time. It seems likely that neither parent wished to involve her initially. Katherine, in spite of her decision to take a stand, would have considered it a needless raising of anxieties and perhaps also an embarrassment. How do you explain to an 11-year-old princess that her father considers you have been unlawfully wedded to him for seven years before she was even born, and that he wishes you to disappear off the scene so that he can marry properly for the first time? Nor would Henry, already dismayed by his wife's tearful and defiant response to his announcement, have contemplated summoning Mary and explaining the position. The princess's separate household made it easier to conceal from her the sordid nature of the dispute, while her daily routine, her lessons and pastimes, could continue undisturbed.

Yet those closest to her, the countess of Salisbury and Richard Fetherstone, undoubtedly knew what was happening, and the household servants, coming and going more often in the outside world, would also have picked up rumours and gossip, even if they were given no official information. Wolsey, Mary's godfather, knew only too well, but he never enlightened her. To do so without his king's permission risked Henry's wrath and, besides, Wolsey was too caught up in the affair professionally to concern himself with a child's questions. What probably happened is that Mary grasped the reality of the struggle between her parents gradually, over a considerable period. There was plenty of time for understanding to dawn, since the conclusion to Henry's dilemma was not reached until 1533. Much had changed in England by then and Mary had left childhood well behind. Whether there came a point when someone, most likely Katherine herself or Margaret Pole, sat down with the princess and explained to her the basics of a struggle that was the talk of Europe, we can only speculate. Eventually, she would have to take sides, but that inescapable burden was postponed by the protracted nature of the dispute. The arcane and tendentious arguments used by the ranks of academics, theologians and lawyers who wallowed in its detail but carefully avoided swift decisions spurred her father's eventual determination that he would break permanently with Rome, never to be maddened by its double-dealing again. He also became increasingly convinced of the need to reform the English Church, not on the Lutheran model, but to rid it of corruption and the effects of superstition and idolatry.[3] But for Mary, her decision was based on purely personal considerations. She came to see her mother as the wronged party, a great European princess and queen of England who had been despicably treated. But, tellingly, it was not until her own status was directly threatened that she publicly opposed her father. She knew that her mother had fought vigorously for what was

right and was inspired by her example to do the same. The consequences of such an approach she did not adequately foresee because Mary,
like Katherine, had failed to appreciate the extent of the changes in her
father's personality.

This was not just naivety on Mary's part, the hopeless strategy of a
spirited but pampered girl who loved her mother but could not grasp
reality. For the first four years of the struggle, she had seldom been far
from her parents and she had seen their civilised behaviour towards each
other in public, almost exaggerated courtesies that utterly amazed
foreign observers. The Venetians could not hide their perplexity. Why, if
Henry and Katherine were involved in a dispute that was rocking Christendom, did they still continue to attend functions together, to dine
together in public and to behave, with their daughter present, as if
nothing was going on at all? In June 1530, the Signory in Venice were
told that Henry and Katherine were together at Hampton Court, where

> they pay each other ... the greatest possible attention ... as if there had
> never been any dispute whatever between them; yet has the affair not
> slackened in the least, although at this present but little is being done
> here, as both parties are collecting votes in France, Italy and several
> other places, but it is not yet known with what success. At any rate, this
> most virtuous Queen maintains strenuously that all her king and lord
> does, is done by him for true and pure conscience' sake and not for any
> wanton appetite.[4]

Maybe this is the line that Katherine took with Mary, absolving her
husband of blame, emphasising that conscience was the key to the difficulties that Henry faced. It would certainly explain Mary's otherwise
misguided confidence in her father, whose conscience was actually one
of the most self-serving and self-pitying in history. At an impressionable
age, Mary learned that conscience was the most important justification
for behaviour that anyone could make. It became her guiding principle
– a clear conscience was what you owed to yourself and God – and the
cause of much of her unhappiness.

The Venetian ambassador had remarked on the air of unreality that hung
over the English royal family in the year 1530, but he also noted that

there were strong currents flowing underneath. Katherine may have wanted to believe the king's protestations that if the pope found that his marriage was lawful, no one would be more delighted than he, but the sensible side of her knew otherwise. Nevertheless, she began her own process of seeking learned counsel as soon as she was officially informed by her husband of his intent; she was committed to the intellectual side of the fight every bit as much as Henry. Katherine was not going to let tears get in the way of producing a robust case to bolster her position, and she would give her daughter the example of how educated women could defend themselves, using the same weapons that men employed against them. This had serious consequences for both the queen and her daughter, because although it was brave and intellectually sound, it relied too much on theory and ignored politics. Katherine was isolated in England and her friends in the nobility, as well as the small number of English humanist thinkers who stood up for her, found themselves imperilled. In fact, the conservative reformers among English humanists, who shared some of the king's concerns about the state of the English Church, never recovered from their involvement in the divorce. Katherine began her campaign by commissioning Sir Thomas Wyatt, who had lost Anne Boleyn to Henry, to translate for her Petrarch's treatise on the remedy of ill fortune. An apt choice for both queen and Wyatt, but in the end it did not make any difference.

The queen then began to consult more widely in Europe. Both she and Henry tried to involve Erasmus, but the ageing scholar, bruised by his involvement in the Lutheran controversy, wisely preferred to stay aloof. Katherine did send again for Vives, but his presence in England was not welcomed by Henry, who put him under house arrest and had him interrogated by Wolsey. The Spaniard left the country but was courageous enough to return with two Flemish jurists sent by Katherine's sister-in-law, Margaret of Austria. Unfortunately, his pragmatic advice did not please the queen, who was not ready to be told that she might better defend her position if she allowed the English courts to condemn her unheard. They parted on bad terms, though she eventually followed his advice, at least in part.

Katherine did have friends in England, but, as the years went by, fewer in high places. The families of the old nobility, the Staffords, the Nevilles and the Courtenays, never deserted her, though their effectiveness was diminished by the rise of the supporters of Anne Boleyn. The queen's English chaplain, Thomas Abell, defied Henry by declaring that those who advised the king were iniquitous. The religious orders such as the Observant Franciscans and the Carthusians, who were sympathetic to the new learning, dared to declare for the queen and were heavily punished, the Observants by dissolution in 1534 and two groups of the Carthusians by death in 1535. Oxford University found for Henry only after great pressure was exerted, and the Cambridge humanists also put up opposition. But among the leading clergy, only Bishop John Fisher of Rochester openly defended the queen. He also refused to acknowledge Henry's supremacy over the Church in 1534 or to take the oath to the act of succession. So did Thomas More, but his attitude towards Katherine and the divorce was more equivocal.

Most of those at court who dared to support Katherine, and later Mary, were women. The influence of this on the princess has been underestimated. She saw that her mother had friends who were not self-serving, like their menfolk, but brave enough to stand up and be counted. Initially, the most significant support for Katherine came from her sister-in-law, the duchess of Suffolk, a close companion in happier days. The elder Mary Tudor was not afraid to show her contempt for Anne Boleyn or her disapproval of her brother's course of action.[5] Unfortunately, the practical assistance she could give was minimal. Court life had begun to weary her and her presence was much less frequent than in the early years of the reign. She preferred to stay on her country estates with her two daughters, and by the early 1530s was not in good health. In 1533, a bitter year for the queen's cause, Mary died, depriving Katherine of one of her staunchest allies.

There were others, not of such high rank, but equally determined to stay true to their queen and their princess. Margaret Pole herself would not be swayed. Her friendship with Katherine was too deep and her responsibility for Mary's day-to-day welfare the main focus of her life. Also in the queen's camp was the redoubtable duchess of Norfolk, wife of the premier nobleman of England. Born Elizabeth Stafford, she was the daughter of the executed duke of Buckingham and sister-in-law to Margaret Pole's daughter. As the wife of Thomas Howard she survived, but only at huge personal cost, one of the most spectacularly unhappy marriages in early Tudor England. In many respects, it mirrored what had happened between Henry and Katherine, though Elizabeth Howard was younger than the queen at the time her husband began to flaunt his infidelity. Up until 1527, their union had apparently been a success, but when in 1527 her husband took as mistress Bess Holland, the daughter of his secretary, the duchess's Plantagenet blood was repelled. She was no more going to take this insult to her birth and her marriage than was the queen, openly betrayed in the same year. Elizabeth Howard's refusal to play the submissive wife gave her common cause with Katherine, one of whose ladies she had been for many years. It may well have actively encouraged her commitment to the queen, deep-seated though this already was. Anne Boleyn was her husband's niece, but the duchess was angered by the idea, vigorously supported by Anne, that her daughter Mary Howard should be married off to the king's illegitimate son. Her relationship with her husband deteriorated still further and she began to accuse him openly of consistent physical abuse. In May 1531 she was dismissed from court 'because she spoke too freely and declared herself more than they liked for the queen'.[6]

Even when Elizabeth Howard was sent away, there were others willing to risk a great deal for the queen. Gertrude Courtenay, marchioness of Exeter, acted in the *Chateau Vert* masque with Anne Boleyn on Anne's debut at the English court and had known her for some time. But they were not friends and Gertrude, who attended Katherine of Aragon at the Field of Cloth of Gold, was loyal to the queen. She acted as a useful go-between from the court to Katherine, via the imperial ambassador. Her family's position was a difficult and rather inconsistent one (Gertrude's husband had signed the petition of the English nobility to the pope to have the king's marriage to Katherine annulled), but the marchioness herself was clearly sympathetic on a personal level to Katherine and Mary. The Exeters were religious conservatives who found the progression towards separation of the English Church from Rome, as the divorce questioned dragged on, disturbing. This may explain Gertrude's interest in another woman, from a very different background, whose opposition to the divorce disturbed Henry far more than the independent outlook of a few court ladies, irritating though they undoubtedly were in his eyes. Yet none of them had spoken openly of a threat to the king's life if he did not abandon his plans to repudiate the queen. That chilling message was contained in the prophecies of a young nun at Canterbury, Elizabeth Barton.

The Nun of Kent was a well-known figure by 1528 and sufficiently regarded for the king himself to seek the views of Thomas More on her sayings and visions. More was unimpressed, finding nothing exceptional in Elizabeth's utterances. He commented that he saw in them only something that 'a right simple woman might, in my mind, speak of her own wit well enough'. Wolsey, who had two meetings with Elizabeth, may have been the person who suggested to the king that it was worth hearing from the nun herself. Henry agreed and Barton was given access to the very pinnacle of Tudor power.

Such proximity to the great fed delusions of invincibility. Elizabeth Barton was now far removed from the humble social sphere in which she had begun life. Yet with her celebrity status came a growing sense of unreality that was to be her undoing. By the late 1520s her prophecies contained much more overtly political content. There were declamations that papal authority must be maintained and heresy rooted out. Most seriously of all, from Henry's perspective, this uneducated woman who had discussed her visions with him now made a sustained onslaught on the divorce itself. She emerged as a major supporter of Katherine of Aragon.

The visions concerning the king and his marriage were detailed and specific. An angel told Elizabeth Barton that if Henry put aside Katherine of Aragon and married Anne Boleyn, God's vengeance would overtake him: 'then within one month after such marriage he should no longer be king of this realm, and in the reputation of almighty God should not be a king one day nor one hour but would die a villain's death'.[7] Even more chilling was the nun's revelation that she had seen the precise spot prepared for the king in hell. This was strong stuff. Henry was an intelligent, well-educated prince, but he was also a man of his times. Languishing in hell was the ultimate dread and the nun's conviction that she knew the site of his eternal torments, delivered to his face, was deeply unsettling. Determined that her prophecies would be known in high places, Elizabeth Barton did not back off; both archbishop Warham and Wolsey were informed that they would also be destroyed if they countenanced the king's marriage to Anne Boleyn.

Some people were repelled by these increasingly violent denunciations but others at least wanted to meet the Nun of Kent themselves. Gertrude Courtenay, evidently aware of the risk she was running, came in disguise to meet her at Canterbury and subsequently Gertrude and her husband received the nun at one of their properties in Surrey, where the young woman fell into a trance. Elizabeth Barton did not disappoint. For so long as she was viewed as a genuine seer, speaking the true word of God, the nun and her advisers might have expected that her uncompromising stance was permissible under the guise of 'frank counsel'. For a while, even the king wondered whether the Nun of Kent might be divinely inspired.

The queen was well aware of the efforts of her supporters and the tenacity of the women who supported her cause. She also realised that the personal risks they took would have only a minimal impact on the outcome of her struggle. The key to Katherine's campaign, and the cause of growing bitterness between herself and Henry, however polite they may have seemed at official functions, was the queen's decision in June 1529 to ask that her case be heard in Rome. Henry had always wanted, indeed expected, papal involvement, but on his own terms. He greatly resented the idea of being summoned to Rome and interrogated by the pope. This was not just annoyance at what the king and his party regarded as troublesome gamesmanship by a fractious woman; papal interference of this sort was an affront to his authority and what he increasingly saw as his unchallengeable position as sovereign of both England and its Church. And there was, too, the disquieting prospect that because Katherine had also played the imperial card, his domestic problems might be used as the excuse for military action by the emperor.

Katherine always maintained, even after Henry married Anne Boleyn, that she sought her nephew's moral support to save the king from error and the country from excommunication and heresy. Even at moments of desperation, she did not want imperial troops invading England in her defence. She was fighting a war, but it was a war of argument and strategy, not swords. In the end, it did become brutal, but the brutality was Henry's, not Katherine's or the emperor's. Charles's response to Katherine's situation was a pragmatic one, inevitably fashioned by the dictates of his imperial role. To the queen he wrote letters expressing his indignation and concern, but they were more proper than fiery: 'I cannot express it otherwise than by assuring you that were my own mother concerned I should not experience greater sorrow than in this your case,' he wrote at the end of August 1527.[8] Not much comfort here, then, as his own mother was very much still alive but widely regarded as mentally unbalanced and living in retreat in Spain. Katherine most definitely would resist a similar fate.

In the summer of 1527 Charles was much more concerned to salvage his international image, badly shattered by his armies' behaviour in Italy.

He issued a manifesto to all the princes of Europe, protesting at the calumnies spread against him, 'as if he could be the author of the Sack of Rome'. In an indirect way, he was, and he knew it. The marriage difficulties of Henry and Katherine did not figure high on his list of priorities, though there was always the possibility that it was all part of some French-inspired plot against himself. Yet his Habsburg sense of family loyalty was piqued by the insult to his aunt, though he hardly knew her personally and had met his cousin, Mary, only once. 'We cannot desert the queen, our good aunt, in her troubles and intend doing all we can in her favour,' he wrote to his ambassador in London. Discretion and moderation were the best way forward, and he had told Henry this in a letter. He could not believe 'that having, as they have, so sweet a princess for their daughter [the king] would consent to have her or her mother dishonoured, a thing so monstrous of itself and wholly without precedent in ancient or modern history'.[9] In this description of Mary, whom he cast squarely as the person most likely to be adversely affected by Henry's behaviour, there is, perhaps, just the hint of guilt for his own treatment of a young princess. Denied her opportunity to be empress, she was now threatened with illegitimacy. It must be a terrible blow, and he would undoubtedly do all he could in bringing pressure to bear on the pope, so that Katherine and Mary would have justice. But he was never going to fight. Upheaval in his northern European domains and the constant threat of war with France were far more pressing concerns.

And so the divorce, the King's Great Matter as it was called in English circles, dragged on for six years, far beyond the worst fears of the king and his supporters. It became a European *cause célèbre*, as the best theological and legal minds of the day were put to work on it and the pope, escaped from Charles V's direct control to Orvieto in Italy, decided that the safest course of action for him was to play off each side against the other for as long as possible. Determined that right was on his side, Henry spent large sums of money on canvassing the opinions of the universities of Europe, rather as senior executives in large corporations now employ consultants to tell them things they want to hear. The universities were only too happy to receive this unlooked-for funding, but they did not give the English king the definitive answer he hoped to get. Katherine also dug her heels in and fought with ferocity a rearguard action, knowing full well that she had few influential friends in England, though popular sentiment appears to have been on her side.[10] But her determination, though understandable, did not mean that what she was doing was ultimately the right thing for her daughter.

Katherine always maintained that her stand was as much about Mary and Mary's future as it was about herself, but in this she was deceived. An understandable self-deception, in the circumstances, but it was not the whole truth. The queen may have been a deeply religious woman, but she was not meek. She refused to accept any compromise, partly out of moral certainty but also because she was the queen and the daughter of great monarchs. Anne Boleyn was so far below her that she would never concede to such a person. Yet at one crucial stage in the convoluted proceedings, as early as 1528, Katherine was offered a way out that promised Mary security. She refused to take it.

Pride, intense attachment to her marriage and also a degree of suspicion that assurances given might not be honoured all swirled in her mind when the Italian cardinal Lorenzo Campeggio put to Katherine in October 1528 the possibility that there was a solution to her dilemma: 'In order to do away with the scruples and other greater evils which the discord between her and her husband was likely to produce … and in order to remove any difficulties as to the succession to the crown of England, he [the pope] thought the best expedient to be adopted was that she should profess in some religious community and take vows of perpetual chastity.' Katherine could end all the unpleasantness by taking the veil. This would leave the king free to marry again and did not call into question Mary's legitimacy or her claim to the throne. The queen was not impressed. She 'at first showed a little irritation … and spoke some angry words to Wolsey, hinting that he was the cause of all of her misfortunes'. After time for reflection, she calmed down and delivered a withering riposte: 'she held her husband's conscience and honour in more esteem than anything in this world; that she entertained no scruple at all about her marriage, but considered herself the true and legitimate wife of the king … the proposal just made in the name of His Holiness was inadmissible'.[11] She would not be pushed aside, either into a rural retirement, as the king had first suggested, or a religious one. First and foremost, she clung to the idea that her marriage was legal. She was a queen and a wife, not a nun. Even raising the doubt that her daughter might be illegitimate was an insult to Katherine's personal integrity. Yet both Mary and England itself might have been spared much trauma if the queen had followed the precedent offered by the first wife of the French king, Louis XII, and entered a convent. But Katherine would not compromise and so Mary's future was inextricably linked with her mother's fate.

Certainly the circumstances of Campeggio's proposal did not improve the queen's frame of mind. He was sent to London to preside, with Wolsey, over a legatine court that would adjudicate the annulment of the marriage. Henry expected that the court would find for him, but he did not know that the pope had given Campeggio instructions that he was to stall as long as possible and that he was definitely not to reach a decision. The cardinal, who was very ill with gout and had endured an awful journey to England, must have prayed that the queen would agree to his suggestion, thus sparing him months of fruitless going through the motions. If so, his prayers went unanswered, though he was much more successful when it came to delaying proceedings.

Following her rebuff to Campeggio, Katherine believed that, if she was not winning, she was not, at least, losing. But it was a strange existence that she led over the next two years. She and Mary were normally with Henry for the religious festivals and great days of state. They all spent Christmas 1528 together at Greenwich, in a show of family unity that was entirely false. On the second day of January 1529 they both attended a reception for the new Venetian ambassador, and it was noted that the queen was accompanied by 'her handsome and virtuously-educated daughter'. Was this meant to imply that Mary was already publicly committed to her mother, or was it merely the result of court etiquette? The report back to the Signory in Venice left out a detail that the Doge and his council might have found more titillating. Also at Greenwich that Christmas, though in a separate establishment, was Anne Boleyn. She had survived a serious bout of the sweating sickness in the summer and was now fully restored to health. Anne kept well away from the queen and the princess but her presence was widely known. Katherine ignored it. There is no evidence that she made an issue of Anne personally when she was with Henry. It is possible that Mary was still in the dark about what was happening. So Anne Boleyn in many ways held the advantage over the two women who stood in her way. She had the king's love, her influence was growing and she was not going to disappear. Katherine was clinging to an illusion, but Anne's power was in the ascendancy. She had no qualms about using it to defeat the queen and to deny the young princess her birthright.

The objective was clear, but the means to achieving it less so, and the time it took galling. Anne was well aware that the woman she meant to supplant had a flair for the public occasion and a lingering hold on the king himself. There was the unavoidable fact that Anne might spend a great deal of time at Henry's side, while her family received favours and political advancement, but still Katherine was queen and recognised as such by the king himself. The king did not like confrontation, least of all with women, and he avoided it whenever possible. Yet it was Henry, encouraged by Anne's steadfastness, who wanted a resolution of his case by Cardinals Campeggio and Wolsey. On 30 May 1529 he gave them authority to proceed with the trial. This provided Katherine with the opportunity to plead her own cause in person. Determined not to go quietly, she would have her day in court.

The cardinals required the king and queen to attend a hearing scheduled for 18 June, in the Parliament Chamber of the Dominican Friary of London, familiarly known as Blackfriars. Two days earlier, Katherine made her formal appeal for the case to be heard in Rome. She would appear before the legatine court having, in effect, already rejected its authority. But she wanted to be seen and, angry though she knew Henry would be, she wanted to make a direct appeal to him. For Katherine, this was not about Anne Boleyn, waiting to occupy her place in the royal bed. It was about her own conscience and the utter conviction that her time spent as England's queen was not built on a lie, but was sacred in the eyes of God.

The trial of a royal marriage, dramatised to great effect in Shakespeare's last play, *King Henry VIII*, was unprecedented in English history. Everyone was seized by the momentous nature of events when the queen and her supporters made their entry on 18 June, and Katherine having read aloud her challenge to the competence of the cardinals to hear her case and confirmed her appeal to Rome, was told that the court would answer her on 21 June, when the king himself would also appear. There, before an audience that included ordinary Londoners, many of whom were women who were open and vocal in support of the queen, Henry and Katherine faced each other on a public stage. This was Katherine's moment, and she still cut a regal figure, despite her girth. She denounced Wolsey and Campeggio as interested parties not competent to hear the case. Wolsey was one of her husband's ministers and had directly benefited from office. Campeggio also held an English bishopric. How could she expect to receive justice from them? When the king spoke he told the judges he could no longer live in mortal sin, but Katherine's response was bitter and sceptical. Why, she challenged, had Henry been silent so long, if, as he claimed, it was his conscience which pricked him? How could she, a foreigner, expect justice in England?

The king's attempts to parry this opening salvo with the feeble assurance 'of the great love he had and has for her', and his earnest desire that the marriage should be declared valid, were a tactical mistake. If that was what he was going to maintain, then she would take the argument literally to him. Crossing the crowded courtroom, with its floor packed with lawyers and its gallery filled with the common people, Katherine made her way directly to where Henry sat: 'The queen rose and throwing herself on her knees before the king, said aloud that she had lived for twenty years with his majesty as his lawful wife ... and that she did not deserve to be repudiated and thus put to shame without any cause.' And though Mary was not there, she was not forgotten. In her broken English, which only added to her air of vulnerability, the queen reminded the king that he knew she had been a virgin when she married him. So she pleaded with him 'to consider her honour, her daughter's and his; that he should not be displeased at her defending it, and should consider the reputation of her nation and relatives, who will be seriously offended'.[12]

Mary did not hear her mother's passionate plea nor see her father give way under this emotional onslaught and apparently concur that the case should be decided in Rome. Yet it is evident from her subsequent behaviour that the aftermath of the Blackfriars trial had a profound impact on her. Her own future was now in the public domain. It could not be evaded. And her mother, increasingly isolated, had scored a historic victory. Katherine, having gained the initiative, did not wait to hear the court's reaction. She swept out, past the cheering women, ignoring the king's attempts to have her called back. On 23 July, Campeggio adjourned the legatine court, pronouncing that the case could be resolved only in Rome. There would be no easy solution to her husband's quest and she and Mary were safe for the time being. Her daughter could continue with her preparation to be England's queen. But there was still Anne Boleyn.

· ❖ ·

She may have been constrained by social conventions and frustrated by the lack of progress but Anne never gave up in her determination to be queen of England. Little is known of her actual relationship with Katherine of Aragon, but Anne evidently underestimated the queen's character and intellect. Like many women in her situation, hearing the complaints of a besotted lover about the inadequacies of his wife, the dire state of his marriage and his undying love for her, Anne probably did not want to think much about Katherine at all. The queen's day was over and replacing her must have seemed a straightforward step, since she and Henry were never legally married. Anne would be his first true wife. This simple scenario was very appealing to a young woman who stood on the brink of a magnificent transformation of her life. It says much for Anne Boleyn's self-belief that when the vision dissolved, she did not accept defeat. But her dismissal of Katherine as a rival, perfectly comprehensible on an emotional level, was unrealistic. She ignored the bonds that had grown up between Henry and his wife, as well as being far too dismissive of the kind of person that Katherine really was. Anne had been part of the queen's entourage for some years but clearly did not understand her. It is almost as if all she saw was the dumpy, rather melancholy woman who prayed a great deal and amused herself by sewing her husband's shirts. She overlooked Katherine's regal bearing at state occasions, her knowledge of politics and international diplomacy; indeed, she does not seem to have taken any account of the queen's European status and influence at all. Katherine was trained to be a queen whereas Anne Boleyn, for all her undoubted intelligence, was trained to be a courtier. If the distinction was lost on Anne, it was not for one moment lost on Katherine of Aragon.

Anne's early belief that she would be queen in a matter of months shows that she did not consider how, or even whether, Katherine would fight. The queen and her daughter were an irrelevance and their fate, which would be decided by the king, did not directly concern her. The combination of Henry's love and her ambition was a heady one, and Anne already knew too much about court politics to waste any time on remorse. The fact that her elevation would bring untold distress to a blameless woman and a young girl brought up as the heir of England never seems to have troubled her at all. Neither did the realisation that she would certainly make enemies of some of the most powerful men in England. Instead, she began to work on the advancement of her own family, particularly her father, Thomas, and brother, George. She could not succeed with the king's love alone, though the absolute certainty of his commitment to her gave her the confidence to carry on. When

Henry faltered, she remained firm. And she believed she knew who stood in her way.

After the disaster at Blackfriars, Anne, who had been close by throughout proceedings, though not overtly living with the king, sat down with him to discuss the next steps. Clearly, the approach that Henry's ministers had been following was not working and a new one was needed. The most convenient explanation for what had gone wrong was not Katherine's intransigence, or the strength of her legal arguments, but the failure of Cardinal Wolsey, as Henry's chief minister, to bring about the desired ruling from the pope. Henry was increasingly troubled by being dependent on papal authority for the ordering of his own affairs, and Anne was convinced that Wolsey no longer supported her, if he ever had. So the cardinal became the first major victim of the divorce. During 1529, his position became more and more untenable. Katherine considered him a long-standing enemy who sought to ruin her because he was pro-French. Anne, who for a while saw him as the person most likely to deliver Henry's annulment, lost faith in him and believed, with some justification, that he had become an obstruction. He was damaging her chances of ever becoming queen.

Wolsey fought a rearguard action that delayed, but could not prevent, his fall. The king was at first as reluctant to dismiss him as he was to take any irrevocable steps in the domestic sphere against Katherine. Wolsey was accused of having overstepped his legatine authority and deprived of the chancellorship on 17 October 1529. The French and imperial ambassadors concurred in thinking this was the work of Anne Boleyn, and Wolsey himself had no doubts; he knew he had mightily displeased the Lady Anne, but still he hoped some means might be found to regain her good opinion: 'This', he wrote, 'is the only help and remedy. All possible means must be used for attaining of her favour.'[13] Wolsey was clutching at straws. He had been so long in power that he could not recognise at first that he had lost it irretrievably. There were others, who had waited long in his shadow, only too pleased that he was gone. Power on the new privy council passed to the dukes of Norfolk and Suffolk, neither of whom had Wolsey's political experience, and the Boleyns' star continued to rise. In December, Anne's father was created earl of Wiltshire and her younger brother, George, sent as ambassador to France. The French ambassador to Henry's court, the astute prelate Jean du Bellay, thought George Boleyn's youth would give rise to some amusement in France. But in England no one was laughing at Anne Boleyn when she celebrated her father's elevation at a feast attended by the leading nobles of the realm. Their wives, including Henry's own sister Mary, were required to give precedence to Anne. She is unlikely to have displayed much humility in accepting their curtsies, but she must have felt their contempt. It was one thing to sit by Henry's side at a banquet and another to become queen. The process by which she would achieve this ultimate goal was still far from clear.

And Wolsey might be deprived of much of his wealth, of his London palace and his role in government, sent off back to his archbishopric of York, but he would not lie down. Now he harboured a grudge against Anne as deep as her own against him. In the last year of his life he reversed his support for the king's divorce, espoused the queen's cause and kept open his channels of communication with the French government and the imperial ambassador. Whether this amounted to treason is not clear but his enemies certainly thought so, and Anne wanted him dead. She got her way, though Wolsey was spared the judicial proceedings and the public executions of other key figures who stood out against the king. On his journey south to face the charges against him he was taken ill at Leicester and died there in November 1530. Henry's many other victims would have welcomed such a natural end.

Wolsey had never been much of a mentor to Mary and his concern was only ever for the temporal power he relished for so long, but if he could have evaded Anne Boleyn's continued wrath, he might, conceivably, have been a useful adviser to the princess. The years were passing and, as Henry's commitment to Anne did not waver, so Mary's to her mother was bound to grow. How could it have been otherwise? All of Europe knew that Mary was going to be the chief victim of the divorce, but her father never seems to have wanted to face this truth. Bastardisation did not, in Henry's mind, mean that she would be treated dishonourably. She would always be his daughter and live the life of a great lady. It would be a diminished role but not necessarily an unpleasant existence. Children must obey and Mary would do as he required because she had no choice. Her opposition did not fit into his plans.

So outwardly, their relationship proceeded as it had always done; she saw him at regular intervals, attended court when summoned and was treated as a princess. She lived a separate life, still with her own household and finances, still being educated as the king's daughter. But Henry, for all his apparent paternal affection, did not want her to succeed him. It may not have been acknowledged by either father or daughter, but he had already rejected her. As time went by, and Mary left childhood behind, Anne Boleyn also needed to readjust her thinking. Depending on how Mary behaved, she could pose a threat to Anne just as serious as the one presented by Katherine of Aragon herself.

While the countess of Salisbury strove to maintain a peaceful and secure environment for the princess, Mary did not live in a bubble. Coming to court as often as she did, she saw the new faces, knew that her godfather had gone, sensed, for all their courtesy, the tension between her parents. By 1531, the stresses and strains were too obvious to be overlooked and Mary succumbed to them, too. In April of that year the Venetian ambassador reported that she had been ill for several weeks with 'hysteria'.[14] This was the first obvious sign that Mary was being affected by the wearying struggle that consumed her parents. She was 15 years old in February 1531 and her illness may have coincided with the onset of menstruation, or, at least, been an indication of menstrual difficulties. She seems to have suffered from painful periods and the accompanying emotional fluctuations that went with this troublesome condition. During the rest of her life, she was beset by what she herself described as times of melancholy, and these bouts of depression brought her low. Concern about the outcome of the divorce only worsened this. When Mary recovered from her illness, Katherine requested that the princess be allowed to visit both her parents at Greenwich. This was refused, possibly vetoed by Anne Boleyn. The imperial ambassador thought that Anne already hated Mary more than Katherine, because she still had her father's affection. Although all negative developments were imputed to Anne Boleyn, who was very firmly a figure of hatred with the imperialists, it is from about this time that Anne's attitude to Mary became more defensive. Did she fear that Mary could still salvage her parents' marriage? For whatever reason, the king was not disposed to have Mary at Greenwich at that point, but he did give Katherine permission to visit her daughter. In fact, he told her very rudely that she could stop there for all he cared, but Katherine continued to ignore these attempts at intimidation. She did spend several weeks with Mary and saw her again later in the summer. But Katherine herself, who had fought so doggedly and never doubted that God and right were on her side, could not avoid the unpalatable truth that the king would not tolerate her presence for much longer. As late as the end of 1530, she was still absolutely convinced that if she could only spend an uninterrupted period of time with him, she could free him from the baleful influence of false ministers and Anne herself. Just before Christmas, she wrote to the pope: 'One thing I should like Your Holiness to be aware of, namely, that my plea is not against the King, my Lord, but against the inventors and abettors of this cause. I trust so much in the natural goodness and in the virtues of the King … that if I could only have him two months with me, as he used to be, I alone should be powerful enough to make him forget the past; but as they know this to be true, they do not let him live with me.'[15] So much confidence and such inability to face the truth. Katherine was back in the early days of her marriage, when her very young husband was guided and shaped by her and all the world was good.

A year went by, and still nothing changed in Katherine's mind. In June, a 30-strong delegation of nobles and churchmen was sent to try, one last time, to get her to yield on the referral of her case to Rome and accept that her marriage to Henry was invalid. She refused all their arguments and pressure, and they left more overawed by the queen than she was of them. One of them, the king's old friend, the duke of Suffolk, now set his face against the divorce.

Henry, however, had had enough. His wife's stubbornness and refusal to submit to his authority, the persistence of Anne Boleyn, his own resentment of imperial interference and papal vacillation, all provoked him into making a decision that had been years coming. As the summer hunting season gathered pace, he and Anne Boleyn visited a number of places in southern England, without Katherine, who normally went everywhere with Henry but who was now left behind at Windsor. She seems to have been unsure of her husband's movements, and when she sent him a message expressing regret that she had not taken her leave of him before his departure, he made it quite clear that his patience was exhausted. He could not give a fig for her goodbyes. In a state of great alarm, Katherine sent for Mary and they stayed together till early August. There is no way at this point that Mary could have been shielded from what was happening. Her mother's anguish must have been all too apparent, and she needed to be sure that Mary understood her side of the story. Yet, even so, the queen would surely not have represented her position (and therefore Mary's) as hopeless. They must hold firm. They had friends who would not desert them and the king might yet change his mind.

Sadly for the two women, he only hardened his heart. Katherine was banished from court and told to remove to The More, once Wolsey's home and the place from which her daughter had set out for the Welsh Marches in 1525. Mary was ordered back to Richmond. When they parted, apprehensive but not despairing, they could not have known that they were saying their final farewells to each other. The queen set up a separate court at The More. It was a considerable size, and she had over two hundred people in her household. But she was removed from the centre of power, marginalised in the country as Henry had wanted four years earlier. Katherine of Aragon never saw him or Mary again.

Her godfather, with all his power and influence, was dead. Her mother, banished and humiliated, she was not allowed to see any more. Anne Boleyn's power was growing, and with it came vindictiveness against the princess herself. Mary made Anne nervous, a nervousness that took the form of more open hostility. In April 1531, Anne and Henry quarrelled angrily over Mary, and though they soon made up, the tension that Anne felt in connection with the princess was still there at Christmas, when she demanded that Mary be lodged as far away from court as possible. Though Anne did not always get her way, Mary was becoming increasingly isolated, as her mother's rival intended her to be. Henry's motives in keeping the queen and Mary apart, however, may not have been entirely dictated by Anne's resentment. He had ample reason to think that Katherine was a bad influence on his daughter and he wanted that link broken. But this does not mean that his affection for Mary was spent. For two more years, he continued to see his daughter regularly, sent her New Year's gifts and appears to have acted as if, from his perspective as a firm but loving father, nothing had changed. Such outward normalcy may have deluded both of them; theirs was a relationship always based on Henry's terms, and when those terms changed, Mary was expected to accept without demur. Her father's love was conditional on her obedience, and the example of her troublesome mother was something that the king needed to correct. It is impossible to know what passed between them at their meetings or how much Henry talked to her about his own affairs, but the likelihood is that their time together was largely social and the conversation centred on topics of the king's choosing. Henry did not need Mary's approval and his own attitude towards her was bound to be ambivalent. She, like her mother, seems not to have understood how much the father whom she associated with the happy times and grand occasions of her childhood was changing. The dispute with Rome over the divorce was pushing Henry to establish his own theories of regal authority and government, and his ego, at first deflated, was growing. His bonhomie was still there but his hardness increased, and with it came a capriciousness that left many of those around him not knowing where they stood. He was slow to withdraw affection, but when he did, he never looked back. Anne Boleyn herself would find this out in time. Mary, who experienced it first, was wholly unprepared for the emotional damage her father could inflict.

Meanwhile the familiar rhythms of life continued, despite the official separation of her parents. Mary was allowed to correspond regularly with Katherine and such communications were a great source of mutual comfort. The countess of Salisbury remained constant in her care towards the royal child she had shaped, even though she knew which way the wind was blowing. There were some new faces in Mary's household, but nothing that suggested that it would be in any way downgraded: Lord Hussey replaced Sir Philip Calthorpe as chamberlain, and his wife, Lady Anne, joined the shrinking circle of those who were later willing to risk royal displeasure in their support for the princess. Richard Wollman, the king's almoner, left Henry's service to add his weight to Mary's education.

Most welcome was the arrival of her cousin, Lady Margaret Douglas, who took over the role of chief lady-in-waiting in 1530. Margaret was the daughter of Henry VIII's elder sister (also Margaret), the dowager queen of Scotland, by her second husband. She and Mary were of a similar age and both enjoyed the affection of their aunt Mary, duchess of Suffolk, who used her influence to promote Margaret's appointment. A strong bond formed between the girls, which lasted all Mary's life. Margaret's prospects were uncertain and her background was troubled, but she herself was outgoing and light-hearted. She brought a breath of fresh air into Mary's life at a difficult time.

There was even the lingering possibility that Mary could escape altogether from the uncertainty of her situation in England through marriage. Henry, aware that the princess was still useful in diplomacy, had not ruled out finding an appropriate match for her. The likelihood of a French husband was receding, but there were other possible suitors mentioned, in places as far apart as Cleves, Transylvania and Scotland.

Nothing came to fruition. Henry's own marital affairs were his absolute priority and he did not want to consider whether he was ruining Mary's prospects by the air of uncertainty that now hung over her birth. A king's illegitimate daughter with no place in the English succession was a far less attractive prospect for a husband in the first rank of European princes. England itself, teetering on the brink of a breach with Rome and now obviously embracing heretical beliefs, was an unattractive source for a royal bride. The lady might be personally devout but her father's schismatic tendencies were likely to make him a pariah.

Henry no longer cared. By 1532 his decisions were becoming more focused and his timetable more urgent. It was perfectly obvious that he would not get satisfaction from Rome. The odds were too heavily stacked against him; Katherine's case was well supported and regarded as legally watertight and Clement VII could defer a decision as long as he wanted. The process of the divorce opened Henry's eyes to the wider disadvantages of papal domination in ecclesiastical matters. It moulded his views on the issue of kingship itself and the idea of royal supremacy. The king wanted to control the Church in England. It needed reforming and its bishops should be answerable to him, not some distant Italian who could be pushed around by Charles V. He also still desired Anne Boleyn and he wanted to marry her. Encouraged by Anne, the king saw ways in which he could adapt the new ideas to his advantage. Anne's supporters, some attached to her by family ties, many others convinced that she was close to winning her long struggle and eager for her patronage, were joined by churchmen such as Thomas Cranmer, who became archbishop of Canterbury at the beginning of 1533, and Thomas Cromwell, a rising politician who had once been on Wolsey's staff. In a further sign that she was close to achieving her goal, Anne was created marchioness of Pembroke at Windsor, on 1 September 1532. The duchess of Norfolk, defiantly loyal to Katherine of Aragon, refused to demean her Stafford blood by carrying Anne's train.

Late in October, Henry took Anne with him for an important meeting with Francis I in Calais. It was Anne's first time back on French soil since she left the French court in 1521. Superbly dressed and attended like a queen consort, Anne was also now in possession of the jewels of a queen of England. Katherine of Aragon had reluctantly surrendered them only at the king's express command, not wanting them to 'adorn the scandal of Christendom'. This was her only public outburst against Anne Boleyn, the woman she would not deign to name.

The French summit was a great success in public relations terms and, finally confident that they would soon be man and wife, Henry and Anne evidently slept together, if not for the first time, then certainly after an abstinence of many years. By January 1533 Anne was pregnant. She and Henry were secretly married by Cranmer at the end of the month. On 23 May 1533, Cranmer pronounced the king's marriage to Katherine null and void on his own authority and on Whitsunday, 1 June, Anne was crowned queen at Westminster Abbey, after several days of carefully orchestrated magnificence. But the splendid entry to London, the pageants, the feasting and display, do not seem to have caught the imagination of a populace who had loved Katherine of Aragon and who were more curious than demonstrative. Only the oldest of London's citizens remembered the entry of a pretty Spanish princess as a royal bride more than 30 years ago, but most Londoners were not entranced by the new queen. Perhaps they were thinking of the woman she had dethroned and pondering its impact on the princess Mary, who took no part in proceedings.

Mary learned of her father's marriage at the end of April, about the same time that the king publicly acknowledged Anne as his 'most dear and well-beloved wife'. The imperial ambassador reported that the news was communicated to her at the same time that she was told of the king's commandment forbidding all further contact with her mother. Mary was naturally very distressed, 'although the princess has since begged and entreated him to appoint someone next to her person to give evidence that her messages to her mother are only in reference to her health, and proposing that her own letters and the queen's may previously pass through the king's hands, her prayers have been completely disregarded'. The ambassador went on to add: "This prohibition [I hear] was read to the princess the very same day that the king caused his new marriage to be announced to her.' It would have been so very easy to be provoked, but Mary steadied herself. She probably also knew of Anne's pregnancy, by then more than obvious, but this was not a reason to panic or over-react. Anne's triumph could be short-lived. She might not survive labour (at 31 she was comparatively old by Tudor standards to be facing her first delivery); she could have a stillbirth or a child that did not survive its early weeks, as had so tragically happened to Mary's mother. So the princess held herself in check: '… she was at first thoughtful and then, as the very wise person that she is, dissembled as much as she could and seemed even to rejoice at it. Without alluding in the least to the said marriage, and without communicating with any living soul, after her dinner the princess set about writing a letter to her father ... on its being shown to the king ... he was marvellously content and pleased, praising above all things the wisdom and prudence of the princess, his daughter.'[16]

The letter has not survived, which is a pity. It must have cost some effort to write. Henry, meanwhile, was only too happy on the basis of this piece of filial obedience and good sense to let things lie. The girl was not going to present any of the problems her mother had plagued him with for so long. She could be afforded a little time and space before the birth of her half-sibling. When that happened, he would have no choice but to make a decision on her status.

Chapter Four

Mary Abased

'I think you are the most obstinate woman that ever was.'

Thomas Cromwell to Mary, June 1536

The first half of the year 1533 promised a false reassurance of normality for Princess Mary. At the customary exchange of gifts that characterised the New Year, rather than Christmas, in Tudor England, her father gave her a gilt cup and a 'gilt cruse with a cover'. These may not seem very imaginative presents. Mary, as befitted her status, already possessed an impressive collection of such items, going back to her early childhood. Similar valuable pieces of plate were part of Mary's tangible wealth. They were not household items but symbols of privilege, their value indicating the power and riches of the donor and the favoured position of the recipient. Carefully entered into the accounts of the princess's household by her financial controller, Henry VIII's largesse provided glittering evidence of who Mary was. It seemed as if nothing had changed.

At the end of May, Mary spent several weeks at the archbishop of Canterbury's palace at Otford in Kent. She seems to have liked it there and had also visited the previous autumn, when she was joined by her cousin, Frances Brandon. But that summer, Frances's mother was dying and there was no question of the cousins sharing each other's company. When the duchess of Suffolk died in June 1533, Mary and her own mother lost a staunch friend. The king had not forgiven the little sister on whom he once doted for her very public disapproval of Anne Boleyn, and the two of them were never really reconciled. Mary Tudor died away from court, on her estate in East Anglia, but her daughter Frances remained close to Mary throughout an eventful life which saw her own daughter usurp Mary's throne.

Despite this family bereavement and the uncertainties about her own future, Mary's time in Kent passed pleasantly enough. She had sufficient leisure to occupy herself with problems faced by members of her household and to ask favours on their behalf. Still styling herself 'Marye Princess', she wrote to Thomas Cromwell, Henry's chief minister, requesting his understanding if the 80-year-old father of one of her servants did not come to London in person to receive the knighthood he had recently been awarded.[1] Mary was a concerned and considerate mistress to her servants and their families throughout her life, a trait that she must have inherited from her mother, since her father never showed the slightest sense of loyalty to those around him. Her life unruffled, or so it seemed, the young princess was happy to be able to use her influence for the benefit of others.

Having handled her father's new marriage with sense and diplomacy, perhaps Mary allowed herself to believe that her own situation was still secure. The court remained at Greenwich, where Anne Boleyn was finding the last months of pregnancy difficult, and Henry did not go on his normal summer progress. Mary had good information on what was happening from the marchioness of Exeter and from the imperial ambassador. She could do nothing but wait. But there were ominous signs of what was to come.

In mid-July, Lord Hussey, her chamberlain, was required by Cromwell to obtain Mary's jewels. Placed in a most uncomfortable position between the demands of the king and the determination of his daughter not to give up a key element of what made her a princess, Hussey squirmed with embarrassment. He was anxious that Cromwell should know of his attempts to carry out the royal command, but he met with a wall of obstruction from Mary and the countess of Salisbury. First, they stalled, saying that no inventory of Mary's jewels could be found; then the princess announced that she would not hand anything over unless she saw the king's letter expressly ordering this. Hussey struggled for more than a month. Naturally, there was exactly the same lack of cooperation when he tried to obtain the princess's plate, being dismissed by the countess with the curt observation that the plate 'cannot conveniently be spared', as if this was a begging neighbour asking for a loan of crockery, not a king demanding return of his possessions. No wonder Hussey vented some of his exasperation on Cromwell: 'Would to God that the king and you did know what I have had to do here of late.'[2] Mary was an intelligent, stubborn girl, and her passion for finery, which must already have been developed by the age of 17, was an essential part of her character. She loved her jewels for their beauty as well as the rank they conferred, and she would not give them up meekly. She was also proud and born to command, not to be ordered about by her chamberlain. The rational part of her already knew what was happening, and she had passed the first test, her father's remarriage, with considerable maturity. But the emotional strain was beginning to tell. Her mental and physical well-being could not be separated. Everything now depended on the child Anne Boleyn was carrying. For Mary, this would be a far greater challenge to her composure than the humiliation of her mother, heartbreaking though that had been.

Katherine was naturally concerned for her daughter's welfare. Although she had not seen her for two years she knew from Mary's letters how the princess was faring and she had a further, much-appreciated source of information and support in Charles V's ambassador, Eustace Chapuys. In dangerous and fast-changing times, Chapuys was Katherine's link with the outside world, the visible face of her nephew at the English court. He was also to become a mentor to Mary and, although it is an exaggeration to say he was a father-figure to the princess, since the differences in their social rank would have made that an unrealistic description of their relationship, still he was a very important constant in some of the most difficult years of her life.

Chapuys replaced Inigo de Mendoza as imperial ambassador in the summer of 1529. Mendoza was a Spaniard, the bishop of Burgos, and an old-style diplomat who combined representation of his country abroad with religious office. This was not at all uncommon at the time, and a number of French and English diplomats held religious posts as well. The alternative source of income was an attraction, given that ambassadors were seldom well paid and had to find ready money for their own expenses and networks of informers. But Mendoza, who complained of constant ill health, was viewed as too hot-tempered and tactless to handle the increasing complications of the situation in England. He was, in fact, the last Spaniard to represent Charles in London for the rest of the emperor's reign. Henceforward, imperial diplomats came from other parts of the emperor's domains, either the Low Countries or eastern parts of modern France. They were civil servants rather than church grandees and were often accomplished professionals. Mary would work with four different imperial ambassadors during her life, but none of them played a more crucial role in her development than Eustace Chapuys.

Katherine had specifically requested Chapuys as Mendoza's replacement because of his legal expertise and prowess in Latin. She believed he could help her over the divorce but, in the end, it was her daughter to whom he rendered the greater service. He was a Savoyard, born in Annecy, around 1490. One year before Mary's birth, he left the University of Turin with a doctorate, and began to establish himself in the government service that was to be his life. In 1517, the bishop of Geneva put him in a key post in the diocese, dealing with the Swiss cantons, where Latin was the official language. On an intellectual as well as a linguistic level he was also highly regarded, being perfectly in tune with the humanist ideas of his day. Chapuys corresponded with Erasmus and counted Heinrich Cornelius Agrippa of Nettesheim, a leading European figure, as one of his closest friends.

His professional life was varied. He progressed through the service of the duke of Savoy and the constable of Bourbon until, in 1527, he entered the employment of Charles V. Two years later he was given the difficult and by no means attractive posting to England. There he remained for 16 years, a faithful servant of his master and a committed opponent of the French, whom he hated because of their designs on his homeland, though he spoke and wrote French fluently. He is also one of the most detailed sources of information that we have on Mary's life at this period. The impact of the divorce and subsequent sweeping changes in religion in England come alive in his fluid if sometimes rambling dispatches. Charles V did not always agree with him and Chapuys' interpretations of what was happening were not always correct, but he was a shrewd observer of men. Though he thoroughly disapproved of the king's treatment of Mary, as well as the chaos into which he had plunged England, he personally found Henry VIII courteous and affable. To say he liked him might be an exaggeration, but there was definitely respect.

Of course, Chapuys is far from being totally reliable, though criticisms of him often miss the point. He did not like England or the English and this seems to have offended later commentators on his diplomatic correspondence. But why should he have liked this small, chilly country on the north-west fringes of Europe with a devious and increasingly domineering monarch? The ambassador's role there, at the time Chapuys took it up, was something of a poisoned chalice, difficult because of the sensitive and uncharted nature of the unfolding domestic drama. From the perspective of those advising the emperor across the North Sea in Brussels, English affairs often seemed peripheral to the multiplicity of considerations faced by Charles V on the wider European stage. England had strange customs and a greedy, venal and violent ruling class. This was not a plum assignment, but it was a demanding one. Henry may have been concerned about the lack of a son, but Charles and those about him were frequently more worried about the proximity of the Turks and the designs of the French.

Chapuys' attitude towards the country in which he was to spend the better part of his professional life was no different from that of many educated Europeans who were his contemporaries. It would never have occurred to him to study English because it was not an international language, though by the end of his assignment he must have picked up a reasonable amount, having heard it spoken by servants and in private exchanges between the politicians he frequented.

Besides, when all of those he dealt with spoke Latin, the common language of the day, or French (and sometimes both), he had no need to grapple with the native tongue of the country. Like all ambassadors, he employed spies and informers and he knew that their information was not always accurate. Some of what he passed on to Charles V and to Granvelle, the bishop of Arras, responsible for much of imperial diplomatic policy, was overstated or misguided. Occasionally, it was just plain wrong. Quite a lot of it was repetitive, a common problem when ambassadors were expected to report weekly and in detail. Coding and decoding were time-consuming and isolating, requiring literal burning of the midnight oil in rooms that were stuffy in summer and draughty in winter. Subordinates did some of this work, but the ambassador often did it himself. Chapuys' grasp of English proper names, the towns and districts and the leading individuals often appears laughable, at least until we remember that there was no uniform spelling at the time. In the 1550s, Elizabeth, Mary's half-sibling, would variously address her as 'Dear Sister' and 'Dear Sistar', so Chapuys can hardly be blamed for getting Jane

Seymour's surname wrong when she was first mentioned in court gossip.

It is true that he represented what was happening in England almost entirely from the perspective of the central government. He only rarely travelled outside London and knew little of the rest of the country, but he saw no need to stray from the seat of power. Throughout his long stay, he resided near to the court at Greenwich, in the pleasantly rural and green outskirts to the east of London. Always he was close to the River Thames, the main artery of transport. In 1533, when Mary's need of him suddenly became greater than her mother's, he was living in the house of Sir Giles Cappel, west of Tower Hill. He was seldom, however, allowed to see the princess. The contacts were through servants and trusted intermediaries, who had greater freedom of movement. Those who came and went, facilitating vital communications between Mary and the ambassador, were almost never named. The king must have known about the existence of these contacts but he let them continue. It would have been difficult to put a stop to them altogether, unless Mary was put under 24-hour watch.

Sometimes Chapuys' activities and advice could easily have been viewed by the king and his council as fomenting discord and rebellion. Considerable forbearance was exhibited, but he does not seem to have been regarded as a serious threat, even when he advocated invasion by imperial troops to support Katherine of Aragon or made tentative plans for the escape overseas of Mary. How much faith he himself had in these schemes is a moot point. There is a feeling about them that he was occasionally frustrated by his inability to do anything practical to help Katherine and her daughter. Perhaps he also wanted to get Charles's attention. Whatever the reason, it made no difference. The emperor himself had long since determined that he could be of very little direct assistance to his aunt and cousin.

We owe much to Eustace Chapuys and his sense of duty and commitment to the task he had been given. Sixteen years in a court that was seldom genuinely welcoming, where nothing and no one could be taken at face value, put a premium on resourcefulness and self-discipline. He had few friends in England, particularly after the death in 1532 of Archbishop Warham, but he was consoled by his continued exchange of letters with Erasmus. Without him, we would know far less than we do about this tumultuous period of English history. And Mary would have been deprived of the one figure she believed she could trust when her world crumbled. He tried to support her in a way that he believed appropriate to her rank and condition and to adapt his advice to keep pace with developments, while never losing sight of his imperial role. It was a difficult balance. She, no doubt, saw Chapuys as a wise counsellor, but in his genuine concern for her welfare, his outrage at the treatment she received and his pity for her mother, there is more than a hint of genuine affection. His own family, of many nieces and nephews and one acknowledged illegitimate son, were far away in Annecy, a town that he never saw again after 1529. He, like Mary, was basically alone.

He also shared her distaste for the rise of new religious ideas. By education and temperament, he was attuned to the humanist ideas of Erasmus and other leading thinkers, but he would have no truck with heresy. For much of his long stay in England, Mary was one of his chief concerns. Her father might call her 'The Lady Mary'; for Chapuys, she was always 'the Princess'. He saw the changes that tragedy and pressure wrought in her and was dismayed. What he could do for her was, obviously, circumscribed, but he did his best. And it may be that, in the summer of 1536, when her relationship with her own father reached crisis point, he saved her life.

As autumn approached in 1533, Mary moved to New Hall, one of her father's country houses in Essex. The mansion was known as Beaulieu at the time, and it was one of Henry's finest residences outside London. It was here that Henry had met his advisers to go over the arrangements for what he thought would be a quick annulment of his marriage to Katherine of Aragon, six years earlier. Now, there soon arrived the announcement that was the distant finale to those discussions. Queen Anne had given birth on 7 September. Rejoicing, however, was subdued. The child was a girl. Henry put a brave face on it, but the truth was that his search for a son to succeed him was still unfulfilled. For the time being, he must content himself with another daughter. The baby was named Elizabeth, and it was clear from the outset that she would supplant her elder sister. In Henry's eyes, Anne's girl was his heir (though he hoped that brothers would follow) and England's only princess. Perhaps he did not care to think back to 1516, and his confident remarks that boys would follow after Mary. Anne Boleyn was actually a year older than Katherine of Aragon when she gave birth to Elizabeth, though she did not have her predecessor's history of failed pregnancies and dead princes.

In fact, Elizabeth's birth did not solve anything. But its impact on the two women it most directly affected, Anne herself and Mary, was profound. Anne's position would have been immeasurably strengthened if she had produced a boy, though the assumption that Mary would have recognised the precedence of a prince born of a union she regarded as adulterous is open to doubt. She might well have regarded him as another illegitimate half-brother, like the duke of Richmond. Or she might have bided her time and waited to see how her father treated her. What seems beyond belief is that she would ever have accepted that she was not a princess of the blood. So Elizabeth's arrival made her decision easier. She simply would not give way to a younger sister. There was no agonising over the course of action to be taken as there was no alternative. Anne Boleyn had destroyed her mother's life and now Mary, utterly certain that she was the king's only true heir, set herself up deliberately as the focus of opposition to Anne. She would not go away, she would not back down. There was widespread sympathy for her, inside England and abroad. Anne always suffered from the fact that she never established a broad base of support, either at court or in the country as a whole, and her main source of foreign support was France, England's traditional enemy. When Anne first came on the scene, Mary did not possess the skills or experience to trouble her and was kept well away from confrontation. Over the years of her mother's adversity, she had behaved with caution and tact, but she had been learning all the while. It is a mistake to view her reaction to Elizabeth's birth as a straightforward case of hysteria and *amour propre*. She knew what the stakes were, as did Anne Boleyn. The rivalry between the two women was as implacable as Anne, who was often given to hyperbole, described it: 'I am her death and she is mine.'

What Mary did not adequately understand was the likely reaction of Henry VIII. And her father, because he was king and all must obey him, did not trouble himself with worries about how she would respond to his commands regarding her. In fact, they showed a wilful lack of mutual comprehension. Mary claimed she would obey her father but defied him for three years. The king would no doubt have preferred not to hurt her (though his affection for her is hard to quantify), but there was no way he could humour her. A king who allowed a daughter to dictate to him on matters of state was no king at all. He sought to make the situation abundantly clear within days of Elizabeth's birth. Mary was to cease using the title princess immediately and her badges, the green and blue livery her servants had used since she was born, were to be removed and replaced with his own. Mary reacted with an incredulity that was almost sneering, writing to her father:

> This morning my chamberlain came and informed me that he had received a letter from Sir William Paulet, controller of your House, to the effect that I should remove at once to Hertford Castle. I desired to see the letter, in which was written 'the Lady Mary, the king's daughter', leaving out the name of princess. I marvelled at this, thinking your grace was not privy to it, not doubting that you take me for your lawful daughter … If I agreed to the contrary, I should offend God; in all other things, you shall find me an obedient daughter.[3]

This rebuke, which implied that the king did not keep track of correspondence sent out in his name and was being manipulated, provoked a swift response. If she wanted her father to spell out her change of status, he would meet her challenge. A deputation, led by the earls of Oxford, Essex and Sussex, was sent off to face down this impudent young lady. They delivered a message phrased in unequivocal tones:

> The king is surprised to be informed, both by Lord Hussey's letters and his daughter's own, delivered by one of her servants, that she, forgetting her filial duty and allegiance, attempts, in spite of the commandment given her … arrogantly to usurp the title of princess, pretending to be heir apparent … declaring that she cannot in conscience think but that she is the king's lawful daughter, born in true matrimony, and believes that the king in his conscience thinks the same.

To prevent what was called Mary's 'pernicious example' spreading, the earls were commanded to represent to Mary 'the folly and danger of her conduct and how the king intends that she shall use herself both as to her title and as to her household'. It was further pointed out that she had 'worthily deserved the king's high displeasure and punishment by law, but that on her conforming to his will, he may incline of his fatherly pity to promote her welfare'.[4] Though there was a hint of the carrot as well as the stick in this pronouncement, it outlined the relative positions of the king and Mary very precisely. In Henry's eyes, his elder daughter was illegitimate. She would be treated as a king's acknowledged offspring, but she was not a princess of England. He had not endured the upheaval of years of argument about his first marriage to leave any doubts unanswered now. Mary's feelings did not enter into it. His will was law, applicable to all his subjects, without question.

Yet a challenge to his authority was exactly what Henry now faced. Mary was standing up to him just as her mother had done. If she had succeeded, he would have been weakened in his own eyes and the eyes of the world. In some ways, it is astonishing that he let Mary's defiance last as long as he did. Yet his patience, or indecision, did Mary no good. She had the spirit of her Castilian grandmother but not her armies. The support, often only tacit, of a handful of courtiers could not help her win her battle. In retrospect, it might have been better for her if Henry's eventual brutality had been administered at once. The delay raised false hopes and developed in her a pattern of opposition based on conscience and self-identity, where suffering almost became a goal in itself. This was unhealthy and damaging to a woman subject to depression, who never subsequently understood that to be strong, rather than pragmatic, was not always the best option.

Chapuys, reporting the christening of the child that he consistently referred to as 'the little Bastard', betrayed his anxiety that the withdrawal of Mary's title was only the beginning: 'In fact a rumour is afloat … that her household and allowance are to be shortly reduced. May God in his infinite mercy prevent a still worse treatment!' But, he added, Mary was taking it all well and her first thought was for her mother: 'meanwhile the princess, prudent and virtuous as she is, has taken all these things with patience, trusting entirely in God's mercy and goodness. She has addressed to her mother, the queen, a most wonderful letter, full of consolation and comfort.'[5]

The ambassador's characterisation of Mary's response was highly misleading. She had accepted nothing, and she was far from prudent. In this first great crisis of her life, she showed how much she was her mother's daughter. For the choice that Henry compelled her to make was not so much between himself and Katherine, as it has often been characterised, but between her rightful heritage, as she saw it, and denial of who she was. It was also an overtly political choice, and it set her on a collision course with many of those close to the king, who were much more seasoned political campaigners. At a meeting in the second week of September with Cromwell and the duke of Norfolk, at which George Boleyn, Anne's brother, skulked in the vicinity but took no direct part,

Chapuys reiterated his concern for Mary. Disingenuously, he told the chancellor and the duke that he understood the proclamation made at the birth of the king's new daughter, but 'I was only afraid that by so doing the rights of the first-born might be impaired ... Hearing this, the duke and the chancellor looked at each other for a time without knowing what to say.'[6] It was, of course, perfectly evident what they were thinking; Mary was serving notice that she took precedence over Elizabeth. Even as she recovered from the birth, Anne Boleyn already knew that Mary would not acknowledge her or her child.

Henry's first move was to implement the threat to reduce the number of Mary's household. This was more of a gesture than a fixed intention to deprive her of all her servants. The privy chamber staff remained more or less untouched and her establishment still numbered about 160 persons. The countess of Salisbury, Richard Fetherstone and Lord Hussey stayed in post. Everything now hinged on Mary's acceptance of her father's orders. Compliance with his commands would have left Mary to continue her life much as she had done before. But it would also have meant acknowledging her own illegitimacy and the invalidity of her mother's marriage. This she could never accept, and by 10 October it was obvious to Chapuys that the situation was deteriorating. Mary would not be told what to do by a deputation of elderly aristocrats, sent to convey her father's instructions. When they left, she

> wrote a long letter to the king, her father, saying that she would as long as she lived obey his commands, but that she really could not renounce the titles, rights and privileges which God, Nature and her own parents had given her. Being the daughter of a king and queen, putting aside other circumstances, she was rightly called princess. The king, her father, might do his pleasure and give her any title he liked, but it could not be said of her that she had expressly or tacitly prejudiced her legitimacy or the rights of the queen, her mother, whose example she was determined to follow, by placing herself entirely in the hands of God, and bearing with patience all her misfortunes.[7]

So the die was cast. It is hard to imagine an answer that would have displeased Henry more. It was defiant, supercilious and contemptuous of Henry's authority. As long as she lived, she would obey his commands, but only when these suited her. And he had no right to deprive her of her title. Only God could do that. But Henry knew that what God gaveth, he, as king, could take away. Having used the word of God as his excuse for defying the pope, the emperor and anyone else who disagreed with him, Henry could not stomach it being thrown at him as a justification for brazen disobedience by a 17-year-old girl. And he had had enough of her prim, unyielding letters. By 3 November, Mary's household was being dismantled and the countess of Salisbury was dismissed. Her offers to continue with Mary at her own expense were rebuffed. The king believed that the countess and others of those around Mary were responsible for encouraging her stance and he wanted her separated from them. 'This the king has done, as he says, to daunt and intimidate her.' He would put both his daughters in the same household, partly for reasons of economy but also to keep Mary in check. Whether he or Anne Boleyn actually proposed that Mary should serve Elizabeth as a maid of honour is not clear, though it is the sort of remark that Anne might have made. Nor would it have been entirely inappropriate for an illegitimate daughter, if she had been brought up as such. But Mary had not and she was appalled. 'Both the queen and the princess', reported Chapuys, 'are marvellously disturbed and in great trouble. They sent to me … for advice in this emergency and begged I would speak to Cromwell and see what could be done to arrest the blow.'

Katherine exhorted Mary to be strong: 'Almighty God will prove you; and I am very glad of it, for I trust He doth handle you with a good love … I pray you, good daughter, to offer yourself to Him … for then you are sure armed.' Isabella of Castile would have approved of such zeal in the face of the enemy. Whether Mary really embraced what was happening to her so enthusiastically is debatable, but she followed as closely as she could her mother's precepts. Katherine, in her own way, kept up as much pressure on her as her father did, imploring her in tones very reminiscent of Juan Luis Vives 'to keep your heart with a chaste mind, and your body from an ill and wanton company, [not] thinking or desiring any husband for Christ's passion; neither determine yourself any manner of living till this troublesome time be past'.[8] How long it would be in passing neither mother nor daughter knew.

If Mary had not fully appreciated what he might do when she confronted her father in writing a few weeks earlier, she could have no illusions now. She recognised that if she was to get something of what she wanted, she would need to work through Cromwell, as well as Chapuys. But Cromwell could not (or would not) see Chapuys at this point, so the ambassador sent his secretary with veiled threats that imperial friendship might be withdrawn and expressing astonishment at the treatment of Mary. Cromwell's answer was studiously opaque:

> ... He begged to be excused and pardoned if he did not reveal to me in particular what he knew of the princess' affair. This having been discussed in the Privy Council with the greatest possible secrecy, he could not reveal it to me or to anyone else unless he had the permission and consent ... of the king. He could, however, assure me in general terms that the king was an honourable, virtuous and wise prince, incapable of doing anything that was not founded on justice and reason.

The ambassador's secretary was told that there was no one in the whole privy council who laboured more assiduously than Thomas Cromwell to foster good relations with Charles V. Up till now, he had done 'all that was within his power' in relation to the treatment of Katherine and Mary, 'and would still do so in the future'.[9]

This was certainly what both Chapuys and Mary hoped, for Cromwell was their only effective channel to the king. The wily politician now began to figure prominently in Mary's life. Cromwell, a Londoner and son of a cloth merchant, was a highly able lawyer, then in his late forties. Over the centuries, historians have seen him as the driver of the Reformation in England, the author of the legal changes that separated the English Church from Rome and the destroyer of its monastic life and institutions. His true role and importance have recently been questioned.[10] Yet even if the king, and not Cromwell, was the moving force behind many of the changes in government and religion during the decade, 'Good Master Secretary', as Mary always addressed him, convinced his contemporaries of his influence. It is hard to imagine how the Reformation in England might have taken shape without this former member of the House of Commons, a property lawyer who had ably served Wolsey. Showing great skill in networking, Cromwell survived the cardinal's fall. His growing interest in new religious ideas and his administrative competence made him extremely useful to the king. Ruthless and cynical, by 1533 he was chancellor of the exchequer, but everyone knew that he was destined for greater office. Certainly Mary thought he was important and Chapuys could not function without him. The two men came to know one another well and their relationship was one of wary respect. Neither trusted the other but circumstances forced them to work together. Cromwell was a difficult man to know, and the image he projected was of the consummate minister, trying to accommodate the desires of his monarch in a search for the best solutions for England. He was self-effacing but in a way that left no doubt that he was someone to be reckoned with. Despite avowals to the contrary – his professed desire to be of service, to smooth things over, to make Mary's life easier – one is left with the strong impression that he was utterly indifferent to Mary personally. She was part of a problem that needed to be solved. Ameliorating her situation and restoring her finally to a better relationship with her father was one way forward, but it was not the only possible outcome. During 1534 he told Chapuys more than once that if her ill health continued and it pleased God to take her, well, so be it. Perhaps he said this only with the intention of alarming Chapuys, but it is equally possible that he meant it.

Three months after Elizabeth's birth, a household was set up for the infant princess at Hatfield House, in Hertfordshire. When she moved there, in the dark days just a week before Christmas, Lady Anne Shelton, Anne Boleyn's aunt and the baby's lady governess, was already aware that Elizabeth would not be her only charge. Mary was expected to join them imminently.

The news was delivered with his habitual brusqueness by Norfolk. The duke 'went himself to the princess and signified her father's pleasure that she should attend the court and enter the service of his other bastard daughter' (Chapuys' words), whom he referred to, quite deliberately, as princess of Wales. 'Upon which Princess Mary replied: "that is the title which belongs to me by right, and to no one else."'[11] She then proceeded to explain politely but firmly how unfitting the proposals being made to her were. It was not what Norfolk wanted to hear and he cut her short: 'he had not gone hither to dispute but to see the king's wishes accomplished and his commands executed'. Mary then asked for half an hour alone and used the time to draw up a formal protest, probably using a wording suggested earlier by Chapuys. When she emerged, still apparently in command of her emotions, she asked Norfolk to give those of her servants who were being dismissed one year's wages and asked how many she could take with her to Hatfield. The reply was not encouraging. There would be plenty of servants where she was going, so no great train was needed. Margaret Douglas was removed from Mary's service and sent off to join Anne Boleyn's entourage. The attractive and popular Margaret, a favourite of her uncle, the king, adapted immediately and got on surprisingly well with the new queen. For Mary, the prospects were much less encouraging. She was left with just two ladies and a small number of male retainers from her staff. Her farewells to the countess of Salisbury must have been painful, and Margaret Pole, who been her guide for many years, no doubt shared Chapuys' concern as to how Mary would cope.

Mary arrived at Hatfield forlorn and apprehensive, dreading what lay ahead and convinced that she would not find friends there. Norfolk, still doggedly carrying out Henry's instructions, asked whether she would like to 'see and pay court to the princess'. This was deliberate provocation of a vulnerable young woman, stripped of all the certainties of her existence. From the very outset, she was placed in a hostile relationship with Elizabeth. But, even at this moment, she strove to retain her dignity and deflect any animosity that she might have felt for the baby. 'She answered that she knew of no other princess in England but herself. She would treat her as a sister, but that was all.' Mary was then asked whether she had any message for her father and replied: 'None, except that the princess of Wales, his daughter, asked for his blessing.'[12] It was a vain hope and probably Mary knew it. Henry, when he heard, was angry with Norfolk, reproaching him for treating his stubborn daughter too mildly. This was not the way to make her see sense. 'He would soon find the means of humiliating her and subduing her temper.'[13] Perhaps if he had seen her he would have realised that he had made a good start. Mary, often in tears, passed a miserable Christmas at Hatfield.

At the New Year, Anne Boleyn presented her husband with 'a goodly gilt bason, having a rail or board of gold in the midst of the brim, garnished with rubies and pearls, wherein standeth a fountain, also having a rail of gold about it garnished with diamonds; out thereof issueth water, at the teats of three naked women standing at the foot of the same fountain'.[14] This lavish and slightly risqué gift (Anne may not have condoned lax morals among her ladies but she evidently had a broader sense of humour where Henry was concerned) was beyond the reach of Mary, whose finances were entirely dependent on what her father chose to give her. In any case, there is no record of the king and his wayward daughter exchanging any gifts at the start of 1534. Too much had come between them. Mary was not merely in disgrace; she was now effectively under house arrest.

· ❖ ·

Anne Shelton did not see herself as a jailer. She was about 50 years old
and a mother of six children when she found herself in charge of the
joint household of Elizabeth and Mary. At a time when she might have
expected to concentrate on her own family and enjoy the comforts of
her home in Norfolk, this younger sister of Sir Thomas Boleyn found
herself in charge of the king's two daughters. Despite the salary and
status, it was a task she often found unrewarding. In theory, Elizabeth was
her primary responsibility, and though the baby's day-to-day welfare was
in the hands of an experienced team (as Mary's had been, at the same
age), Lady Shelton knew she would shoulder the blame if the little
princess fell ill, or – an even more uncomfortable thought – died.

Mary, though, was a quite different case. The general assumption that
Anne Boleyn engineered her aunt's appointment in order to make
Mary's life a misery has an element of truth, but Mary gave as good as
she got. From the moment she arrived at Hatfield, she radiated resentment and the stubbornness that came with her pride and sense of loss.
She was determined to be treated differently, requiring meals at times
that did not fit in with the rest of the household, a separate and more
expensive diet and the freedom to take copious amounts of exercise. This
was believed to be good for her menstrual problems and was undoubtedly of great psychological importance to her, as well as physical benefit.
From Lady Shelton's point of view, though, it was a vexing demand. She
could not allow Mary to ride, or even walk, unsupervised. The girl's
fragile health merely added to her difficulties. How serious was it? How
should it be treated? Supposing, as Chapuys pointed out, Mary died in
her care? Then there would be accusations of poison. The lady governess
was horrified. It was difficult enough to follow the king's commands
where his daughter was concerned, and Mary's uncooperativeness exasperated her. But to be suspected as a poisoner was too much.

Strained as their relationship often was, Lady Shelton actually admired
Mary. She knew that she was a great lady brought low, and when she failed
to follow some of the nastier orders for breaking Mary's spirit, it was
because she baulked at the idea of grinding a king's daughter into the
ground. At the end of February 1534, she was told off by the duke of
Norfolk and Lord Rochford, Anne's brother, 'for behaving to the
princess with too much respect and kindness, saying that she ought only

to be treated as a bastard'. Anne Shelton gave a robust reply: 'Even if the princess were only the bastard of a poor gentleman, she deserved honour and good treatment for her goodness and virtues.' In other circumstances, the new governess might have been a suitable replacement for the countess of Salisbury, but Mary was never going to trust a Boleyn. Nor could the queen's aunt extend too much tolerance, given that her instructions were to keep Mary closely watched and to try, whenever she could, to get her to acknowledge the precedence of Anne Boleyn and her daughter. Whether Mary did this freely or reluctantly did not much matter.

A sensible woman, Lady Shelton recognised from the outset that she was unlikely to meet her niece's wishes in that respect, but she was vigilant in barring access to Mary by Chapuys and his servants. This would have been too obvious a dereliction of duty and, besides, she must have known that Mary had means of communicating with the outside world. She could not afford to keep an open house. The king's wrath if Mary escaped was an ever-present concern. But there is no evidence, despite Anne's threats and the imperial ambassador's fears, that Mary was ever physically assaulted. Anne might order her aunt to 'box her ears as a cursed bastard' if Mary continued wilfully to refer to herself as 'princess' but the lady governess did not resort to violence. Letting Mary know what had been said would have been enough to cause great distress, and Anne Shelton soon learned that provoking Mary never produced the desired effect. There was no poison at Hatfield, as Chapuys dreaded there might be, but the atmosphere was constantly tense and harsh words were often exchanged. Mary's temper was not helped by the fact that she had very little to do except dwell on her situation. Her formal education came to an end in 1533. There was no schoolroom with the attentive Dr Fetherstone at Hatfield. The contrast with the domestic tranquillity of Mary's life as a princess could not have been more marked. If her emotions frequently got the better of her, it is hardly surprising. And Anne Shelton, having to cope daily with her charge's hostility, did not have an easy time of it.

Henry and Anne now had Mary where they wanted, but they could not get her to do what they wanted. Henry demanded Mary's obedience and he was getting tired of being told how to manage his family. Charles V may have felt there was nothing to be done while his aunt lost her throne and his cousin her inheritance, but even he seems to have been stung by the desperate, bitter letter Katherine of Aragon addressed to him in February 1534. She begged the pope to do her justice and the emperor to take action in the matter. She and Mary, she said, were imprisoned 'like the most miserable creatures in the world'.[15] Her rebuke developed in the emperor a high-minded intention that he would become a father to Mary since her own had evidently abandoned her. Naturally, this did not sit at all well with Henry VIII. The emperor's efforts to find Mary a husband, as a way out of her troubles, caused especial offence. They were also unlikely to succeed for, as James V of Scotland, a potential bridegroom, pointed out, Charles was not in a position to deliver Mary and her own father had declared her to be a bastard. But Mary was grateful for the emperor's support and she did, indeed, begin to think of him as a father from this time. Charles's most lasting contribution to the entire divorce episode was to widen the breach between the king and his daughter.

When Chapuys finally obtained an audience with the king at the end of February, the ambassador protested about the treatment of Katherine and Mary. Henry must have expected this and he responded 'graciously' at first, remarking that Chapuys knew he was legally married to his present wife. The first marriage, Henry reminded him, had been pronounced unlawful, so Katherine could not be called queen and Mary could not succeed. And he added, significantly: 'Even if she [Mary] were legitimate, her disobedience merited disinheritance.' But Chapuys was not deterred. He pointed out that Parliament could not make Mary a bastard. Legitimacy cases could be decided only by ecclesiastical judges, and, besides, Mary was legitimate 'owing to the lawful ignorance of her parents. The king himself had considered her as the true Princess until the birth of his new daughter.' This may have been the truth, but it was definitely not what Henry wanted to hear, and he grew irritated. According to English law, he told Chapuys, Mary could not succeed: 'there was no other princess except his daughter Elizabeth, until he had a son, which he thought should happen soon'. In other words, time would solve the problem and Henry did not consider Elizabeth as a serious successor, either.

Perhaps he thought this would disarm the imperialists, but Chapuys boldly pushed for better conditions for Mary and asked that she be allowed to live with her mother. He raised the possibility of unpleasant rumours if Mary fell ill. This upset the royal equilibrium altogether.

Mary, Henry claimed, 'was well and in a good place, and he might dispose of her as he wished, without anyone laying down the law to him, and without giving account to anyone'. Later he was to state that children owed some obedience to their mothers but more to their fathers. There was nothing remarkable in this. Henry was a king and a man of his times. Mary owed him unquestioning loyalty and she had forfeited all due consideration by refusing it. To place her with her mother would mean that she could never be brought to see reason. Neither king nor ambassador emerged fully satisfied from this encounter, and Chapuys continued to believe that the king's 'amie' would press for harsher treatment still.[16]

He was right to be fearful. Mary stood between Anne and her husband, as well as threatening the queen's security. The relationship between Anne and Henry was always tempestuous. Her outspokenness and involvement in politics did not make her an easy spouse; there was a great deal of love but also a great deal of temper. And Anne, for all her declamations, was less confident than she seemed. There had been many attacks on her and she stood at the centre of a storm that showed no sign of abating. Despite what Henry had told Chapuys, there was a notable defensiveness about official pronouncements on Henry's marriage. Suspiciously fulsome depictions of the new queen appeared in instructions given to the churchman Nicholas Heath when he prepared to go on embassy to the German princes. Anne was described as a person

> whose approved and excellent virtues, that is to say, the purity of her life, her constant virginity, her maidenly and womanly pudicity, her soberness, her chasteness, her meekness, her wisdom, her descent of right noble and high parentage, her education in all good and laudable thewes and manners, her aptness to procreation of children, with other infinite good qualities … cannot but be most acceptable unto Almighty God, and deserve His high grace and favour, to the singular weal and benefit of the king's realm and subjects.[17]

Was it truly necessary to depict Anne as such a paragon to the already disaffected vassals of Charles V in Germany? Even if the wording was intended to be used in other countries as well, its air of special pleading indicates that Henry strongly felt the need to underline Anne's credentials as queen. She was deliberately being positioned against Katherine and Mary. There had always been universal praise for Mary's virtues and achievements, and Anne's credibility needed a boost. She was not, after all, of royal blood, and the mystery that attached to royalty always eluded her, anointed queen consort though she was. The queen herself was acutely aware of the intangible nature of the ties between Henry and his daughter, and she worried about them. She was determined to isolate Mary and to stiffen Henry's resolve.

Her persistence is understandable, since the signs are that Henry was at first minded to bring matters to a head by speaking to Mary in person. In mid-January 1534, when Mary had been at Hatfield for only a month, Henry set out from London with the intention of visiting both his daughters. 'One of the principal causes of his going was to persuade or force the princess to renounce her title.' But, once he had gone, Anne grew anxious. She sent Cromwell after the king to dissuade him from seeing Mary. She feared, probably justifiably, that at best the meeting would be inconclusive; more worryingly, Henry might be persuaded by his daughter's pleading to give way. The king followed Cromwell's advice and sent the minister himself to press Mary to renounce her title. It is not clear whether he had ever spoken directly to Mary before, but he could have been left in no doubt of her firmness of purpose. She told him 'that she had already given a decided answer, it was labour wasted to press her and they were deceived if they thought that bad treatment or rudeness, or even the chance of death, would make her change her determination'.

Aware that there might not be many such chances to appeal directly to her father, Mary asked for leave to come and kiss his hand. This was refused, but still she was not to be entirely thwarted. She must, at least, make sure he saw her, so that he would retain in his mind the imprint of a gesture of submissiveness. 'When the king was going to mount his horse she went on to a terrace at the top of the house to see him. The king, either being told of it, or by chance, turned round, and seeing her on her knees with her hands joined, bowed to her and put his hand to his hat.'[18] This courtly response was second nature to Henry VIII, but it did not mean that his heart was melted. His ambivalence remained. He told the French ambassador that he had not spoken to the princess because of her obstinacy, which came from her Spanish blood. Yet when the ambassador politely remarked that Mary had been very well brought up, 'the tears came into his eyes and he could not refrain from praising her'. But he continued to heed his wife's concerns. Mary did not see her father again for more than two and a half years.

Anne Boleyn got her way. She succeeded in keeping them apart and never wavered from this course. A more subtle woman might have considered outmanoeuvring Mary by occasionally bringing her to court, treating her with kindness and consideration and letting her show the world that, if she continued to defy her father, she was just a sulky, jealous child and a disobedient daughter. The new queen, who liked to be the centre of attention, feared Mary too much to follow such a strategy. Their meetings during Anne's reign, though few, followed a predictable course. Anne attempted to reason with Mary, holding out the promise of better treatment; Mary invariably responded with scathing rudeness, as only someone brought up as a princess could; Anne, her temper barely in check at most times, then got very angry indeed. But the moral victory was clear. It was always Mary's. A striking example of this is their confrontation in March 1534, when Anne had gone to Hatfield to see Elizabeth. 'She urgently solicited the princess to visit her and honour her as queen, saying that it would be a means of reconciliation with the king, and she herself would intercede with him for her, and she would be as well or better treated than ever.' Mary's response was icy: 'she knew no queen in England except her mother', but if 'madame Anne Boleyn' would speak to her father on her behalf, she would be much obliged. Anne tried again, to no effect, 'and in the end threatened her', but Mary was unmoved.[19]

It did her no good. Her defiance clouded her judgement and led to humiliation. Lacking any other form of protest, obstruction was the only course she could follow. This caused her to concentrate on the distinction between herself and Elizabeth; she was absolutely determined not to recognise the child's superior status. This resolution went to the core of her being. Sometimes it gave rise to tantrums that may have been deliberately calculated, as well as providing an outlet for venting frustrations. At the end of March, Elizabeth's household removed from Hatfield and Mary refused to accompany Anne Shelton in the litter provided for their transport. To follow after Elizabeth would have meant an acknowledgement of her precedence and this Mary was adamant she must avoid. Eventually, one of the gentlemen present had to lift her up and put her bodily in the litter. Often portrayed as an act of gratuitous violence, it may have actually suited Mary quite well. 'She made a public protestation of the compulsion used and that her act should not prejudice her right and title.' She would do this whenever she could. Still, it seems ignominious and Chapuys disapproved. 'I should not have advised the princess to have gone to this extreme, for fear of irritating her father and consequently suffering worse treatment'.[20]

Her treatment remained about the same, with Henry's outlook being more generous at some times than others. For Mary and her mother there was an empty triumph when the pope finally ruled in Katherine's favour in April. Henry was personally angered but it merely confirmed his determination to deny Rome any further role in English affairs. The pope was a distant figure without authority, his pronouncements no longer recognised in England. There was already a new Act of Succession with an oath attached that required all to acknowledge the Boleyn marriage. This placed a further burden on Mary, though she was not forced to take the oath immediately. Any respite she enjoyed was only temporary and the pressure on her, and members of her former household, was maintained. Lady Anne Hussey, wife of Mary's chamberlain, was questioned in the Tower of London about her contact with Mary 'since she lost the name of princess', and whether she had continued to refer to Mary by her title. In July, Anne Boleyn's father, the earl of Wiltshire, pressed Mary to renounce her title, promising that, if she did, the king 'would treat her better than she could wish'. Still, Mary held firm.

There was, however, a price to be paid for her principles. Few people could have come unscathed through the trauma and stress that Mary had suffered. Her world had collapsed, shrunk to a handful of faithful servants and the letters of a desperate mother and a largely powerless imperial representative. Nobody else dared to acknowledge her any longer as a princess. The fear of execution was already there. God alone knew what lay in the future. As the summer came to an end, Mary became seriously ill. Her sickness continued, at varying intervals, over the next two years. Poor health was something Mary had endured since her mid-teens, but this was more severe, more alarming than anything seen before. Chapuys decided to make a major fuss. Mary must not be neglected. He appealed directly to the king and Henry responded by sending his own physician.

On 2 September, Dr William Butts reported to Cromwell on his examination of Mary:

I came to my Lady Mary this day at 7 o'clock, whom I find in a mean state of health, *but at the beginning of her old disease* [emphasis added]. I have caused her mother's physician to be sent for, with the apothecary. The cause of this rumour by the ambassador, as I can learn, comes of two things: that she [Mary] being diseased in her head and stomach, my lady Shelton sent for Mr Michael, who gave her pills, after which she was very sick and he so much troubled that he said he would never minister anything to her alone; and thus signified sharply to the ambassador.[21]

This brief note indicates that Mary, probably suffering from bad headaches and stomach cramps at the start of her period, had been so unwell that Lady Shelton decided to see whether she could get her some medication to ease the discomfort. Mary then suffered a severe reaction to the pills prescribed by the apothecary and was very nauseous. The apothecary, afraid that he would be accused of poisoning the princess, was thoroughly alarmed, as no doubt was Lady Shelton.

It is significant that Katherine of Aragon's doctor was also consulted by Dr Butts. One of the arguments that Katherine used to try to get permission for Mary to join her was that she could cure her illness: 'The comfort and cheerfulness she would have with me would be half her cure. I have found this by experience, being ill of the same sickness.' She repeated this request in 1535, saying that she would nurse Mary in her own bed. The queen did not get her wish, but the involvement of her doctor in Mary's treatment in September helped. Restrictions were applied, however, even in these circumstances. The physicians were not allowed to speak to Mary without witnesses and they were to converse only in English. Nowhere was the precise nature of the illness spelled out. Current medical opinion suggests that Mary suffered from dysmenhorrea (acute period pain). This may have been linked to endometriosis or other conditions such as ovarian cysts, but a precise diagnosis is impossible, given the very fragmentary nature of the evidence. At the time, a mixture of ignorance and embarrassment surrounded the topic.

Mary recovered by the end of the month, but was subjected to recurring bouts of indisposition for the rest of the year and throughout 1535. Though these may have all been caused by her gynaecological condition they were undoubtedly made worse by stress. Dr Butts himself made this clear to the king, when he told Henry that 'her illness arose only from sorrow and trouble; and that she would be well at once if she were free to do as she liked'.[22] This frank assessment troubled the king, who 'heaved a great sigh, saying that it was a great misfortune that she remained so obstinate, and that she took from him all occasion to treat her as well as he would'. But Henry was ambivalent in his attitude, and the opinion of his medical man that Mary's health problems, no matter how nasty, were partly self-inflicted was not calculated to bring anything other than a temporary remission of pressure. When Dr Butts boldly advocated sending Mary to her mother, the king was firm in his refusal to countenance such an idea. There would be no way of getting her to renounce her title and claim if he gave way. It was distressing, but the solution was entirely up to Mary herself.

There were times when Mary experienced relief from her symptoms and then she appeared in surprisingly good health and spirits. During 1534, Chapuys saw her twice, each time at a distance. In the late summer, he saw her when she came to Greenwich and commented on her striking appearance: 'It was a great pleasure to see such excellent beauty accompanied by heroic bearing.' This was shortly before she became seriously ill, but at the end of October he saw her again. The restrictions on her freedom of movement were temporarily lifted, and she had arranged to be rowed along the Thames, so that Chapuys could see her from his house 'in the fields by the river between Greenwich and this town'. He reported that she was in good health and seemed to be happy and very cheerful.

Perhaps some of this was bravura, a performance put on to demonstrate to her cousin the emperor that, as a true princess, she was not cowed by months of harassment. Or maybe she was genuinely pleased to be out on the water and to glide in tranquillity for a while. It was only a brief respite and it changed nothing. The king and his daughter remained at loggerheads. The French ambassador even reported that Henry 'hates her [Mary] thoroughly', and another French diplomat, visiting London on a special mission with the admiral of France, added that the English king was unrepentant in his attitude. Mary was in his power, and would remain so. There was no chance of her becoming queen or claiming any right to the throne.[23] While it is important to remember that Henry wanted to give the impression to the French that Mary counted for nothing (there was already discussion of a marriage between Elizabeth and the third son of Francis I), he never budged from his original position. Mary would be brought to submission. It was never a question of if, only of when.

During 1534 and the following year, Mary watched with growing fearfulness as her father, determined to assert his newly gained authority as head of the Church in England, sent political and religious opponents to their deaths. First to suffer were Elizabeth Barton and those closest to her. The Nun of Kent was made to confess that she was a fraud, manipulated by others. She was hanged and beheaded at Tyburn. The religious orders that had supported Katherine, especially the Carthusians, fared even worse, suffering the horrible traitors' death of hanging, drawing and quartering. The steadfast Bishop Fisher, her only true champion among the clergy, died on the block, his body emaciated from sorrow and imprisonment. 'From age and suffering he was more like a shadow than a man' was the comment of an Italian on his execution. This courageous and honourable churchman was as good as dead already, but Henry wanted his head. He also wanted that of his former chancellor. Thomas More famously put his God before his king and so earned himself a golden place in history.[24] Mary and Katherine, in common with much of Europe, were horrified. In Chapuys' dispatches there is almost an air of disbelief about what was going on in England. It was from this time that Mary began to contemplate escaping to the safety of the imperial court. The notion recurred again at times of crisis, but it appears to have been more of a fantasy than a realistic option. Chapuys dutifully thought about it, but concluded that it would be very difficult. Mary's health continued to be erratic and Cromwell repeated his view that the death of the princess 'would do little harm'. Such a coldly pragmatic observation from the king's closest adviser made Chapuys very uneasy. No doubt this was the intention.

In one respect, however, Henry was still unsuccessful; the original impetus for all this bloodshed and upheaval remained. There was no male heir. Unknown to Mary, Anne Boleyn miscarried in the summer of 1534. It would be more than a year before she conceived again.

The year 1536 was the darkest of Mary's life; a time of violence and rebellion, of political skulduggery on a breathtaking scale and, for Mary herself, irreplaceable loss. It began with death and ended without joy. What happened in between damaged the eldest child of Henry VIII permanently. To understand Mary, it is necessary to relive the events of this murderous year through her eyes.

The New Year was hardly begun when Mary lost her mother. Katherine of Aragon, who had fought so unflinchingly for herself and her daughter, died at Kimbolton Castle on 7 January. Here, on the edge of the Cambridgeshire fenland, she had gone downhill rapidly in the last weeks of 1535, probably as the result of a heart condition. Informed that the princess dowager, as he called his first wife, was very ill, Henry VIII at last allowed Eustace Chapuys to go and visit her. He arrived on 2 January and spent four days with her. She was in pain, eating only with great difficulty and sleeping hardly at all. But she was perfectly lucid, and his presence evidently comforted her. They talked of the past, and when she wondered aloud whether the course of action she had followed was the right one, he offered what words of support he could. She told him she intended to bequeath to Mary her furs and the gold cross she had brought with her from Spain in 1501. Few other possessions remained to her. By the time Chapuys left, she seemed to have rallied, but the improvement was only temporary. Sensing that the end was near, she dictated one last letter to the husband who had cast her aside like an object for which he had no further use: 'My most dear lord, king and husband,' she wrote,

> the hour of my death now drawing on, the tender love I owe you forceth me, my case being such, to commend myself to you, and to put you in remembrance with a few words of the health and safeguard of your soul which you ought to prefer before all worldly matters, and before the care and pampering of your body, for the which you have cast me into many calamities and yourself into many troubles. For my part I pardon you everything and I wish to devoutly pray to God that He will pardon you also. For the rest, I commend unto you our daughter Mary, beseeching you to be a good father unto her, as I have heretofore desired. I entreat you also, on behalf of my maids, to give them marriage portions, which is not much, they being but three. For all my other servants, I solicit the wages due to them, and a year more, lest they be unprovided for. Lastly, I make this vow, that mine eyes desire you above all things.[25]

In its dignified pathos and remembrance of a great and, for the writer, enduring love, it is one of the most moving farewells in the English language.

Mary was devastated by grief. The love she always felt for her mother had deepened during their mutual adversity, and the realisation that she would never see her again was enormously painful. While Katherine lived, mother and daughter encouraged themselves with the faint glimmer of hope that Henry would relent and allow them, however briefly, to be together. Now Mary expected that the pressure on her from her father 'to subscribe to their damnable statutes and detestable opinions', as Chapuys put it, would intensify. The princess's vulnerability at this time would make her even more of a target, or so Charles V and Chapuys at first thought. The emperor wrote to his wife, the empress Isabella, that Mary was apparently inconsolable, 'especially when she thinks of her father's past behaviour towards herself and of the little favour she can expect for the future'. He hoped that God would take pity on her, a sure indication that he would do little enough himself. Yet the expected pressure did not materialise, and Mary's situation slightly improved. She seems to have been too absorbed in sorrow to notice this.

Part of the reason for this alleviation was that Katherine's passing came as a great relief for Henry. It also brought with it the promise of better Anglo-imperial relations, since the emperor's obligations to Mary were, in reality, no more than polite concern for her welfare. This might be turned to diplomatic advantage at times, but basically Charles did not want to get involved in Tudor family politics. At court, Henry and Anne were reported to have danced for joy when they received the news that Katherine had died. This shocked Chapuys less than the meagre arrangements for the former queen's funeral and burial at Peterborough cathedral, totally inappropriate, he thought, for her rank and lineage. Royal protocol would have kept Mary away from her mother's obsequies in any case. The chief mourner at the funeral was Frances Brandon.

Henry, meanwhile, was delighted to have just one wife. He celebrated with Anne Boleyn and paraded little Elizabeth. Vague rumours, picked up earlier but generally dismissed by Chapuys, that the marriage had soured, that Henry's eye had fallen on another, were apparently scotched by the queen's third pregnancy. Her position seemed stronger than ever, and Anne sought to capitalise on this where Mary was concerned. Through Lady Shelton, she tried once more for an improvement in her relations with the king's elder daughter. Again, to her chagrin, she was rebuffed. Anne's response was to write a letter to her aunt spelling out that the effects of the king's displeasure could be permanent, especially if Mary eventually took the oaths expected of her under duress. The letter was deliberately left where Mary could find it, an unpleasant form of bullying that showed Anne's lack of understanding of her quarry. Mary copied the contents of the letter and forwarded them to Chapuys.

Then she put the letter back down where she had found it, in her oratory, and carried on as before. She must have seen the hand of God in what happened next. On 29 January, the day Katherine of Aragon was laid to rest, Anne Boleyn miscarried. In that moment, Anne's hold on her throne became suddenly much less secure.

Various reasons have been proposed for the loss of Anne's unborn child.[26] She may have been agitated by an injury sustained by Henry VIII during a bout of jousting, something that the increasingly heavy king still enjoyed. Four days before the miscarriage he had fallen badly and was unconscious for a while, to the consternation of his courtiers. That Anne was dismayed by the injury to her husband seems likely, more so than the story that went around subsequently that the real cause of her miscarriage was that she had discovered the king with one of her ladies sitting on his lap. She had lost a child late in the first trimester of pregnancy in 1534, however, and given that she herself believed that she was about 15 weeks pregnant at the time, perhaps she had some underlying problem with spontaneous abortion at this stage of pregnancy. Whatever the cause, the outcome was to destabilise Anne's position. Henry, feeling much more sorry for himself than his wife, began to wonder whether he would ever have a son. The seed of an idea, that God did not favour his second marriage any more than his first, was planted in his mind. Still, not too much should be read at this stage into the king's musings or the queen's emotional response to her condition. There were external influences already in play that would destroy their marriage and lead to Anne's downfall. Of these, one of the most important was the constancy of Mary herself.

Katherine's death meant that Mary became the focus of opposition to Anne. She was a doughty opponent, still fighting and defiant after two and a half years of pressure to deny her birthright. Anne's threats were an inspiration to Mary to hold firm. If only Henry could be induced to acknowledge that his first marriage was made in good faith, then Mary would take precedence over Elizabeth in the line of succession. Mary's supporters saw in the queen's predicament an opportunity to exploit the king's doubts and destroy the Boleyns. They had waited a long time for the chance that was now presented to them, risking all the while the possibility that the king's displeasure would take a more extreme turn.

Now the Poles and the Courtenays, the families that most wanted to see Mary restored and her position as heir clarified, found a useful ally in Sir Nicholas Carew, one of Henry's long-standing boon companions. Carew disapproved of the divorce but thought it prudent to hold his tongue while Katherine was alive. Like his fellow-conspirators he was a religious conservative who disapproved of the advance of new ideas in England. This, too, he kept quiet. But from January 1536, he used his influence on the king to turn Henry's mind against Anne Boleyn. He and his wife had stayed in touch with Mary throughout her ordeal and they were in her confidence.

The conspirators knew that Mary's tacit support was vital if they were to achieve Anne's removal; this she was willing to give, without asking too many questions as to the means to be employed. Her friends were careful not to implicate her in the fine detail of their plans. Chapuys, representing the main international guarantor of Mary's claim, inevitably became involved. He, in turn, set about lobbying Thomas Cromwell. The ambassador had picked up things from conversations with Cromwell, nuances here and there, statements that might or might not be taken at face value, which led him to believe that the minister and the queen had their differences. Chapuys knew that Cromwell had always favoured a better relationship with Charles V. He would use this to bring the minister round to the side of Mary's supporters. Or so he thought. Only later did he find out that Cromwell had a quite different agenda of his own.

Meanwhile, there were other means of encouraging friction between Henry and Anne. Aware of the king's roving eye and the passionate but often abrasive nature of his relationship with his wife, the charms of a quieter, more submissive lady were carefully cultivated by Anne's enemies. It would be a good idea to have a replacement waiting. This rival was Jane Seymour, the daughter of a country gentleman from Wiltshire. Her brother was ambitious, she was tractable and in every way a contrast to Anne Boleyn. She seemed, in short, ideal.

The story that it was Jane Seymour who had been discovered by Anne in a compromising position with the king, thus precipitating the queen's miscarriage, is unlikely. It was probably made up after the events of 1536. Everything we know about Jane (and she remains the most opaque of Henry's six wives) points to her being a well-schooled and prim observer of the proprieties, not an abandoned hussy. Her reputation would have been severely dented by involvement in royal horseplay.

She and her tutors knew far better than to let her be alone anywhere with the king.

The mystery is why Henry was attracted to her at all. Contemporaries agreed that she was plain. Nor did she have a sparkling personality. Henry's tastes in women stupefied people at the time as much as they do now. The only surviving portrait of her, by Holbein, confirms the view of Eustace Chapuys, who reported to the emperor that she was 'of middle stature and no great beauty, so fair that one would call her rather pale than otherwise'.[27] The face, under the heavy gable hood that Jane favoured, in contrast to the French hood that Anne wore, looks cross and wary. For someone supposed to be sweet-natured, Jane's sharp features, with her mean little double chin, come as a surprise. It is just possible that, when animated and smiling, she may have been transformed. No one, except for the woman she supplanted, seems to have actually disliked her. It is easy to think that someone so colourless must also have been lacking in character, a malleable puppet in the hands of others. What we know of her virtuoso performance in winning Henry's heart suggests otherwise. At the very least, she was an accomplished actress who learned her part well. She could have been under no illusions about the prize. Jane Seymour wanted to be queen every bit as much as those at the court who pushed her into the king's company.

Chapuys knew her brother, Edward Seymour, who had undertaken an earlier mission to the imperial court. While the Boleyns remained in power, Seymour's chances of further advancement seemed small. His sister, still unmarried in her late twenties, had been at court since 1529, first as an attendant to Katherine of Aragon and then Anne Boleyn. There was evidently still no prospect of finding a husband, which perhaps tells us indirectly quite a lot about Jane's charms, though it may also reflect on the Seymour family themselves. Her father had seduced Edward's first wife and their affair could scarcely have enhanced the chances of his eldest daughter. When she described herself, in rejecting Henry's clumsy attempt to buy her favours, as the daughter of 'good and honourable parents', she must have hoped her father's peccadilloes were forgotten.

She nearly was herself, until she became the object of 'courtly' pursuit by the king, in the early stages of his wife's third pregnancy. Jane Seymour might have remained the platonic object of these chivalric courtesies had her brother not scented an opportunity. With careful coaching and help from others who wanted to see Anne Boleyn removed, he could turn Jane from a meek lady-in-waiting into a queen. To achieve this, he needed friends at court, and his political intelligence told him that now, while the queen was low and the king uneasy, was the time to begin his campaign. But Jane must be wholly committed in order to play her role to perfection. She could have declined, or muffed the part she was given. Instead, she held her nerve and carried everything off with consummate skill. When Henry sent her a letter and a purse of gold at the beginning of April, she declined to accept the money, telling the king's messenger, on her knees, 'there was no treasure in the world she valued as much as her honour, and on no account would she lose it, even if she were to die a thousand deaths … if the king wished to make her a gift of money, she requested him to reserve it for such a time as God would be pleased to send her some advantageous marriage'.[28] Henry was touched by her modesty, captivated by the quietness she radiated in stark contrast to Anne's sound and fury. Jane was a clever little mouse.

But for all her cleverness and her brother's ability, with the help of Carew and Mary's supporters, to manipulate the king, Jane Seymour's success was far from certain. Anne, typically, chose to fight and to do so very publicly. She would not be ousted, and the Boleyns ruined, by a scheming goody-two-shoes whose backers lacked any real power or influence. But beyond her immediate family, Anne could command few friends herself. Her uncle, the duke of Norfolk, was disgruntled that the Howards had profited less than he had expected. His daughter, Mary Howard, was married to the king's illegitimate son, the duke of Richmond, at Anne's behest, but he did not see this as any reason to be grateful, and his estranged duchess was infuriated by it. But the real danger to Anne, as April approached, was not from her own proud uncle or pasty Jane Seymour, or even from the unconquered spirit of Princess Mary. It came from Thomas Cromwell. And he was an enemy more formidable than all the rest put together.

So why did Thomas Cromwell, that assiduous servant of the crown and Anne's ally throughout the tortuous process of the divorce, decide to 'think up and plan', as he put it, the coup against Anne Boleyn, in Easter Week 1536? Recent scholarship, especially the work of Eric Ives, has clarified much of the mystery that, for centuries, surrounded the fall of

Anne. But some questions, particularly about the degree of Henry's fore-knowledge and involvement in the plans against his wife, remain. One thing seems certain, however. Thomas Cromwell had fallen out with Anne (or, at least, believed that their disagreements on policy matters were serious enough to threaten his life) and he saw, in Mary and her supporters, a means of defeating the queen. They welcomed him to the cause. Chapuys remained slightly suspicious, never entirely sure of Cromwell's motives, but he acknowledged that nothing would be achieved on Mary's behalf without him. So the stage was set for one of the most audacious plots in English history.

Anne's relationship with Cromwell foundered on religious policy rather than his attempts to ingratiate himself with Charles V, though these later added to the tension. A fundamental disagreement developed between the queen and the minister during the first months of 1536 over the legislation to confiscate the wealth of the smaller monasteries. Up to this point, Anne and Cromwell had much in common on religious matters. Both were supporters of new ideas, of promoting the reading of the Bible in English and emphasising the individual's relationship with God as opposed to the oppressive structure of the Church. The queen had not disapproved of the attack on monastic wealth, but she fiercely opposed the idea of its passing into the hands of a small, self-serving group of individuals at the expense of the wider community. She hoped to influence Henry to use the money for educational purposes. Suddenly, Cromwell saw the possible ruin of all his plans. If Anne prevailed, she would effectively negate the Dissolution Bill. He had visions of going the same way as Wolsey, but perhaps without a natural end. And he had also realised that his discussions with Chapuys on improving Anglo-Imperial relations were likely to leave him further exposed. Charles V was willing to give support 'for this last matrimony or otherwise' (a splendidly vague phrase), but only so long as Mary was legitimised and recognised as heir presumptive. Cromwell now knew that Henry VIII would never agree to such an outcome and he did not need to imagine Anne's reaction if she discovered the emperor's terms for a rapprochement. His sanctimonious assurance to Chapuys at the end of February that 'he would not, for anything in this world, be held as a liar and dissembler' sounded very hollow now.

On 1 April a meeting took place between Chapuys and Cromwell in which the ambassador sought to play on the rumours he had heard. He told Cromwell he had avoided meeting him personally for some time, in order to avoid the queen's further anger: 'I recollected well his telling me that she would like to see his head off his shoulders. Such a threat, I said, was constantly before my eyes … and I sincerely wished him a more gracious mistress than she was, and one more grateful for the immense services he had rendered to the king.' Piling it on, Chapuys continued that Cromwell must be careful not to 'offend or over-irritate' Anne, and he hoped that the minister's 'dexterity and prudence' would protect him from what had happened to Wolsey. A fresh marriage for the king would surely be the way of 'preserving him from many inconveniences'. Not, Chapuys added, that Anne Boleyn had ever done *him* any harm personally.

Cromwell thanked him rather sourly, observing that 'he was well aware of the precarious nature of human affairs, to say nothing of those appertaining to royal courts'. He went on to talk about Jane Seymour, describing her rejection of the king's advances, saying she had been 'well-tutored and warned'. At least he could assure Chapuys that a future wife for the king would not be French. Chapuys departed feeling very positive about developments. He had been asked to lend his support to the moves against Anne Boleyn and believed these would give Mary better security, even if male heirs were born of a new match. He wrote to the emperor: 'I shall again inform her [Mary] of what is going on, and, with her advice, will act in such a manner that if we cannot gain, at least we shall lose nothing.'[29]

Charles V was also more interested than he had been for some time in improving his relationship with England, and, more to the point, getting Henry VIII's active support in his eternal struggle with the French. Over the course of the decade since the catastrophe at Pavia, Francis I had never fully abandoned his claims on northern Italy and he had eventually recouped his military strength. With Katherine of Aragon no longer a factor, Charles hoped that Henry might be inclined to commit himself to imperial support. After several meetings, both Chapuys and Cromwell believed they had a workable set of proposals. All that remained was to present them to the king and gain his approval. Chapuys was summoned to court for 20 April. He was pleased by his gracious reception and by the attention shown him by Viscount Rochford, who had been assigned to escort him. He was careful, though, not to enter into any discussion with the queen's brother about his 'Lutheran principles'. The imperial ambassador was taken to the chapel at Greenwich before dinner and there, for the first and last time, he bowed to Anne Boleyn. He had earlier politely declined Henry's invitation to be received by the queen and kiss her hand. But his bow amounted to some kind of formal acknowledgement. Did he, given his knowledge of what was afoot, privately regard it as an empty gesture?

To the disappointment of both Chapuys and Cromwell, the meeting went badly. The king seemed more irritated and capricious than anyone had anticipated. One of the sticking points was Mary. Henry made it quite clear that he would not tolerate the interference of Charles V over her future. She was, he said, his daughter, 'and that accordingly as she was obedient or disobedient he would treat her; nobody had anything to do with that'. If Chapuys reported these words to Mary and her partisans as well as Charles V, it is surprising that they did not take more notice of them. Henry had consistently followed the same approach to Mary since the birth of Elizabeth, and it could be argued that, in the broader frame of his dynastic requirements, his stance had not changed, where she was concerned, since 1527. Mary's supporters were too focused on plotting against Anne to heed the very clear signals coming from the king. Instead, Sir Nicholas Carew exhorted the princess to be of good cheer. The Boleyns were about to get their comeuppance: 'shortly the opposite party' (his own) 'would put water in their wine'.

With prospects for improved Anglo-Imperial relations now looking much less certain, Cromwell represented himself to Chapuys as a man in despair. He may also have been a man in fear of having overstepped the mark where Henry was concerned. In trying to explain and justify his inability to deliver, he made a revealing remark to Chapuys: 'He declared to me that although he had all the time dissembled and made me believe that what he said to me was his own private view of the affair, not the king's, he could assert – nay swear – that he had done or said nothing without his master's express commands.' When Chapuys asked what could have brought about so radical a change in the king's mind, Cromwell professed to having no idea. But the minister ended this awkward exchange by observing 'that princes were endowed with qualities of mind and peculiarities unknown to all other people ... whoever trusts in the word of princes, who one day say one thing and on the next retract it, relies on them, or expects the fulfilment of their promises, is not a wise man'.[30] Just how unwise he was not to find out for four more years, but his comments on the role Henry had played prior to the audience with Chapuys must raise the question of how much – and when – Henry knew about the moves against Anne Boleyn. Cromwell may have had an increasingly urgent personal need to get rid of the queen, but his master was fast succumbing to Jane Seymour's pallid charms.

There is much that remains confusing about the precise timings of Anne's destruction, though evidently Cromwell began to work on it in earnest at the end of Easter Week. He had taken the legal steps that would allow him to proceed, including the preliminaries for the recall of Parliament, but he needed an occasion, something on which a case could be built. Then, on 30 April, Anne herself supplied the first piece of ammunition he was seeking. She had a heated and very public row with Henry Norris, the king's groom of the stool and one of those closest to Henry in his privy chamber, about his feelings for her. Though Anne was a flirt she may not have intended to encourage Norris to contemplate anything beyond the accepted moves of the game of courtly love. Now, she put him very firmly in his place. Perhaps she had been attracted to him and sensed the danger. For whatever reason, she seems to have wanted to deter him in no uncertain terms. Piqued, Norris denied that he was lovestruck, but the damage had been done.

The confrontation was witnessed by a fascinated audience, not all of whom were well intentioned. It seems likely the story got back to the king, and Anne was alarmed that it could be misconstrued. The next day, she appealed directly to Henry for understanding, with Elizabeth in her arms. Such behaviour was not calculated to win the king's confidence. His anger and unease were aroused. But this, in itself, was not enough. Cromwell knew that they fought frequently and were always reconciled. More evidence was needed before the queen could be apprehended. And then, suddenly, luck was on his side. The ammunition was unintentionally provided by one of Anne's musicians, Mark Smeton. He also seems to have harboured feelings for Anne, and, like Norris, she slapped him down, reminding him scathingly of his lowly position. She would have done better to ignore him, but she was very conscious of her rank and evidently on edge.

Smeton's lovelorn posturing in her apartments again attracted the attention of those who wanted to topple Anne Boleyn. Finally, Cromwell had a target and he struck. Smeton was arrested and subjected to 24 hours of fierce torture that may have had a physical as well as a psychological element. When it was over, he had confessed to adultery with the queen. On 2 May, Henry VIII received a message, presumably about Smeton's confession, that caused him to leave Greenwich in a hurry. The previous day, he and Anne had attended the May Day jousts together. Now he left her behind, to be interrogated by the duke of Norfolk and other members of the council. Later that day, she was taken to the Tower of London. She never saw Henry or Elizabeth again.

Thereafter, events moved swiftly. Anne suffered from a nervous collapse once she entered the Tower and could not stop talking. Sometimes she laughed almost hysterically. Her desperate thinking aloud about the possible causes for the calamity that had overtaken her provided the resourceful Cromwell with all the remaining evidence that he needed. So the ramblings of an innocent woman, implicated by some of her personal servants and paying the price for the years of resentment she had aroused, were used against her. Viscount Rochford was also arrested, as were Norris and several others who served in the privy chamber. Cromwell wanted their collective influence destroyed, and he saw in Anne's plight the means of being rid of them all. The charges against the queen, of adultery with three gentlemen of the privy chamber and Smeton, were given even more spice by the additional accusation of incest with her brother. One of the people who gave evidence to support this charge was George's own wife, Lady Jane Rochford. Her motives for this terrible act of revenge have never been made clear, but she must have hated her husband and her sister-in-law a great deal. Cromwell made sure she was well taken care of financially once it was all over.

The charges against Anne seem preposterous. Even Chapuys, scarcely a well-wisher, commented on the lack of evidence against the queen and those accused with her. As well as the sexual element, she was also accused of having tried to poison Katherine of Aragon and Mary. At the time, Archbishop Cranmer, always close to the queen, refused at first to believe these accusations. He thought she had always been a virtuous woman: 'I am in such perplexity', he wrote to Henry, 'that my mind is clearly amazed; for I never had better opinion in a woman, than I had in her; which maketh me think, that she should not be culpable … I loved her not a little for the love which I judged her to bear toward God and his gospel.'[31] Many others, titillated by the lurid details of the accusation, wanted to believe otherwise. And Cranmer's first duty was to do Henry's bidding. Once Anne was condemned, he speedily annulled her marriage, as he had done Katherine of Aragon's. This left Elizabeth a bastard, just like her half-sister Mary.

The queen defended herself with courage and dignity at her trial, and her brother with considerable energy and defiance at his. There was

Portrait of a lady thought to have been Mary Tudor, inscribed and dated 1546. (By kind permission of Viscount De L'Isle from his private collection.)

Katherine of Aragon, first wife of Henry VIII. Her inability to produce a male heir destroyed her marriage, plunging her daughter Mary and the entire country into a period of painful upheaval.

King Henry VIII, between 1535 and 1540. A striking portrait of Mary's father, painted at a time when her relationship with him was compromised by his determination to divorce her mother, Katherine of Aragon.

The first of Mary's five step-mothers, Anne Boleyn was hated by the princess as the usurper of her mother's place as queen and the author of all her misfortunes between 1533 and 1536. Anne's occasional attempts at reconciliation were con-temptuously repulsed. But her disgrace and execution only increased the king's deter-mination to subdue his elder daughter.

Mary aged 28 in 1544, the year she was restored to the succession by Act of Parliament. Her fine complexion is evident, as is her love of the latest fashions in rich russet and crimson brocade and velvet.

Edward VI, probably painted in 1546, the last year of his father's reign. Intellectually capable, committed to religious reform and fond of sports, the young king was not the weakling of popular imagination. He was determined to cut both Mary and Elizabeth out of the succession when he realized he was dying.

Jane Seymour, quiet but clever enough to play an effective role in bringing about the downfall of Anne Boleyn. Jane was a religious conservative who champ- ioned Mary's cause but died after giving birth to Henry VIII's heir, Prince Edward.

KATHARINE PARRE

ABOVE LEFT The intelligent and companionable Katherine Parr, Henry VIII's sixth and last wife. Her friendship with Mary transformed the princess' life in the mid-1540s, but Katherine's impulsive remarriage to Thomas Seymour after the old king's death cooled their relationship.

ABOVE RIGHT The hastily divorced Anne of Cleves. In this famous painting by Holbein, the German princess appears personable. Henry VIII married her unwillingly and never overcame his aversion in the six months that she was his consort. Mary remained on excellent terms with her till Anne's death in 1557.

ABOVE LEFT Mary's Lady Governess, Margaret Pole, countess of Salisbury. A vital influence in Mary's upbringing, this niece of Edward IV was one of the great ladies of the English court. Handsome, devout and devoted to Mary, she was imprisoned by Henry VIII and executed in 1541.

ABOVE RIGHT Cardinal Reginald Pole, Margaret's son, papal legate and archbishop of Canterbury. He spent years in exile in Italy when he opposed Henry VIII. In 1554 he restored the English Church to the papacy, ending twenty years of schism.

LEFT The Emperor Charles V as a young man. The head of the Habsburg dynasty, Charles V ruled a vast swathe of Europe and the Americas, often through his relatives. Mary viewed him as a father figure after Henry VIII rejected her, but his support for her was often half-hearted and driven by political rather than personal considerations.

never the slightest doubt about the verdict. Tudor state trials did not allow for sudden and miraculous acquittals. Anne was spared the flames, the prescribed means of death for an adulterous queen, and faced her execution with resignation. On 16 May, Cranmer heard her confession; she seems to have asked him to watch over the education and upbring-ing of her daughter and to have then assumed, wrongly, as it happened, that her death would follow the next day. It was not until 19 May that she went to the scaffold. Before her death, she addressed the crowd, as was the custom. She was dutifully loyal to the king, but she refused to confess any wrongdoing: 'According to the law and by the law I am judged to die, and therefore I will speak nothing against it. I am come hither to accuse no man, nor to speak of that whereof I am accused and condemned to die, but I pray God save the king and send him long to reign over you, for a gentler and more merciful prince was there never and to me he was ever a good, a gentle, and sovereign lord.'[32] Was this said just to ensure better treatment for Elizabeth, or did she go to her grave remembering only the happier moments that had characterised her love affair and marriage with Henry VIII? Then she prayed. She was still praying when the Calais swordsman took off her head.

Among the spectators that spring day in 1536 was Thomas Cromwell, the man who had destroyed her in the space of less than three weeks. The day after her death, Henry VIII was betrothed to Jane Seymour, who had been tactfully lodged at Sir Nicholas Carew's house during Anne's trial. It was a short engagement. Jane and Henry were married on 30 May and Anne Boleyn's name was not spoken again at court for more than 20 years.

Henry's unquestioning acceptance of the guilt of the woman he had lived with for nine years is remarkable. Theirs had been a great love and he abandoned it on the basis of evidence that even Anne's enemies found incredible. He must have wanted to believe it. According to Cromwell, he had 'been authorised and commissioned by the king to prosecute and bring to an end the mistress's trial, to do which he had taken consider-able trouble'.[33] But who was managing whom? It all depends when Cromwell's commission was received. And even supposing that it was after revelations that shocked the king, was he putting the responsibility for solving the problem on his chief adviser out of distress or guile? Emotionally he was a strangely fragile man with an infinite capacity to feel sorry for himself. He also knew how to get others to do his dirty work and he expected complete, unquestioning loyalty. Opposition made him ruthless, but Anne's opponents, and Mary above all, did not learn from the lessons of her fall.

Mary was at Hunsdon in Essex, with Elizabeth, when Anne was executed. Her immediate reaction to the news is not known but her supporters believed they had triumphed. The princess herself undoubtedly expected to be restored to her father's favour imminently. Her steadfastness would be rewarded now the concubine was dead. She waited for a week, perhaps expecting to receive some word from London. Then, on 26 May, she addressed herself to Cromwell, asking him to be a channel for her to the king. She said she would have asked him before, but 'I perceived that nobody durst speak for me as long as that woman lived, which is now gone: whom I pray our Lord, of his great mercy, to forgive.'[34] Little did she know that the most terrible phase of her own ordeal was just beginning.

The arc of Mary's summer of hell, from unrealistic hopes, through fear and confusion to abject humiliation, can be traced in her letters. Many of these, in the collection of the 17th-century antiquarian Robert Cotton, were badly damaged by fire in 1731. The British Library still holds their remains, some of them little more than charred fragments. Fortunately, Mary's correspondence was printed before the fire by another antiquarian, Thomas Hearne, in 1716.

The letters show a young woman who, through a mixture of pride and naivety, completely misjudged her situation. This was not entirely her fault; her friends, rejoicing at Anne Boleyn's removal, did not realise they had been used, either. But used they were. Cromwell never intended that the old, conservative, Aragonese faction (so called because its principals were supporters of Queen Katherine) should triumph. Now that they had served their purpose, he intended to remove the conservatives. And it was easy to do this, by depicting them as disloyal subjects who were plotting to overturn religious change and restore Mary, the king's illegitimate and disobedient daughter, to the succession.

Chapuys, who always regarded working with Cromwell to overthrow Anne Boleyn as something of an unholy alliance, remained unconvinced. 'I must say however', he wrote to Charles V, 'that as yet the king has shown no intention of bringing about the said re-instatement but has on the contrary obstinately refused to contemplate it'.[35] Nor did he trust

Cromwell's assertion that in the next meeting of Parliament, Henry VIII would have Mary declared heiress to the crown, especially when, in almost the same breath, Cromwell earnestly requested him not to make any reference to the princess when he next had an audience with the king. It seemed to the ambassador that nothing about Mary's underlying dilemma had really changed. Henry would surely not move 'unless she previously swears to, and conforms with, the irritating statutes concerning the king's second marriage as well as against papal authority; which act of acquiescence, in my opinion, it will be extremely difficult to obtain from the princess.' He felt Mary ought to agree 'so long as her conscience is not aggrieved, nor her rights and titles impaired through it'. But this was palpably impossible. The whole point of getting Mary to swear was so that she acknowledged that she had no rights or titles of any sort.

But Mary did not yet see this at all. Buoyed by obtaining permission to send a letter directly to her father, Mary wrote cheerfully to Cromwell at the end of May, thanking him for 'the great pain and labour that you have taken for me and specially for obtaining of the king my father's blessing and licence to write unto his grace; which are two of the highest comforts that ever came to me … I trust you shall find me as obedient to the king's grace, as you can reasonably require of me'. She foresaw that, with Cromwell's continued help, her father would withdraw his displeasure and allow her to come to see him, at last.[36]

Cromwell must have sighed when the letter reached him. She was hardly in a position to dictate terms on what might reasonably be required of her. The king wanted complete submission; the only terms being offered were his. So he summoned Chapuys and told him that he had prepared a minute that Mary could use as the basis of a letter to her father. It would be taken to her 'by a lady in her utmost confidence' (this was Lady Kingston, wife of the lieutenant of the Tower of London), who would, nevertheless, make it quite clear to her that if she refused to sign 'she will be ill-treated and severely punished'.[37] Chapuys also understood that Mary's supporters would suffer unless she gave in and that her submission was not just the price of improvements in her own life, but in Anglo-Imperial relations as well. Most of all, he realised that he needed to save Mary from herself.

She was still holding out in the second week of June, but becoming increasingly disturbed that she had received no reply to her letters to her father. On the first day of the month she had written to the king desiring his blessing and asking forgiveness for 'all the offences that I have done to your grace, since I had first discretion to offend'. She was, she said, 'as sorry as any living creature'. So far, Henry might have been pleased with the apology, but there was a qualification: 'Next unto God, I do and will submit me in all things to your goodness and pleasure … humbly beseeching your highness to consider, that I am but a woman and your child, who hath committed her soul only to God and her body to be ordered in this world, as it shall stand with your pleasure.' She also congratulated him on his marriage and asked to be allowed to see the new queen.[38] It sounded good, but Henry wanted specific, unequivocal surrender to the laws that he, not God, had instituted. He made no reply because none was needed. He left it to Cromwell to ensure that Mary finally did what she was told.

A week later, she again addressed her father, apparently under the delusion that 'he has forgiven all her offences and withdrawn his displeasure long time conceived against her'. By this time, she had received the draft letter from Cromwell that she was to sign and return. But when she sent an amended copy back to the minister, on 10 June, she pleaded with him that she had given as much ground as her conscience would allow. She would not deny her mother's marriage, nor her own title: 'You shall perceive', she wrote,

> that I have followed your advice and counsel, and will do in all things concerning my duty to the king's grace, (God and my conscience not offended:) for I take you for one of my chief friends, next unto his grace and the queen. Wherefore I desire you, for the passion which Christ suffered for you and me, and as my very trust is in you, that you will find such means through your great wisdom, that I be not moved to agree to any further entry in this matter than I have done. For I assure you by the faith I owe to God, I have done the uttermost that my conscience will suffer me: and I do neither desire nor intend to do less than I have done. But if I be put to any more (I am plain with you, as with my great friend) my said conscience will in no ways suffer me to consent thereunto … For I promise you (as I desire God to help me at my most need) I had rather leave the life of my body, than displease the king's grace willingly. Sir, I beseech you for the love of God to take in good worth this rude letter. For I would not have troubled you so much at this time, but that the end of your letter cause me a little to fear that I shall have more business hereafter.[39]

It was desperate, eloquent stuff, and her fear was justified. She had sensed the truth – that, finally, she would be compelled to submit utterly. But she still could not bring herself to admit it.

Not even a deputation from the council, sent with uncompromising instructions, could sway her. She had 'sundry times and of long continuance shown herself so obstinate towards the king's majesty and so disobedient unto the laws' that she could scarcely expect forgiveness. It was only her father's inordinate goodness and patience which saved her, 'such is his majesty's gracious and divine nature, such is his clemency and pity, such is his merciful inclination and princely heart'.[40] And what had this paragon of forbearance and saintliness done? He had dispatched a group of aristocratic thugs, headed by the ubiquitous Norfolk, to induce her to yield. When Mary got the best of the argument, they resorted to a vicious verbal assault. The cold brutality of the threats they made to a defenceless girl was stunning. The earl of Essex voiced their conviction that 'since she was such an unnatural daughter as to disobey completely the king's injunctions, he could hardly believe that she was the king's own bastard daughter. Were she his or any other man's daughter, he would beat her to death, or strike her head against the wall until he made it as soft as a boiled apple; in short, that she was a traitress and would be punished as such.'[41] While this may be highly revealing of the overall view of women as disposable chattels of men in Tudor England, it was still remarkable language to use to someone born a princess. But, despite these threats of violence, the king's bullies left empty-handed. Mary, frightened, alone and suffering from headaches and toothache, was almost at the end of her tether. Yet she would not sign.

Cromwell was exasperated. This could not be permitted to continue – her wilfulness was a danger to all around her. The king expected him to deliver, and the longer she held out, the more his ire would increase. Even Jane Seymour had totally failed when it came to gentle persuasion on Mary's behalf. The king and his minister had not disposed of Anne Boleyn for Mary's sake. She had no bargaining power and the tender state of her conscience was not relevant.

Chapuys was informed that he must persuade Mary to sign the articles that her father had drawn up. Her stubbornness was just making things worse, for her supporters and herself. The ambassador, his tongue firmly in his cheek, responded that he thought Mary would take more notice of Cromwell, who was like a second father to her. In fact, Cromwell was more like a wicked uncle. He sent Mary a letter that was both uncompromising and threatening. Her discomfort, he said, could be no greater than his. Having told the king that she would do his bidding, he was now ashamed and afraid of what he had done, 'in so much that what the sequel thereof shall be, God knoweth. Thus with your folly you undo yourself, and all that have wished your good ... to be plain with you, as God is my witness, like as I think you the most obstinate and obdurate woman, all things considered, that ever was.' She deserved punishment for her 'ingratitude and miserable unkindness', and he would not speak on her behalf again until she had signed 'a certain book of articles' he was sending her. These were to be accompanied by a letter demonstrating 'that you think in heart what you have subscribed with hand ... if you will not with speed leave all your sinister counsels, which have brought you to the point of utter undoing, without remedy, and herein follow my advice, I take my leave of you forever'.[42]

The prospect of abandonment by Cromwell and the likely fate of her supporters, if she continued to hold out, finally broke Mary's resolve. Chapuys also encouraged her, for the sake of her own health and future, to comply with her father's commands. He advised her to sign the articles without reading them. Papal understanding could be obtained through imperial influence at a later date. The priority now was her security, not her soul.

On 22 June 1536, the princess signed her submission. In it, she said: 'I do now plainly and with all mine heart confess and declare mine inward sentence, belief and judgement, with a due conformity of obedience to the laws of the realm'. She humbly beseeched the king to forgive her offences and sought his mercy. Then she acknowledged him as sovereign and as supreme head of the Church of England. But it was the third article that was the most bitter. She acknowledged, but only under extreme duress, her mother's marriage 'to have been by God's law and man's incestuous and unlawful'.[43]

Mary's health had suffered badly during years of strain and sorrow. Now the elation of Anne Boleyn's disgrace had been swiftly supplanted by five weeks of ruthless psychological abuse. Her courage was remarkable, but she was only human. She longed for peace of mind, a calm existence and her father's acceptance. So she signed away everything she had stood for during the dismal years of her banishment – her beloved mother's marriage, her own legitimacy, papal authority over English religious law. This supreme act of denial remained on her conscience for the rest of her days.

Four days after her capitulation, Mary wrote to her father: 'I cannot express my joy or make my return for your goodness but my poor heart, which I send unto your highness to remain in your hand, to be for ever used, directed and framed, which God shall suffer life to remain in it, at your only pleasure. I beg you to receive it as all I have to offer.'[44] It was the first of a series of letters so abject they are almost embarrassing. They seem to have been written of her own free will, or perhaps she thought she could not sink any lower and was anxious to convince Henry that her love was unconditional. Having made the sacrifice, she wanted the benefits she had always been assured awaited her. Certainly, she now understood that this was the tone her father expected. Mary was also careful to establish a close relationship with the new queen as soon as possible, thanking her for her 'most prudent counsel for my further proceeding'. More than anything else, she wanted to see her father.

On 6 July, Mary left Hunsdon at night for a private meeting with her father and Queen Jane. She had not spoken to Henry in five years but now there was an outpouring of fatherly affection. He said he felt deep regret for having kept her so long away from him and made 'brilliant promises for the future'. No father, reported Chapuys, could have behaved better towards his daughter. Henry proffered 1,000 crowns for her immediate expenses and Jane gave her a fine diamond ring. The king assured her that Cromwell and others would soon come to talk to her about her 'state and household'; when he himself returned from a visit to Dover, she could reside again at court.

It all sounded wonderful, but it was not the whole truth. 'Mixed with the sweet food of paternal kindness, there were a few drachmas of gall and bitterness. But after all, we must set that down to paternal authority,' commented Chapuys. A good deal of Henry's bitterness had been aimed at Charles V: 'he said to the princess ... that her obstinate resistance to his will had been encouraged and strengthened by the trust she had in you; but that she ought to know that your majesty could not help or favour her in the least as long as he [the king] lived'.[45]

Mary was also affected by family developments closer to home in the summer of 1536. Her half-brother, the duke of Richmond, died unexpectedly after a short illness on 23 July. For the king, the loss of his 17-year-old son, whom he seems to have genuinely loved, was unnerving. Two illegitimate daughters were all he had to show for his desperate search for an heir, and Jane Seymour had yet to conceive. Chapuys, on the other hand, thought it 'not a bad thing for the interests

of the princess', and Cromwell, rather sickeningly, actually congratulated Mary on Richmond's death. Her reaction is not recorded. She was,
though, keen to remind her father that he had another child: 'My sister
Elizabeth is well and such a child toward as I doubt not but your highness shall have cause to rejoice of in time coming.'[46] It was a sweet
tribute to a little girl whose precedence she had resented but who was
now as abandoned as she herself had once been. Mary felt sorry for her
and may have hoped to jolt Henry's conscience about Elizabeth's treatment. If so, she did not immediately succeed. In mid-August, Cromwell
was specific in his instructions that 'my lady Elizabeth shall keep her
chamber and not come abroad'.

Once a greater degree of respect and status was restored to Mary,
Chapuys began to acknowledge the full extent of the agony she had
suffered. He told the bishop of Arras: 'this affair of the princess has
tormented her more than you think'. A few weeks later, he wrote to
Empress Isabella that Mary was in good health and kindly treated. But
he did not conceal that she had 'escaped from the greatest danger that
ever a princess was in, and such as no words can describe'.[47] He exaggerated, of course, but only somewhat.

The danger might be gone, but considerable pressure remained.
Charles V's influence over Mary continued to rankle with Henry. In
early October, she was being pressured by her father to write to the
emperor, his regent in the Netherlands (Mary of Hungary) and the
pope, saying that she had signed the articles of her own free will.
Presumably this was just a public relations exercise, since Henry must
have realised that they were all well informed about the circumstances
of Mary's submission. It reinforced his authority over her, however, and
reminded her that she had no power, however much her cousin might
appear to take up her cause. Mary heard, but apparently did not accept,
what her father had to say about her Habsburg connections. For the rest
of her life, she consistently overestimated imperial support because she
had no other source of external comfort.

But now her father had much else to occupy his mind at home. The
most serious uprising of his reign was upon him, and for a while it
looked as if he might lose control of the north of England and possibly
his throne. The great rebellion known as the Pilgrimage of Grace was
fuelled by widespread discontent at Henry's religious reforms, and
against the dissolution of the monasteries in particular. Ominously, the
rebels had not forgotten Mary, either. One of their demands was 'that the

Lady Mary may be made legitimate'. It proved that she retained a place in popular affection and that she was still a political presence.

The Pilgrimage of Grace was suppressed with ruthlessness and duplicity, two qualities that Henry (and many of his court) had in spades. Its failure marked the end of a momentous period. On 22 December, the king, his wife and daughter rode through the City of London in a splendid procession, on their way to spend Christmas at Greenwich. The streets were superbly hung 'with rich gold and arras', and the priests of all the London parishes, carrying their best crosses, candlesticks and censers, stood on the steps of St Paul's.[48] Mary enjoyed the pomp of such occasions, so she would not have minded the bitter cold. 'The cause of the king's riding through London was because the Thames was so frozen there might be no boats go on there for ice.' It was a fitting end to a chilling year.

Chapter Five

The Quiet Years

'She would be, while her father lived, only Lady Mary, the most unhappy lady in Christendom.'

Mary's view of her situation in 1542, reported by the French ambassador, Marillac

On 15 October 1537, Mary stood at the font in the Chapel Royal at Hampton Court while Archbishop Cranmer performed the rites of baptism over her brother Edward. As befitted a lady of royal birth – and the child's godmother – she was wearing a kirtle of cloth of silver, richly embroidered. Yet though her appearance was carefully considered, her behaviour showed that this was a family ceremony as well as a state occasion. Mary was the much older sister of two small children who would never know their own mothers. If she was not exactly maternal, she still represented a warmth and approachability that the more remote figure of the king, their father, lacked. She was attentive both to the baby prince and to the four-year-old Elizabeth, who carried the chrisom-cloth. When the ceremony was over, Mary left holding her little sister by the hand.

She may have reflected that life was now more straightforward for both Elizabeth and herself. The birth of a son to Jane Seymour finally gave her father the heir for whom he had ruined many lives, including her own, and changed the religious and social spectrum of his realm. The prince seemed healthy and, provided he survived the inevitable perils of childhood illness, he would, in due course, ascend the throne. It was perfectly possible he would have other brothers, making the prospect of Mary ever becoming queen of England remote indeed. Now she could look forward to a period of stability, perhaps even to marriage, if her father could be induced to let her wed. Queen Jane's softening influence had definitely worked in Mary's favour, and the two women liked each other. During Jane's pregnancy, Mary was pleased to be able to send the queen cucumbers from her own gardens and gifts of quail. Jane was also a conservative in religious matters and no friend to the reformers, which increased her appeal to Mary and those who had supported the princess in the summer of 1536. Their relationship looked as though it would continue to be cordial and a source of comfort to a young woman who had been through a prolonged and harrowing ordeal.

But it was not to be. On 24 October, Jane Seymour died after suffering severe internal bleeding, probably caused by a placenta that failed to detach properly after her son's birth. Mary was too distressed to participate in the first part of the ceremonies following the queen's demise, and her place was taken by the marchioness of Exeter. By the date of the actual burial, on 12 November at Windsor, Mary had composed herself sufficiently to fulfil her duties as the chief mourner. She rode alone at the head of the cortège, her train held up by Lady Jane Rochford, Anne Boleyn's sister-in-law. Thereafter, her public appearances were few and far between. Henry VIII remained a widower for more than two years. He does not seem to have looked for solace in the company of his elder daughter, even though she might once more have been viewed as the first lady in the land. Mary was still not summoned back to court on a permanent basis and she continued to pass her time either by herself, at Richmond, or with Edward and Elizabeth, moving between the stately homes of the south-east. Whether, if Jane Seymour had lived, she could have brought about a closer rapprochement between Mary and her father we shall never know. Mary was officially forgiven, but neither she nor Henry could entirely forget the past. The king never fully trusted her, wondering often whether her capitulation had been genuine and whether she was concealing her true feelings every time she met him. He suspected that she no longer loved him. Whether she did or not is impossible to say. Perhaps there was some residual affection, but Henry's behaviour as time went by diminished even that. Mary adopted towards her father an attitude of respectful but remote quietness, a kind of stillness that would not attract attention. The king's bouts of sentimentality were unpredictable and his basic requirement of Mary was unquestioning obedience. In fact, he made sure, in his treatment of her friends over the next five years, that she understood fully her utter dependence on him, not just for bed and board, but for life itself.

· ❖ ·

Though the threat was always in the background, Mary's situation improved quickly in the last half of 1536. With Cromwell's help, she began to plan her household, adapt to her reduced status and start to manage her finances again. When the secretary asked her to make suggestions for the ladies she would like to serve her, the abject tone of her reply was, at first, grating. He was, she said, too good to her: 'How much am I bound unto you, which hath not only travailed when I was almost bound in folly to recover me before I sunk and was utterly past recovery?' Since the time that he had saved her from herself he had not ceased to proffer advice, to ensure that she did not relapse into being 'too wilful and obstinate'; so that now 'there is no spark in me'. Perhaps not, but she went on to address the matter of her sister Elizabeth's title, still a sensitive issue, with some subtlety: 'Concerning the Princess (so I think I must call her yet, for I would be loathe to offend)', she acknowledged that she had been extremely unyielding, but this was a mistake, she realised. On the other hand, now Cromwell had advised that it would be perfectly proper to call Elizabeth merely by the name of sister, she would never call her anything else. Did a smile cross her lips when she wrote this? Was she just teasing Cromwell, playing to his sense of self-importance with her flowery turn of phrase? She would gladly accept 'what men or women soever the King's highness shall appoint to wait on me'. It was almost like a script she had learned and could recite when occasion demanded it.

Yet she went on, quite briskly, to put forward names of those 'I would have about me', who had done faithful service to herself and the king: 'Margery Baynton and Susan Clarencius have in every condition used themselves as faithfully, painfully and diligently as ever did women in such a case; as sorry, when I was not conformable, as became me, as glad when I inclined any thing to do my duty, as could be desired.' In other words, these were women who had been with her throughout most of her difficulties and who she wanted to share her new life. And she added a third name, that of Mary Brown, 'that was sometime my maid, whom for her virtue I love and could be glad to have in my company; and here be all that I will recommend'.[1] It was a modest and very personal request to be with those who had served her well, perhaps the closest she came to having a family. Susan Clarencius would be with her till the day she died, becoming the most influential of her gentlewomen during Mary's reign. She seems to have already been a widow in the 1530s and was devoted to Mary, though her advice could be unreliable. Mary did not ask for the restoration of Margaret Douglas or any great ladies; that might have seemed too presumptuous. Besides, Margaret was in disgrace for having entered into a secret engagement with Thomas Howard, Anne Boleyn's uncle. This led to both lovers being confined for a time in the Tower. Howard died there in 1537, but Margaret survived the ordeal and was released to the care of the nuns at Syon convent on the outskirts of London. She did not emerge for another year, and after a further amorous escapade with another Howard (Charles, half-brother to Henry's fifth queen) she was again sent back to Syon.

Minus the lively Margaret, Mary's new household eventually numbered 42 people, a far cry from the time when, as a nine-year-old, she had set off for the Welsh Marches with three hundred people in her retinue. Henry VIII made her a basic allowance of £40 a quarter (roughly £13,000 today), and Mary found it impossible to live within her means, especially at Christmas time, when she often had to ask for more. She did, however, ensure that accounts were kept, and it is from these that a fascinating picture of her life in the period 1537–43 emerges. While she still suffered from intermittent ill health (she was unwell several times in the summer of 1537, before her brother's birth), and was certainly no longer at the centre of events, her existence was comfortable and she was by no means always discontented.

Mary Tudor was a king's daughter and she lived a privileged life. Her privy purse expenses, signed in her own hand, reveal a woman who loved clothes and jewels, ate well, was generous to her friends and gambled rather more than was seemly. Music continued to be one of her favourite ways of relaxation. In March 1538, Chapuys reported that he had spent some time at Richmond, 'talking with her and hearing her play on the lute or on the spinet in so admirable a manner that I really believe she is the most accomplished musician that could be found'.[2] It seems he was not exaggerating, as his opinion was supported by the French ambassador, who described Mary as playing 'singularly' well.

She also revived her instruction in languages and was able to indulge her interests in drama and literature. She retained the loyalty of one of the great wits and entertainers of the period, John Heywood, a devoted admirer of his 'most noble lady', whose 'beauty twinkleth like a star within the frosty night'. For him she was not 'a thin, frail woman with tight lips' but a princess in appearance, if not in name.

Others also praised the 'fayre lady Mary', and although there may be poetic licence in these descriptions, it seems that Mary did not lose her looks overnight.[3] Her complexion, in particular, was regarded as very fine: 'she looks not past 18 or 20', wrote the French ambassador in 1540, 'although she is 24'.[4] In many respects, he reported, she resembled her father, and she spoke and laughed like him. But, unexpectedly, she had a deeper voice. Whether this means that Henry actually had a rather high-pitched voice, in contrast to his daughter's lower register, we shall never know, but the idea of a light voice issuing from that increasingly massive frame is quite strange.

The grandeur of Mary's dress and the magnificence of her jewels must have added considerably to the effect she produced as a young woman. Even in adversity, the princess had paid a great deal of attention to her wardrobe, ensuring that furs, collars and dresses were mended and that her garments were decorated in the latest fashions. She had been deprived of almost all her jewels in March 1534, as a punishment for her continued intransigence, and was just beginning to build up her collection and her wardrobe again when Jane Seymour died. After the period of mourning, she was given some of the jewellery that had belonged to the queen, but Lady Kingston, in charge of Mary and Elizabeth's household, felt she should check with one of Cromwell's men whether it might be acceptable for Mary to wear again 'her white taffety edged with velvet', even though this dress had earlier met with the king's approval.

But such hesitancy was only temporary. Mary became a fashion trendsetter. In her twenties, she favoured French gowns with turned-up sleeves which often revealed a rich velvet facing. The square, open neck of the French gown could be filled in with a partlet, either in the same silk or in a contrasting colour and texture. Mary's gowns were often of cloth of gold and silver and were already high-collared by 1544 and open at the neck to show 'a wrought lining of coloured silk embroidery on linen'. The earliest visual evidence we have of this style depicts it a good ten years later, so Mary was definitely leading, not following, fashion in the 1540s.

Elements of this look, though not the partlet, can be seen in the 1544 portrait of Mary by Master John. She is wearing a gown of crimson damask cloth of gold, brocaded with a looped piece of silver thread. It had paired gold aglets for fastening the foresleeves and a girdle jewelled with rubies and pearls. The headdress was also richly adorned with pearls. Crimson was a favourite colour, which must have looked good with her complexion. Early the previous year the royal accounts noted that she had ordered 'a coat of crimson satin embroidered with pearls and gold'.[5] Mary also wore other colours associated with royalty, such as the stunning gown of 'purple satin, embroidered with parchment of gold and purple sarcenet for the pulling out of the sleeves', which would have set off her red hair very effectively.[6]

These dresses, especially if they featured long trains, were very costly. Mary's accounts show that she regularly bought silks, cambric, satins and caffa, a kind of silk that cost 12 shillings a yard. She also purchased pairs of sleeves in gold and silver. The cost of cloth of gold and silver varied but was generally about 40 shillings a yard. Prices were high but clothing was also adaptable, even recyclable. Pairs of French sleeves were made into Venetian sleeves when the Italian style temporarily gained precedence over the French in the mid-1540s, and pearls used as decorations for garments and headdresses could also be reused. This was just as well, since Mary had purchased a hundred of them at a cost of over £66, well above her entire monthly allowance, in December 1537. Mary was also very fond, as were other ladies of her time, of 'night gowns'. These sumptuous garments were perhaps intended for more relaxed evening wear but they were most definitely not for sleeping. One listed in the wardrobe accounts for this period took 15 yards of black velvet, lined with satin, and another required 12 yards of black damask, edged with 3 yards of black velvet and lined with fur. Mary's attitude to dress is entirely at odds with the negative historical image of a dowdy, dour woman incapable of enjoying life. The love of clothes probably developed in her early childhood, with its memories of her betrothals in appropriate finery to the French dauphin and later to Charles V, as well as the elaborate costumes she wore at court masques.

The jewels that enhanced these dresses were equally important to Mary. She had many pieces set with diamonds, pearls, rubies and emeralds, as well as individual rubies, known as balaces, that hung on chains. Some were in the shapes of crosses, others of flowers; her inventory for 1542 lists 'one flower with a great emerald set in a dolphin, one ruby on it and one great pearl pendant'. Many were brooches, often of gold and diamonds, on religious themes, such as the history of Moses, Noah's flood and Christ healing the man with palsy. She also possessed a fine collection of what were known as 'abillements', chains of goldsmiths' work worn round the neck or bosom and set with precious stones.[7]

At this stage of her life, little of the jewellery Mary wore was actually owned by her. The king made provision for his daughter out of the royal collection, but he could request pieces back or even, as in 1534, require everything to be returned. Mary's income did not permit her to purchase expensive jewels, so gifts from Henry's later queens must have been especially welcome. Shortly after her marriage in 1543, Katherine Parr, Henry's sixth wife, gave her new stepdaughter a beautiful pair of golden bracelets, set with diamonds, rubies and emeralds.

Mary's surroundings were graciously furnished and comfortable. There were tapestries, velvet hangings and an extensive inventory of bedlinen, cushions, chairs and carpets, crockery and drinking vessels. Her dining was also sophisticated, washed down with wine and ale. At table, she was offered a varied and healthy diet, quite out of the reach of all except the most favoured. There was an abundance of fresh, seasonal fruit such as cherries, peaches, raspberries and pomegranates, as well as apples and pears. In the summer, she enjoyed strawberries and cream. Vegetables were readily available and Mary had artichokes, leeks and cucumbers to accompany a wide variety of meat, fish, crustaceans and game. She ate everything from carp and pike to oysters and sturgeon, and was fond of venison and partridge. Bacon, eggs and cheese were also featured at the less glamorous end of her consumption. For dessert, there could be pancakes or marchpane, a kind of marzipan macaroon. Mary also liked a type of hard candy known as Manus Christi, made from white sugar, rosewater and powder of pearls, decorated with gold leaf. This could also be made into cakes and gilded. It was sometimes used for medicinal purposes, but was probably popular because of its sweetness and attractive appearance.[8]

When the grim regime that had characterised Mary's life for three years was lifted in the second half of 1536, she returned to her favourite pastime, betting on cards and dice, with a vengeance. In the accounts, there are 23 different entries up to December 1538 for money delivered to the Lady Mary to play at cards; 40 to 45 shillings twice a month was common at the beginning of this period, but this amount diminished by half later in 1537. Perhaps Mary was trying to rein herself in. She was, for a while, spending nearly one-third of her income on gambling.

Her daily life was healthy, even if she herself did not always feel well. Most days she was reported as walking between two and three miles, and she loved to ride and to hunt. The present of a horse from Cromwell almost as soon as she signed her submission provided a welcome distraction from dwelling on the enormity of what she had done. So too, presumably, did the parrot she received as a gift in 1537 and the spaniel she acquired later from a yeoman of the King's Chamber.

Throughout her life, Mary had given money to charity and in alms. This was partly because it was expected of royalty – and although she gave frequently she did not give great amounts, which reflects her lack of direct income – but she does seem to have had a definite interest in London's prisons and poorhouses and in the choristers of the Chapel Royal, whose singing she enjoyed. The largest single sum she donated during this period was 40 shillings in alms on the day her brother Edward was born.

To her family and friends she was generous and thoughtful in the gifts she provided. Those to Elizabeth ranged from 20 shillings to buy her playthings to five yards of rich yellow satin for a kirtle, as well as pieces of jewellery. Mary evidently believed, quite rightly, as it turned out, that her sister would like clothes as much as she did. But what to give her father? The choice of present for Henry must have posed a problem at the beginning of every year. As a king, he lacked for nothing, but his children were expected to provide him with original gifts. Elizabeth's attempts to think creatively about this in 1545 produced an impressive Latin translation of her stepmother's religious writings and nearly cost Katherine Parr her life when the king realised the extent, and content, of his wife's literary attainments. Mary managed to avoid such pitfalls. One year she opted for a beautifully upholstered and decorated chair, commissioned from the leading specialist in London. Although a competent needlewoman herself (she sometimes made cushions for members of the court at Christmas time) she clearly decided that an expert was needed in this case.

Yet although she was able to fill her time mostly as she wished, in the company of those who were sympathetic to her situation, there is a pervasive air of sadness about Mary in her twenties. This is very apparent in the 1544 portrait, which shows a woman still youthful for 28. The eyes, though, lack sparkle and the downcast mouth betrays what she has suffered. It is still possible to see the attractive princess she once was, but she is visibly fading. She knows that life is passing her by. At the time of the painting, she was firmly established back at court, but much had happened in between to explain the underlying dejection caught so well by the painter.

Before Katherine Parr's influence brought Mary finally back into Henry VIII's favour she lived comfortably, but uneasily. Her relationship with her father was like that of a well-treated hostage, and she was only too aware of this, as her resigned and rather bitter comment to Marillac shows. There was much talk of marriage – in fact hardly a year went by without some negotiation – but Mary's assessment that her father would never find her a husband because he did not want to let her go was correct. He treated her exactly as he had done when she was a child. She was a diplomatic tool, convenient to support his increasingly unrealistic attempts to be a major player in Europe.

In the autumn of 1536, as she struggled to come to terms with her reduced status, she was still being referred to as 'the princess' in letters from Henry to his ambassadors in France. It did not take long for discussions to resume about a possible marriage with the duke of Orléans. The use of the term 'princess' was a brazen piece of double-talk, presumably intended to reassure the French that they were not getting devalued goods, even though Mary herself had just been browbeaten into giving up the title that had been hers since birth.[9] She realised that she was only a pawn in her father's efforts to retain his influence as a power-broker in Europe. The wonder is that the emperor and the king of France continued to play the game at all. Their suspicion of each other outweighed any rational analysis of the harm – or help – that Henry could offer. Meanwhile, if he could be induced to part with his daughter on favourable terms, there was always the possibility of her claim to the throne being validated. So they continued their embassies and proposals, mindful of the fact that the German princes were also expressing an interest. In 1541, the French went so far as to make discreet enquiries about Mary's childbearing prospects and were reassured by an informant described as a lady of Mary's chamber. If Henry had really wanted to find a husband for Mary, there was no shortage of potential suitors.

The name that occurred most frequently, right up to the time when she became queen, was Dom Luis of Portugal. This brother-in-law of Charles V was a widower ten years older than Mary, and the efforts to bring about a marriage between them were almost farcically protracted. It was natural for the emperor to support Dom Luis as a candidate for his cousin's hand. He was Catholic, a family member and could provide Mary with a stable and comfortable life. Away from the constant tensions of her existence in England, Mary might have become a Portuguese princess and recaptured some of her mother's Iberian inheritance. She knew better than to express any opinion where marriage was concerned, however, and Dom Luis did not press his suit vigorously. In fact, he never remarried, which looks like a preference for the single state.

But while marriage discussions were carried on with France and the empire at diplomatic level, one aspiring bridegroom decided to stake his claim in person. This was highly unusual and raised a few eyebrows. Duke Philip of Bavaria, a German prince who proudly announced that he never heard mass, came to England in the winter of 1539, offering his military service to Henry VIII and his hand to Mary. He evidently made quite an impression, so much so that Thomas Wriothesley was dispatched to Hertford Castle, where Mary was living, to raise the matter with the princess herself.

It must have been a strange meeting, this able servant of the Crown and one of Cromwell's closest associates, discussing with the Lady Mary the possibility of her marrying a Lutheran. Mary already knew Wrio-thesley well, and if he had established a rapport with her he would have been a good choice for a rather delicate mission. Wriothesley was a handsome man with a commanding presence, and although he became associated with religious conservatism in the 1540s, he was there to try to gauge her reactions to a possible match with a heretic.

If opposition had been anticipated, none was offered. Mary did observe, in respect of Duke Philip's beliefs, that 'she would prefer never to enter that kind of religion', but she would obey her father's will in the matter. And she agreed to meet Philip, who was keen to woo her without an intermediary. Perhaps her curiosity was aroused by this romantic gesture. The more realistic part of her nature may also have reminded her that she was 23 and that no one else had made such an effort to gain her hand. The duke offered a means of escape from her father, and there was little enough to keep her in England.

On 26 December 1539, Mary walked with Philip of Bavaria in the gardens of the abbot of Westminster. The wintry surroundings were a contrast to the warmth of the duke's approach to his intended bride. She spoke no German and he no English but, as educated people, they were able to converse in Latin. An interpreter filled in any gaps when Latin did not suffice, and they seem to have communicated effectively. Philip gave her a magnificent diamond cross with a pendant pearl as a token of his affection and repeated that he wished to marry her. He was also bold enough to kiss her, something which no man who was a stranger had ever done. Mary, whether disarmed or merely disconcerted, did not repulse him. It was for the king to decide, she said, and she would obey him. At no time did she show actual dismay. Perhaps she was a little flattered, despite her pride. He was 13 years older, but he was the only man ever to make a personal appeal to marry her.

A delighted Philip returned to Henry at Greenwich convinced that he could move things to a swift conclusion. A marriage treaty was drawn up which stated that Mary would waive all her rights to the English succession and bring with her a dowry of £7,000 (just under £3 million). The French and the imperialists, both taken by surprise, expected that the marriage would be celebrated within weeks. By mid-January 1540, Chapuys believed it had already taken place. It was distasteful and worrying, but it would have to be accepted. The rumours, however, were wrong. Something in Henry's terms did not sit well with Duke Philip and he had already left the country, without his bride. Discouraged but not defeated, he tried twice more during the year, but by then attention was entirely focused on the king's disastrous fourth marriage to Anne of Cleves, which may have ruined Mary's chances. In 1543, the duke resumed his quest, when he and Mary met for a second time. Again, he departed without her. The wait for a husband continued.

Mary's passivity during the fruitless rounds of marriage discussions does not necessarily mean that she was happy to remain unmarried. It was, more likely, a prudent way of keeping emotions in check, of preventing the dashing of hopes. Nor did she wish to convey anything to her father other than complete obedience. The small amount of diversion offered by Duke Philip was a brief enough lifting of dark clouds. All around her, as the new decade dawned, were the reminders of how unpredictable and dangerous life at court could be. Her father was ageing and not in good health. But this only increased his ruthless and revengeful nature. Seeing what he had done to those she counted as friends, she had no intention of testing his patience herself.

There were clear reasons why she took the path of least resistance. By 1541, five of those who had been her supporters in 1536 were dead, accused of conspiracy and treason. Henry Courtenay, marquess of Exeter, Lord Montague (the eldest son of the countess of Salisbury), Sir Edward Neville and Sir Nicholas Carew were executed in 1539.

Gertrude Courtenay, marchioness of Exeter, the faithful friend of Katherine of Aragon and Mary, was imprisoned for a while in the Tower and her young son, Edward, for much longer. But much worse for Mary than even the loss of these representatives of the old Catholic nobility was the execution in 1541 of Margaret Pole. She had been arrested at the same time as the others, when fears of a Catholic backlash and attack from Europe caused a climate of fear at court. Her position was compromised because her exiled son, Reginald Pole, was sent by the pope to try to persuade both Francis I and Charles V that the time was ripe for a concerted attack on the heretical kingdom of England. He failed, but his attempts cost his family and their associates dear. Margaret Pole, countess of Salisbury, languished in the Tower for two years until, one June morning, she was peremptorily told that she was about to die.

And it was to be a terrible death, not the swift oblivion that this elderly noblewoman, her entire life passed in the shadow of suspicious kings, deserved. She told the officers of the Tower, who came to fetch her, that she found the sudden pronouncement of the death sentence very strange, not knowing what crime she had committed. But she was composed when she walked to the small block, and there 'she commended her soul to God and desired those present to pray for the king, queen, prince and princess'. Her last thoughts were of Mary, the girl she had prepared for the throne of England. Then an apprentice executioner, a young lad with slight experience and less skill, butchered her, hacking her head and shoulders to pieces. The extreme violence of her end mirrored that of her father, Clarence, and the turbulent century into which she had been born. She was the last aristocratic victim of the Wars of the Roses.

The knowledge that the woman who had brought her up had ultimately paid with her life, and in such a barbarous way, was too much for Mary to bear. For some time after the news of the countess's death was brought to her, she was very ill.

The extinction of key members of the old aristocracy was only partly the result of invasion scares. There was also a settling of scores, both for Henry VIII and Cromwell. They had not forgotten 1536. But neither had other men on the increasingly divided council, and they were no friends to the newly created earl of Essex. By the summer of 1540, a combination of circumstances at home and abroad allowed Cromwell's opponents, led by the duke of Norfolk, to move against him. It was not merely his power they disliked but his continued support for new religious ideas. Their success, which seemed unlikely at the beginning of 1540, was blessed by the conjuncture of a set of events reminiscent of Cromwell's coup against Anne Boleyn, and having about as much justification in reality.

It used to be said that Cromwell's fall was brought about by the debacle of Henry VIII's fourth marriage, to the German princess Anne of Cleves, but this sorry affair was the occasion rather than the cause. True, the king held his minister responsible for the excruciating embarrassment that the marriage caused him, but he was more concerned by Cromwell's attempts to push the Reformation still further in England. Greater doctrinal reforms were opposed by Henry and by Norfolk's affinity, which included the clever but irascible churchman Stephen Gardiner. Cromwell knew his danger and he tried, with all his habitual cunning and resource, to fight back. At one point in the spring of 1540, it looked as if he might have turned the tables, but Norfolk had an unsuspected advantage; he could provide the king with an alternative wife.

She was another of his nieces and her name was Katherine Howard. Very young (possibly no more than 15), petite but with a full figure, she was as sexually attractive to Henry as the unfortunate Anne of Cleves had been repellent.[10] It is ironic that Cromwell's fall should have been hastened by this pert though not very bright girl, but her charms proved the impetus Norfolk had been looking for. When Cromwell was arrested in the council chamber on 10 June 1540, Norfolk himself pulled the badge of St George from the minister's neck. He was taken to the Tower and executed on 28 July. The last of the innumerable services he had done for Henry VIII was to provide the detailed information needed to secure the Cleves divorce.

The man Mary viewed as her saviour was gone and with him her political anchor. Though she mourned Margaret Pole more, she had needed Thomas Cromwell for guidance. Only Chapuys and her own judgement were left to her now. Part of that judgement needed to be applied to her relationships with the two women who were briefly her father's fourth and fifth wives.

· ❖ ·

Mary and Elizabeth attended the wedding of Henry and Anne of Cleves and both subsequently got on well with her. But Henry married her only with the most extreme reluctance. The causes of his aversion have never been entirely clear. He had found the celebrated portrait of her by Holbein pleasing, but the lady herself did not meet expectations. It was not love at first sight, but utter revulsion. Anne was unsophisticated and lacked small talk, and she committed an unfortunate blunder when she did not even recognise the king when he first came to meet her at Rochester. This was hardly Anne's fault – Henry had indulged in his rather juvenile penchant for disguise and was dressed up as Robin Hood, probably not a well-known figure in Cleves – but it was a bad start. Yet it seems to have been her body odour as much as anything else which deterred him. As nobody else commented on this we can only assume that Henry had a very sensitive nose. After consulting with his ministers as to whether the marriage could be stopped, and being told it could not, he took the plunge and married her early on the morning of 6 January 1540. Preoccupied with his own situation, he was not going to give much attention to dealing with Mary's marital prospects, even though he was being pressed by Philip of Bavaria. Perhaps he felt that one German match was enough for the time being.

Anne was a tall, slim woman with fair hair and a face described by the French ambassador as 'confident and resolute'. Even allowing for some licence with the paintbrush, it is hard to understand, looking at Holbein's portrait, why she unnerved – and apparently unmanned – Henry so. Whatever the cause, he could not consummate the marriage and even told his lords that he thought, because of Anne's 'slack belly and breasts', that she was not a virgin. This ungentlemanly verdict sealed the fate of their brief union. By late spring Katherine Howard had been dangled in front of Henry and Anne was divorced, after some initial opposition, with a comfortable settlement. Once she was no longer in his bed, Henry seems to have got on rather well with her. There are varying accounts of whether Anne was happy with her divorce or not, but in view of what happened to her successor, any anger she felt must surely only have been temporary.

Mary remained on good terms with Anne of Cleves but her relationship with Katherine Howard began uneasily in the hot summer of 1540. Katherine may have been as much as ten years younger than Mary herself, an age gap that made her status as stepmother almost ridiculous. The young Elizabeth was given trinkets and petted by the new queen, but it was much harder to win Mary over. In the autumn of 1540, four months after her marriage to Henry, tension between the two women was high enough for the king to threaten the removal of two of Mary's favourite maidservants. Chapuys reported that Katherine was offended because Mary did not treat her with the same respect as her two prede-cessors. This sounds perfectly plausible; it would be surprising if Mary did not have reservations about Katherine, who had been, up till then, an obscure member of a clan that Mary had no cause to love. But common sense prevailed. There was no point in feuding with Katherine Howard, and the queen was essentially good natured. Mary's personal dislikes could be deep-seated, but Katherine must have won her over. By early 1541 any ill feeling was put behind them and Mary was finally given permission to reside permanently at court. In the summer she accompanied Henry and Katherine on part of their progress through the north of England. How much she enjoyed this we cannot tell, but its acknowledgement of her prominent place in royal circles must have been a relief. To Mary, like almost all those around the court, her father must have seemed blissfully happy with his young and lively wife. She – like him – knew nothing of Katherine Howard's steamy past.

The revelation of the sordid goings-on in the household of the dowager duchess of Norfolk, where Katherine lived as a girl, were prompted by those who disliked the ascendancy of the Howards and the brake that had been put on further religious changes. There was also an element of settling scores, as Katherine had dealt rather heartlessly with some of the men in her past. But her behaviour as queen, when she conducted an intense relationship with Thomas Culpepper, was aston-ishingly reckless. Even more bizarre was the support and encouragement she had received in this liaison from Lady Jane Rochford, the closest confidante among her ladies.

Cranmer, one of the prime movers against Katherine Howard, was discomfited when Henry at first refused point blank to believe the charges laid out against his 'jewel of womanhood'. Further evidence, much of it acknowledged by the terrified queen herself, convinced Henry that he had married a promiscuous little strumpet who could not have loved him at all. Katherine was hastily removed to the convent at Syon House. Like her cousin Anne Boleyn, she may have clung to the hope that she could avoid death but known in her heart, from the first moment of her interrogation, that she would not be allowed to live. As early as 11 November 1541, when details of the queen's detention were seeping out to international observers, Marillac told Francis I: 'The way taken is the same as with Queen Anne who was beheaded.' Katherine's exhilarating but brief reign as queen consort was over: 'she has taken no kind of pastime but kept in her chamber, whereas before she did nothing but dance and rejoice, and now when the musicians come they are told that it is no more the time to dance'.[11] On 10 February 1542 Katherine was taken by river to the Tower. Knowing that this really did signal the end, she put up some resistance and had to be manhandled on to the boat. Three days later, subdued and proper in her final speech, she was executed with Lady Rochford. This sinister and enigmatic woman, who had a perverse delight in compromising others, had been on the fringes of Mary's circle of friends. It was as well for Mary that she did not get any closer.

In 1536 the poet Thomas Wyatt the elder had written despairingly of the 'bloody days' that took the lives of Anne Boleyn and those accused with her. At least they had a trial; Katherine Howard was condemned by Act of Attainder. With her passing came to an end a period of three years that was bloodier still.

Henry decided it would be better to have Mary away from court while the proceedings against the disgraced queen were completed. She was sent to join Prince Edward, escorted on the journey by Sir John Dudley, a soldier and politician who had briefly served Anne of Cleves as her master-of-horse. Disappointed by the Cleves divorce, Dudley began to wonder whether his career at court would ever prosper. He may not have regarded accompanying the Lady Mary on this occasion as a significant step in the right direction. Neither could have anticipated that, 11 years later, when he was the most powerful man in England and she was a rebel, he would ride out of London to meet her again.

The king was very low for much of the following year, as he struggled to adjust to the knowledge that he had been so mistaken in Katherine Howard. But, as 1542 drew to a close, the ever-vigilant Chapuys noticed that he seemed to have moved on: 'now all is changed and order is already taken that the princess shall go to court this feast, accompanied with a great number of ladies; and they work night and day at Hampton Court to finish her lodgings'.[12] The imperial ambassador evidently believed that Henry's desire to have his daughter with him for the

Christmas season was a positive indication that he was better. He had clearly decided that Mary would help him forget the past, and this was a sign of her much-strengthened position. Perhaps the king did look forward to Mary's company, to hearing her sing, watching her dance and entertain him with her musical talents. On the other hand, he may have been even more interested in the ladies who surrounded her. One, especially, caught his attention at around this time. This was Lady Latimer, the wife of a northern lord who had made up for being implicated in the Pilgrimage of Grace by fighting with the royal armies on the Scottish border in 1542. He was much older than his wife, and it was widely known that he was very ill, so ill, in fact, that he was unlikely to survive. When he died in February 1543 his wife, born Katherine Parr, became a widow for the second time. She had already determined to stay in London, at court, and appears to have joined Mary's household shortly before Lord Latimer's death. Suddenly, it was remarked that the king came at least once a day to see his daughter. Mary may have found this increased parental attention gratifying, but she may also have guessed that she was not actually the main reason for her father's sociability. Henry was clearly interested in Lady Latimer.

He was not the only one. Pleasing in appearance – to modern eyes she appears the most attractive of Henry's wives – and warm in personality, Katherine Parr was a trim redhead with a considerable sense of style. Much has been made of the fact that she appealed to Henry because she was 'mature', but she was certainly not matronly. At 30, she was younger than Anne Boleyn had been at the time of her marriage to the king. There was also a passionate and impulsive side to her nature, for she had fallen deeply in love with the king's brother-in-law, Sir Thomas Seymour. A rather disreputable charmer at whose feet sensible women seemed to swoon, Seymour was still unmarried at 34 and looking for a wife, preferably as high born and rich as possible. Katherine Parr did not fit into either of those categories; she was the daughter of a courtier from Kendal in Westmorland and the money she inherited from Lord Latimer was adequate rather than generous. As Thomas Seymour gave every appearance of reciprocating her affection, it must be supposed that he wanted her for herself. Unless, of course, he saw her as an entrée to Princess Mary. He had previously tried to woo the young Mary Howard, the duke of Richmond's widow, but was rebuffed by the duchess and warned off by the earl of Surrey, her brother. The Howards were not keen to be allied with the Seymours, whom they considered upstarts.

It is possible that Seymour's obvious courtship of Katherine Parr heightened the king's own feelings, in a manner reminiscent of his brush with Sir Thomas Wyatt over Anne Boleyn years before. A rival in love made the lady all the more desirable. When she was told that the king wanted her as his sixth wife, Katherine's reaction was, at first, despairing. The opportunity of a love match with a handsome, virile man was suddenly replaced by the contemplation of her name being added to the list of Henry's wives. The precedents for surviving this dubious honour were discouraging, even if the unkind advance of the years suggested that the king would not, himself, see his dotage. Age had not withered Henry; instead, it had fattened him. Pain and ill health made his notorious temper still more unpredictable and his reputation as a husband was the talk of Europe. Unhappily for Katherine Parr, she could not afford the delicious quip attributed to Christina of Lorraine, once mentioned as a bride for Henry, who said she must decline because she would rather keep her head. Katherine's desire to stay at court had come back to bite her in the most unexpected way. There was no practical line of escape. She must have known she could not turn him down. Her sister Anne had served most of Henry's queens and her brother William was ambitious. Their lives, as well as her own, would be ruined if she did not acquiesce. After an agonising period, she also convinced herself that her marriage was the will of God. Already attracted to the ideas of the religious reformers, she decided she would use her position as queen to influence the king away from the conservatism of the Howards and their allies. So Katherine Parr, well educated, twice married and, though childless, an experienced stepmother of adult children, married Henry VIII in the Queen's Closet at Hampton Court on 12 July 1543. The Lady Mary was one of only 20 people who attended the ceremony, and she looked on with pleasure. The new queen's mother, Maud Parr, had been one of Katherine of Aragon's ladies-in-waiting, and Mary must surely have remembered her. It is highly likely that Henry VIII's first wife was godmother to his last. Finally, here was someone that his elder daughter could call a friend.

Katherine Parr is often remembered for her religious interests and supposed nursing skills, as well as her success in re-establishing family harmony between Henry and his children. Her portrait in Lambeth

Palace is of an intelligent, almost intense woman. Perhaps she is not quite lovely, but she is undoubtedly compelling. All of which makes her sound worthy but rather dull, but there was another side to her, the side that Thomas Seymour had already seen. She was also sensual, careful to make sure that her bedchamber was perfumed delicately and her person adorned with beautiful gowns and jewels. Katherine took her marriage vows, to be 'bonny and buxom, in bed and in board', seriously. There were many advantages, as she soon discovered, to being queen of England, and she was determined to make the most of them.

There followed for Mary three and a half years of stability, the longest uninterrupted period of happiness that she would know for the rest of her life. Her stepmother was a cultured person with a warm heart, whose company was a delight, not a duty. When Mary and Elizabeth both accompanied the king and queen on the summer progress that followed the marriage, the atmosphere was familial, in contrast to the time exactly three years earlier when Mary had travelled with her besotted father and Katherine Howard. In the wider family circle, Margaret Douglas benefited from the arrival of the new queen as well. She had recouped her position again by 1543, when she became first lady-in-waiting to Katherine Parr. The following year, Henry finally found a husband for Margaret in Matthew Stewart, the Scottish earl of Lennox. But his own daughter remained unwedded.

She may not have minded. Katherine and Mary were often together, sharing their love of clothes and precious stones, dancing and music, reading and conversation. Chapuys recognised from the outset the benefits to his princess of this affectionate relationship, and he was equally gratified by the queen's pro-Habsburg stance. She went out of her way to make sure she saw him when he came to court and she made a superb impression on the duke of Najera when she entertained him, with Mary, in February 1544. And in this year, the last of his long sojourn as ambassador to England, Chapuys saw his princess legally restored, in name but not title, to her rightful place in the succession to the English throne, behind her brother and ahead of her sister. This belated acknowledgement of reality on the part of Henry VIII owed a great deal to his last wife's influence.

Mary observed a tactful public silence about the revival of her prospects. Whether she spoke of the changes in private we do not know. The assumption must be that she was pleased, at least as much by the implied approval she now enjoyed in the eyes of her father, as in any contemplation that she might one day rule herself. That still seemed a prospect too distant to be worthy of much consideration. She may also have been absorbed at this time in her participation in another of the queen's projects, a major work of literary translation inspired by Katherine's interest in new learning. This was a translation into English of Erasmus's Latin *Paraphrases upon the New Testament*. Mary undertook, at her stepmother's request, the challenge of translating the paraphrase of St John's gospel. The work kept her occupied for some while, until illness meant that her chaplain, Francis Mallett, had to complete it, but her contribution was much praised by Nicholas Udall, the editor of the series. This 'peerless flower of virginity', he wrote, 'doth now also confer the inestimable benefit of furthering both us and our posterity in the knowledge of God's word and to the more clear understanding of God's gospel'.

How could Mary, the contrary Catholic queen of popular history, have become involved in such an undertaking and earned the approbation of those in the reforming circle around Katherine Parr? The answer lies in her humanist education and upbringing. Education and religion were so closely intertwined in 16th-century England that it appeared quite natural for a woman like Mary, who had always prided herself on her ability in Latin, to turn her attention to such a task. After years of relative intellectual deprivation, she would not shy away from the stimulus being offered. It has been suggested that she did not finish her translation of St John because she was deterred by the queen's own evangelical leanings and the strongly reforming interests of all the other ladies in Katherine's circle, with the exception of Lady Margaret Douglas.[13] But she was definitely unwell again at the point that her completed input was expected. Her subsequent reluctance to be credited as the author, because she had not finished it, suggests scrupulous modesty rather than distaste. Katherine stepped in, determined to give Mary her due. After all, she had undertaken most of the work: 'I do not see why you should repudiate that praise which all men justly confer on you,' she told the princess.[14]

But Katherine's confidence in her hold over her husband, fuelled by a successful interlude as regent when Henry went in person to prosecute the last of his wars in France, came close to destroying her. The religious conservatives, led by Bishop Gardiner (who had actually married Katherine to Henry), moved against her in the summer of 1546. Encouraged by a further decline in Henry's health and his evident irritation at this wife's literary prowess, her attempts to dispute with him and push him further down the road of reform, they nearly managed to get her arrested and put in the Tower. How the queen found out about the plot against her is not certain (John Foxe's account of it makes dramatic and entertaining reading, though some elements of it may be fabricated), but she managed to remain surprisingly level-headed, despite her undoubted fear.[15] Pleading illness and contrition, asserting that she had only ever intended to distract her husband from his pain when they discussed religious matters, Katherine got herself back into Henry's arms and saved her life.

His attitude towards her, in the remaining months of his life, was at first one of indulgence. Then, as he realised that he was more seriously ill, he distanced himself from the queen and his children, concentrating his mind on the arrangements that would need to be made for his son's minority. He passed his final Christmas at Whitehall, apart from Katherine and Mary, who were at Greenwich. On 11 January, the queen's apartments were prepared for her arrival but it is not known whether she saw her husband after that date. Neither she nor any other members of his family were with him when he died on 28 January 1547, aged 56.

Mary was not told of his death for several days, as the new men of the council nominated by Henry to govern in his son's name took elaborate precautions to ensure that all was in place before the public announcement was made. She was angered by their dissimulation but there was nothing she could do about it. For the time being, she remained with the dead king's widow, who had learned, to her chagrin, that she would not become regent for Edward VI. True to his lifelong convictions about the inadequacy of women as rulers, Henry made sure Katherine Parr would have no role in the government of the country. Yet however wary the young king's councillors were, nothing could alter the fact that Henry's elder daughter was the heiress to the throne. He had reiterated this in his will. And he had also left her a rich and independent woman. All her life, she had been his property. Now, she was free at last.

PART THREE

The Excluded Heiress
1547–1553

Chapter Six

The Defiant Sister

'If we were to grant you license to break our laws, would it not be an encouragement to others to do likewise?'

Edward VI to Mary, 1551

Mary was three weeks short of her 31st birthday when her father died. His passing was momentous for her on a personal level, as well as for England, now facing the uncertainty of a long royal minority. Henry VIII had been the major figure in her life, the cause of much unhappiness and oppression. He defined who she was – a king's daughter and a great lady, though not a princess of England. Yet in her own eyes, and those of her cousin, Charles V, she had never ceased to be a child born in true matrimony. The imperial court did not immediately recognise Edward VI as king, because he had been born to a father who had broken with Rome and the legitimacy of his succession was not assumed, even though Henry commended his son to the emperor on his deathbed. Writing from Brussels, Charles' sister, Mary of Hungary, who was regent of the Netherlands, preserved a carefully non-committal air: 'We make no mention at present of the young prince,' she wrote to Ambassador Van der Delft in London, 'as we are ignorant as yet whether or not he will be recognised as king, and we await intelligence of the emperor's intentions.' She was equally reticent about Mary, noting: 'We likewise refrain from sending you any letters for our cousin, the Princess Mary, as we do not yet know how she will be treated.'[1] The regent's caution was understandable but also unnecessary. Charles soon discovered that Mary was not going to challenge for the throne; she considered her brother the rightful heir and she accepted the Henrician religious settlement, which made the monarch supreme head of the Church, but had not embraced the more extreme forms of the new religious ideas, such as the abolition of the mass. What she does not seem to have anticipated adequately is that the men who now held power were determined to move forward with religious reform, quickly and comprehensively, and that their policies would make her life extremely uncomfortable once again.

Whether she felt deep sorrow at the old king's death we shall never know. Her reaction seems to have been measured, at least for public consumption. She was apparently more irritated by the delay in receiving the news than prostrate with grief on hearing it. Probably her reaction was one of relief mingled with regret; she could not have avoided thinking about the past and the treatment she and her mother, as well as many others, received at her father's hands. But if she did not mourn Henry with tears, he was still her parent and she did feel his loss, which was, as she put it four months later, 'very ripe in mine own remembrance'.

The most immediate consequence of her father's demise was financial security. Within a few months of Henry's death, as grants of land were made to them, Mary and her sister, Elizabeth, became two of the wealthiest people in the country. They both had an income of £3,000 a year (just under £1 million today), the promise of a dowry of £10,000 (£3 million) when they married and extensive holdings of property. Mary was the owner of 32 houses and manors in the east and south-east of England and one in Cheshire. A number of these, in East Anglia, were previously lands held by the Howards, but the attainder of the duke of Norfolk and execution of his son, the earl of Surrey, in the weeks just before Henry VIII's death, allowed them to be handed over to Mary. It is somewhat ironic that she was able, so many years later, to profit at the expense of a family that had never really wished her well, but the outcome was that Mary effectively owned most of Norfolk, Suffolk and considerable lands in Essex. This part of England was to become greatly significant in her life, for with the lands came men as well as money, giving Mary something that she had consistently lacked before – an affinity, as supporters with local ties were known. So many acquisitions inevitably required professional management, the 'sage officers and ministers for ordering thereof' that Henry had required his councillors to appoint for his daughters in his will. After a gap of nearly 15 years, Mary could once again expect to head a household that befitted her status, for she was, as she had been at the start of 1533, the heiress to the throne of England, and second person in the realm.

The changes in her situation did not come about all at once and were, in part, the result of other developments affecting people close to her. For several months, until about the middle of April 1547, Mary remained in the household of the widowed Queen Katherine. There is no evidence that she attended either her father's funeral or her brother's coronation on 20 February. During this period of mourning, Mary had the opportunity for quiet reflection. She was able to observe the behaviour of the men who were appointed by Henry VIII to govern for his son, and learn, to her growing discomfort, the direction in which their policies might lead. She already knew many of them, of course, for although she had never participated in the government of the country, she had a great deal of experience of the vortex that was English politics, a fact that has been overlooked by historians who have cast her in the role of political ingénue. While her father lived, she knew better than to pass judgement on his advisers, preferring to see herself as their client rather than their critic. Now she was not afraid to voice opinions, especially when the behaviour of Edward's council had a direct impact on her. And she did not think much of those who ruled in her brother's name.

Henry's will, which Mary never saw, named 16 executors to act as privy councillors and 12 assistants, who were probably intended to form a further pool of advisers without having to be privy councillors themselves. It was carefully devised to prevent the abuse of power and to negate, as far as was possible, the inevitable instability of faction. The council had absolute authority and was supposed to be 'hermetically sealed'.[2] The only way out of it was death, and there was no way in. As such, it was a clever solution to the very real problems posed by the character of Tudor political life and the requirement to have an effective executive until Edward VI could assume power himself, a reality that was nearly a decade away.

Much has been written on whether the will was altered in the days just before Henry's death but, even if it was, this does not really matter.

Henry could not impose himself from the grave and everyone knew that power would reside with Edward Seymour, earl of Hertford, the king's maternal uncle. Just how much power, however, remained to be seen. Aided by the capable William Paget, the dead king's secretary, and his ally, John Dudley, Hertford kept the king's death (and the will, which he had in his possession) secret for three days after Henry died. Mary was only one of the majority who were not informed until after Seymour had told Edward and brought the young king to London. On 1 February, the executors rejected de facto the terms of the will by appointing Hertford Lord Protector of the realm and governor of the king's person. In so doing, they made him the most powerful subject that there had ever been in Tudor England. A little more than two weeks later they added to his prestige by giving him the title of duke of Somerset. He was to rule England, with increasing disregard for the kind of collective govern-ment envisioned by Henry VIII, for two and a half turbulent years.

Van der Delft's observations on the new power structure were shrewd and prophetic. He believed that power would effectively be executed by four men: the Protector himself, Thomas Wriothesley (who had shed tears when, as Lord Chancellor, he announced the old king's death to the House of Lords), John Dudley and William Paget. A career diplomat and politician who served Henry and each of Henry's children in turn, Paget was highly rated by the imperialists: 'It is ... most desirable that we should keep Paget in hand, for his authority in this country is great,' was the opinion of the ambassador. But he also noted that Somerset and Dudley were likely to fall out, principally because Dudley was 'of high courage' and not likely to submit for long to Somerset. He was also known for his 'liberality and splendour', presumably an indication that he was aiming for something more than a place alongside Somerset and the others on the council. The Protector, Van der Delft said, was a 'dry, sour, opinionated man'.[3]

Mary seems, however, to have had a soft spot for the duke of Somer-set and his wife, even though their religious beliefs and practices soon began to diverge alarmingly from her own. She had known the duchess for some years, when she was a lady-in-waiting to Katherine Parr, and appears to have been one of the few people who actually liked this controversial woman. 'My good gossip Nan', she called her, and she seems to have anticipated that their friendship would continue, writing to ask for favours for one of her servants in the spring of 1547. No one else seems to have looked so kindly on Anne Somerset, who was depicted as a scheming, overbearing harridan. Paget, in discussion with Van der Delft, would later sum up the troubles of the duke in the memorably pithy phrase: 'He has a bad wife.' That was, indeed, a contemporary comment, though it may say as much about views of strong women in a male-dominated world as it does about the lady herself. Certainly, she was not popular, but Mary never forsook her. After her husband's final fall from grace, in 1551, the duchess remained in the Tower of London as a prisoner until released by Mary when she became queen. And Mary, for all her reservations about the quality of Edward's council, apparently preferred Somerset to the regime that replaced him. Perhaps it was the family connection to Jane Seymour, the queen who had spoken on her behalf in the terrible summer of 1536, which explains what seems otherwise to have been a surprising generosity of spirit towards the man who caused her much unhappiness over religion.

One of the many areas of contention outside the council (which speedily relieved Wriothesley of his role in March 1547) was a dispute within the Protector's own family. This nearly drew in Mary as well, and was the reason that she left the dowager queen's household towards the end of April. Within weeks of becoming a widow, Katherine Parr had renewed her liaison with Thomas Seymour, the Protector's younger brother. Disappointed that he did not have as great a role in the running of the country as Somerset, Seymour decided that a dowager queen was a prize worth winning. It is quite possible that he did genuinely love her. Katherine had narrowly survived four years of marriage to Henry VIII, and she now allowed her heart to overrule her head. The possibility that she might be happy for herself, since she had no further political role, turned the earnest religious commentator into the reckless lover of a high-profile rogue. So began an affair that was hard to conceal. The precise date of Katherine Parr's marriage to Thomas Seymour is unknown as the ceremony was conducted in great secrecy, probably around the middle of May. The queen took her sister into her confidence but not Mary, though the circumstantial evidence, including the timing of Mary's departure from Katherine's household, suggests that her stepdaughter was uncomfortable with her behaviour.

Katherine's new marriage may have been solemnised by God, but it was not sanctioned by king and council. Admittedly, there was nothing in Henry's will to say that the queen could not marry again, but it was clearly impolitic to have done so very quickly, and without the king's formal consent. Edward was very fond of his stepmother and the errant couple realised that they needed to get his support and preferably that of other members of his family as well. So they embarked on a letter-writing campaign, hoping to win hearts and minds for a proposed match that they knew only too well was already a fait accompli. One of the people that Seymour approached to press his supposed suit with the queen was Mary.

Dismayed by what she had observed while still with Katherine and apparently smarting at the insult, however unintentional, to her father's memory, Mary firmly declined to become involved. She began her letter politely enough, by thanking Thomas Seymour for his role in obtaining various payments for her, but went on to say:

> I have received your letter, wherein, as me thinketh, I perceive strange news, concerning a suit you have in hand to the Queen for marriage, for the sooner obtaining whereof, you seem to think that my letters might do you pleasure. My lord, in this case I trust your wisdom doth consider that if it were for my nearest kinsman and dearest friend ..., of all other creatures in the world, it standeth least with my poor honour to be a meddler in this matter, considering whose wife her grace was of late, and besides that if she be minded to grant your suit, my letters shall do you but small pleasure. On the other side, if the remembrance of the King's Majesty my father (whose soul God pardon) will not suffer her to grant your suit, I am nothing able to persuade her to forget the loss of him ... Wherefore I shall most earnestly require you (the premisses considered) to think none unkindness in me, though I refuse to be a meddler in any ways in this matter, assuring you that (wooing matters set apart, wherein I being a maid am nothing cunning) if otherwise it shall lie in my little power to do you pleasure, I shall be as glad to do it as you to require it, both for his blood's sake that you be of, and also for the gentleness which I have always found in you ... Your assured friend to my power, Marye.[4]

The letter, in Mary's strong, clear hand, is both clever and revealing. It contains an implied reproof, to Seymour and to Katherine, and the strong suggestion that the princess knew very well what had been going on under her nose, even if she did claim to be 'nothing cunning' about 'wooing matters'. Mary's other-worldliness has been overstated in the past. She knew Seymour's reputation with women and was not fooled by his appeal to her innocence. Later she claimed that she had met him only once, but this letter suggests otherwise.[5] What she did have was the measure of him, and considerably more so than her half-sister, whose reputation was nearly ruined by her later association with Katherine Parr's fourth husband. A letter attributed to Elizabeth at this time, by the unreliably inventive 17th-century Italian historian Gregorio Leti, refers to correspondence between the sisters that may or may not have taken place. In it, Elizabeth expresses very pompously 'how much affliction I suffered when I was first informed of this marriage' and of the necessity to 'use much tact in manoeuvring with her [Katherine], for fear of appearing ungrateful', but her disdain, if genuine, was not sufficient to keep her out of the queen's household, with all the problems that ensued.[6] What was true, even if the words put into Elizabeth's mouth by Leti are a fiction, was the observation that neither she nor Mary could offer any obstacle to the marriage. And neither, as it turned out, could the Protector and his formidable wife. But they did not take kindly to finding that the queen was now their sister-in-law, and ill feeling between the Seymour brothers was intensified by the quarrel over jewels and precedence that broke out between their wives.

Mary was glad to be apart from these squabbles, as an independent woman, setting up her own household with trusted servants. For much of Edward's reign she lived at either New Hall or Hunsdon in Essex, though in the autumn of 1547 she went to East Anglia to inspect her lands and was an occasional visitor thereafter. The officers of her household were well chosen, unswervingly loyal and willing to give Mary, upon occasion, unwelcome advice. Chief of these men was Robert Rochester, who became the controller of her household. He was, according to a contemporary, 'a man of few equals in steadfastness, loyalty and wise counsel'. All these attributes would be put to the test in his service of Mary during her brother's reign. By 1549, Rochester had been joined by Sir Francis Englefield, who does not seem to have had a specific role, but who was clearly viewed as having significant influence on Mary, and by Edward Waldegrave, who was Rochester's own nephew.

These men had much in common. They were all religious conservatives from eastern England and all were devoted to their mistress, not just personally, but dynastically. Waldegrave also had family ties. His wife, born Frances Neville, was the daughter of Sir Edward Neville, executed with the Courtenays and the Poles in 1538. When her husband took up his office with Mary, Frances became one of her ladies, so underlining her family's long and often dangerous tradition of service to the princess.

Rochester and his colleagues were willing to suffer imprisonment and hardship for her sake, not just so that she was able to follow her religion, but because they wished to ensure her place in the succession. Collectively, they checked Mary's tendency to make the dramatic gesture; she might subsequently say that she was willing to embrace martyrdom rather than give up the mass, but her officers were determined that she should live to claim her throne, when the opportunity arose. They also acted as a vital counterweight to imperial influence, reminding Mary that she was Henry VIII's daughter more than she was Charles V's cousin, and that her future lay in England. Fortified by their support and convictions, Mary faced the future with more confidence.

But in one important respect, Katherine Parr's final marriage left a gap in Mary's life. It deprived her of the company of a woman whom she regarded as an equal. Now there was no one to fulfil that role. Margaret Douglas, much more inclined to enjoy the court than Mary and aware of the importance of being seen, came down to London from Yorkshire with her young son, Lord Darnley. Much as she wanted the boy to meet Edward VI and for his role in the English succession to be recognised, she did not stay long. The countess of Lennox shared Mary's devotion to the old religion and felt uncomfortable among the reformers of Edward's regime. She soon retired to her husband's northern estate at Temple Newsam. This left Mary with only her ladies-in-waiting to provide female company. They were loyal and affectionate but they were subordinates, not friends. Her sister might, in other circumstances, have become her confidante. Instead, they grew apart and a tension developed between them that was never resolved.

Though there were many factors that influenced the development of the sisters' relationship, including the inescapable one of geographical separation, the greatest and most fundamental can be simply stated. Elizabeth was no longer a child, but a person of substance with a mind of her own. Potentially, she was a rival. At 13 years of age she was a highly intelligent young woman who had benefited from a superb education, part of it shared with her brother, and informed by a greater breadth of learning and enquiry than Mary's. Mary's education was certainly impressive by the standards of its day, but those standards had changed by the time Elizabeth entered the schoolroom. She was taught by men who had questioned established orthodoxies, and the power of new ideas inclined her away from her older sister intellectually. Mary had been proud of Elizabeth's precociousness while she was growing up (as indeed she was of Edward's) but what was attractive in a child was suddenly less so in a woman. Elizabeth shared Mary's emotional fragility, as did all the Tudors except the founder of the dynasty, Henry VII, but, over time, she learned to use it to better effect. Never having known her mother, she was not encumbered by the sense of loss and resentment that inevitably coloured Mary's adult life. Her past, her origins, was unspoken, and she lived very much in the present, pampered by her adoring household staff and her foolish but loving governess, Katherine Ashley.

When Mary left Katherine Parr's household, Elizabeth stayed, unwisely, as it turned out. Henry VIII's last queen died a few days after giving birth to a daughter (named Mary, after the princess) in September 1548, by which time her younger stepdaughter had already moved out, apparently under a cloud. The whisperings about the real reason for her departure became clear in early 1549, when, suddenly, lurid details surfaced about Thomas Seymour's behaviour towards Elizabeth while she was under his roof; they were part of the evidence gathered against him which resulted in an accusation of treason. He was never brought to trial but attainted and executed in March 1549, without his brother lifting a finger to save him. Chastened by the knowledge that she had escaped real danger mostly because of her ability to live on her wits, Elizabeth now realised only too well the perils she and Mary faced at the hands of the unscrupulous power-seekers of Edward's reign.

But the Seymour episode did not bring the sisters closer together – if anything, it pulled them further apart. Elizabeth emerged with a dubious reputation, while Mary's was unsullied. Mary kept her own counsel about what had gone on, but at the back of her mind was probably the question that increasingly haunted her as Elizabeth grew towards maturity – what was to be expected, seeing that she was Anne Boleyn's daughter? That thought was more than sufficient to threaten the basis of their relationship and to cancel much of the affection that Mary had once felt.

A chilliness was developing between the sisters, who saw little of each other during the six years that Edward was king. They exchanged letters but were seldom at court together, and there is no record of either having entertained the other at any of the many houses they both owned. They soon came to represent different strands of the political and religious fabric of their brother's kingdom, and it was Mary's relations with the young king, rather than Elizabeth, which mattered more. To Edward's increasing frustration and Mary's near-heartbreak, they were at odds for most of his reign.

· ❖ ·

Edward was only nine years old when his father died and had spent much of his short life trying to impress the rather distant figure of his parent, for whom he probably felt as much fear as affection. Yet though often depicted as a cold, even heartless child, he seems to have loved both his sisters. Elizabeth was close to him in age and had shared his lessons and his household. Mary, though, was old enough to be his mother, and she always treated him with respect but as if he were a child. This gave her a convenient excuse for disagreeing with the edicts of his ministers, when, as became more frequently the case, they did not suit her. Edward hated the confrontations with Mary, and on one occasion they both ended up in tears, but he found her tone patronising and was increasingly impatient with it as he grew into his teens. This creeping disenchantment with a difficult woman whom he could not help loving when he was a little boy may explain his attitude towards her when he knew he was dying in 1553.

But six years earlier, there was no reason to suppose that he would never attain his majority. He was a healthy, active child with a good mind and a determination to be a good king, to govern his people with the God-given powers that Archbishop Cranmer had so radically described at his coronation. Perhaps his academic attainments at so young an age were overstated. The imperial ambassador was dismissive of the paragon's linguistic abilities when introduced to him. He began to greet the king in French, but Somerset told him to address the king in Latin, 'which he said he understood better than French, but, truth to tell,' added Van der Delft, unkindly, 'he seemed to me to understand one just as little as the other, although the archbishop of Canterbury had assured me that the king knew Latin as well as he [the archbishop] did himself'.[7] It does not seem to have occurred to Van der Delft (who admittedly was disenchanted with the entire state entry from the Tower into London) that a small boy meeting all manner of dignitaries for the first time in public might be momentarily tongue-tied, or just plain bored.

Edward survived the arduous ceremonies of the coronation and the subsequent feasting with a becoming dignity. He did not see much of Mary in the first year of his reign; she went off to Norfolk in mid-July to inspect her estates there and did not return till September. She was expected in London in early November but she was still in Essex at the beginning of the next month, suffering from ill health. The physicians called it melancholy and it seems to have afflicted her, by her own admission, every year at about this same time. When Van der Delft went to see her she told him she did not expect to return to London that winter. But the reasons for her depression (perhaps a form of what would nowadays be known as seasonal affective disorder) may have been intensified by the changes in religious practice that were increasing in England. Mass was no longer being celebrated in the house of the Protector, his brother or John Dudley, now earl of Warwick. But Mary was devoted to the mass, a ceremony central to her daily life. She already knew she would never give it up, even if it meant public opposition to the laws being made in her brother's name.

So what had once been a comforting ritual, but probably nothing more, became the touchstone of Mary's life. She embraced it almost ostentatiously, hearing four masses a day as early as June 1547, well before the full extent of Somerset's religious policy became clear. Mary hated everything the reformers, led by Thomas Cranmer, epitomised: their evangelical support of the vernacular Bible and church services, their unseemly marriages, their acquisition of former Church lands (though many Catholics, including the Howards, had profited equally). To her they were hypocrites and time-servers who sought to overthrow centuries of faith in the pursuit of personal profit and power. But more than anything else, she hated them for their commitment to the communion in both kinds and their assertion that nothing miraculous happened when the host was elevated and the priest received the body of Christ. Doctrinal arguments she eschewed, but the Latin mass and its central mystery were her chief points of reference in an uncertain world. She would not yield on them. Her defiance meant that she became, whether intentionally or not, the focus of opposition to the Edwardian regime.

Perhaps she did not set out to define herself that way and she was certainly not personally implicated in armed opposition, but the Lady Mary became an intractable problem for Edward's ministers. The reason was straightforward. However much she might storm and protest, she was breaking the laws of the land. This had the most serious of implications: 'If the king and his sister, to whom the whole kingdom was attached as heiress to the crown in the event of the king's death, were to differ in matters of religion, dissension would certainly spring up. Such was the character of the nation,' Somerset informed Van der Delft. 'He hoped the Lady Mary would use her wisdom and conform with the king to avoid such an emergency and keep peace within the realm.' But he added, significantly for the manner in which the disagreement intensified in the early 1550s, 'he would not enquire into her private conduct if she had not yet come to their way of thinking'. The Protector and the king clung at this stage to the quite unrealistic belief that, left to herself, Mary would come round and embrace religious change. In this, they were completely deluded. Their laws were helping Mary discover, again, her own identity. She would never change. Her conscience transcended statute law and was perfectly clear. Her brother and his advisers were breaking the law of God and propelling England on the road to perdition.

The clash between these two positions was never entirely resolved while Edward lived, but its seriousness ebbed and flowed as other considerations absorbed the attention of the politicians. Mary was not the only influential figure who opposed religious change. Margaret Douglas's house became a centre for Catholic opposition in the north of England. Other prominent Catholics such as the duke of Norfolk and Edward Courtenay remained as prisoners in the Tower of London. In 1548, they were joined by Stephen Gardiner, the irascible bishop of Winchester. Gardiner had fallen from favour with Henry VIII in the 1540s and been very pointedly cut out of the king's will. He served early notice that he would not accept the direction Edward's council was setting. After preaching an uncompromising sermon justifying transubstantiation, he was swiftly deprived of his liberty. Mary seems not to have commented on this herself, and there is no evidence of any communication between them. This may partly be explained by a recognition that it would not be wise, though both Mary and Gardiner were not shy of speaking out. But she had never been really close to him and could not forget that he had changed sides in the 1530s and supported the divorce.

Edward's councillors, daily beset with the business of running a country, faced difficulties far more serious than the embarrassment of disaffected public figures. Committed to major religious change most of the council certainly was, but it also grappled with huge economic problems: the expense of war, a debased coinage and rising agrarian discontent. Foreign policy was a constant source of pressure. Relations with both France and Scotland were bad. The French wanted the return of Boulogne and the Scots never forgave Somerset for attacking them in 1547. In revenge, they sent the five-year-old Mary Queen of Scots to France. There she was to be betrothed to the dauphin and brought up as a French queen-in-waiting.

All these developments were watched with interest by Charles V. The

emperor and his advisers did not derive much comfort from the spectacle of a weak and divided England and were concerned about the
triumph of heretics in government, which would only encourage similarly deluded and evil people in the Low Countries. But Charles soon
realised that his cousin's stand on religion gave him a powerful influence
over English politics. In supporting her unequivocally he could threaten
dire – though mostly unspecified – consequences if she was not allowed
to follow her religion. Somerset's policies would have made him a
natural ally of the imperialists except in this one, insuperable respect. It
clearly troubled the duke, who expressed concern as early as the summer
of 1547, that the emperor reportedly found his government 'displeasing'.
In May 1549, as the country prepared for the introduction of the new
prayer-book and service in the vernacular, Somerset emphasised that all
that had so far been undertaken was for the good of England: 'These
[religious changes] were greatly needed to repress and stifle the dissen-
sions bred within the realm, and although His Majesty may be
convinced that our right course would have been to leave things as they
were in the late king's time until the termination of the Council of
Trent, yet if the causes and considerations that moved us to act were
known to him, and how soberly we have proceeded in this matter, he
would impute less blame to us.'[8]

But Somerset did not satisfactorily explain what the 'causes and
considerations' were and, in any case, Charles would probably not have
been convinced. It was easier to remind the English of their frailty by
building up Mary as a principled opponent of the regime. Her natural
inclination in every crisis was to turn to her mother's family for help. For
years, they had been the only people she felt she could trust (even if her
trust was misplaced) and they were powerful. The Habsburgs also had a
strong sense of family obligation, though when it came to his relatives in
England, Charles was much more impressive with words than deeds. In
the spring of 1549, however, he could hardly have ignored Mary's deeply
felt plea for his support.

She was, she said, 'sincerely grieved' to hear about the extent of his ill
health, and especially touched that he had taken the trouble to write to
her 'entirely with your own hand, though ill'. One of her greatest
comforts in the world was to hear news of the emperor, 'and particularly
now in these miserable times, for, after God and considering the tender
age of the king, my brother, your Majesty is our only refuge. We have
never been in so great a necessity and I therefore entreat your Majesty,

considering the changes that are taking place in the kingdom, to provide, as your affairs may best permit, that I may continue to live in the ancient faith, and in peace with my conscience.' She feared that the new act of parliament would not allow her so to do, but she would hold firm: 'in life and death I will not forsake the Catholic religion of the church our mother, as I more fully declared to your Majesty's ambassador, when I asked him what help I could look for if they attempted to compel me with threats or violence'.[9]

Was Mary overreacting? Perhaps. Less open defiance might have been more prudent but Mary was not a pragmatic person. She had suppressed her conscience when she bowed to her father's will 13 years earlier and she would not do so again. The parallels with 1536 were inescapable and must have brought back wretched memories. Once again, she was under attack, fighting for right, this time against the dark forces manipulating her brother. But this time, she was not a dependent, defenceless girl. With men and money of her own and the assurance of the emperor's support, she clearly felt that she could survive. It would not be pleasant, but it could be endured and it would make her a stronger person. Though she did not say so she knew, from the reaction of ordinary people in East Anglia, that it would also reinforce her reputation as the upholder of the true faith. Legislation did not necessarily mirror popular sentiment and the majority of Englishmen had not yet made up their minds about the new liturgy. Mary was a powerful example to those who were un-decided.

Her cousin assured her of his protection; he would not let her be bullied. He instructed his ambassador to seek a written assurance, 'in definite, suitable and permanent form', that Mary would be permitted to practise her faith as she had always done. Later, he would state still more flatly that he would not have allowed her to abandon the religion that her family had followed for centuries, even if she had been inclined to temporise. He did not say so explicitly, but the embarrassment would have been too great. A heretic Habsburg was not something Charles V could countenance. Nor had he entirely abandoned the idea of promot-ing a marriage for her with a bridegroom of his choice. Again, Dom Luis of Portugal was mentioned, though it soon became obvious that the emperor's brother-in-law was interested only in Mary's dowry. The possibility of marriage was used by Somerset as an opening for a visit to the emperor by William Paget. Before his departure, the canny statesman sought to downplay the significance of religious change in England, tellingVan der Delft:'I will tell you something I would tell no other man alive, for it might suit me ill to do so. I think with time matters that cannot be touched now may yet be mended. If the emperor is lenient, it will help in this.'[10]

It was a vain hope, this expression of a moderate man who cared for his country more than any ideology or religion. But, experienced *politique* though he was, Paget achieved nothing and actually produced difficulty for Edward's government. Charles V subsequently stated categorically that Paget had given him, while they were together in Brussels, an assurance that Mary would be left undisturbed to follow the form of religion she preferred. Paget could not, of course, acknowledge this, and given his natural caution, and his underlying concerns about the stability of English politics, it seems unlikely that he would have committed himself so clearly, even if it seemed to him an eminently sensible course to follow.[11]

The reality was that nobody could give any assurance for the future in the troubled summer of 1549. Social and religious discontent produced widespread rebellion, in the south-west and in Norfolk, which threatened the Protector's survival. Somerset had compounded these difficulties by his highly autocratic and increasingly irrational personal style of government. The commons may have been in revolt about enclosures and the resulting economic hardship they faced, but the Protector's colleagues had themselves reached breaking point. The 'Good Duke' was actually hot-tempered and high-handed, combining venality (which his colleagues must have known something about) with a dangerous propensity to appease the rebels in order to hold on to power. Maybe he did have some real sympathy for the populace, but it was his policies which had increased the hardship of their lives. For some time, he had abandoned all pretence of consultation with the council; discussion made him impatient and his determination to rule in an arbitrary fashion was causing increasing alarm. He was certainly warned, in frank terms, by Paget, who wanted to remain loyal but saw which way the wind was setting. His letter to the duke, written on 7 July 1549, paints a vivid picture of a rudderless, divided England at the halfway point of the 16th century:

... I see at hand the king's destruction and your ruin. If you love me
or value my service since the king's father's death, allow me to write
what I think. Remember what you promised me in the gallery at
Westminster before the late king died ... planning with me for the
place you now occupy – to follow my advice before any other. Had
you done so, things would not have gone as they have.

Society is maintained by religion and laws: you have neither. The
old religion is forbidden and the new not generally imprinted. The law
is almost nowhere used: the commons have become king ...

He went on to urge Somerset to ride out himself and deal with the
revolts through exemplary justice.[12]

The duke did not follow Paget's advice. He let John Dudley, by this
time earl of Warwick, deal with the Norfolk rebellion. Two thousand of
the rebels were killed in fighting outside Norwich on 27 August, and
though Warwick did not follow up his military success with many judicial executions, his ruthlessly efficient dispatch of so many local men
provoked a hatred long remembered by the citizens of East Anglia. Their
resentment explains why many of them supported Mary four years later.
Opposition to the 1549 religious changes was also a powerful underlying factor that Somerset had chosen to ignore. It is interesting to note
that Mary herself remained silent while the revolt raged around the lands
she had recently acquired from the unpopular Howards, though the
council claimed that her servants were implicated in both Cornwall and
Norfolk, a charge which she indignantly denied.

Publicly, she also stayed aloof as the final drama of the Protector's rule
was played out. For nearly a week, in October 1549, England teetered on
the brink of civil war, as Somerset tried, and failed, to survive a coup that
had been long brewing. By late September, Warwick, Thomas Wriothesley, earl of Southampton, and Arundel (an unlikely triumvirate of two
conservatives and a man who had long been Somerset's friend) could
stand no more. They persuaded other members of the privy council to
support them and Somerset was finished. Removed as he was from his
fellow-politicians, it was not until 5 October that the Protector fully
accepted the gravity of his situation and commanded all subjects to
Hampton Court, to protect the king against 'a most dangerous conspiracy'. Warwick still had an army in the Home Counties and Somerset did
not control the Tower of London. Alarmed for his own survival and
afraid he would lose his property, he took the desperate gamble of

removing Edward VI to Windsor, which was more defensible. There he was joined by Archbishop Cranmer and the thoroughly disillusioned Paget.

But his actions could easily be misrepresented as kidnapping of the monarch, and the king himself seems to have been genuinely scared when he was bundled away from Hampton Court. Cranmer's 'young Josiah', divinely appointed to build a new Church in England, was just a frightened little boy in that autumn of 1549. The king's discomfort was intensified by the fact that he caught a terrible cold on the journey to Windsor and felt very unwell. To the credit of all concerned, however, Edward VI and his country were spared an actual outbreak of violence. Somerset realised that his power was gone and Warwick and the others did not want an armed conflict.

The real casualties of these troubled times were friendship and trust, neither of which was to be easily found in mid-Tudor England. As Somerset lamented when he wrote to Warwick, so long his political ally: 'My Lord, I cannot persuade myself that there is any ill conceived in your heart as of yourself against me; for that the same seemeth impossible that where there hath been from your youth and mine so great a friendship and amity between us, as never for my part to no man was greater, now so suddenly there should be hatred.'[13] This poignant letter demonstrates the political naivety of the king's uncle, whose long experience of the hatreds and deceptions of Henry VIII's court had not taught him the lesson he now learned the hard way. Accepting defeat, he surrendered to the inevitable. On 14 October he was taken to the Tower and the king, who was desperate to get away from Windsor, returned to Hampton Court.

Mary was not in London to offer comfort to her brother while his uncle's regime collapsed, but she knew more than most people about what was happening and the manoeuvrings behind it. She told Van der Delft that she had been approached to give her support to Somerset's overthrow, but had declined to get involved. While things remained uncertain, this was wise, and it may also have increased her stock with the council, who continued to view her as someone who must not be ignored. They wrote to Mary and Elizabeth on 9 October (though the letter was primarily intended for Mary, as the heiress to the throne): 'Because the trouble between us and the Duke of Somerset may have been diversely reported to you, we should explain how the matter is now come to some extremity. We have long perceived his pride and ambition and have failed to stay him within reasonable limits.' They had been alarmed by the duke's accusation that they wished to destroy the king and his behaviour at Hampton Court, where he had 'said many untruths, especially that we should have him removed from office and your Grace made regent, with rule of the king's person, adding that it would be dangerous to have you, the next in succession, in that place. This was a great treason and none of us has by word or writing opened such matter. He concluded most irreverently and abominably, by pointing to the king and saying that if we attempted anything against him, he [the king] should die before him.' No wonder Edward had been petrified. The council went on to explain that they had 'quietly taken the Tower for the king and furnished ourselves with the help of the City of London, which was loyal to the king before the Tower was ours'. They reported that the duke had removed Edward to Windsor and hoped that God would help them 'deliver [the king] from his cruel and greedy hands. If it should come to extremity', they added, 'which we will work to avoid – we trust you will stand by us.'[14]

The council's communication to Mary referred directly to a question about the coup, and the confused months of wrangling that followed it, that has never been fully resolved. Was Mary, at any point, offered the regency? Nowadays, such a robust denial would be taken by a cynical media as proof positive that an approach had been made. Merely by acknowledging the possibility that she could undertake such a role, the council were giving it credence. It seems likely, then, that feelers were put out and that some, at least, of the new privy council considered her a viable candidate. The imperialists would certainly have backed her and, for a time, Van der Delft and others believed that the removal of Somerset was a victory for conservative forces and presaged a return to the old faith. The princess could come out of her semi-exile and use her influence to reimpose the religious settlement of Henry VIII. They were, however, deceived. For two months, the direction that the new government would take hung in the air, as a struggle for power on the council ensued. When it was over, Warwick emerged as the leader of England's government. He soon made it plain that he had no intention of abandoning religious change; in fact, he would press forward, with Cranmer's support. All mention of Mary as a regent disappeared.

In truth, she had missed her opportunity. Yet it was a decision taken deliberately. The assertion that Mary would have been an ideal choice because she would not have interfered with the normal process of government is hard to justify. She was known for being a hard-headed woman of strong views, and it seems inconceivable that she would have been content to act as a royal figurehead.[15] Arundel was still in touch with her at the beginning of November, but she could not be persuaded. Though she had been a political outcast for most of her adult life, Mary was no shrinking violet. She would have done much to return her brother to the religion in which she herself had been raised. The reason she failed to grasp the nettle was dislike and distrust of one man above all: John Dudley. 'The earl of Warwick', she told Van der Delft in January 1550, 'is the most unstable man in England. The conspiracy against the Protector has envy and ambition as its only motives.'[16]

Maybe she was allowing herself the luxury of demonstrating to an imperial diplomat that she had foreseen Warwick's ascendancy and had been wise not to become embroiled in a dangerous political intrigue that could have damaged her reputation. By mid-December, the earl had emerged as the strongest man on the council and those who wanted to call a halt to further religious reform were in retreat. The very day that Mary indulged in her character assassination of Warwick, Wriothesley and Arundel were removed from the council.

Yet if, as seems likely, Mary had privately held this view of John Dudley for some time, it is hard to know why. Nor is it apparent that the antipathy was always mutual. Perhaps she viewed him with the same haughty disdain that many of her brother's advisers inspired in her. In 1551, at the height of her persecution by Edward's council, she would tell a deputation of Dudley's colleagues: 'you should show more favour to me for my father's sake, who made the more part of you from almost nothing'. She never bothered to conceal her contempt for this upstart ruling class.[17] But the princess's remarks bring into sharp relief the new strongman himself, for Dudley was one of the most important servants of the Crown in the 16th century. As maligned after his death as Mary was after hers, he remains one of the most fascinating and elusive figures in an age full of intriguers. It has been said that Mary feared only two men in her life, her father and John Dudley. By 1553 she had every reason to hate and fear the man who was by then duke of Northumberland, but there is no obvious explanation for her determination to stay well away from him in 1549.

They had known each other, though hardly on close terms, since at least 1540, when Anne of Cleves came to England. During Anne's brief marriage to Henry VIII, Dudley was her master-of-horse and Mary would have seen him at court. The only recorded instance of their having spent any time in each other's company was when Dudley accompanied Mary to Windsor in 1541, at the time of Katherine Howard's downfall. Though neither was inclined to indulge in small talk, perhaps Mary observed something then that displeased her. Despite Somerset's reference to the bonds of a long friendship, Dudley did not socialise much and no one, apart from his devoted wife Jane and his family of eight surviving children (of whom six were sons, enough to cause envy in the unprolific Tudors), felt much affection for him. His childhood had been very nearly blighted by the execution of his father, an unpopular financial adviser to the first Tudor king, soon after Henry VIII's accession. If he held a grudge it was suppressed and he worked very hard, over a long period, to secure his own advancement at Henry's court. Often, he was frustrated by the slowness of his attainment of high office, but by the time Katherine Parr became queen, he was well on his way. Allied as he was to supporters of religious change, his beliefs may have been another reason Mary disliked him, though the depth of his religious feeling is hard to judge. He was known for a quick temper, and his hand would go to his sword when discussions in council irritated him. Ill health, which some thought was feigned, meant that meetings were often held at his London house, Ely Place, on the Strand. Perhaps this gave him greater control, bringing the other councillors to him and underlining his power, but it may well have been a response to the pressures of office.

None of this adequately explains Mary's startling comment that he was the most unstable man in England. In reality, she was to find him uncomfortably consistent in his treatment of her for the next three years. As he bullied and tormented her in his attempts to deprive her of the mass, she came to despise him even more.

John Dudley took over the reins of power because he did not see his own future, or England's, safe in conservative hands. And the country he now directed, whether from the council chamber or his bed at home, when stress overwhelmed him, was in grave need of a firm guiding hand. The wars had left a debt of £300,000 and inflation at 75 per cent was running out of control. The reassurance of centuries of religious practice had gone, leaving a gap in people's daily lives that could not be filled by legislation or the accessibility of services in their native tongue. Edward VI and Mary, though occupying two ends of the religious spectrum, were sure of their faith. Most of the populace remained to be persuaded. Dudley saw with admirable clarity what must be done. This meant staunching the bleeding of resources for unwinnable wars and making peace with France and Scotland. So he gave Boulogne back to the French, in return for badly needed cash, and began negotiations for a marriage between Edward VI and Princess Elisabeth of France, daughter of Henry II. The king was enthusiastic, despite the obvious difficulties of his prospective wife's religion.

As far as English politics were concerned, once his position was established, he aimed for conciliation with the duke of Somerset, who was restored to the council in April 1550. Two months later, Somerset's daughter, Anne Seymour, married the younger John Dudley, Viscount Lisle, in a very public attempt to underline improved relations. But there was always a question mark over how the new balance of power would work out, and this extended to other members of the council, such as Arundel, who came and went pretty much at Dudley's pleasure over the next few years.

For Mary and Charles V, however, there was nothing good in the new regime. A rapprochement between England and France was never going to endear Dudley to the emperor, and his commitment to continue with religious reform soon became clear, to Mary's despair.[18] He had made two influential enemies. This was unintentional in Charles's case, but an inevitable result of England's new foreign policy. Where Mary was concerned, the confrontation was deliberate. By March 1550, the council realised it could not be rid of the problem Mary posed by arranging her marriage. Dom Luis of Portugal, the councillors said, had insufficient land and wealth 'wherewith to provide a suitable estate for so great a lady and for their children'. A great lady she may have been, but she was also a great headache for Dudley. He saw her position as direct defiance of the rule of law. The practice of mass in her household was not to be tolerated. She must be made to submit.

Mary was not surprised but she was distressed. Her first thought was to appeal directly to her brother and pre-empt any moves to limit her freedom of religion. So though she did not like London, she came in the second week of February and was allowed, after two attempts, to see the king. The meeting did not give her the comfort she wanted and she came away filled with gloom. As she contemplated her situation, distress

turned to desperation, and she became convinced that, since marriage
was not an option, another, even more extreme course must be considered.

On the evening of Monday, 30 June 1550, three imperial warships
arrived off the coast of Essex. Further out to sea, they were supported by
four larger vessels. This little fleet, commanded by the Dutchman
Cornelius Scepperus, had encountered 'much bad weather' as it crossed
the North Sea, but as soon as the vessels anchored, the sea changed to a
flat calm. The next day one of the ships made its way to Stansgate and a
small boat, with two men in it, rowed ashore. They claimed to be grain
merchants and took with them a sample of their corn, but when they
got ashore they found things unnervingly quiet. There was no one to
meet them and they were obliged to return to their ship without having
spoken to any local people. They had, however, been observed, and by
quizzical eyes.

   People living round about, especially in the small port of Maldon at
the head of the Blackwater estuary, knew of the rumours and wondered
about the true motives of these Flemings who had materialised
overnight. They were not convinced that the grain vessel was alone or
that it had come with innocent intent. Though there was a long history
of problems with Scottish pirates plundering the imperial merchant
fleet, which might explain the need for an adequately defended ship,
something about this vessel seemed wrong. The real purpose, they feared,
was altogether more sinister. Nearby at Woodham Walter the Lady Mary
had been in residence since early May. Her confrontation with the
government was well known and the possibility of her attempting to flee
England had been all the talk in this part of Essex for weeks. It was hard
to keep anything secret in a large household, where people came and
went and not everyone was trustworthy, even if they seemed devoted.
Yet few people could have anticipated quite how the enterprise would
finally be abandoned.

   The saga of Mary's abortive attempt to escape from England to what
she hoped would be a secure haven in the Low Countries was well
documented at the time. It has elements of almost surreal comedy:
disguises, frantic attempts to keep something secret of which the authorities were well aware and the final, complete deflation of Mary's refusal

to seize the chance when offered. At its heart was a troubled woman under severe strain, who entertained the fantasy that creeps into the minds of many people who are stressed almost beyond their mental resources – that running away offers a simple solution to all their difficulties. It is less the act itself which matters, more its contemplation. Perhaps this explains the contradictory nature of Mary's behaviour in the summer of 1550. A woman who had shown remarkable fortitude over so many years could not, for a time, cope with yet another assault. To call this weakness would be a harsh judgement of Mary, who could not forget the past. There must have been echoes of her father in the determination of John Dudley to bring her to heel. In 1536 she had everything taken from her: her mother, her status and, most damaging of all, her shattered conscience. Now, in 1550, another man, but this time no king, merely a servant of her misguided younger brother, was trying to take away one of the pivotal parts of her life, her religious faith. Mary had reinvented herself as the most prominent opponent of sweeping religious change but she did not know how great her following, outside her own affinity, might be. Neither did she want to be associated with violent disobedience to the king. This personal crisis, fed by terrible memories and fears for her own safety, reduced the proud princess Mary to observe, in her agony of mind: 'I am like a little ignorant girl, and I care neither for my goods nor for the world, but only for God's service and my conscience. I know not what to say; but if there is peril in going and peril in staying, I must choose the lesser of two evils.'[19]

Charles V also thought long and hard about whether, in agreeing to Mary's repeated requests that he should furnish her with a means of escape, he was doing the right thing. As always with the emperor, his doubts about the wisdom of the enterprise were partly inspired by an uneasiness about whether he would actually be doing his cousin a service and partly overshadowed by political considerations. Aside from the hazardous nature of getting her away by ship, once gone she became financially dependent on him and could not serve his purpose by acting as the rallying force of principled opposition in England. He was also preoccupied with his preparations for leaving Brussels, which he did at the end of May, to go and take up residence at Augsburg. Ill and unhappy, beset with costly wars and rebellious subjects, this weary man who was losing his grip on his vast empire must have found Mary's troubles little more than a minor irritation. His instinct, and his instructions to Van der Delft, pointed towards calming Mary down and persuading her to temporise. Eventually, he reluctantly agreed to help her.

The plan for Mary's flight was put together over a two-month period between May and July 1550 and the princess was very much its moving force. She had convinced herself that not just her religion but her life was in danger. This was the answer she gave to Van der Delft, when he pointed out to her that, if the king died, her absence could deprive her of the crown and would probably ensure the triumph of religious change for good: 'If my brother were to die, I should be far better out of the kingdom; because as soon as he were dead, before the people knew it, they would despatch me too; there is no doubt of that, because you know that there is nobody about the king's person or in the government who is not inimical to me.' The problem with following the emperor's advice on temporising was that her own, grim experience told her quite the reverse: 'I fear I may tarry too long,' she said. 'When they send me orders forbidding me the mass, I shall expect to suffer as I suffered once during my father's lifetime; they will order me to withdraw thirty miles from any navigable river or sea-port, and will deprive me of my confidential servants, and, having reduced me to the utmost destitution, they will deal with me as they please. But I will rather suffer death than stain my conscience.' Her suspicion of the council was profound. They were 'wicked and wily in their actions and particularly malevolent towards me'.[20]

As in her earlier correspondence with the emperor, Mary was probably overstating her case. But what matters is her utter conviction that those in power meant not just to restrict her but to destroy her. This visceral fear explains the contradictions in her position. She would suffer death for her faith and yet the reason she wanted to flee was that she was afraid she would be killed by order of Edward VI's advisers; she was concerned for her household but willing to implicate them in her flight and leave them to their fate; she believed that she had a great deal of support at popular level but would not acknowledge that abandoning England would leave the people deprived of hope.

Mary had given some thought to the details of her escape. Van der Delft acknowledged that the first plan developed was Mary's idea and he believed it could be made to work. Or perhaps it would be truer to say that he hoped it would work, because it relieved him of involvement, and the thought that he might be compromised alarmed him. Like Mary, he had a regard for his own personal security and that of his family. His desire to be of service to the princess was tinged with growing anxiety, especially as he was ill and arrangements were already in hand for him to leave England himself.

The essence of Mary's scheme was that she should be as close to the sea as possible, to facilitate her escape by water. At the beginning of May 1550 she had moved from New Hall to Woodham Walter in Essex, and one part of the plan was already in place. The move could easily be explained. New Hall needed cleaning and with the summer season approaching, she wished to resume taking sea baths for her health. Her house was regularly provisioned by boat and the comings and goings of these supplies would provide ideal cover for a vessel organised by Robert Rochester, the controller of Mary's household, to remove the princess from her native country. As with so many perilous undertakings, the devil of the plan was in the detail. Royal lady as she was, Mary did not initially contemplate going alone. She wanted with her 'four of her ladies whom she trusts more than the rest' (interesting to note that she evidently had reservations about some of them) plus Rochester himself and two unnamed gentlemen, one of whom was 'very rich but would willingly give up all that he possesses to follow my lady to a place of safety'. Apart from these people, Mary would take nothing with her 'except her rings and jewels. The plate she uses belongs to the king,' wrote the ambassador, 'as, I suppose the tapestries and other furniture do.'[21]

Van der Delft said that no one apart from himself, his secretary and Rochester knew of the princess's plan. Whether that was true or not, it involved too many people to be practical. Then the possibility of a boat being procured in England evaporated. The month of May came and went with Mary still in Essex and still exhorting the ambassador and his master to help her leave. Matters stalled when the government introduced restrictions on all movements at night, so that 'no roads or crossroads, no harbours or creeks, nor any passage or outlet' escaped the vigilance of 'good folk who had something to lose'. This was a reference to the possibility of further summer uprisings like those of the preceding year, but a secondary motive for the council may have been to restrict Mary and frustrate her possibility of flight.

The plan that was finally put into action took shape after Charles V had left Brussels and was approved by him on 25 June. Its driving force may have been his sister, Mary of Hungary, the regent of the Low Countries, who was more inclined to make decisions and take action. She also wanted to ensure that any repercussions were minimised, particularly in the event of failure. This meant waiting until Van der Delft had left, so he could not be implicated, and it also required that his successor, Jehan Scheyfve, a man of whom the regent did not think much, was kept completely in the dark. Thus it fell to Jehan Dubois, secretary to the imperial embassy in London, to take on the burden of managing the revised escape plan. He was more than equal to the task; in fact, he carried out his part of it in exemplary fashion. But it did not succeed.

The emperor foresaw difficulties when he gave his sister his guarded approbation. All concerned should be aware of the need for flexibility and not try 'to reckon the thing too exactly from day to day, as if the sea were a fixed and invariable factor, permitting such undertakings as may be carried out on land'. He thought that there was inevitably some danger and that speed was vital, or the details might leak out. 'As for disguising our cousin,' he wrote, 'I will leave that to those in charge … but no disguise need be used as to whether or not I knew of the undertaking, and it will be better to be quite open about it … for we have the best of reasons and have done all we could to protect our cousin's person and conscience … and holding back as long as possible from this extreme measure, which it has now become imperative to resort to because of the attitude adopted in England.' Charles was evidently not given to cloak-and-daggery and he was determined to put the blame on Edward's councillors. He was more concerned that the pursuit of Scottish pirates, the pretext for his ships being in English waters, could lead to difficulties if the ambassadors expected from Scotland at any time arrived in Brussels before the ships set sail.[22]

In the event, none of the difficulties foreseen by Charles V happened. The reason Mary did not leave was straightforward. She had changed her mind. Or, put another way, when faced, at last, with the opportunity to go, she could not bring herself to do it. Conflicting emotions battled within her, but even as she struggled with her packing, she knew she would stay. In the end, she accepted that her future lay in England. It was a momentous decision and it was in no small part due to Robert Rochester, who intervened to save his mistress from herself. Without his influence and his deft direction of her conscience, it would have been harder still for her to ignore what she knew was likely to be her one and only opportunity of flight. At the crucial moment, he relieved her of dealing with the situation by assuming control of it himself.

We do not know exactly what passed between Mary and Robert Rochester, but it can be inferred from what he told the exasperated and anxious Dubois, who had rowed ashore on 1 July. He soon found out that it was the controller who had 'raised several difficulties tending to delay us in taking our load on board'. These would be better explained if Dubois could meet Rochester in the nearby churchyard of St Mary's, and the secretary soon found himself in earnest, if very quiet, discussion with Mary's servant, pretending to bargain over the price of corn.

In order to talk better, and not to attract attention by skulking around among the gravestones, the two men soon went off to a safe house, where they walked up and down in the garden. Here Rochester revealed what was troubling him so much: '... he saw no earthly possibility of bringing my Lady down to the water-side without running grave risks because of the watch that was posted every night ... the suspicions of certain of her household which was not so free of enemies of her religion as she imagined, and the danger she would incur of being held back'. But then he went on to reveal the true reasons for his doubts:

> Also, were she to go now that there was no pressing reason, for she was still as free to live as she liked as she had ever been, it might be imagined a mighty scandal would be raised. He also mentioned that she would lose all hope of the succession were her brother to die, and asserted that she still had plenty of time in which to escape. He was convinced that she would in no way be molested before the end of the parliament that was to meet the following Michaelmas at the earliest ...

And by that time, he said, it would be winter and she would be at her house at St Osyth, ideally placed for an escape by sea should one be necessary. He went on to tell Dubois that 'I would give my hand to see my Lady out of the country and in safety, and I was the first man to suggest it. And if you understand me, what I say is not that my Lady does not wish to go, but that she wishes to go if she can.'[23] This strange sentence, with its undertones of a decision being constantly re-evaluated and deferred, was not lost on Dubois.

Mary continued to prevaricate and to worry about how the emperor would take it if, as she lamented, 'it would be impossible to go now, after I have so often importuned his majesty on the subject'. She did not want to tell Dubois outright that she was staying and her often repeated 'but what will become of me?', a rhetorical question asked of herself rather than anyone else present, shows that the mental turmoil had not subsided. At the last, Dubois was compelled to leave because the local authorities realised what was going on. Their manner of handling the affair showed a sense of consideration for Mary, 'whom we hold as high as the king's person', but their intervention, with its threat to confiscate Dubois' cargo of corn, brought matters to a head. It seems quite possible that Rochester had alerted them. Dubois did not tarry. He knew very well he must avoid further attention.

If Mary thought that this would all blow over and nothing of it would be publicly known, she was badly deceived. As Edward VI himself reported in his diary, 'Sir John Gates was sent into Essex because it was credibly informed that Scepperus was to steal her away to Antwerp.' Gates was a crony of John Dudley's, and his presence with a troop of horse made the strong statement that Mary was being watched carefully. In some parts of the Low Countries it was reported that the princess had already landed and, the following month, the English ambassador to France reported that Henry II had 'confidentially informed him of a design by the Lady Regent to send Scepperus to the English coast to carry away the Lady Mary'.[24] No doubt the French king passed on this snippet with a great deal of satisfaction.

Dubois returned for a while to Flanders and wrote up his report during the voyage back, which was as stormy as the one that had brought him on his unfulfilled mission, and very long. He was unable to deliver his account of what had happened before mid-July. In it, he said that he suspected that Rochester had 'made out the situation in Maldon to be more dangerous than it was in reality'. He was almost certainly right. Now his chief concern was how the regent would take the news that, after all, Mary was still in England.

Mary of Hungary was annoyed by what had happened but most of her ire seems to have been directed at the unfortunate Scepperus, who wrote her an embarrassed letter asking for her pardon for not providing sooner the details of his expedition. The situation was complicated by the fact that Van der Delft died within weeks of returning from England and there was some worry about whether he had let others in on the secret. Charles V regretted that the enterprise was not successful 'because of the danger that may menace the person concerned'. He was rather thrown by his sister's complete denial to the English ambassador at her court of any knowledge of the affair, since he had been prepared to acknowledge it himself. But Mary of Hungary produced a remarkable performance when the subject was raised. She would never receive her cousin unannounced and without Edward VI's knowledge and consent.

To which Chamberlain, the ambassador, confirmed that, of course, the council only wished to treat Mary well 'and serve her as the king's sister and near relative of his majesty'.

But the regent was plainly impatient with her English cousin. She told Scheyfve to pass her words on to Mary in England, 'so that she may better know how to conduct herself in this matter … and in the circumstances she could not do better than live quietly in her own house as she has done up to the present'.[25] It is not surprising she was lacking in compassion, as her own life had been so difficult. Her young husband, Louis II of Hungary, was routed by the Turks at the battle of Mohács in 1526, and she learned of his ignominious flight and death only some weeks later. Young, striking and childless, she nevertheless set her face against remarriage and, in this respect, her brother could not command her. She had ruled the Low Countries on his behalf since 1531, never quite meeting his demands, always conscious of the burden that she knew was getting heavier with time. The effort, and her own no-nonsense character, made her hard on others. She had little time for Mary, whom she saw as a self-pitying ditherer. Her view was that the princess would have to put up with religious restrictions, even the withdrawal of the mass from her household. When summoned to join the emperor in Augsburg at the end of the summer, Mary of Hungary seems to have persuaded Charles that no further rescue attempts should be made. This doughty Habsburg queen was much more concerned in 1550 about constant depredations of Scottish pirates on her fishing fleets than she was about Mary Tudor.

The princess had reason to be grateful to Robert Rochester for guiding her away from a course that would probably have made her a permanent exile. Apart from his sincere commitment to his lady, he also, like other members of Mary's household, must have wondered what would happen to him if she fled. During the following year, he found out to his cost what happened when she stayed.

On the surface, one of the most surprising features of the whole affair was that everyone concerned pretended it had not happened. Maybe it would have suited Warwick and the council better if Mary had slipped away, to become someone else's problem. It would have been easy to represent her as a traitor to her brother, to point to her history of opposition to her father and dismiss her as a weak and benighted woman who could never be trusted again. Instead of disciplining the princess, other tactics were tried. Mary's chaplains were targeted for infringing the king's statutes on religion, though no immediate penalties were enforced against them. At the same time, a charm offensive was launched, whereby Mary found herself the reluctant recipient of invitations to court and visits from the chancellor, Richard Rich, importuning her to join him on hunting trips, to attend a selection of sporting events and generally partake of his hospitality.

Mary knew there was a hidden agenda behind all this sudden attention. But how was she to handle these senior officers of her brother's government without landing herself in more trouble? Refusing an invitation to court would put her in the most awkward position and might deprive her of the opportunity of going when she felt she really needed to see the king. Privy council secretary William Petre and Rich arrived with letters of credence from the king and his council, signed by twelve of them, 'to the effect that they had special orders and commission to request her to go to court and visit the King's majesty, her brother'. Professing great astonishment and clearly caught off guard, Mary produced a rambling series of unconvincing excuses:'... her indisposition, the distance at which she found herself from his majesty's court, the smallness of the house [whatever that meant – presumably she was suggesting that Edward VI was not living somewhere spacious enough to receive her] and the fact that she had been with him not long ago'. In fact, it had been six months since she had seen the king, though her visitors seem not to have corrected her on that score. They did, however, counter with the cheery observation 'that if my Lady were poorly, a change of air and abode would be beneficial to her and improve her health'. To which Mary replied, with much more honesty than political tact, that if she needed a change of air, she would rather go to one of her own houses.[26]

For the rest of 1550, the council held back from inflaming the situation with the heiress to the throne, and the action against her chaplains was deferred. The hardening of attitude may well have been triggered by the king himself. Mary came to court, as did Elizabeth, for the Christmas season, the last time all three of Henry VIII's children were together. Elizabeth, who was certainly higher in favour than her sister, arrived with a great show of support and stayed throughout the Twelve Days of Christmas. Mary did not. She left early, distressed and alarmed by an incident that did not bode well for her future.

She must have come with some anxiety, as she had managed to evade the festivities altogether the previous year, and the summons in August 1550 had unnerved her considerably. The attack on her religion that took place over the holiday was not unexpected but the ferocity and source were. Edward VI chose to reprove her for hearing the mass, unequivocally and in public. The king was 13 years old and a child no longer. He had had enough of his sister's disobedience and condescension, her constant references to his being too young to know his own mind. Now she was with him, he decided that she must be made to understand that enough was enough. She must stop protesting and do as she was told.

Precisely what he said is not recorded, but the manner of its delivery did more than make Mary wince. It made her cry. She later wrote to the council, clinging to the belief that allowed her to keep going throughout the ordeal of Edward's reign, that her brother was badly advised. They had turned him against her and she could not forgive them. 'When I perceived how the king, whom I love and honour above all things, as by nature and duty bound, had been counselled against me, I could not contain myself and exhibited my interior grief.' Then, in an instant, the realisation that he had reduced his sister to tears destroyed Edward's own composure. He wept himself. He '... benignly requested me to dry my tears, saying that he thought no harm of me'. The councillors present also tried to put a positive gloss on Edward's harshness. Mary was told that her brother intended only to 'inquire and know all things', and there, she claimed, matters had rested. But her pride was shattered. She also believed that this row signalled a new onslaught, and she was not mistaken.

On 17 January 1551, the council wrote to Mary that mass must no longer be heard in her household. She sent an uncompromising reply, but her weariness of mind and body and her sense of underlying hopelessness are obvious. 'My general health and the attack of catarrh in the head from which I am suffering do not permit me to answer them [the letters] in detail, sentence by sentence.' She disputed their assertion that no promise had been given to Charles V where the exercise of her personal religion was concerned:

God knows the contrary to be the truth: and you in your own consciences (I say to those who were then present) know it also ... You accuse me of breaking the laws and disobeying them by keeping to my own religion; but I reply that my faith and my religion are those held by the whole of Christendom, formerly confessed by this kingdom under the late king, my father, until you altered them with your laws. To the king's majesty, my brother, I wish prosperity and honour such as no king ever enjoyed and I confess myself to be his humble sister and subject and he my sovereign lord, but to you, my lords, I owe nothing beyond amity and good will, which you will find in me if I meet with the same in you … I do not follow the belief in which I have been nourished all my days for love of his Imperial majesty.

This was, she said, her 'final answer to any letters that you might write me on matters of religion. Were you to know what pain I suffer in bending down my head to write … for love and charity you would not wish to give me occasion to do it. My health is more unstable than that of any creature and I have all the greater need to rejoice in the testimony of a pure conscience.'[27]

Neither the council nor the king was at all moved by her plea to be left alone. On 28 January she received a stinging rebuke from her brother. Her understanding of the situation, she was told, was 'fruitless and wayward'. She was his nearest sister and yet she wished 'to break our laws and set them aside deliberately, and of your own free will'. The leeway she had been given was awarded, for a time, 'in order that you should do out of love for us what the rest do out of duty'. This approach had clearly failed and Mary was doubly in error. She was 'using and perpetuating the use of a form of worship to the honour of God, which in truth is more like dishonour', and she had refused to open her mind to new knowledge. This grieved him more than anything but he would, nevertheless, listen to 'all you have to say, you and your partisans … you shall be permitted to speak frankly, and what you or they say shall be listened to, provided you undertake to listen to the answers and debates that shall ensue. You perceive that I lay aside my estate of sovereign king and lord and commune with you rather as your brother.' She would be angry, he asserted, if one of her household openly disregarded her orders, 'and so it is with us, and you must reflect that in our estate it is most grievous to suffer that so high a subject should disregard our laws. Your relationship to us, your exalted rank, the conditions of the times, all magnify your offence.' Her constant carping about his age was no argument. 'In truth, sister, we think our youth is an advantage, for perhaps the evil that has endured in you so long is more strongly rooted than we suppose … If we were to grant you license to break our laws and set them aside, would it not be an encouragement to others to do likewise.

These things are so evident that we would have been able to judge them six years ago.' He could not let pass her impugning of his authority: 'we hold ourselves to possess the same authority our father had for the administration of the republic, without diminution of any sort ... You must forbear being so bold as to offend again in this matter.' Finally, almost as an afterthought, he commended her to God's keeping and wished her health as God's gift. In a kind of postscript written in his own hand, he lost some of the majesty of his expression but none of its impact: 'Sister, consider that an exception has been made in your favour this long time past, to incline you to obey and not to harden you in your resistance.' It was his reading of the word of God and he would see to it that his laws were loyally carried out and observed because he was himself a true minister of God. He would not 'say more and worse things because my duty would compel me to use harsher and angrier words. But this I will say with certain intention, that I will see my laws strictly obeyed, and those who break them shall be watched and denounced ...'[28]

Mary was appalled. His comments, a fine example of the eloquence possessed by all the Tudors, struck to her very soul. The contents of his letters 'have caused me more suffering than any illness unto death ... I hope I may in the end prove myself to be as truly loyal to your majesty as any other subject, no matter who he may be. I will in nowise enter into any disputation ... but in the humblest manner possible, beseech you for the love of God to suffer me to live as in the past'.[29]

Did she know, deep down, that she had already lost him? He was not quite a man but no more a boy, and she had offended him more than she ever intended. Robert Rochester had pulled her back from the brink of self-destruction six months earlier but he could not teach her the guile of her sister Elizabeth, that marvellous ability to play with words and say nothing incriminating. She was too frank for her own good and knew no other way. No doubt she did sincerely believe, and perhaps with justi-fication, that a promise had been made to the emperor that she would not be harassed on religion. She could never credit that this would be so flatly denied, or appreciate her brother's position as an evolving rather than a stationary one. They now represented two opposing sides of a dispute over religion and sovereignty that would not be resolved in Edward's lifetime, or hers. And their relationship could never really be restored, though an effort was made on both sides. Mary was back at court in mid-March for further discussions with her brother and a punishing exchange with Dudley at a full council meeting, when he accused her of trying to discredit the king's councillors. 'How now, my Lady?' he remonstrated. 'It seems that your Grace is trying to show us in a hateful light to the king, our master, without any cause whatsoever.'[30] She was so unwell during this visit that the more conciliatory Dr Petre, trying to assure her a few days later of 'the cordial affection' of the king and council, was received by a bedridden princess. By the time she and Dudley met again, the following January, he was an even more over-mighty subject, with the title of duke of Northumberland. But he had not forgotten another aspect of her visit of the previous March, one somewhat at odds with the image of a sickly, defenceless princess. The power behind her was carefully displayed as she rode through London with 50 knights and gentlemen before her and 80 ladies and gentlemen after her. They were all ostentatiously wearing rosaries. And there were many more of their persuasion in East Anglia, and indeed throughout England.

For the remainder of 1551, the government used different tactics to force Mary's submission. Where direct intimidation had failed they launched an attack on the leading members of her household. Rochester had been required to attend the council and questioned about the hearing of mass in her household even before the exchange of letters between Mary and the king. In August he, Englefield and Waldegrave were all summoned before the council and told that they were 'the chief instruments and cause that kept the princess in the old religion'. Rochester and his colleague of course rejected this accusation, saying that they were 'but the lady's ministers in what concerned the management of her house-hold and temporal goods; but as for her religion and conscience she asked nobody's advice and, what was more, not one of her ministers dared broach the matter in her presence'. Their description of their roles, though a touch disingenuous, since they clearly had considerable impor-tance in a wider consultative sense, rings absolutely true, however, on religious matters. It also indicates that Mary was someone to be feared as well as loved.

She took very badly indeed the nasty attempt to humiliate her by using her servants as messengers for the king's instructions and she sent them back to London, where the council promptly incarcerated them in

the Tower when they refused to go back with a second order. There
Rochester stayed throughout the winter, suffering for his lady, until 18
March 1552, when he was released on grounds of ill health. Englefield
was freed at the same time. Both men immediately returned to Mary's
service. Waldegrave was allowed out of the Tower, under house arrest,
somewhat earlier, because of a serious attack of ague, but he did not
return to the princess until the end of April.

Mary knew that her servants were suffering entirely because the
council did not wish to go to the lengths of incurring criticism by
imprisoning her. In August 1551 she had her last acrimonious argument
with members of the council when Rich, Petre and Sir Anthony Wingfield came to Copthall to deliver yet another ultimatum from the king.
They found her furious but determined not to give way. 'It was not', she
informed them, 'the wisest counsel to appoint her servants to control her
in her own house.' If an attempt was made to replace Rochester with a
new appointee, she would leave. 'And I am sickly,' she added, 'yet I will
not die willingly … but if I shall chance to die, I will protest openly that
you of the council be the causes of my death. You give me fair words,
but your deeds be always ill towards me.' Her parting shot was one they
did not forget, delivered with true dramatic flair from an upstairs
window – she told them she wanted Rochester back. His absence meant
that she had been compelled to become her own controller. Though she
had learned 'how many loaves of bread be made of a bushel of wheat …
my father and mother never brought me up with baking and brewing,
and, to be plain with you, I am weary with mine office'.[31] With this
rebuke ringing in their ears, the conciliar deputation departed without
having achieved anything.

Still, the pressure on her eased considerably, as Northumberland
decided that there was no advantage in going after her any more. The
king was only a few years short of his majority and was being carefully
groomed for that day by greater involvement in government. He proved
an apt pupil and Northumberland a responsible and even sensitive
mentor. The duke certainly had much experience of raising boys.
Edward was keen on sports, like his father, and his frame was filling out.
He survived both the measles and the smallpox in 1552, both diseases
that could bring death. There was nothing to suggest that he would not
enjoy a long reign.

Mary did not spend Christmas 1551 at court. Instead, she entertained
her cousin Frances and her husband Henry, recently made duke of

Suffolk. During 1552 the princess came to London in June to see the king at Greenwich and for the rest of the year she found the council yet more conciliatory, with Northumberland keeping her briefed on foreign affairs during the autumn. On 6 February 1553 Mary, again with a substantial force, was once more at court for her winter visit to the king. She was greeted outside London by Northumberland's son, himself now earl of Warwick, and Lord William Howard, an uncle of Anne Boleyn. The family connections of these two gentlemen were no doubt forgotten in the splendour of her reception. When they rode into the city Mary's forces and her escort were three hundred strong.

She did not visit Edward immediately because he had caught a chest infection. As someone who frequently suffered from colds herself, she probably thought nothing of it. When they parted, she had not the slightest inkling that they had met for the last time.

Chapter Seven

Mary Triumphant

**'My resolve is to disown and disinherit Mary
together with her sister Elizabeth.'**

Edward VI to his council, June 1553

The pressures of her brother's reign combined with the long-term effects of her own indifferent health aged Mary. Some time around 1550, William Scrots painted her in a magnificent and very expensive dress of black velvet and satin, with distinctive blackwork embroidery decoration on the collar, cuffs and sleeves and a gold-edged French hood. The dress itself makes a statement about Mary's power and wealth and her image of herself. She is composed but distant, as if her mind is somewhere else. And she is still a handsome woman. The contrast with her portraits as queen is considerable though perhaps not surprising, considering all that lay between.

Despite the respect accorded to her when she came to court, Mary was still uneasy about her position as her brother edged closer to his majority. When the duke of Northumberland had opposed her outright, she knew where she stood. Now he seemed more obliging she needed to be careful not to drop her guard. The ill-defined truce on religion troubled her, and she wrote to Charles V asking that 'when a season shall appear more propitious in your majesty's eyes' the imperial ambassador should 'by all possible means try to obtain that the hearing of mass in secret may be permitted and granted to me'.[1] Charles, who saw no reason to stir up trouble, evaded the issue. He was preoccupied with the

French, and they always came before Mary. Since the princess did not enjoy the kind of confidential relationship with Jehan Scheyfve that she had with his predecessors, she did not press the point. This absence of imperial input was actually an advantage for Mary's English advisers, the loyal gentlemen of her household who cherished her best interests, because they knew she would not be distracted by outside influences. And soon there were matters of the utmost importance to command their mistress's attention. As the unparalleled crisis of the summer of 1553 developed, Mary found herself once more in the cockpit of events.

There had been rumours circulating in the diplomatic community since the early spring about the king's inability to shrug off his February chest infection. Up until now, he had seemed vigorous and increasingly strong-willed. Edward VI had developed into an active boy who loved sports and spectacles. He was not at all the sickly Tudor swot that has so often been depicted. And he was very conscious of what it meant to be a king, anticipating the arrival of his French bride and her very large dowry with enthusiasm. By the age of 15 he was taking an active part in council meetings and decisions on matters of state; he looked forward eagerly to the day he would fully assume the reins of government. His diary for 1552 is full of references to diplomacy with the French, comments on trade matters and on the war between the French and Charles V. Carefully guided by Northumberland, the foundations for his assumption of power seemed well laid. Yet as the leaves began to turn green, there was anxiety in London. The king ventured out of doors for the first time in two months in early April, in his park at Westminster, on a day of 'soft and bright' weather. He was, though, under strict medical supervision, and a few days later he went by river to Greenwich. There he remained, and tongues began to wag more than ever. His indisposition was turning into something very sinister indeed.

At the time no one knew for sure what was happening to Edward, and though there was concern, there was nothing like panic. Nor was there any attempt, in the early stages, to conceal his condition from Mary. Northumberland wrote to her personally about her brother's health in March and again the following month, 'though not with so much detail as heretofore'. No doubt he had his reasons for this reticence, and they may not have been entirely to spare Mary the increasingly gruesome reality. Scheyfve, on the other hand, with little to do but keep his ear to the ground, was more forthcoming. 'I hear from a trustworthy source that the king is undoubtedly becoming weaker as the time passes, and wasting away. The matter he ejects from his mouth is sometimes coloured a greenish-yellow and black, sometimes pink, like the colour of blood. His doctors and physicians are perplexed and do not know what to make of it.'[2]

Still, it was not felt that Edward was in any immediate danger. In early May, he seemed to rally briefly and Northumberland wrote to William Cecil: 'Our sovereign lord doth begin very joyfully to increase and amend, they [the royal physicians] having no doubt of the thorough recovery of his highness.'[3] To Mary, he continued to be conciliatory, sending her the full coat of arms as a princess of England, 'as she used to bear them in her father's time'. Mary's response to this gesture is not known, but her reservations about the man behind it remained.

The duke himself was, for a time, very occupied with other considerations. Recently arrived as a senior member of the aristocracy, he was keen to underwrite the future of his numerous progeny. From late April onwards, preparations for a double wedding in the family demanded his attention. Guildford Dudley, the fifth of his sons, was to marry Lady Jane Grey, daughter of the duke and duchess of Suffolk. At the same time, his daughter Katherine would become the wife of the earl of Huntingdon's son. These alliances strengthened his position, but if is doubtful that he had thought beyond that. Indeed, Jane Grey was not his first choice for Guildford. He wanted the earl of Westmorland's daughter, but the earl was not interested in a close association with Northumberland, even if he was the most powerful man in the kingdom. The Suffolks were more amenable, and on Whitsuntide, 21 May, Mary's 16-year-old cousin became Lady Jane Dudley. Perhaps she wore some of the 'rich jewels and ornaments' the king had sent her as a wedding present. There was great magnificence and feasting, as well as games and jousts, at Durham Place, the duke's latest property acquisition in London.

Scheyfve, suspicious and concerned, read a great deal into this: 'The duke and his party's designs to deprive the Lady Mary of the succession to the crown are only too plain. They are evidently resolved to resort to arms against her, with the excuse of religion among others,' he wrote at the end of May. Mary herself was said to be 'in great trouble and perplexity' because of the illness of her brother.[4] She had her own lines of communication into the court, maybe even into the council chamber, so she was well informed. It is impossible to say whether she fully shared the imperial analysis of her situation at this point; certainly, she wished to convey an impression that she was reactive, even biddable, until circumstances dictated otherwise. It was the safest course. The ambassador, for his part, had actually guessed correctly, and the strange thing is that he probably knew Northumberland's mind before the duke did. But the precise means that might be used to exclude Mary, beyond the vague threat of violence, were unclear to almost everyone. The driving force for what happened next seems to have been as much the king himself as his mentor.

By the second week of June, it was obvious to Edward VI that he was dying. The cause was probably not tuberculosis, as used to be thought, but a bacterial pulmonary infection contracted months earlier. It was most likely a complication of the chill he was reported to be suffering from in mid-February. As he was previously a strong young man, the disease took some time to reach its awful, but inexorable, conclusion. The symptoms show that renal failure and septicaemia eventually overwhelmed his entire system. Today, a simple course of antibiotics administered early in his illness would have prevented this deadly infection. Instead, he was condemned to a painful and protracted passing from a life that had seemed full of promise.

The last weeks were dreadful. Edward could not rest unless strong sleeping draughts were administered, and his head and feet swelled. His scalp was shaved, his nails fell out and the stench of the sputum he continued to bring up nauseated even his most devoted servants. Though little could be done to alleviate the indignities of death, his intellect remained clear. His one consolation, amid all this suffering, was that the country he ruled was now freed for ever from the yoke of the papacy in Rome and the uncertainties over religious practice his father had bequeathed him. Those men in whom he had confidence, principally Cranmer and Northumberland, would, he believed, uphold his uncompromising devotion to the new religion. But there was one vital question of state that demanded his attention, as his life ebbed away. To be sure that there was no going back, he must take an audacious step. He must alter the succession to the English throne.

It had begun as an intellectual exercise, the sort of hypothetical problem suitable for the clever mind of Edward VI. There could be no more important consideration than the future of his own dynasty. We do not know whether the topic was entirely of the king's choosing or whether it was developed following discussion with William Thomas, an Oxford graduate of reformist ideas who was working with Northumberland in training the king for government. For many years, historians drew a direct line between the document entitled *My Devise for the Succession* and the crisis of summer 1553. It was viewed as the moving force for a sinister plot, masterminded by Northumberland when he knew Edward was mortally ill. But this is to confuse cause with effect. The duke was not so cunning, nor nearly so well organised, as those who sought to vilify him after his fall believed. Archbishop Cranmer told Mary subsequently that Northumberland had never raised with him the idea of changing the succession. He said the impetus came from the king and other council members, and he had no reason to protect Northumberland once Mary was on the throne. As with the moves against Anne Boleyn nearly two decades earlier, Cranmer merely wanted to represent the truth as he saw it.[5]

The *Devise* was originally written no later than January 1553, at a time when there was no reason to expect the king's imminent death. It proposed a radical change to the order of succession laid out by Henry VIII and put on the statute books by Parliament in 1543. At one stroke, Edward disinherited both his sisters, stipulating instead that the throne pass to the male heirs of Frances, duchess of Suffolk, and then to the male heirs of the Lady Jane, her eldest daughter. Jane was educated according to the new religious ideas and she was staunchly anti-Catholic. This made her an attractive alternative to Mary. The king had realised for some while, perhaps since the disastrous Christmas of 1550, that his elder sister would undo all the religious changes of his reign if she were ever to succeed to the throne. He was not willing to die in that knowledge. His reasons for rejecting Elizabeth as well were logical rather than theological. Given the order of succession in the 1543 act and Henry's will, disinheritance of Mary implied disinheritance of Elizabeth too. This textbook exercise did not allow family feelings to get in the way of the needs of the state. Edward was perfectly willing to trample on the rights of Mary, who had loved him all his life, and Elizabeth, who had shared his schoolroom and his religious ideas. They were women and as such inferior. Though the 16th century produced many capable women rulers, Edward's views were entirely in tune with the times in which he lived. Nor should it be supposed that, when he first wrote the *Devise*, he saw any inconsistency in bringing forward the claim of the women of the junior branch of the Tudors. He merely assumed that his cousin Jane would, when she married, produce male children. The nearest male heir, Margaret Douglas' son Lord Darnley, was no more than eight years old and a Catholic. The king would never have passed his throne to a child being raised in the old religion.

All this had already taken shape in Edward's mind when Mary came to court four months earlier. But no one else knew of it, except perhaps for William Thomas. The king would hardly have provoked his sister by inviting her thoughts on what he had written. In fact, he was already seeking to marginalise Mary through observing a polite indifference to her Catholicism, thus minimising the damage she could do publicly as the regime's main opponent. At the same time, he took steps to remind his other sister of her doubtful status by giving Elizabeth's main property in London to Northumberland. Durham Place, the scene of Jane Grey's nuptials, had very recently been Elizabeth's town residence, and she was not amused by its loss. All this was part of the king's flexing of his muscles, readying himself for a time when power was entirely his.

When it became obvious to Edward that he did not have long to live, the *Devise* assumed an altogether different significance. It was no longer a dissertation on what might happen; it was a practical blueprint for England and a balm for his troubled spirit. Robbed of his own future, he would now take the step that would make his sisters historical footnotes. For were they not both bastards as well as females, and therefore doubly unfit to rule? They would remain for ever as his father had originally intended at the time of Edward's own birth, the Lady Mary and the Lady Elizabeth, not princesses of England. It required only one small change in the wording of the *Devise* to bring about the result he so fervently desired.

Northumberland may not even have known that the *Devise* existed before June, but he now saw a way in which he could safeguard his own position and calm his king, as Edward struggled to fend off death for a few weeks longer. Instead of 'the heirs male of the Lady Jane', the phrase 'the Lady Jane and her heirs male' was inserted, probably at the duke's suggestion. Edward's Protestant cousin would become queen, even though her mother, the closer claimant, was still alive and still of child-bearing years. Quite why Frances of Suffolk was written off in this way has never been explained, but she must not have tried to push her claim over her daughter's. Her subsequent behaviour gives the impression of someone who was always rather anxious for her own skin, so perhaps she reasoned that if the venture did not succeed, she would be better off at one remove from it. She would obviously have been a less attractive proposition to the duke of Northumberland, who saw in this manipulation of the succession a way in which his ascendancy could continue, uninterrupted. Through a happy accident of timing, the duke's new daughter-in-law provided him with the means to retain power when Edward was gone. Once seized by the idea, he committed to it wholeheartedly. He did not have the luxury of a period of reflection or doubt. The changes to the succession must be put in place swiftly and with unanimity, to ensure a smooth transition from Edward to Jane. There might be doubts raised, voices murmuring in corridors and corners, and they needed to be silenced. Mary and Elizabeth would object, but what could they do? And both resided close enough to London for them to be easily apprehended. When the hour of the king's death was close, he intended to summon them to court and, once there, they would be in his power.

There were now two difficulties to be overcome and they were almost mutually contradictory. The first was to change the succession legally, with the consent of council and then through Letters Patent. More time and wider support would have been needed to get the changes agreed by Parliament, and this was clearly not an option. As it was, many of the council, and the law officers in particular, were greatly disturbed by what was being proposed. On 12 June, the Lord Chief Justice, Sir Edward Montagu, caused consternation by announcing that he would not be party to anything involving changes to the succession. There was, he said, succinctly, 'the danger of treason'. His delicate conscience and legal obstinacy infuriated Northumberland, who was never slow to offer violence in word and demeanour when opposed. He called Montagu 'traitor before all the council and said that in the quarrel of that matter he would fight in his shirt with any man living'.[6] His aggression made many present uneasy for their own safety, but still there was sufficient opposition for a compromise to be proposed. Mary should be offered the crown but must undertake not to change religion or replace any of the current ministers. This proposal showed a regard for legitimacy but was not met with much enthusiasm.

The legal wrangling angered the king. Edward refused to be thwarted; Mary must not inherit his throne, he told the judges when they appeared before him on 15 June. Neither would he countenance

Elizabeth, the daughter of an adulteress, as his heir. His cousin Jane was a lady of high virtue and sound religious convictions. She would support the growth of 'the religion whose fair foundation we have laid'. The sight of this angry, desperately ill youth summoning up the last shreds of his energy to berate them swayed the judges. No doubt they were also conscious of Northumberland scowling in the background. They capitulated, agreeing to help the king draw up his will.

When it was known that the legal establishment had submitted to the king's demands, the doubters gave way. Reluctance was suppressed in the comfort of collective responsibility, which the king absolutely required. Opposition would have been treason, giving an excuse for a wide-scale purge that would have removed anyone who questioned the king and Northumberland. The argument that both Mary and Elizabeth were illegitimate probably carried more weight than highlighting the religious issues surrounding Mary personally. The Letters Patent were already drafted before the king's confrontation with the judiciary. They stated that the marriages of Katherine of Aragon and Anne Boleyn were 'clearly and lawfully undone'. This meant that Mary and Elizabeth were 'unto us but the half blood, and therefore by the ancient laws, statutes and customs of this realm be not inheritable unto us, although they were legitimate, as they be not indeed'. It was also easy to play on old fears about the effect of a foreign marriage, should either woman become queen. A 'stranger' would impose foreign laws on England, 'which would then tend to the utter subversion of the commonwealth of this our realm, which God defend'.[7] But this was not a new argument and, whatever the convoluted legalisms about the status of Edward's sisters, the provisions of the Act of Succession of 1543 and Henry VIII's will were being flouted. Edward VI was actually attacking legitimacy by claiming to uphold a different interpretation of it.

Northumberland also knew his colleagues on the privy council. He had it in his gift to reward as well as bluster. In mid-16th-century England, a delicate conscience meant political annihilation and personal ruin. So the duke appeased his critics with grants of lands, always so much more attractive than principles. Eventually all the council and the judges, with the exception of Sir James Hales, signed the Letters Patent, as did the mayor and alderman of London. The victory was facilitated by Northumberland, and served his own purposes, but it was still very much the king's. Using a mixture of persuasion and threats, Edward was able to stage his own coup d'état in the final weeks of his life.

There was, however, a major difficulty, and it could not be overcome by personal pleas or the spectre of the scaffold. Although the council was sworn to secrecy, so momentous a change to the succession was impossible to conceal. Those troubled by the machinations, whether supporters of Mary or enemies of Northumberland, were careful not to be caught in open discussion, but word, inevitably, got out. The unity Northumberland tried to invoke was, as he well knew, fragile. The other steps he took to underwrite his power, the arming and provisioning of the Tower of London and the readying of the fleet, were impossible to conceal. Rumours about what would happen after Edward's death began to circulate in southern England. Too many people knew what was intended. Northumberland's courting of the French was also bound to attract attention in the diplomatic community. The new ambassador in London, Antoine de Noailles, relayed to Henry II what Northumberland had told him on 26 June: 'that they had provided so well against the Lady Mary's ever attaining the succession, and that all the lords of the council were so well united, that there is no need for you, Sire, to enter into any doubt on this score'.[8] This Anglo-French cosiness made the emperor very edgy. Mary had wondered for some time why her cousin was silent. It was just as well that she remained unaware of Charles V's real assessment of her situation, since she would not have found any encouragement there.

The truth was, he gave her little chance of success. Everything he heard made him think she would be lucky to survive, let alone become queen. On 23 June he issued a long set of instructions to a special mission of three ambassadors, who were to depart immediately for England. Scheyfve was tiring of the inconsequential nature of his role in London. Mary of Hungary used him mainly in a consular, rather than an ambassadorial, capacity, and the satisfaction of sending out lurid bulletins about Edward VI's decline, which he had done indefatigably in recent months, was beginning to fade. One of the three men sent by Charles was Scheyfve's replacement, Simon Renard, an energetic native of the Franche Comté who had previously been the imperial representative in Paris. Accompanied by Counts de Courrières and de Toulouse, who were there to add gravitas, Renard set out for England, charged with finding out as much as possible about Edward's condition.

The emperor's chief concern was not to bolster Mary's chances of becoming queen but to minimise or even neutralise French influence in England. Once arrived, they should seek an audience with the king as soon as possible. 'We are', he wrote, 'unwilling to allow the French to appear quicker with their sympathy … and we stand in need of no example to teach us the offices of friendship.' But supposing it turned out that Edward was already dead when they got there? 'In that case you must deliberate among yourselves according to the turn events shall take, and decide on the wisest course to be adopted for the safety of our cousin, the Princess, and, *if it is possible*, to assist her to succeed to the crown.' His main concern was for her personal safety, not her rights, and he feared that the charge that she would marry a foreigner if she became queen would be raised against her. The ambassadors must make it clear that the emperor favoured an English match for Mary. The English lords would need plenty of reassurance on this point, 'loathed as all foreigners are by all Englishmen'. Charles V considered it impossible for Mary to have the slightest chance of being a serious contender for the throne unless she agreed to make no changes in government or religion and undertook to pardon all offences committed by those currently in power. 'If she is asked to make a promise in this sense she must make no difficulty about it, for she has no choice in the matter.' He summed up his requirements as follows: 'your principal objects will be to preserve our cousin's person from danger, assist her to obtain possession of the crown, calm the fears the English may entertain of us, defeat French machinations, and further a good understanding between our dominions and the realm of England'. All this was to be done without money or men, in times of great uncertainty. It was a very tall order.[9]

The emperor's natural caution tied the hands of his servants. It was not even clear how they could ensure his cousin's welfare, and once they left Flanders they were very much on their own. As they made their way to London, an eerie calm settled over England. There was no option but to wait and see what was going to happen. Yet before they could even speak to Mary, nature intervened. On the evening of 6 July Edward expired in the arms of Sir Henry Sidney. 'I am faint,' he said. 'Lord have mercy on me and take my spirit.'

Mary had passed the spring and early summer quietly at Hunsdon. Yet though there was no sign of any unusual activity there must have been much going on behind the walls of the manor. The appearance of normality, of passivity, was a feint. The princess knew from her own sources that her brother's illness was fatal. She was also well aware of the steps that had been taken to deprive her of the crown. Closeted with her advisers, Mary decided that there was, in reality, only one course open to her: she must proclaim herself as queen and she must prepare to fight. Much of her adult life had been passed in opposition, but now there was a need for clear thinking and boldness, not protests and tears. The supreme moment had crept up on her, like the lengthening days of summer. In the last weeks of June, she could trust only Robert Rochester and his network of Catholic gentlemen – and her own conviction that God was with her. Religious faith, as well as the Tudor heritage, kept her strong. She was the daughter of Henry VIII and Katherine of Aragon and she would prevail. The throne of England was hers by right of law and of descent. Her courage occasionally faltered when her father was alive and she had good reason to fear the duke of Northumberland, but she did not waver now. If she stayed, he would come for her and she would almost certainly be imprisoned, perhaps worse. She commanded no army, no backers of any importance among the nobility, and Charles V had all but abandoned her. The only people who believed in Mary were her household, and even they, no matter how much affection they bore her, must have been apprehensive. But if her affinity in East Anglia would rise for her then others might follow. There could be just a glimmer of hope. Around that speck of light, careful plans were made to evade and outwit the authorities, to wrestle the initiative from the preoccupied council in London. At the very least, this would buy her time.

The decision to move was taken before Edward's death because it was felt to be too dangerous for Mary to stay at Hunsdon. The idea that she and her advisers were naive enough to respond to the council's summons to London, and actually got as far as Hoddesdon before being warned that it was a trap, is not borne out by contemporary sources. Instead, Mary and her small party turned north and then east on the night of 4 July. A plausible excuse for this sudden departure was invented, to the effect that her physician, Roland Scurlock, had been taken ill with a suspected attack of the plague, making it imperative for her to leave swiftly. Safe houses, owned by trusted sympathisers, had already been prepared along the route that would take her to Kenning-hall in Norfolk, the former Howard house chosen as her headquarters. Riding through the hours of darkness, Mary covered almost 40 miles before she arrived at her first resting place, Sawston Manor in

Cambridgeshire, the home of Sir John Huddleston and his family. When she left the next day she may have felt it safer to adopt a disguise, as some reports have her riding dressed as a servant behind one of Huddleston's own people.

When she got to her next destination, Euston Hall, near Thetford, she was greeted by its chatelaine, Lady Burgh. It was here, on 7 July, that news of her brother's death was first conveyed to Mary, apparently by Robert Reyns, her London goldsmith. But it could not be verified and she knew that she must wait until there was no shadow of a doubt. A premature proclamation that she was queen would be treasonable and those around her, having laid the groundwork so well, could not let her play into the hands of her enemies. The privy council, who must have hoped that she would be in their power by now, deliberately concealed the king's death for two days. Northumberland had learned well from the experience of keeping Henry VIII's death secret but, despite his precautions, the news was difficult to suppress. The imperial ambassadors reported it themselves on 7 July. Probably Reyns was tipped off by a friendly source within the king's household or the privy council. Later, Sir Nicholas Throckmorton claimed that he had been Reyns's inform-ant. His loyalty to Mary was, however, equivocal, and by 1554 he was implicated in plots to overthrow her. She would have been entirely justi-fied in treating his news with the greatest of caution.

By 9 July there was no longer any doubt. Mary was established at Kenninghall and the news of Edward's death was confirmed. She had escaped Northumberland's clutches and was ready to put the next part of the plan into action. But first, she wanted to address her household. They were gathered together, no doubt awaiting with rising excitement their lady's entry. Many of them had been with her since the grim days of her disgrace, often fearful for her health and her safety, never quite knowing what the future held. Now she was to impart wonderful tidings. Her brother, she told them, had departed this life. 'The right to the crown of England had therefore descended to her by divine and by human law.' Some of those present once feared they would never hear such words from the lips of Mary Tudor. Great cheering followed as they all 'proclaimed their dearest princess Mary as queen of England'.

There was no such enthusiasm when Mary's letter to the privy council arrived in London the following day. She came straight to the point. Upon their allegiance, they were to 'cause our right and title to the crown and government of this realm to be proclaimed in our city of

London, and other places as your wisdom shall seem good'. Further letters and proclamations announcing her accession were already drafted and were also sent on 9 July. They called on loyal subjects to proclaim her and requested forces to come to her aid. The council were taken aback by this brisk confidence but incredulity soon gave way to unease. Following the stipulations of Edward VI's Letters Patent on the succession, Jane Grey had been proclaimed queen in London the day before Mary's own announcement. No woman had ever ruled England in her own right before. Now, in the space of 24 hours, the country had two rival queens regnant. And it was not at all clear which of them would eventually be crowned.

Jane Grey was recuperating from an unpleasant stomach ailment at the royal manor in Chelsea when, according to tradition, one of Northumberland's daughters came to take her to Syon House. There, where another queen, Katherine Howard, learned that her past had caught up with her in 1541, Jane was told that her future in the year of our Lord 1553 was to be the first female English monarch. It was not exactly a shock, since she had known about the proposals to change the succession for several weeks, but the enormity of it disturbed her a great deal. She neither relished nor sought the throne. But she did not refuse it, either. If God had willed her this burden, then she must bear it humbly and to the best of her ability. And that ability, at least intellectually, was considerable. Protestant writers, seeking to make mileage from the picture they painted of an innocent girl sacrificed to the forces of political opportunism and religious reaction, regarded Jane with a reverence that nearly turned her into a saint. That image has lost nothing with the passing of the centuries, but it is far from accurate. A more measured view, based on what we know of her from her own words and behaviour, reveals a devout but surprisingly hard-headed young woman. Her priggishness is unattractive but should not be viewed too harshly. Like most girls of her age in 16th-century England, she was required to grow up fast and to accept that who she was posed a danger to others, as well as to herself. Proximity to the throne was a dubious privilege. Mary had learned a comparable lesson at the same age.

So Jane could not avoid what she most certainly did not desire. On 10 July, at three o'clock in the afternoon, she was brought downriver by barge from Syon House to take up residence as queen in the Tower of London. Her mother carried her train and her husband walked beside her, apparently paying her a great deal of attention. A small crowd had gathered, but it was quietly curious, not full of vociferous joy. Most of them probably had no idea who she was, and even those who knew had never seen her before.

The onlookers saw a slim 16-year-old, short, like the cousin whose claim to the throne she denied, and with the same red hair. She was dressed, as if to reinforce her credentials as the rightful queen, in the Tudor colour of green, richly set off with gold. It was a fine symbolic gesture, rendered all the more touching by the need to raise the diminutive Jane on platform shoes, so that she could be better seen.

Her childhood had been short, strict and loveless. Jane's mother, who, as Frances Brandon, passed pleasant summer days with Princess Mary, was an overweight heiress with none of the beauty or wit of her own mother, the other Mary Tudor. In portraits she looks harsh and sullen. Yet her marriage seems to have been happy enough. Her husband, Henry Grey, was a crony of Northumberland's, and his loyalty was rewarded by the granting of the duchy of Suffolk, the title that had belonged to Frances's father. There seemed little likelihood, alas, of his passing it on. The sons born to the couple had not survived; Jane was the eldest of three sisters. As small children they were all subjected to physical chastisement and a family atmosphere notably lacking in affection. Frances was not a sentimental mother and she consistently put her husband's interests before those of her children. The girls' manners, however, were carefully watched and they were under strict instruction to refrain from such unladylike failings as breaking wind at mealtimes. Not surprisingly, Jane grew up to be a rather humourless girl, though she was very well educated. Contemporaries described her intellect and scholarship in glowing terms, though many of these accounts were written after her death. She was also committed to the new religion.

As the great-niece of Henry VIII, she would always be an attractive target for the unscrupulous, politically ambitious, new men of mid-Tudor England. Her parents never made the slightest effort to protect her from the predators of the court if they thought they saw an advantage. Yet neither of them had any political acumen. They were perfectly content when Jane was removed from the family at the age of ten to join the Lady Elizabeth in the household of Thomas Seymour and Katherine Parr. Jane found the dowager queen an affectionate guardian and probably enjoyed the respite from the strictures of home life. Fortunately for her, she was too young to receive the kind of dubious attentions from Seymour that brought Elizabeth such trauma when he was disgraced. There is no record that the cousins spent much time in each other's company or that they had any great feeling for each other, but Elizabeth must have known her better than Mary did.

Jane is often represented as an unwilling victim, an unhappy child-bride and a reluctant queen. The truth is less straightforward. There was nothing uncommon in being married at 16 in those times and no one expected a love match. Jane's resentment of the Dudleys was more likely the result of being second choice. Northumberland had wanted an alliance with the powerful Clifford family, in the north of England, but the earl of Westmorland would not oblige. Jane was proposed as a last-minute substitute and it was probably the timing and manner of her union with the duke's son which offended her, rather than the lad himself. Their temperaments were very different, Guildford being something of a mother's boy and generally immature, whereas Jane was self-contained and prim. The Dudleys were a very close-knit family, in complete contrast to the Greys, and Jane does not seem to have warmed to the duchess of Northumberland, the matriarch of the clan. It is true that the duchess had a strong influence on the household, but Jane was not her first daughter-in-law and she had girls of her own, so was experienced in guiding young people. Since 1548 she had been in bad health, and as she was not a frivolous woman, but a faithful follower of the evangelical religious ideas she had picked up in the service of Anne Boleyn, she and Jane might have been expected to get on well. But they did not.

None of this is especially surprising in any marriage, let alone an arranged 16th-century match. Jane and Guildford might well have worked their way through this initial sticky patch if they had been given the opportunity. Instead their relationship, brought about in haste and destroyed by political developments beyond their control, was never allowed a chance to blossom. There is no way of knowing whether it was even consummated.

She may not have sought the throne but Jane believed, as did Mary, that God's will must be done. In her brief reign of nine days, there are signs that she had an aptitude for government and that she knew her own mind. All the advantage seemed to be with her. The political and religious establishment was firmly on her side; prominent citizens of London swore their support and Bishop Ridley preached to the people at St Paul's Cross, with a clear public relations message. He underlined that both Mary and Elizabeth were bastards and since neither was married, the possibility of foreign domination by any European husband they might choose was a dangerous threat. Queen Jane was married to an Englishman and so the realm was secure. It was an argument that had been rehearsed before, by the dead king, but it does not seem to have changed any minds. Ridley's audience was notably unwilling to show any display of public approbation for this queen who had been imposed on them. Like everyone else, the bishop assumed that, though Jane was the one with the claim to the throne, Guildford would be named king alongside her. Ridley did not know that Jane had already refused this possibility, greatly irritating Northumberland and upsetting her husband so much that he had run off to his mother for comfort.

Northumberland may have felt that she would change her mind, after a few days of reflection. But time was not on his side. He could not force a swift change of heart on her and there were other, more pressing considerations. The duke appeared, at Edward's death, to have all the power and authority necessary to fulfil Edward VI's wishes and maintain his own position as the de facto ruler of the country. But he had over-looked, or perhaps misjudged, the one factor that would have made him impregnable. He had failed to secure Mary herself. The princess's depar-ture from Hunsdon caught the council off guard. Their immediate response was to send out letters to the lords lieutenant and other worthies of the counties branding her as a potentially subversive outcast. This was the first shot in a battle for hearts and minds in which Mary engaged as fully – and more successfully – as her opponents. Then, as now, public opinion was important, and there was a scramble to influ-ence it. But initially the council were in an uncomfortable position, caught on the back foot. When they wrote, on 8 July, Edward VI had been dead for two days, but there was no official announcement yet of his demise and Jane Grey had not been proclaimed. Obviously Mary needed to be discredited, and quickly, but nothing specific could be said about the cause. 'This shall be to signify you', the councillors wrote,

> that the Lady Mary being at Hunsdon is suddenly departed with her
> train and family toward the sea coast of Norfolk, upon what occasion
> we know not, but as it is thought either to flee the realm or to abide
> there some foreign power, intending by such ungodly means and ways
> to disturb the commune quiet of this realm and to resist such

ordinances and decrees as the King's majesty hath set forth and established for the succession of the imperial crown.

Local officials were exhorted to

> be ready upon an hour's warning with your said power to repair unto
> us and to stand fast with such ordinances as be subscribed unto us by
> his Majesty, signed with his own hand and sealed with the great seal of
> England, the which we shall cause to be imparted unto you with as
> convenient speed as we may ... in the mean time we require and pray
> you to take such good orders for the maintenance of the continual
> watches in every place within that shire as no stir or uproar be
> attempted but that the doers thereof be by your industries stayed ...[10]

The problem with this hastily conceived missive is that it begged more
questions than it answered. Why had Mary bolted? The inference was
that she had been cut out of the succession, but, if so, why? Her religion
was alluded to, as was the spectre of foreign involvement, without any
specifics being given. And what about her sister Elizabeth, a follower of
the new religion, who was nowhere mentioned? The letter also seemed
to assume that there would be trouble, with its references to 'stir' and
'uproar', and it claimed a legitimacy for the Letters Patent that was false;
they had never passed the Great Seal. It does not seem to have caused
great alarm at local level, but neither did it inspire outpourings of loyal
devotion. The privy council had signalled to the shires that all was not
well at the seat of government and, outside East Anglia and the Thames
Valley, most counties waited on events.

The council's primary concern at this point was that Mary would try
to flee the country altogether, using one of the east coast ports close to
her own lands. Past experience, as much as wishful thinking, could have
influenced this interpretation. She had considered flight before, when
she was in less obvious personal danger. Still, it would be better to apprehend her rather than have her slip out of England, and Robert Dudley,
Elizabeth's future favourite and one of Northumberland's many sons,
was dispatched with a force to try to intercept the fugitive. He failed and
Mary remained at large.

The council were at dinner on 10 July when Thomas Hungate,
Mary's messenger, delivered her letters demanding their allegiance.
Hungate was promptly 'lodged' in the Tower for daring to carry such a

subversive message. He had, though, succeeded in ruining the meal. There were mutterings of concern around the table and the duchesses of Northumberland and Suffolk broke down in tears, as well they might, since they were as ambitious as their menfolk. Neither had wasted any emotion on Mary's feelings or the justification for denying the princess and her sister their birthright. Personal loyalties between women were as fragile as they were among men in these times of intrigue.

At first, the council held firm. The next day, they sent an uncompromising rebuke. It stated categorically that Jane was queen of England by Letters Patent endorsed by the realm's leading nobles. Mary was nothing but a bastard who could not inherit the throne. At the same time, Jane was being proclaimed all over England, in a coordinated campaign in every county. Instructions were also given to Sir Philip Hoby, the ambassador in Brussels, to inform Charles V that Jane's accession was a fait accompli and that Mary stood no chance of success.[11] It sounded good, but the anxiety remained, and with good reason. Family frictions were soon the least of Queen Jane's problems. By 13 July it was evident that a full-scale rebellion in support of Mary Tudor had broken out in eastern England. Weeping duchesses or no, Northumberland knew that she was not going to go away. He could not avoid resorting to arms.

When Mary arrived safely at Kenninghall, the first part of her plan had succeeded. Having managed to evade capture, she could now move forward into the positive phase of her strategy. Kenninghall was a good choice for the headquarters of a war council, accessible to her supporters but not too close to the towns of East Anglia, whose fealty was much less certain than that of the Catholic gentlemen of the countryside. The house had once been the showpiece of the Howard family's wealth, its 72 rooms stuffed with tapestries and elegant furnishings. There was an irony in Mary basing herself in the former home of the man who had so often, and so brutally, tried to get her to submit to her father. But now Norfolk was an old and ailing prisoner in the Tower, musing on the untimely death of his brilliant but irresponsible son, the earl of Surrey, the final victim of Henry VIII's many judicial murders. He who was once the highest peer in the land had little enough left when the inventory of his home was made in 1547. The house must have looked bereft when Mary first visited it in the summer of 1547.

Mary was a wealthy woman by then, and though she could have afforded to raise it back to the sumptuousness of its glory days, there is no evidence that she spent much money on it, or a great deal of time there. Her preference in Edward's reign was for her Essex homes. Someone who suffered such regular ill health would not have found north Norfolk, where the winds blow in from the North Sea, an attractive destination, especially in winter. But the fact that the house was not cluttered with prized possessions made it ideal for Mary's purposes in the summer of 1553. An infrequent visitor she may have been, but her household advisers, with their strong local links, had been careful to maintain their contacts and boost their lady's image with the country gentlemen who formed her affinity. There was much genuine affection for Mary, and this goodwill was a powerful weapon when effectively exploited.

The second phase of the plan to put Mary on the throne swung into action even before she established herself at Kenninghall. On 8 July she summoned the heads of three leading East Anglian families, Sir George Somerset, Sir William Waldegrave and Clement Heigham, to join her cause. Waldegrave and Heigham were with her when she arrived at Kenninghall, and they had been joined by others – Sir John Mordaunt, husband of one of her long-serving gentlewomen, Sir William Drury, John Sulyard and the earl of Bath, at that stage the highest-ranked supporter of her claim. It was far from being an impressive host, but it was a start.

From Kenninghall, Mary sent out prepared letters to the knights and gentry of Norfolk and Suffolk, calling them to her side. Her communications strategy was considered and effective. One of its essential components was the spoken as well as the written word. Well-briefed local men were sent out to persuade and inspire by verbal means, enabling them to reach not just the landowners but their tenants and household staff as well.[12] These personal appeals had a powerful impact. But her concentration was not solely fixed on East Anglia, since her advisers knew that they must mobilise in the Thames Valley as well. So Sir Edward Hastings was also ordered to deliver support in Middlesex and Buckinghamshire, and his obedience galvanised other partisans of Mary in the neighbouring counties of Berkshire, Oxfordshire and Northamptonshire. This westward expansion of the rising was to prove a major element of its success.

She wrote, her network of messengers spoke on her behalf, and she was answered. Over the next five days the loyal knights and gentlemen of eastern England, primed by Mary's personal staff, came with their own followings and their arms, pledged to uphold her cause. Their names were a roll-call of the leading families of the region: the Rochesters, the Jerninghams, the Waldegraves, the Whartons, the Bedingfelds, the Sheltons, the Southwells, the Poleys, the Nevilles, the Huddlestons and Henry Radcliffe, son of the earl of Sussex. As the contemporary account of Robert Wingfield records, 'every day ... the countryfolk of the two counties flocked to the support of their rightful queen'. Mary rewarded 125 of these men with annuities. Of the high nobility of England, there was not one single representative.

The men who stood for Mary were, of course, risking a great deal. Revolts in the English provinces were nothing new but few succeeded. The great northern rebellion of 1536, the Pilgrimage of Grace, was the result of a similar groundswell of discontent at religious change and Mary's exclusion from the succession. Its leaders were given fair words and then ruthlessly extinguished. In East Anglia itself, Northumberland had demonstrated only four years earlier the kind of mercy rebels could expect. Mary's supporters had not forgotten, but still they were willing to rally to her call. Their determination to stand up to the centre, to combat the politicians in London who cared nothing for local interests, is demonstrated by the scale of their response. The Edwardian government's attempt to legislate out of existence their long-held beliefs was a source of underlying resentment. It has been said that legitimacy was not a major issue in influencing support for Mary, but for her supporters it was inextricably linked with her Catholicism. To them, she was the unquestioned heir. So this woman, who was a rank outsider at the beginning of July, a disinherited princess whose opposition figured so low on the scale of considerations in London that those in power had overlooked the need to arrest her, held firm as her bid for the throne entered its crucial phase.

By 12 July, she had sufficient momentum and a large enough force to move her headquarters to Framlingham in Suffolk, a moated castle more easily fortified than Kenninghall. There, in the deer park below the castle, more local worthies awaited her. But her success was not yet assured, despite the defection to her cause of the earl of Sussex and Sir Thomas Cornwallis. No Protestant family had offered its support and the urban areas of East Anglia were either opposed, in the case of King's Lynn, or divided, as in Ipswich, where both Mary and Jane were proclaimed on the same day. Nor was the countryside unanimous in its support for

Mary. The marshland areas of East Anglia had suffered terribly the effects of spiralling prices and drought. They did not welcome quartermasters from Mary's forces looking to relieve them of what few victuals they had.

And there were ominous signs of the violence that might lie ahead. Robert Dudley had a small but effective military force in the area which was keeping up resistance and threatening those known to support Mary. As he awaited reinforcements from London, he did not back down. A slightly larger force could have transformed his chances.

Throughout all this time, Mary showed remarkable courage and commitment. The miserable, indecisive princess who could not quite bring herself to cut her ties with England in 1550 was nowhere to be seen. Instead, she had rediscovered the implacable girl who resisted, for three years, a king's determination to make her deny who she was. This was the supreme struggle of her turbulent life. But it had a clear goal, a prize worth fighting for, and it was evident that there were many who were willing to die for her. The knowledge galvanised her as never before. She already saw the hand of God at work and she responded. Mary was no passive observer of events, and the idea that she knew very little about the planning behind her fight for the throne underrates her intelligence and diligence. Mary was not the sort of woman who sat in the background where matters of such importance were concerned. Her direct, very personal involvement is stamped all over the summer of 1553. By 14 July, she had won over Lord Wentworth, who arrived 'clad in splendid armour and accompanied by a not inconsiderable military force' to join her troops. But, at the same time, two other developments immensely strengthened Mary's prospects. The fleet at Great Yarmouth, which Northumberland was counting on to prevent her escape to the Continent, had mutinied, probably with the encouragement of Henry Jerningham, who was very influential in the town. And the duke himself had left London with two thousand men and a substantial amount of artillery, intending to engage her forces. He expected more to arrive when he reached Newmarket, but he was to be disappointed. Once he had gone, the council began to fall apart.

The ruling elite in London were not alone in their astonishment at Mary's stand. The imperial ambassadors, marooned in uncertainty, were equally amazed. On 7 July, Renard and his colleagues were more concerned about Mary's survival than anything else. They gave her no chance of success whatsoever, assuming that she had retired to Kenning-hall as a defensive measure only. Mary, they said, felt safer there, local people were devoted to her and she 'hopes she will be able to shelter herself … and not be as easily arrested as if she were near Court'. But there was no anticipation that she would fight for the throne and the ambassadors foresaw 'small likelihood of being able to withstand the duke's designs … her promotion to the crown [will] be so difficult as to be well nigh impossible in the absence of a force large enough to counterbalance that of her enemies'.

In fact, they became irritated by what they saw as sheer wrong-headedness in Mary's approach to her predicament. Although they had not managed to see her, clearly information was exchanged and they did not like what they heard: 'She came to the conclusion that, as soon as the king's death should be announced, she had better proclaim herself Queen by her letters; for thus she would encourage her supporters to declare for her … My Lady has firmly made up her mind that she must act in this manner and that otherwise she will fall into still greater danger and lose all hope of coming to the throne.' Such a course seemed to the ambassadors hopelessly unrealistic: 'We consider this resolution strange, full of difficulties and danger,' they sniffed.[13]

Their advice thus far was to do nothing until she was absolutely certain of Edward's death. They remarked: 'The actual possession of power was a matter of great importance, especially among barbarians like the English.' They did not allude to the fact that family history could already have taught Mary such a lesson. The grandmother she and Charles V shared, Isabella of Castile, needed no such admonishments when she deprived her own niece, the rightful heir, of the Castilian throne. No one had ever dared to call her barbaric, except perhaps the Jews and Moors whom she persecuted with such single-mindedness. Needless to say, the ambassadors did not advocate lifting a finger to help Mary, mindful as they were that Charles V had instructed them 'to avoid throwing England into confusion to the disadvantage of your majesty and your dominions'. But it was important to avoid giving Mary the impression that they had abandoned her entirely, 'for then she might take opportunity to put the blame for disaster upon us'. And with this honest assertion of the importance of watching their own backs, they sat on their hands and waited to see what would happen.

Councillors William Petre and William Cecil came to see them on 10 July to announce the king's death, though the ambassadors knew of it three days earlier. A polite stand-off ensued, though they did feel moved to ask the council to 'remember my Lady Mary, cousin german to your majesty, to receive her under their protection and shelter her'. The council could scarcely help remembering her and would have very much liked to shelter her, as a closely guarded prisoner, but she was out of their reach by then. Ever cautious, the trio merely noted to the emperor that, if they were summoned to the new royal presence – and they naturally assumed that Guildford Dudley would be king and it would be to him, not Jane, that they would address themselves – they would say nothing in support of Mary's claim to the throne.[14]

The following day Charles wrote underlining his general support for their handling of the crisis in England. He wanted them to 'recommend' Mary and to dispel any notion that he wanted to marry her to a foreigner, or that she might introduce radical changes into religion or government. But beyond that he would not go, 'because our hands are full with France'. And he dismissed the value of private persons professing loyalty to his cousin: 'unless a number of the most powerful nobles took her side it would be impossible to undermine the carefully prepared course of action that Northumberland is working'.[15]

The duke thought so, too, until reports of Mary's growing army convinced him otherwise. He then faced a difficult decision. Should he take the fight to Mary himself or entrust the task to others? If he left London he would no longer be able to direct the process of government and he had reason, good reason, as it turned out, to suspect that there might be defections from the council once he had gone. He mistrusted his colleagues. Paget and Arundel, whatever they might say to his face, held grudges against him for his treatment of them in recent years, and Arundel had refused to sign a personal undertaking to uphold the succession as laid down by Edward VI. Northumberland's initial preference was to put the duke of Suffolk in command. Jane was his daughter and it was in his interests to fight for her. The Grey family, however, had other ideas.

Tradition has it that Jane, frightened by the danger and loss of her father's protection, implored him not to go. This story fits in well with the view of a child-woman at the mercy of events beyond her control, but Robert Wingfield in the *Vita Mariae Reginae* states that it was the duchess, not her daughter, who became hysterical at the thought of Suffolk's departure; Jane, he asserts, encouraged her father to go.[16] Perhaps Henry Grey, a blusterer who achieved high rank and office through trading on his wife's family connections, was privately less than keen to go himself. Northumberland reluctantly accepted that his hand had been forced. One of his sons was already in the field and a kinsman, Henry Dudley, was about to set off for France to seek help there if it should prove necessary. There seemed no alternative but to lead a force against Mary in person. It was a decision he took with notable reluctance.

In the late morning of 13 July, the duke gave a sombre speech to his fellow-councillors, betraying a lack of confidence in the situation which did little to steady their nerves. He commended his family and fortune to their safe-keeping and pointed out that Jane was entirely dependent on them. The queen, he said, was 'by your and our enticement ... rather of force placed therein [meaning on the throne] than by her own seeking and request'. Then he issued a stark reminder that they were all in this together – a theme to which he would return at his trial. 'Consider', he warned them, 'also that God's cause, which is the preferment of his words and the fear of papacy's re-entrance, hath been as ye hath heretofore always alleged, the original ground whereupon ye even at the first motion granted your goodwills and consents thereunto, as by your handwritings evidently appeareth.'

An unnamed councillor hastened to convey their collective loyalty: 'My lord, if ye mistrust any of us in this matter, your grace is far deceived; for which of us can wipe his hands clean thereof? And if we should shrink from you as one that were culpable, which of us can excuse himself as guiltless? Therefore herein your doubt is too far cast.' Northumberland replied, with less than total conviction: 'I pray God it may be so; let us go to dinner.'[17]

He left the next morning, noting as he rode by the silent citizens of London that no man wished him Godspeed. There were still little hard fact about Mary's rebellion and he had left Suffolk in charge in the heavily fortified Tower, with instructions to keep the council there in a form of unspoken detention. There was every prospect that he would prevail. But his political sixth sense already told him that he had gambled and lost.

· ❖ ·

At Framlingham, meanwhile, a substantial host was gathering below the castle's stout walls, commanded by the elderly earl of Sussex. There was also welcome news on 16 July from Sir Edmund Peckham, the treasurer of the Mint, who had been instrumental in the Thames Valley rising. Mary's cause was prospering west of London and reports began to circulate that Peckham had 10,000 men ready to march on London, to seize the Tower and it armaments. All this increased Mary's confidence, even as Northumberland's began to waver. The duke reached Cambridge on 16 July and was joined by Sir Edward Clinton and the earl of Huntington. But no further troops came from London, where the rumours of Peckham's host caused consternation. The duke's force set off towards Bury St Edmunds, sacking Sawston Hall in revenge for Huddleston's sheltering of Mary. It was an ineffective gesture; the men began to desert and Northumberland was forced to turn back to Cambridge. There he waited and hesitated, uncertain whether to make the push to confront Mary's troops. His eventual decision to refrain from causing bloodshed was crucial. At the time, he was given no credit for it, but Northumberland, despite his prickliness, was not, at heart, a bloodthirsty man. As in 1549, he did not relish the prospect of civil war.

The final boost for Marian supporters, and the one that probably assured her success, was the decision made by John de Vere, earl of Oxford, to declare for Mary on 18 July. The story was told at the time that he had been persuaded to change his mind only by a spirited household rebellion among his servants, but that may have been a convenient cover.[18] The 16th earl, a Protestant sympathiser and notorious womaniser, was a complex man. He could hardly be considered a natural ally but, as he controlled most of Essex, his defection was of paramount importance. No doubt it was military prudence rather than personal distaste for someone with a very irregular private life which caused Oxford's troops to be sent off to bolster the defence of Ipswich, rather than join Mary at Framlingham. She did not need him there, in any case. Convinced now that success was hers, she issued a memorable proclamation the same day. It was signed: 'Marye the quene'.

The original document, on a large square leaf of paper, has been in the possession of the Bedingfeld family for over 450 years, but has been overlooked by Mary's biographers until now. In it, Mary announces her succession on the death of Edward and makes very clear that she is speaking with regal authority, true dynastic right and from a position of military strength. It begins: 'By the Queen. Know ye all good people that the most excellent princess Mary, elder daughter of King Henry VIII and sister to King Edward VI, your late sovereign Lord, is now by the grace of God Queen of England, France and Ireland, defender of the faith and very true owner of the crown and government of the realm of England and Ireland and all things thereto justly belonging, and to her and no other ye owe to be her true Liege men.'

Having asserted her legitimacy, she makes clear her strength of arms. She is, she says, 'nobly and strongly furnished of an army royall under Lord Henry, Earl of Sussex, her Lieutenant General, accompanied with the earl of Bath, the Lord Wentworth and a multitude of other noble gentlemen'. And she goes on to attack Northumberland and his ambitions without even deigning to name her cousin Jane Grey or mention her claim to the crown – her wrath is squarely aimed at the man she knows has sought to deprive her of her right: '… her most false traitor, John, duke of Northumberland and his complices who, upon most false and most shameful grounds, minding to make his own son king by marriage of a new found lady's title, or rather to be king himself, hath most traitorously by long continued treason sought, and seeketh, the destruction of her royal person, the nobility and common weal of this realm'. The contempt for the Greys as claimants and the political opportunism that has made them usurpers of the true succession is very clear in these carefully chosen words of condemnation.

The proclamation ends with a rallying cry: 'Wherefore, good people, as ye mindeth the surety of her said person, the honour and surety of your country, being good Englishmen, prepare yourselves in all haste with all your power to repair unto her said armies yet being in Suffolk, making your prayers to God for her success … upon the said causes she utterly defyeth the said duke for her most errant traitor to God and to this realm.'

More, however, than just defiance is thrown at Northumberland. Mary is implacable in her determination, as she puts a price on his head: 'Anyone taking him, if a noble and peer of the realm, to have one thousand pounds of land in fee; if a knight, five hundred pounds in lands, with honour and advancement to nobilitie; if a gentleman under the degree of knight, five hundred marks of land in fee and the degree of a knight; if a yeoman, 100 pounds of land in fee and the degree of a squire.' The tone makes it quite clear, though it does not say so explicitly, that

Northumberland's fate, if he is taken, will be death.[19]

Still, no one in Mary's camp knew whether there would be a military engagement and the mustered forces grew slightly restive with inactivity and anticipation. It was decided that a personal appearance by Mary was required. On 20 July, her splendid white horse was saddled and she rode out to make an inspection at four o'clock in the afternoon. An inspiring sight awaited her. The standards were unfurled, the military colours set up and battle lines divided into two, under Wentworth and Sussex. For the first time as queen, Mary saw her forces arrayed, ready to fight and die for her. But the press of men and arms was too much for her horse and it became frisky. She was a fine horsewoman but she could not afford the ignominy of being unable to control this nervous animal, so she dismounted and continued her inspection on foot. Moving among her men, she spoke to them 'with an exceptional kindness and with an approach so wonderfully relaxed as can scarcely be described ... she completely won everyone's affections'. After she inspected these divisions, a large detachment of cavalry streamed forth, making a splendid sound. 'The queen was much delighted with this show and spent three hours there before returning to the castle.'[20]

It was there, in the old Howard fortress on the evening of 20 July, that Mary received Lord Paget and the earl of Arundel, who had ridden post-haste from London. They brought her the news that she and her advisers had been hoping, praying and working for all summer. The privy council had proclaimed her queen the previous day and Northumberland had surrendered without even drawing his sword at Cambridge. After two weeks of confusion and intrigue not one drop of English blood was shed in bringing Mary Tudor to the throne of England. In London, bonfires were lit and church bells rung in one of the greatest spontaneous outpourings of joy that had ever greeted the accession of a new monarch. 'Men ran hither and thither, bonnets flew into the air, shouts rose higher than the stars, and all the bells were set a-pealing,' wrote an anonymous Italian in London, adding, with a fair infusion of hyperbole, 'from a distance the earth must have looked like Mount Etna. The people were mad with joy, feasting and singing, and the streets crowded all night long. I am unable to describe to you, nor would you believe, the exultation of all men. I will only tell you that not a soul imagined the possibility of such a thing'.[21] Nor, until the last couple of months, had Mary, but now, suddenly, the distant dream of her childhood was reality. The sorrow, the suffering, the fears of a life spent in uncer-

tainty were all part of her past. She instructed her chaplains at Framlingham to give thanks to God for her bloodless victory, saying that she
'wanted the realm cleansed of divisive parties'. With God's help, she had
triumphed against all the odds. She took this as a sign that He would
bless her through all the years of her reign.

What had happened back in London, that brought Paget and Arundel to
Mary with letters full of contrition and assurances of unswerving devotion? The simple answer is that, without a firm hand at the centre, there
had been a collective loss of nerve. Northumberland himself had given
voice to fears of such a development and it had come to pass, almost as
if he had, perversely, willed it into existence. Suffolk was no war leader,
and though he might lock his fellow-councillors in the Tower, as a
protective measure, this form of polite imprisonment made it easy for
doubts and resentments to fester. The duke was also an ineffective jailer.
The marquess of Winchester managed to get out on 16 July but was
brought back. He was clearly unhappy with the restrictions placed on
him and it seems highly likely that he was already moving towards Mary.
His example, allied to the highly disturbing rumours reaching London
that Peckham's forces were coming to invade the capital and that Mary
had 30,000 men under her standard at Framlingham (in fact, she probably had no more than 6,000), provided the impetus for others to take
more direct action.

There were also signs that the mood of the population of London as
a whole might be shifting. Despite the growth of Protestantism in the
capital, there was no outpouring of support for Queen Jane, who was
not seen by anyone after her arrival at the Tower on 10 July. As the days
went by, the upholders of Mary's claim became more vocal. On 13 July
a tract was printed and distributed in London by one 'Poor Pratte' which
tells us a great deal about how public opinion could be influenced in the
days when no other mass media existed.

Pratte wrote his epistle to Gilbert Potter, a drawer (the 16th-century
equivalent of a barman) at the St John's Head tavern, within Ludgate.
Then, as now, public houses were places where political opinions were
voiced and Potter had spoken too freely for the liking of the authorities.
He had been pilloried and lost both his ears for saying that the Lady
Mary had a better title to the throne than the Lady Jane. His beliefs,

whether spontaneously expressed or coached as part of wider effort to discredit Jane at popular level, provided Potter's defender with the ammunition for a stunning piece of propaganda. In a positively biblical style, Pratte warmed to his theme:

> What man could have shown himself bolder in her grace's cause, than thou hast showed? Or who did so valiantly in the proclamation time, when Jane was published queen (unworthy as she was) and more to blame, I may say to thee, are some of the consenters thereunto. There were thousands more than thyself, yet durst they not (such is the fragility and weakness of the flesh) once move their lips to speak that which thou didst speak. Thou offerest thyself amongst the multitude of people to fight against them all in her quarrel, and for her honour did not fear to run upon the point of the swords. O faithful subject! O true heart to Mary, our queen.

The heroic Potter is compared to various Old Testament figures, such as Daniel cast to the lions, and the writer continues in mixed religious and classical vein for some time. But he is convinced, even so, that Mary would rather her brother lived than become queen, but, as a virtuous princess and rightful heir, the throne is hers. At the end of the epistle is a reference that may provide a clue to the backers of this broadsheet, which would have been easily distributed, posted in public places and read out to those who were interested but illiterate. The writer has heard, he says, that in respect of those who exercise power, the earl of Arundel 'will not consent to none of their doings'. He beseeches God to keep the earl steadfast.[22]

Whether Arundel had prior knowledge of 'Poor Pratte's' epistle is impossible to say. The precise chronology of the council's betrayal of Northumberland is hard to determine. On 16 July, the councillors sent out a long and impassioned letter to the counties which marked their final attempt to uphold Queen Jane. This time it pulled no punches in castigating Mary or calling upon every xenophobic and religious prejudice to discredit her. She was the

> bastard daughter of the noble prince, king Henry VIII, seeking daily more and more by all ways and means she can to stir and move sundry of the nobles, gentlemen and others the Queen's Majesty's subjects to rebellion, [and] ceaseth not to spread and set further most traitorously

sundry untrue reports of our sovereign lady Queen Jane and falsely also some of us of Her Majesty's privy council ...

Edward VI had considered that the crown could only pass to someone of 'the whole blood'; otherwise would have meant the 'bringing in of strangers, whereof was like to have followed the bondage of this realm to the old servitude of the Antichrist of Rome, the subversion of the true preaching of God's word and of the ancient laws, usages and liberties of this realm'. The unanimity of the ruling elite in their support of the king was emphasised: 'long before his death, not only we and every of us being of His Majesty's privy council did consent and subscribe ... so do we still wholly remain and God willing mind always to remain of that concord, and to maintain and to defend to the death our said sovereign lady Queen Jane's just title during our lives'. The blame for all 'these unnatural seditions and tumults' was laid squarely on 'the said bastard daughter'. Mary was an ingrate, who should have been content with the honourable state in which she was left by her father and allowed to live by her brother. 'But,' they went on, 'through the counsel of a number of obstinate papists she forsaketh as by her seditious proclamations may appear the just title of supremacy annexed by the imperial crown of this realm, and consequently, to bring in again the miserable servitude of the bishop of Rome, to the great offence of almighty God and utter subversion of the whole state of this realm'. And if this was not enough, there was a sweetener at the end, for those loyal to Queen Jane could be assured that they would find her a good and gracious lady, 'and us most willing to further any your reasonable suites when occasion shall serve'.[23]

Arundel signed this appeal to the shires but, the truth was, occasion did not serve. He already saw his future with Mary, not with Jane, no matter how good and gracious she might be. And he was not alone. Some time after 16 July, he and Pembroke were able to slip out of the Tower and establish themselves at Pembroke's London residence, Baynard's Castle, in the City. Suffolk either did not, or, more likely, could not, control them. Pembroke was Katherine Parr's brother-in-law and a courtier of long standing. He was joined in the relative security of his home by half a dozen other key councillors, including Paget. Most of these men had worked with Northumberland without demur, but they now believed he could not win. Galvanised as much by fears for their own future as by a rousing speech in support of Mary's claim by Arundel, they now formed a rival faction that would sweep Jane Grey from her rocky throne.

Others, though, were not of the same mind. On the morning of 19 July the councillors were still split, with Cranmer in particular unwilling to embrace the idea of Mary as queen, with all its implication for the Edwardian religious legislation. During a day of heated exchanges, the outcome hung in the balance until late in the afternoon, when the archbishop and a dwindling group of Janeites reluctantly agreed that Mary should be proclaimed. The text of their newly discovered loyalty was agreed, beginning with the assertion: 'We your most humble and obedient subjects, having always (God we take witness) remained your highness's true and humble subjects in our heart'. These correct but totally unconvincing sentiments would, it was hoped, save many political careers.

In the Tower, the duke of Suffolk interrupted his daughter's evening meal with the removal of her colours and the stark announcement that she was no longer queen. It could not, by then, have been entirely unexpected. Popular tradition has it that she expressed relief but, even if this were so, the implications could not have been lost on her. As an intelligent young woman who well understood the harsh realities of mid-16th-century politics, she knew the fate of usurpers, and that was what she had become. She had no cause for joy. Even as the bells rang out in London and street parties took place to celebrate Mary's accession, Paget and Arundel snatched up the letters for the new queen and took horse to her Suffolk stronghold. Jane's brief period of rule had ended in victory for Mary and disaster for the Greys and the Dudleys.

The two councillors who were ushered into the royal presence on 20 July were a good choice to represent the astonishing volte-face of the privy council in its most positive light. Both were Catholic sympathisers, personally uncommitted to the changes of Edward's reign, though they had not sought to draw further attention to themselves by publicly challenging Cranmer and Northumberland on this issue. They also had good reason to dislike the duke, who had humiliated them and caused them heavy financial loss on vaguely specified charges of corruption. Paget was stripped of his Garter in 1552 and imprisoned for a period in the Tower, while Arundel was fined £12,000 and sent off to cool his heels (and murmurings of discontent) among his affinity in Sussex. But both were later restored to the council, further evidence of Northumberland's pragmatic rather than vengeful approach to opponents. Paget, risen from humble origins and ever the committed public servant, may have understood. Arundel, the holder of the premier earldom in the country, could trace his Fitzalan ancestors back to the Norman conquest, and his resentment was much less easily assuaged.

Nevertheless, it is hard to believe that their explanations sounded sincere to Mary and unlikely that she received them with anything other than a businesslike welcome. She needed them, but this did not mean she suddenly trusted them, or anyone else on the council. Yet the country had to be governed and she could not dismiss the men who had sought to keep her from the throne, however personally distasteful she found their malleable consciences. Her priority was also theirs. And that was to apprehend the duke of Northumberland.

He had stayed at Cambridge, in the house of Sir John Cheke, provost of King's College, while his colleagues in London dissembled and finally disowned him. His inaction is curious, but, again, in keeping with the man. Failure, which had been so long a stranger, paralysed him. But it also seems to have deluded him into thinking that if he abased himself, he might, just possibly, be allowed to live. When Mary was proclaimed in Cambridge it is said that he, too, threw up his cap as a sign of rejoicing. He could have tried to escape but the desertion of most of his troops and the sudden triumph of Mary's cause left him an isolated and forlorn figure. When Arundel came to arrest him on 23 July, he expressed the hope that the queen would show him mercy. 'My lord,' replied the earl grimly, 'ye should have sought for mercy sooner.' Two days later he was brought under armed escort into London and imprisoned in the Tower. Fearful for the fate of his wife and family, he had to wait for his trial while Mary established herself on the throne.

That process began on 24 July when Mary left Framlingham for Ipswich. She then moved at a leisurely place towards London, stopping at New Hall, where her first council met at the end of the month, and later at Ingatestone in Essex, the home of Sir William Petre. While at New Hall, she received one anguished petitioner but refused to see another. The favoured supplicant was her cousin Frances. The panicked duchess of Suffolk had pleaded to be allowed to speak to the queen, and was received at two o'clock in the morning. She was desperate to make restitution, to implore Mary for understanding and forgiveness. But it turned out that her request was only for herself and her husband, not for her daughter. Jane, still in the Tower, but now as captive, not ruler, would have to fend for herself. Frances was more fortunate than the duchess of Northumberland. She also asked to speak with Mary, but was refused. Desperate to save her husband's life, she wrote an impassioned and disorganised letter to William Paget's wife, Anne, imploring her to use her influence with the ladies close to Mary. If she was not allowed to speak to the queen herself, she placed all her hope on the two women she believed stood the best chance of pleading her case: 'Now good madame,' she wrote, 'for the love you bear to God forget me not: and make my lady marquess of Exeter my said "good lady" and to remember me to Mistress Clarencius to continue as she hath begun for me.' She also asked for help for her sons, though she added with a frankness that speaks much for the depth of her love for her husband: 'I do not so much care for them as for their father who was to me ... the best gentleman that ever living woman was matched withal'. Neither Lady Exeter nor Susan Clarencius succeeded in saving Northumberland, but there is interesting indirect evidence that Susan, at least, may well have tried. When the duchess died in 1555 she left her 'tawny velvet jewel coffer' to Mistress Clarencius and her 'high-backed gown of wrought velvet' to Anne Paget.[24] But in August 1553, as for her daughter-in-law, Jane Grey, the Tower of London became her prison. It was clear where Mary's retribution would lie.

And now the one figure who had been missing throughout the crisis of July 1553 emerged from the shadows to make her move. Princess Elizabeth was at Hatfield House in Hertfordshire when Edward died. A distance of 15 miles separated her from Mary at Hunsdon, but there is nothing to indicate that the two women had any contact until Mary was proclaimed queen. Like Mary, Elizabeth was summoned to London, ostensibly to visit her sick brother, but she stayed put. Given that her own prospects and, indeed, probably her life depended on how her sister fared, her inaction could easily have put her in danger. She would surely not have been overlooked for long if Northumberland had succeeded in capturing Mary. Did she know of Mary's plans but resolve to remain aloof until there was a definite outcome? Perhaps she did not rate Mary's chances any more than the council in London did.

There could have been an opportunistic aspect to her inaction. Perhaps she believed that, if Mary failed, she could pursue her own claim to the throne, since she was not a papist. Apparently she never considered giving unreserved support, either publicly or practically, to her sister though if it had come to a fight the number of men she could have supplied from her own affinity might have been crucial. Given the unpredictability of the situation and her own natural caution, far greater than Mary's, her wait-and-see attitude is not surprising. She had her own reasons, based on hard experience, to fear the inconstancy of politicians in London. On top of this, Edward's attempt to cut her out of the succession was a bitter blow in view of the almost flamboyant affection she had always shown him.

Once it was certain that Mary had prevailed, Elizabeth wrote with congratulations. She was preparing to come and greet her sister but, with an attention to detail that may have been somewhat irritating, she was equally concerned with what she should wear. Must it be mourning for Edward VI? she wondered. [25] Apparently she was informed that this was unnecessary. The dictates of fashion and decorum satisfied, she then moved back into London, where she established herself in advance of Mary's planned entry into the capital. On 29 July, accompanied by 2,000 of the well-armed men she had conspicuously failed to offer her sister, Elizabeth rode through the City of London, sporting the Tudor colours, to take up residence at Somerset House. She was met with great popular acclaim. Her ability to muster such an impressive force belies the image of the defenceless princess so beloved of historical novelists. This was a powerful young woman, a Tudor to her beautifully manicured fingertips, fully conscious of who she was. After this splendid show, she left the next day to meet her victorious sister at the royal manor of Wanstead. They had great cause to celebrate Mary's success together, since it restored the direct line of their father. In one of the charming acts of generosity that were typical of Mary, she gave jewels to her sister's ladies. Later, Elizabeth herself received white coral beads trimmed with gold and a ruby-and-diamond brooch telling the story of Pyramus and Thisbe, both from the queen's personal collection.

But there were undercurrents between the sisters, tensions not yet acknowledged openly but also not far below the surface. The clever little sister that Mary loved as a child was gone, replaced by a woman she did not really know. At 20 years old, Elizabeth was in full bloom. Her adult presence – and she had plenty of it – disturbed Mary. How could it not? The spectre of Anne Boleyn haunted her still. When Mary looked at Elizabeth, she saw someone who could have been a younger, taller version of herself. The two women bore a striking resemblance to each other, with their red hair, long noses, heart-shaped faces and thin lips. They shared a love of fine clothes, the latest fashions and jewels. No one who saw them together could doubt that they were the daughters of Henry VIII, though Mary herself came to question it when their relationship was at its most difficult. But this was unworthy. Their father may have deprived Elizabeth of her title but he never questioned her birth.

For the present, buoyed up by the joy of her accession and distracted by the many decisions concerning advisers and policy that had to be made in a very short space of time, Mary put aside her misgivings. Elizabeth came to her dutifully and quite properly and they would enjoy Mary's victory together. On 3 August came a moment that only the queen herself and a small group of those closest to her had dared to contemplate a mere month before. Accompanied by an estimated 10,000 men, the new monarch entered her capital. Huge crowds acclaimed her as she rode in her royal chariot. 'Her look, her manner, her gestures, her countenance were such that in no event could they have been improved,' reported the imperial ambassadors. 'She was dressed in violet velvet, her skirts and sleeves embroidered in gold; her face is more than middling-fair; her equipage was regal. She was followed by my Lady Elizabeth, her sister, whom she has welcomed with great warmth, even to kissing all her ladies... her estate has been increased since the Queen's accession.'[26]

The imperialists, and particularly Simon Renard, would soon play on Mary's reservations about her sister. Their agenda was to put the new queen firmly in their camp, not encourage a close relationship with the Protestant Elizabeth, who, by statute, was the heiress to Mary's throne. There was still something of an aura of disbelief among European observers, both French and Habsburg, that Mary had come to the throne at all. The emperor was as delighted as he was surprised. 'These news', wrote Charles V, 'are the best we could have had from England, and we render thanks to God for having guided all things so well ... You will ... offer her our congratulations on her happy accession to the throne, telling her how great was our joy on hearing it.' So how were they to explain his complete lack of support? If an opportunity arose in private audience, without the more cynical councillors looking on, '… you may give her a more detailed account of the reasons that moved us to send you to England, and explain to her that you were instructed to proceed very gradually in your negotiation, with the object of rendering her some assistance, and that we were hastily making preparations, under cover of protecting the fisheries, to come to her relief'.[27] His words are a wonderful example of redefining policy to suit one's own purpose, but whether or not Mary was satisfied with such excuses does not really matter. Charles had every reason to assume she would remain close to him, as she had done all her adult life, and he would not be disappointed. Still, it was probably the nearest he came to embarrassment where Mary was concerned. It did not trouble him for long.

The French had other concerns. They were closely identified with Northumberland's policy and had not relished the idea of Mary, with her Habsburg leanings, becoming queen. Yet right from the start of the succession crisis, they were less convinced of Jane's durability than the imperial representatives. Antoine de Noailles, their cool-headed ambassador, had not been in London long and his dispatches in early July give the impression of someone who was observing rather than predicting events. On 13 July, he made all the right noises about Jane, describing her as 'virtuous, wise and beautiful and who promises much', but he made no attempt to conceal Mary's stance, even helpfully supplying a map showing London, Mary's house at Hunsdon and Norwich, where he believed she was. The next day he reported that her cause was growing and revealed that he had dined with the Venetian ambassador, who spoke warmly of Mary and told him that she was more popular with the people than Queen Jane. On 23 July Noailles, realising that the French must shift their position now Mary's accession was complete, wrote asking for new instructions. These did not come quickly. When the constable of France, Montmorency, did write, on the last day of July, he told Noailles to adopt an approach that the ambassador could well have thought out for himself. He was to emphasise French goodwill towards Mary and state that the French knew she was the legitimate – and popular – choice of the country.[28]

The international situation would loom large from the first days of the reign, but, for the present, it was only one of a myriad of policy areas demanding urgent attention. Mary had no time for contemplation, or to go over quietly in her own mind just how far she had come in the space of a mere fortnight. Her first council, numbering about 20 men, met before her entry to London. It was an interim body, but the business of government was pressing and there was, as she later told Renard, so much to do that she scarcely knew where to begin. Despite their differences and her mistrust of most of them, there was one outstanding consideration that united the queen and her advisers. Northumberland's hour of reckoning was at hand.

He and his sons were honourably treated during their imprisonment, but the Dudleys and their supporters were not among the inmates allowed to present themselves to Mary when she arrived at the Tower of London on 3 August. More fortunate beneficiaries of the old tradition that new monarchs should show clemency were four people who could not have expected early release while Northumberland remained in power. One was a woman, Mary's old friend the duchess of Somerset, who went back to her family. She lived long into the Elizabethan period, dying in 1587. The other three were men. The youngest was Edward Courtenay, a distant cousin of Mary and son of Katherine of Aragon's loyal supporter, Gertrude, marchioness of Exeter. His mother, her hopes suddenly raised for the future, rode proudly with Mary as she came into London. Also there when the queen entered the Tower were Stephen Gardiner, bishop of Winchester, and the old duke of Norfolk, who knelt now to do homage to the woman whose religious views he shared but whose prospects he had sought to destroy. Each man would play a prominent part in the first two years of Mary's reign but, for the prelate and the senior aristocrat, there was no period of recuperation from their imprisonment. Gardiner was named Lord Chancellor and Norfolk, appointed High Steward, found himself on 18 August presiding, once more, over a showpiece trial.

Nearly a month had elapsed since Northumberland's arrest, more than sufficient time for him to decide that he would not submit without defence to a court of his peers. The conduct of his trial, which had as much to do with ritual as justice, impressed foreign observers with its solemnity. The English did these sorts of things very well: 'As your lordship knows,' the merchant Antonio Guaras wrote to the duke of Alberquerque in Spain, 'these proceedings are here conducted with great dignity.'[29] Yet there was not the slightest doubt – except perhaps in Northumberland's own mind – that he would be found guilty and condemned to die. The process by which this decision would be reached, however, was part of the spectacle.

He kept his temper well under control as he faced the men who had deserted him. He came 'with a good and intrepid countenance, full of humility and gravity'. His defence was simple and logical, if no doubt unpalatable to his audience. What had he done but to carry out the commands of Edward VI, in a manner agreed by all the council? If he was guilty of high treason, so were they. His claim that his actions were carried out under the broad seal of England was untrue, but the rest of his argument was perfectly sound. But it was never going to sway anyone. 'His peers beheld him with a severe aspect,' Guaras noted. When the death sentence was pronounced he asked for, and was granted, a nobleman's death. Then he made another, unexpected, request. Faced with the fast-approaching end of his life, he must think about his soul. So he asked 'that I may have appointed to me some learned man for the instruction and quieting of my conscience'. The churchman who counselled him was Stephen Gardiner, a long-standing foe but a man who was suddenly restored to influence and power. Whether through personal anguish or political manoeuvring, Northumberland was about to give the new regime a huge propaganda victory.

The most striking aspect of his behaviour, in the few days left to him, was the duke's rejection of the religious beliefs he had done so much to impose on England during Edward's reign. There has been a great deal of debate over whether his return to the Catholic faith was genuine or affected as a last-ditch attempt to be spared the axe. It is impossible to know what passed between him and the bishop or whether it had any part in the commutation of the death sentence on his eldest son. If he had also been promised mercy, he was to be disappointed. On 21 August, the day fixed for his execution, he took mass in the chapel of the Tower, telling those who came to observe his change of heart: 'I do faithfully believe that this is the very right and true way, out of the which true religion you and I have been seduced these sixteen years past by the false and erroneous preaching of the new preachers, the which the only cause of the great plagues and vengeance which hath light upon the whole realm of England and now likewise worthily fallen upon me'.[30] It is worth noting that his sons made no such expression of a change of faith. The words may have been supplied to him or they may have been his own. But any hopes that they might be the means of sparing his life were soon to be disappointed. The lord lieutenant of the Tower came to him later in the day to tell him to be prepared for death the next morning.

What is more likely is that Northumberland did not want to die, and not just because he feared death, but because, as a servant of the Crown, he viewed it as a waste of his talents and experience. The desperate letter he is said to have penned on the last night of his life may not be genuine. It was addressed to Arundel, a man whom he had wronged and who was scarcely likely to intercede on his behalf, but some of its sentiments do reflect the image he had of himself. John Dudley knew he had misjudged Mary. Very well, it was a mistake, but he had acknowledged it and he could not see it as an impediment to serving her now she was queen. 'Alas my good lord,' the letter said,

> is my crime so heinous as no redemption but my blood can wash away the spots thereof? An old proverb there is and true that a living dog is better than a dead lion. O that it would please her good grace to give me life, yea, the life of a dog, that I might live and kiss her feet, and spend both life and all I have in her honourable service, as I have the best part already under her worthy brother and her most glorious father ... O my good lord, remember how sweet life is and how bitter ye contrary ...[31]

In the end it was Jane Grey herself, the girl who, by his own admission, he had thrust into peril, who summed up his predicament as well as anyone. Her outraged eloquence betrays a depth of emotion that she seldom showed. 'Woe worth him!' she cried.

> He hath brought me and my stock in most miserable calamity and misery by his exceeding ambition. But for the answering that he hoped for his life by his turning, though other men be of that opinion, I utterly am not; for what man is there living, I pray you, although he had been innocent, that would hope of life in that case; being in the field against the queen in person as general, and after his taking, so hated and evil spoken of by the commons? ... Who was judge that he should hope for pardon, whose life was odious to all men? But what will ye more? Like as his life was wicked and full of dissimulation, so was his end thereafter ... Should I, who am young and in my few years, forsake my faith for the love of life? ... But life was sweet, it appeared; so he might have lived, you will say, he did not care how.[32]

Reluctant in the face of death and anguished in mind, Northumberland nevertheless affirmed at the end that his rediscovery of the old faith was personal and not the result of pressure. He said he had 'no shame' in returning to God. When he went to the scaffold on 22 August 1553, there was a large crowd present to see John Dudley die. An eyewitness description of his last moments captures the man, brave in public but still not quite accepting his fate. There are signs that he held out the hope of a reprieve right till the last moments:

> And as the bandage [blindfolding his eyes] was not well fitted when he was about to stretch himself upon the beam, he rose again upon his knees, and surely figured to himself the terrible dreadfulness of death. At the moment when he again stretched himself out, as one who constrained himself and willed to consent patiently, without saying anything, in the act of laying himself out … he smote his hands together, as one who should say, this must be …[33]

So passed from this world one of the most enigmatic men of Tudor England. A competent rather than brilliant soldier but a politician of great skill and resolution, he was undone by one supreme error of judgement. He took longer than most to rise to a position of influence but could not imagine rescinding power once he had gained it. The council chamber was his natural milieu, a confined space where his serious and unyielding personality could intimidate men for whom he personally cared little. He had acquired wealth but lacked an affinity and learned the hard way from Mary, a woman he dismissed as a serious opponent, the value of loyal support. His downfall seemed a disaster for his large family and his wife never recovered from the loss of the man she called her most dear lord. She survived him by less than two years. In 1555 his heir, the earl of Warwick, died within 24 hours of being released from the Tower, to add to the family sorrows. But his other sons lived to restore their fortunes and Robert Dudley became the favourite of Elizabeth I, completing in her reign a century of Dudley service to the Crown. So, in the end, the dying wish of Northumberland, that his 'childer' would not suffer for their obedience to him, was fulfilled.

Mary had shown mercy and restraint in her dealings with the politicians who had tried to keep her off the throne. This policy, advocated by Charles V and her own advisers, was expedient but could not be extended to Northumberland. He was the new regime's priority in August, his execution an exemplary way of sending out the message that there would not be generalised retribution but that treason would not go unpunished. Once he had gone, Mary could move forward with confidence and begin to put in place her vision for England. She was the queen, but first she must be crowned.

PART FOUR

The Queen Without a King
1553—1554

Chapter Eight

Mary's England

'So, for good England's sake, this present hour and day
In hope of her restoring from her late decay
We children, to you old folk, both with heart and voice,
May join altogether to thank God and rejoice
That he hath sent Mary, our sovereign queen,
To reform the abuses which hitherto hath been.'

Prologue to *Respublica – a drama of Real Life in the early days of
Queen Mary*

When Mary was proclaimed in London on the afternoon of 19 July
it was more than a vindication of her courageous and principled
fight for the throne. Her victory underscored the legitimacy of statute
law as laid out in the Act of Succession of 1543 and conformed to the
wishes of Henry VIII that the succession should pass to his own children
before others were considered. The new queen's titles demonstrated the
extent of her power and responsibilities, in matters temporal and spiritual. She was 'Mary by the grace of God Queen of England, France and
Ireland, defender of the faith, and in the earth supreme head of the
Church of England and Ireland'. This impressive statement of regal
might contained elements that spoke to both the past and the present
and was what the majority of Mary's 'true and faithful' subjects expected
to hear. Yet it posed several important questions about how the queen
would rule that would demand answers sooner rather than later.

One part, of course, was little more than wishful thinking. The

English lands in France had dwindled to Calais and its surrounding area, but the claim remained, a survivor of centuries of enmity that would be reignited during Mary's reign. Ireland, on the other hand, was a newcomer to the titular display of the English monarchs. There had been a presence there, often uneasy and fragmented, since the Norman conquest, but only in 1541 did Mary's father, unwilling to settle for just being its Lord, add the title of King of Ireland to his style. The principality of Wales, in which the queen's dynasty originated, no longer merited a separate mention; it, too, was only recently united by statute law with England.[1]

Geographically, Mary's kingdom was small. Scotland was, quite literally, another country, a natural ally of France and a constant thorn in the side of its southern neighbour. The marriage of Mary's aunt, Margaret Tudor, to James IV of Scotland as long ago as 1503 had not succeeded in bringing about a warmer relationship between the courts of Edinburgh and London, and both regarded each other with suspicion when not involved in outright hostilities. The creation of a Great Britain lay in the future.

The realm in 1553 was a hybrid of the Gaelic Irish, the Welsh and the English, but it was the voices of the English which were most often heard, and England was the centre of the monarch's power. It was home to just under three million people, a population that actually declined in the 1550s as the result of famine and deadly epidemics, though numbers recovered strongly by the end of Elizabeth's reign.[2] London, its largest city, had 60,000 inhabitants, but this was unimpressive by European standards; the population of Paris was three times greater. Nowhere else in Mary's kingdom came near to London in size – even at the end of the 16th century, Dublin was a small town of only 6,000 people.

Perhaps because it was small in both area and population, England had a long tradition of unified central government, and in this centrality lay the key to its identity. The country was defined by the things it had in common: its language, its laws and its coinage. In the provinces, local men might have the power to exercise the law, but the commands they enacted came from Westminster, where an assiduous civil service made sure that the justices of the peace and lords lieutenant of the shires knew what was expected of them. Only rarely, as with the East Anglian and Thames Valley risings in support of Mary, did the centre find itself challenged.

It was a strongly administered country, but one that had seen enormous change in the 20 years before Mary's accession. She herself had direct, uncomfortable experience of the impact of the religious upheaval and she now found herself head of a Church whose beliefs she did not share and whose leaders she despised. The Edwardian regime had moved much faster and much further than the majority of the population wanted. In reforming the liturgy it had removed a great deal that was familiar and deprived the congregation of what many of them saw as the mystery and beauty of the experience of worship. Cranmer and others believed passionately that the immediacy of God's word, rendered into English that all could understand, was far more beautiful than the ornaments, altarpieces and carvings that Edward's commissioners stripped from the churches. The religious processions, observance of saints' days, strict adherence to Lenten dieting and, above all, the inaccessibility of holy communion on a regular basis, all these things were viewed as detrimental to a godly society by the supporters of the new learning.

The changes had begun under Henry VIII but their acceleration between 1547 and 1553 was the result of legislation imposed from on high. It could not, in the space of just six years, banish the beliefs or customs of centuries. People were reluctant to break the law, but they resented what had been taken from them. Many still thought as Mary did. They did not view her, as so many historians have done, as going backwards, but as someone who could pick up again the interrupted pattern of religion in their daily lives. The transition for such people was easily achieved. As Lord Rich wrote, in respect of a kinsman who believed that he was not in favour with the queen: 'He is as willing as any man to hear mass.' And so were countless others.

If people's consciences were mobile, so was the society in which they lived. Mid-Tudor England saw much more movement, both up and down the social ladder, than has generally been realised. People did not stay in one place all their lives. They might not go any great distance, perhaps no more than five or ten miles from where they were born, but most moved at least once. Only the very rich or very poor migrated long distances. Those who did tended to leave the north and west for the more prosperous south and east of England, a trend that has not changed in 450 years. The cosy image of close-knit villages dotted over a rural landscape, where generations of the same family lived and died together, is a myth. Extended families were most unusual. Households generally consisted of a husband and wife, their children and their servants. To ensure that they were in a position to establish themselves independently, both men and women often waited until they were in their late twenties to marry. Given that life expectancy was only in the high thirties, death often parted couples before they had much time together.

England was an agrarian society but it was not a subsistence economy with a fixed peasantry. In the countryside as well as the towns, people made things that they could trade. Yet life was far from easy. Wide-scale enclosures, depriving the common people of their rights to forage and graze animals, had led to social unrest, as in the risings of 1549. Prices rose sharply during the reign of Henry VIII and the coinage had been several times debased, a combination that only increased hardship. Both of Mary's predecessors died in debt, mostly as a result of the expensive and inconclusive wars of the 1540s. All the wealth from the religious establishments that Thomas Cromwell had worked so hard to put in the Crown's coffers had been dissipated.

Beyond these man-made difficulties were other disasters that only God, it was believed, could influence. The vagaries of the weather were a constant concern, since failed harvests could cause starvation that decimated large areas of the country. Prolonged periods of torrential rain were a feature of Mary's reign, especially in the years 1554–6. Her future husband, Philip, arrived from the warm climate of Spain in July 1554 to be greeted when he landed at Southampton by pelting rain. The downpours did not let up for their wedding day, either. But the worse was yet to come. At the end of September 1555 the country experienced 'the greatest rains and floods that ever were seen in England. The low countries in divers places were drowned, and both men and cattle. All the marshes near London ... and all the cellars with beers and wine and other wares and merchandise in them drowned also. The rains ... continued to March 18 [1556]: not ten days together fair.'[3]

Those spared by the weather might equally succumb to disease. Epidemics did not always follow bad harvests but their effects were just as devastating. In 1558, the year of Mary's own demise, a virus probably related to influenza caused one of the greatest losses of life in England in a single year since the Black Death.

Outsiders viewed Mary's England as an unattractive place to live. Physically, its countryside was pleasing enough and London, with its skyline of churches, impressive, but there were few other positive aspects. Visitors saw a land fractured by religious dissension, very much prey to its treacherous nobility and unstable climate. It was not, as one Spaniard discovered in 1554, a healthy environment. 'I am', reported Juan de Bara-hona, 'full of furuncles and of the itch, the doctors tell me it is due to the. water, because I do not drink beer and now I drink water boiled with cinnamon, because the water of this country is very bad and becomes putrid in the stomach.'[4]

This was the reason why Englishmen consumed so much alcohol and spent far too long in taverns, a lifestyle that foreigners thought contributed to disorder and moral degeneracy. Scheyfve, the imperial ambassador, spoke for many observers when he noted that 'the subjects of this realm are wont to live in pleasure-seeking and intemperance, haunt taverns and become wholly idle and disorderly'.[5] Nicolaus Mameranus, an imperial commentator on his first visit to England, was shocked by the intemperance he witnessed. He proposed a sweeping remedy for this 'nuisance of public drinking, (introduced by Satan) by both sexes in public taverns'. The solution amounted to a prohibitive levy on anyone who drank just for the sake of drinking, by requiring them to pay the equivalent of what they spent on drink directly into the national coffers. 'This would be beneficial to the commonwealth and public salvation. Such ruinous disgrace exists nowhere else in Christen-dom and ought to be permitted in no Christian state.'[6]

Incorrigible as the lower orders were, the nobility were hardly any better. They were all 'ambitious, revengeful, seekers after novelties, inconstant, given to conspiracies, only held in check by fear of the sword'.[7] Not one of the new men raised up by her father spoke out in defence of Mary's claim or came to her aid. The old families, who supported the princess and her mother in the 1530s, had suffered, some-times with their lives, and seen their power and influence eroded. They disliked the upstarts as much as she did but, until now, were unable to raise their voices without fear of recrimination. Henry, Lord Stafford, the son-in-law of Margaret Pole, tried repeatedly to obtain some restitution from Northumberland that would help him pay off his debts, but got nowhere. He hoped for better things under Mary, and in his heartfelt letter to her of October 1553 he reminded her of all that his family had endured over two decades: 'I am bold to declare my state, remembering that my wife's friends chose death rather than consent to your disinher-itance in your tender years. I desire neither high authority nor dukedom, but the inheritance I was born to if malice had not defeated me … why should I despair, having so merciful a mistress, who daily restores right-ful heirs? Pardon me troubling you; consider the old saying, need and necessity have no laws.'[8] His petition resulted in his being granted one of the two offices of chamberlain of the exchequer four months later.

Yet there was a certain disingenuousness in Stafford's appeal to Mary which mirrors the complications of noble life in mid-Tudor England and also casts light on the queen's suspicions of those she might otherwise, in more stable times, have consulted with confidence. The baron had always been keen to keep on the good side of those who were in power. As a warm supporter of Somerset he supported religious change and would not receive his sister Elizabeth, the duchess of Norfolk, who had also risked much for Katherine of Aragon. And his two children were a dreadful embarrassment. Thomas led an unsuccessful invasion in 1557 and Dorothy, a committed Protestant, chose exile in John Calvin's Geneva rather than live under Mary Tudor. The queen did not restore Stafford to his executed father's dukedom of Buckingham, no doubt mindful of the long-standing uneasy relationship between the Crown and the Staffords. If she wanted guidance, she would have to look elsewhere. In fact, there were, in her mind, very few people she could trust in her unpredictable country. But govern it she must and, with God's help, she would make it a better place.

The picture of Mary as a woman who had little grasp of what was going on, who could not work with her politicians and was essentially run by her cousin, Charles V, is entirely false. From the very beginning, the queen had a clear idea of what she wanted to do and the utter determination to achieve it. She never, even when unwell, shrank from the business of government, and she knew that she must draw on the experience of the men who had tried to deprive her of her throne. Without their expertise, and their very real sense of duty to the Crown, nothing could function, and Mary recognised this from the outset. She did not like them and it is fair to say they probably did not like her, but their need was mutual. Her strong voice and personality, coupled with a notable temper at times, meant that she was no pushover, to be manipulated as they saw fit. On one occasion, she reduced William Paget to tears, something that her father never did. She was naturally outspoken and found it hard to hide her feelings. As queen, she was not obliged to curb her tongue lest she be hectored as she had been by her brother's privy council.

The most pressing priority for Mary was to re-establish the structure of orderly government. Uncertainty over the succession had distracted from the smooth running of affairs, and it was time to address the many issues of day-to-day administration, as well as putting down markers on key policies. On the day Mary was proclaimed, William Cecil, a councillor who she believed bore her little goodwill, set off to meet her at Ipswich, armed with a list of areas for early resolution. Whatever they thought of each other, the past could not be allowed to intrude into the demands of the present. Cecil had a veritable shopping list of matters of state, ranging from the burial of Edward VI (which had not yet taken place) to foreign policy, the economy, the restitution of law, the calling of Parliament and the coronation. There was, interestingly, no specific mention of religion. At the top of his agenda was the need to establish a council. He could have served on it if he had wished, but he declined the offer when it was made and returned to private life. His Protestantism was not of the strident kind, but it was deeply held, and he knew he would be uncomfortable working with Mary.

At the time of her proclamation, Mary had 21 councillors with her in East Anglia. They were her household officers and the leading local men who answered her summons for assistance. None of them had any experience of national government, and though they had been successful in putting Mary on the throne, they were not necessarily well qualified to run the country. Uncomfortable as it might be, only an injection of Edwardian councillors could supply the continuity that the government must have if it was to function effectively and without challenge. By mid-August more than a dozen of them had been nominated. At the same time, various opponents of her brother's policies, churchmen and aristocrats like Gardiner and Norfolk, were also added, swelling the total to 44.

Much was made at the time – and has been subsequently – of the unwieldiness of such a large group of councillors. How could they possibly be effective, especially since many of them could not stand each other, and what might be expected of people like Robert Rochester and the country knights, men who had never functioned at this level before? The answer, like much to do with Mary's reign, is not the most obvious one. The council soon split into two groups, a smaller core of about 20, with regular attendees who handled much of the responsibility, and a wider circle whose presence was much less frequent. Mary could not deprive those who had served her so loyally, and she was faced with their complaints at the injustice of finding themselves sharing power with men who had tried to keep her off the throne. Lord Derby confided in the imperial ambassadors that there was discontent among those who had stood by the queen in her days of adversity, because she had 'admitted so readily to the council those who conspired against her life'.[9] But the first councillors felt, with considerable justification, that the assumption that they had no skills to bring to government was insulting. Rochester was clearly a superb organiser who knew how to call on public support. He had delivered for Mary in a way that completely outclassed anything that the Edwardian councillors achieved in respect of the unfortunate Jane Grey. So he held firm, as one of the inner core.

Paget, Arundel and their colleagues from the previous government, on the other hand, were determined to ignore the past. Like Edward, it was dead and gone. They saw service to the Crown as something to which they had committed their lives, and were pragmatic about whom they served. Confident in their ability, quick to exploit opportunities, they emphasised moving forward. They would compromise where necessary, but only to get their way. Stephen Gardiner, appointed Lord Chancellor shortly after his release from the Tower of London, was a more difficult proposition than the Marian household officers, and tensions inevitably arose. But though he and Paget detested one another, and had done since Paget's abandonment of his former mentor under Henry VIII, the impact of their feuding has been overemphasised.

They appeared to have drifted far apart, these two doughty survivors of Mary's father. Yet their mutual antipathy seemed more serious than was actually the case. It may have been a distraction but it was not automatically an impediment to getting things done. They had more in common than either felt inclined to admit. Both had supported, over many years, a pro-imperial policy, and neither fully enjoyed the queen's confidence. Gardiner's political career was made by his role in the divorce of Katherine of Aragon, when he was sent on mission to Rome by Henry, who expected him to manage the presentation of his case so as to bring about the pope's acquiescence. He failed, but his endeavours and the subsequent support he gave to the idea of the royal supremacy over the Church in England earned him a prominent place among Henry's advisers. None of this endeared him to Mary, but as his fortunes changed, and his disputes with Archbishop Cranmer grew, her opinion of him seems to have modified. Gardiner quarrelled with the reformers throughout the bitterly disputed struggle for power in the 1540s, and under Edward this theme continued, leading to his incarceration in the Tower. He paid for his refusal to accept the new religious legislation with the loss of his liberty, and Mary acknowledged his steadfastness during these difficult times when she raised him to the Lord Chancellorship, but he was never really her man. Gardiner was still more politician than theologian. Mary was soon to discover that, when it came to the question of her marriage, his views were quite different from her own.

Paget's Catholicism was less public but it was the faith that he embraced. In his mind, it bound the people of England together more effectively than Protestantism, and for that reason above all he supported its restitution. Mary remained unenthusiastic about him, lumping him in her mind with the other new men of her father's time, raised up from nothing to assume the greatest offices of the land. But no one could deny his experience, his linguistic ability or his diplomatic skills. The queen knew she could not rule without his input, even if she found him distasteful. He was as committed to the Habsburg connection as she was, and his vision for England's international role was the closest to Mary's of any councillor.

Most of the criticisms of the privy council came from the imperial ambassador, Simon Renard, who had no direct knowledge of how its business was actually transacted and wanted to represent it to Charles V in the worst possible light. He thought the chancellor and Paget were both flawed. For him, Gardiner was too inclined to find an English solution for everything, ignoring the might and influence of the emperor. His view of Paget was even less flattering, and he delighted in depicting the minister as a greedy chancer who wanted only financial reward. This misrepresentation was fuelled by unwarranted ambassadorial pride. Renard's ability to get along with Paget was compromised from the start of his mission by the coolly perceptive but cruel warning of the bishop of Arras that 'he [Paget] is more than a match for you'. Renard, who had a high opinion of himself, did not take the hint. More generally, he interpreted personal friction, which certainly did exist among Mary's advisers, as a sign that the council was incapacitated. It was not. Discussion and debate, however heated, did not equate to debilitation. There had been many and frequent arguments among councillors in the two preceding reigns. Perhaps the most remarkable thing about Mary's council is how well, not how badly, it worked.

She was determined that it should, and that she must swallow her

doubts and establish herself as its head. On 16 August, the imperial representatives were evidently irritated to find their audience with the queen
postponed, because Mary was so heavily involved in council meetings
that if she had tried to fit them in as well she would have lost the tide
that would take her down to Richmond. They viewed Mary's dealings
with the council in an entirely negative light, evidently assuming that
the queen was completely under the thumb of these 'inconstant and
variable' men. 'We perceive by the evidence of our own experience and
by the messages she sends us that she places herself so much under the
authority of her council that she does not grant any except public audiences.'[10] But the assertion they went on to make, that she was afraid of
her advisers, is unsubstantiated. It did not occur to Renard and his
colleagues that Mary might have her own reasons for wanting to appear
transparent in her handling of important matters of state, or that she
could believe that her authority would be enhanced by working with
the council rather than marginalising it. Too many private audiences
with diplomats in these weeks immediately after her accession sent out
the wrong messages. She soon demonstrated that when she wanted to
keep things to herself, she would do so without any fear at all.

Queen and council had much to absorb their attention in these early
weeks of the reign. The state of the economy, the conduct of foreign
policy, the question of religion – all vied as issues for immediate consideration and action. At the same time, the coronation must be arranged,
with appropriate ceremonial and imagery, Parliament called and the
royal household established. The council could advise, but nothing could
be undertaken without Mary's consent. In this strongly patriarchal
society, 20 men had to learn how to deal with a woman as monarch for
the first time. But there was no real time to agonise over what it might
mean, and Mary's gender was not viewed as a barrier to getting things
done, except, interestingly, by her cousin Charles V and the imperial
diplomats. There was much to be learned, and quickly, on all sides, but
the first impressions of Mary's intentions were very positive.

By early September significant moves were being made to get the
finances of the house of Tudor back into good order. A proclamation
fixing the value of newly minted gold and silver coins and the publication of their comparative value with the much-adulterated coinage of

Edward VI produced an immediately beneficial effect, lowering prices by one-third. And on top of this, Mary repaid the debts of her father and brother, which greatly strengthened public goodwill. 'No one', commented the imperial ambassadors, 'expected so much … the publication came very opportunely and will turn many an old servitor, minister, officer, besides merchants, bankers, captains, pensioners, soldiers and others, who had no expectations of the kind and hoped nothing from the queen, from their tendencies to evil.' In general, the public mood could not be better: 'The people … are full of hope that her reign will be a godly, righteous and just one, and help to establish her firmly on the throne.'[11]

For Mary personally, however, an equally pressing concern was religion. The queen heard the advice that was being given from all sides, that she should be circumspect in her approach to undoing the changes of her brother's reign, particularly as Protestant opinion in London itself was strong and there were outbreaks of violence when the mass was reintroduced. But family matters intruded and played on her conscience. Edward's funeral had not yet taken place and she was swayed from her plans to bury her brother using Catholic rites only with considerable difficulty. The part of her that had always thought of him as her godson and a little boy was hard to suppress. He might be dead, but she knew what was best for him, what his soul needed. In life, she was convinced that he had been the tool of schemers who wanted to use religion for their own ends. She could never accept that his beliefs were as deeply held as hers, and she wanted his funeral to be her final gift to him, the expression of her love and desire to return him to the religion in which he had been born. It was what propriety and her father's will demanded, she told the dismayed Simon Renard. 'It would too sorely violate her conscience to allow the late king, her brother, to be buried otherwise than as religion dictated, for she was bound by the late King Henry's will, in which he left instructions for masses and prayers to be said.' If she had got her way it would, of course, have also been a very public, stinging blow to the Protestant cause, and her own words show how much she understood that aspect. 'If she appeared to be afraid, her subjects, particularly the Lutherans, would only become more audacious, and would proclaim that she had not dared to do her own will. She was determined to tell the council that she was going to have a mass said at the funeral'.

But others demurred and eventually prevailed on the queen to think again. At a time when there was still concern about her hold on the crown, those around her thought it was a step too far. She had already been compelled, before she even reached London, to issue a proclamation for the suppression of false rumours, the 'light, seditious or naughty talk' that was still circulating.[12] So a compromise was reached, whereby Edward was buried in Westminster Abbey following Protestant liturgy. The service, on 8 August, was presided over by Cranmer and the bishop of Chichester. With the marquess of Winchester as his chief mourner, Edward was laid to rest, while his sister salvaged her troubled conscience by hearing a requiem mass in St Peter's chapel, in the Tower of London.

In other respects, her first pronouncements on religion indicated moderation. While arguing for Edward to be buried in the observances of the old religion, she also told Renard 'she wished to force no one to go to mass, but meant to see that those who wished to should be free to do so'. She went on to tell him that she would soon issue a public proclamation to that effect, though he noted her emotional attachment to the Holy Sacrament that was kept on an altar in her chamber. Nor did she hide it in the wording of the proclamation itself.

This was issued from Richmond on 18 August and, as Mary's first official pronouncement on religion, it was carefully scrutinised. The wording, which was probably drafted by Gardiner, combines the queen's personal affirmation of her faith with a more pragmatic and − for the 16th century − surprisingly tolerant outlook towards those whose views differed from her own:

... Her majesty, being presently by the only goodness of God settled in the just possession of this realm ... cannot now hide that religion which God and the world knoweth she hath ever professed from her infancy hitherto, which as her majesty is minded to observe and maintain for herself by God's grace during her times, so doth her highness much desire and would be glad the same were of all her subjects quietly and charitably embraced.

Though some, she realised, would not follow her example: 'And yet she doth signify unto all her majesty's said loving subjects that of her most gracious disposition and clemency her highness mindeth not to compel any her said subjects thereunto until such time as further order by common assent may be taken therein'. She closed by commanding everyone 'to live in quiet sort and Christian charity'.

The sting of this proclamation was in its tail. Mary had signalled the direction in which she would go by leaving open the door for further, more direct steps to be taken in the restoration of Catholicism. There was to be no sweeping change imposed just yet, but the impression remained that this was an interim measure, not the end of the story. Other measures spelled out the likely direction. A crackdown on 'those without sufficient authority to preach and to interpret the word of God' was reinforced by a ban on the 'playing of interludes and printing of false fond books, ballads, hymns and other lewd treatises in the English tongue'. The wording may sound quaint, but the intention was clear. Protestantism was equated with sedition. This link was established early and continued throughout Mary's reign.

Nor was this all. The queen had already gone one step further than anyone, even the imperial ambassadors who clung to her so closely, knew. She was already in correspondence with the pope, asking him to lift the edicts that had been imposed when her father broke away from Rome, as a precursor to the full restoration of papal authority. At the beginning of August, a rather startled Julius III received her announcement of her accession, and the first notification that Mary intended to give up her title as head of the Church of England. In fact, he was so taken aback by this personal contact that for a while he did very little about it, beyond sending a cardinal to London with instructions to find out what was actually happening there. The pope's response was cautious but the reaction of Mary's cousin, Reginald Pole, the son of her old lady governess, was one of boundless joy. He wrote to Julius III at the beginning of August: 'I cannot delay congratulating your Holiness until the receipt of further intelligence, the nature of the event appearing to me such that since many years nothing has occurred in Christendom on which one could more reasonably congratulate a Christian mind … and God of his goodness … has chosen to annihilate all these long cherished projects by means of a woman who for so many years has suffered contrary to all justice'.[13]

He had been away many years himself, and scarcely knew the country he left behind in 1532. Margaret Pole's third, cleverest son was now more Italian than English, both in outlook and appearance. Yet though he had spent such a long time in the service of Rome, he signally failed to seize the chance of the papacy which so nearly became his in 1549, following the death of Pope Paul III. Whether through too much complacency or a lack of political skill, he was outfoxed by the Italian cardinal Giovanni del Monte, who became pope as Julius III. Disliked and distrusted by both the French and the Habsburgs, Pole found his career seemingly going nowhere until his distant cousin, Mary Tudor, achieved the apparently impossible and became queen of England. Suddenly, an entirely different prospect opened up, and he hastened to remind the new queen of the sufferings of his family, the Poles, which her father had sought to exterminate. 'Her majesty will perceive', he wrote to Mary, 'that the beginning and cause of all the evil … placed in the heart of the king her father [was] the perverse desire to make the divorce from the queen her mother.' No doubt Mary did perceive it that way, but she may not have known that Reginald Pole had certainly not stood out against the divorce initially and had actually undertaken missions on Henry's behalf to facilitate it. So his subsequent assertion that he had risked his life in Katherine and Mary's defence was a convenient rewriting of his past, a talent that he possessed in considerable measure. He exhorted her to obedience to the Church, something in which she needed little encouragement, and closed by expressing his wish to come at once to England. But he was to be thwarted in this desire by the emperor and by English politicians, who were not keen to see him back on English soil. Eighteen months would pass before he returned as Mary's archbishop of Canterbury, by which time she had put in place most of the central pillars of her religious policy without him.

The evidence suggests that Mary's own view of religion in England when she came to the throne was in the course of development. Her anxiety to be rid of the title of head of the Church may have been as much psychological as devotional. Its connotations with the outcome of the divorce, with her own troubles in the 1530s and, above all, with her father were very uncomfortable. As with the declaration of her own bastardy, something that troubled her greatly and could not be undone except through Parliament, Mary wanted to cleanse her past. But this does not mean that she wanted to turn back the clock to the way religion had been practised in 1529. She had been educated by those who believed in the need for reform in Catholicism and seems to have been perfectly comfortable with many aspects of the Henrician settlement. It was the attempt to impose the much more radical ideas of the reformers under her brother that she had opposed, not the religious framework Henry VIII bequeathed in 1547. The mass satisfied the core of her own spiritual needs, enveloping her in its central mystery of the real presence of Christ. To deny that miracle was to her the greatest heresy of all. She could not understand those who believed otherwise. She cared nothing for what they called themselves: sacramentarians, Lutherans, Calvinists, Zwinglians, any of the still-splintering sects that were bundled together under the catch-all term of Protestant, they were simply unbelievers to Mary and to countless other Englishmen. Hundreds of years would pass before the notion of respecting those who held different ideas became accepted or admired. Mary was a 16th-century woman. She did not think as we do.

Her policies on religion were still evolving in the autumn of 1553. There had been little time to develop a detailed template and she could not ignore the pressing needs of establishing herself as queen. Shortly after her coronation, she wrote to her cousin Cardinal Pole, dashing his hopes of immediate, wholesale change. Acknowledging their kinship (he was, she wrote, 'joined to her by nature'), she nevertheless realised the need to proceed with care, describing 'what pain the queen feels from being as yet unable by any fitting means to manifest the whole intent of her heart in this matter'.[14]

But some of the policies she would pursue were already well formed in her mind. She wanted a more literate clergy, who could inspire the people through good sermons. This had long been felt to be a notable weakness of the Catholic Church in England. At parish level priests were often ill educated and they were not trained to engage their congregations through the power of preaching. The success of the Protestants in this respect was plainly seen. To compete, Mary's clergy must be supplied with material that they could use in the preparation of their own sermons. The printing press, that tool of the seditious, could also be used to propound effectively the ideas of an English Catholicism. Time was taken in preparation, but the Marian period produced a substantial body of homilies and reference material, much of it from the pen of Edmund Bonner, the bishop of London. It was printed by the queen's printer, Robert Caly, from his press in St Paul's churchyard.

Mary also felt strongly about married priests. Her disapproval has been equated with sexual prudery, but this seems too modern an interpretation. It was a distaste that her sister Elizabeth shared, but she has not been criticised for it in such highly coloured terms. Marriage to Mary was an institution blessed by God, and one for which she had great reverence, like all people of her time. But it was not appropriate for priests because it destroyed the uniqueness of their relationship with

God. In that sense, perhaps, she did consider that married priests were defiled, but this does not mean that she nursed lurid fantasies of what went on in priestly bedrooms. The importance she attached to the mass in her daily life meant that she expected complete moral purity in those who administered it. No action was taken in the first nine months of the reign, but in March 1554 Mary issued an instruction ordering every bishop 'to deprive or declare deprived, and remove according to their learning and discretion, all such persons from their benefices or ecclesiastical promotions, who contrary to the ... laudable custom of the church, have married and used women as their wives'.[15] Among those affected by this pronouncement was the 67-year-old archbishop of York, who wrote in bewilderment asking what he should do with his wife, whom he had married only a few years earlier because, he claimed, of pressure from the Edwardian authorities.

But Mary accepted reluctantly, as she informed Reginald Pole, that she could not move too fast. Her advisers were even more concerned about the implications of swift religious change. Some Protestants might wait and see what she would do but others were eager to make their opposition apparent from the first days of her rule. Simon Renard believed that much of this disaffection stemmed from foreign radicals who lived in London: 'Frenchmen, Germans and Flemings exiled and thrust out of their own countries for heresy and other crimes'. Such troublemakers evidently feared that they would now be compelled to leave the country and 'would do nothing except seek opportunities for troubling the queen's reign'.[16] When he gave Mary this opinion, she may well have wondered how someone so recently arrived in England could really know about the frame of mind of its overseas inhabitants. Her own account of the situation was more detailed and accurate than Renard's. She was, she said, well aware of the situation in London and even that one of her own guard had cursed Bishop Gardiner. Security was the responsibility of the appropriate authorities. She had left the mayor and aldermen of London to deal with 'the administration of justice, the police and the maintenance of peace among her subjects'. Until Parliament was called, she would not constrain any of her subjects on matters of religion. This was certainly what the anxious imperialists, afraid that a bombastic approach to religious change might jeopardise a fragile monarchy, wanted to hear. It was not by any means a statement of personal belief. Mary could be pragmatic when the situation demanded it.

· ❖ ·

The reminder that there was a substantial and vocal foreign element in London was unnecessary. Mary was already thinking about the international situation and the importance of diplomatic affairs. There was a flurry of activity about the appointment of an ambassador to France at the end of July, before Mary reached London. This indicates the queen's determination to establish her authority with the French, who had been too close to Northumberland, and to take the initiative in Anglo-French relations in a positive way. Sir Anthony St Leger was sent on a special mission to announce Mary's accession to the French court. When he arrived at Compiègne he found the French willing to play their part in observing the diplomatic niceties, reporting that Montmorency, the constable of France, 'received her majesty's letter very joyously'.[17] The French government was keen to extricate itself from any suspicion of having backed the wrong claimant; Henry II sent new credentials to Antoine de Noailles on 29 July. The day after her triumphant entry into London, Mary received Noailles, together with the French ambassador to Scotland. Noailles, with a charming touch of Gallic gallantry, duly reported in his account of the meeting that Mary and her ladies had been grandly dressed in cloth of gold and bright colours, with very large sleeves in the French fashion. His comments show that Mary knew how to look like a queen, as well as act like one. A few days later, the French ambassador was invited to dine at the Tower with the council. He evidently appreciated these attempts to include him, but though he may have welcomed assurances from Gardiner and Paget that Mary wanted peace with France, he was less convinced by their pronouncement that she would not favour her Habsburg relatives over France.[18]

Noailles himself had been in England only since May 1553, but though his position might seem difficult, he was well provided for by his government, with plenty of money at his disposal and a network of spies and messengers who kept him informed. He was also in close touch with d'Oysel, the ambassador to Scotland, who could give moral support and supply information from his own sources. He clearly was not in a position to influence Mary, nor was he expected to; the main part of his brief was to protect French interests, particularly if they were threatened by closer ties between England and the empire. And he could, through careful management of his agents, influence what was happening in England. As the autumn turned to winter in 1553, his ability to manipulate would become much more apparent.

French concerns over Mary's preferences in Europe were under-standable, and her partiality for the imperialists has been noted ever after. The queen's dependency, so the argument runs, started in her formative years when Charles V became her putative father, continued under various imperial ambassadors, notably Eustace Chapuys and Simon Renard, and reached its height when she married Philip of Spain. In this interpretation, Mary appears as a woman constantly being used by others, trapped by her own emotions and inexperience in a pattern of behaviour that deprived her of any independence of thought, and out of tune with the interests of England. While it cannot be denied that the emperor's main interest in Mary had always been political rather than personal, she was still a member of his family, and dynasty was a concept that overrode everything else with Charles V. He treated his sisters and his daughters in the same way, as extensions of his own power and surro-gates for him in the government of his huge territories. And it was true that he had been the only figure outside her household who took a sustained interest in Mary's life and whose views, particularly on religion and society, matched her own. Theirs was a shared heritage and it was inconceivable that Mary should have wanted to distance herself from it. It is equally a mistake to dismiss her as having no background in inter-national affairs. Much of her life had been spent on the European stage, as the discussions about her marriage ebbed and flowed over the years. She did not take any direct part in the conduct of diplomacy until she became queen but she was a well-informed, if not impartial, observer.

The Anglo-Habsburg alliance, so often described as being damaging to England's international prospects and emerging nationhood, was nothing new. In fact, it was a key element of the foreign policy of Henry VII, Mary's grandfather, and though Henry VIII had stretched imperial patience, he fought wars with England's traditional enemies, France and Scotland, never with Charles V. Mary's desire to align herself with her cousin was a product of continuity, not of regression. But it did also have, for her, a very strong element of loyalty and gratitude. Though a monarch in her own right, she clearly never thought of herself as his equal. She was thrilled when he wrote her letters in his own hand, which apparently he had seldom done before.[19]

Charles V was ruler of much of the Western world in 1553, and Mary's unexpected accession offered him unforeseen possibilities for shoring up his influence in north-western Europe. Yet his cousin's success was a cause for relief rather than unbridled enthusiasm. It removed the threat that England would side with the French, a cause of concern when Edward VI was king, and it opened up the possibility that both the queen and her sister might make useful marriages. Precisely how this might be taken forward would have to wait until after the coronation, but the manoeuvring had already begun. There were candidates both in England and in his own family but, for the moment, the emperor was content not to reveal his hand fully, to anyone. His attention to matters of state depended on his health; more than 30 years of the inescapable demands of warfare and government had reduced him to a physical wreck. The onset of autumn made those around him anxious, knowing the dismal prospects he faced in the cold winters of Brussels. He had gout in every limb, nerve and joint of his body, even the back of his neck. Catarrh meant that he often could not speak and, when he did, he could hardly be heard. Haemorrhoids, it was reported, 'swell and torment him so much that he cannot turn without great pain and tears'. He might be the most powerful man in Europe, but he longed for respite from all these afflictions and the severe depression that accompanied them. This had 'altered his character', and he was often sunk in a melancholy that neither of his sisters, Mary of Hungary and Eleanor of France, could alleviate.[20] Their cousin, who had suffered much herself, was now queen of England, and this provided some small comfort. But it could not disguise the fact that the Habsburg family endured, rather than enjoyed, power.

Mary was aware that Charles suffered from gout, but she probably did not know the full extent of his woes or that business ground to a halt when his health was especially bad. Her memory of him was that of her early childhood, when he was young and vigorous. He was her family and her natural ally; their interests were not always identical but in matters of international importance she was always likely to follow his lead. She needed no encouragement from his ambassadors. Yet Simon Renard, who did not set foot in England till early July and who had no knowledge of the country other than that gleaned from conversations with Scheyfve, was never shy of giving advice to the queen on every aspect of her policy, both national and European. Just how much faith she put in him is not easy to determine, since he was very good at self-promotion and it suited his interests to represent Mary as leaning heavily on him for all sorts of guidance and information. It is clear from the evidence of her own handwritten notes that she did talk to him frequently during the autumn of 1553. These meetings were often, but not exclusively, private, and this has led to the assumption that he was leading her rather than the other way round, but then this is the impression that he wanted to convey when he wrote back to Brussels. There is probably very little that he introduced into their conversations that did not match the way her own thoughts were already developing, even when these encompassed Tudor, as well as Habsburg, family matters. And it was here that he probably did the most lasting damage.

Simon Renard's suspicions of the queen's sister, still not officially given the title of princess, were voiced early and often. It is easy to understand his fears. Elizabeth did not share Mary's religious beliefs and her status as 'second person' in the realm, even if never officially recognised by Mary, meant that she would always be attractive to disaffected persons, whether the French (in whose camp she might already be) or to home-grown rebels. She was young, carried herself with supreme confidence, and was good-looking. But it was mostly her cleverness which worried Renard. Within two weeks of Mary's entry into London, he reported that he had raised with the queen 'the presence at court of the Lady Elizabeth, who might, out of ambition or being persuaded thereto, conceive some dangerous design and put it to execution, as she was clever and sly'. Elizabeth's position had actually been mentioned as part of a wider discussion about what to do with Lady Jane Grey, whose own fate was now in Mary's hands. The queen told Renard 'that she was about to send the Lady Elizabeth away, as the same considerations had occurred to her'.[21] No doubt they had, yet Elizabeth did not leave court for more than three months. Mary seems to have had mixed feelings about letting her go, and her attitude towards her sister remained inconsistent. The part of the queen that had always sought to dominate her brother Edward felt that it was better to have the young woman at court, where she could be supervised. This proprietorial view was accompanied by the hope that Elizabeth could be genuinely brought back to Catholicism and that she was not ill intentioned.

But Renard would have none of it. His dislike of Elizabeth leaps off the pages of his dispatches, and he was determined to poison the relationship between the sisters. Maybe he saw a potential rapprochement as a threat to his own influence. He was a man who trusted no one and saw plots everywhere. Elizabeth had her own following and the danger she posed should not be discounted. The safest course was to assume the worst:

It would appear wise in your majesty not to be too ready to trust the Lady Elizabeth and to reflect that she now sees no hope of coming to the throne [a dubious assertion], and has been unwilling to yield about religion, though it might be expected of her out of respect for your majesty and gratitude for the kindnesses you have shown her, even if she had only done so to accompany you. Moreover, it will appear that she is only clinging to the new religion out of policy, in order to win over and make use of its adepts in case she decided to plot. A mistake may perhaps be made in attributing this intention to her, but at this early stage it is safer to forestall than be forestalled, and to consider all possible results ...[22]

Whatever the queen's doubts, she was not immediately swayed by Renard's advice, and Gardiner believed that Elizabeth would come round in religious matters. Aware that the imperialists were depicting her in a very bad light, Elizabeth appealed directly to Mary: 'Perceiving that the queen did not show her as kindly a countenance as she could wish ... she besought the queen to grant her a private audience ... the queen did not do so at once; but two days later ... the Lady Elizabeth approached the queen and knelt down on both knees; weeping, she said she saw only too clearly that the queen was not well-disposed towards her, and she knew of no other cause except religion.' She went on to point out that she had 'never been taught the doctrine of the ancient religion', and she asked Mary to send her books and 'a learned man ... to instruct her in the truth'.

This sounded very promising, but, as always with Elizabeth, there was equivocation. She would undertake this study so that 'she might know if her conscience could allow her to be persuaded'. Renard believed that this was all an act and reported that when Elizabeth did attend mass, she 'complained loudly all the way to church that her stomach ached' and 'wore a suffering air'.[23] He does not say whether he personally witnessed this display of reluctance, but his reports of what passed between the Tudor sisters in private are either based on detailed revelations from Mary herself, or fabricated. The former interpretation seems the most likely, but the level of detail sometimes given by Renard may at least be embroidered. Nor was he winning the battle against Elizabeth at this point. He believed that she had 'converted' because some members of the council, presumably Gardiner and Paget, had warned her that to do otherwise would mean that she had to leave court. Mary does seem to have been persuaded, even if Renard continued to stoke her own misgivings. There was no question of Elizabeth being sent away before the coronation, in which she was given a prominent role.

Some of the ambassador's dark suspicions may have had to do with his feelings of insecurity about his own position, which he was desperate to regularise. His anxieties would have struck a chord with many in the diplomatic fraternity, though imperial stinginess over financial provision was worse than most. Whatever impression he tried to give Mary and Paget, the minister with whom he had the most direct dealings, he was far from happy when the instruction came from Brussels in late September that he was to continue in the London posting alone. No one had thought about his family and his salary was woefully inadequate. He had, he pointed out, been sent to London suddenly, suffering from ill health, and 'did not provide myself with a secretary, servants or furniture' because he had thought, at the time, he would be gone only for four to six weeks. 'I have a wife and children at Brussels and did not set my private affairs in order before leaving,' he wrote to the emperor. 'Besides which I owe a great deal of money having received no payment for 16 months as your majesty's councillor … Moreover, Sire, I have no money here, and no means of getting any as I possess no credit or friends; … your majesty's letter makes no mention of pay, stipend or any provision whatsoever.'

His pleas did not go unheeded. The emperor wrote at the beginning of the next month that he was, indeed, to stay – there could be no negotiation on that point. His salary up to the end of 1553 would be sent to him, though there would be no increase beyond what was normally paid to ambassadors in England. And he did get the money owed to him from the Burgundian post he held. Beyond that, no decision had been taken about how long he would stay. Charles V knew that Renard's tenure in London was increasingly likely to depend on Mary herself.

While Simon Renard worried about his own household, he could do little to affect the formation of Mary's personal establishment, beyond being asked to convey the emperor's concerns that some of her ladies were using their position to dispense too much influence. 'If you have an opportunity of speaking to her without her taking it in bad part, you might give her to understand that people are said to murmur because some of her ladies take advantage of their position to obtain certain concessions for their own private interest and profit.'[24] These women were clearly more canny than their image, largely derived from the negative comments of Spanish visitors, suggests. Unattractive, over-dressed ladies of a certain age most of them may have seemed to outsiders, but they adapted with great alacrity to the privileges that came with their new-found status. We do not know whether Renard found a tactful way to pass on his master's reproofs, but Mary's household had been on the outside looking in for so long that it is hardly surprising that some took advantage. Their behaviour was no different from that of courtiers down through the ages, but the fact that women could operate so blatantly was viewed with disapproval. That it was known so soon after Mary's accession across the North Sea indicates a high level of resentment, but Charles V did not reveal his source of information.

The truth was that Mary's household, and especially her privy chamber, was a preserve where the queen would brook no interference. Below stairs, the establishment remained much as it had in her brother's reign, and overall the household was not remodelled on the basis that a queen regnant would have different needs from a king. But in the queen's privy chamber, her personal domain, where she sought relief from the pressures of ruling, as well as companionship and security, there was a complete revolution. This traditional preserve of male intimacy became female dominated very quickly after the accession. The main posts were filled in a matter of weeks and they all went to women. Mary had three levels of female servants who supported her on a daily basis, away from the prying eyes of diplomats and politicians: ladies, gentle-women and chamberers. The ladies, who numbered about half a dozen at different times of the reign, included Lady Anne Petre, Lady Eleanor Kempe (a long-serving attendant), Lady Frances Jerningham and Lady Frances Waldegrave. The latter two were the wives of existing members of Mary's household, so their commitment to Mary was well established, though in the case of the Waldegraves that loyalty was put to the test when the queen came to consider the question of marriage. Lady Petre, the wife of former privy council secretary William Petre, had enter-tained the queen during the difficult days of Edward's reign, as her husband owned estates in Essex not far from Mary's. Though this hospi-tality was intended to keep an eye on Mary, she does not seem to have resented Anne Petre at all, and perhaps derived some enjoyment from her company. She would surely not have employed her otherwise. Anne

Petre was the second wife of one of the more notable political survivors of mid-Tudor England. Herself a widow when she married him, Lady Petre probably found herself able to aid her husband through her appointment, though his experience meant that Mary could scarcely have done without him. Not much is known about the others. Frances Jerningham was married by 1536, but this does not mean that she was necessarily much older than Mary, and Frances Waldegrave was a few years younger than the queen.

Those closest to the queen, who had known her longest and never left her side through all the difficult years, were to be found among the eleven gentlewomen of the privy chamber. Here Susan Clarencius, who had served Mary since the 1530s, presided with considerable power and influence. She was not officially appointed chief gentlewoman, but her power in this unspoken role was well understood throughout Mary's reign. Her main importance was that she controlled access to Mary. Born Susan White in Essex, she may already have been widowed when she joined Mary. He husband, Thomas Tonge, held a variety of heraldic posts, though it was his last, Clarenceux king of arms, which gave his wife the 'surname' for which she became more commonly known. Her precise age at the time is uncertain, but she was probably at least six years older than her mistress. Susan Clarencius influenced Mary more than any other of her ladies, or so the imperialists thought. Certainly she did well in monetary terms during Mary's reign, receiving annuities, pensions and wardships of minors who had been left orphaned. She was also an acquisitive lady, constantly making demands of the Venetian ambassador, Michieli, for presents to be given to Mary which subsequently ended up as gifts to Mrs Clarencius herself. Michieli was clearly aggrieved when Susan brazenly asked for his own 'coach and horses and all their furniture' to be handed over to the queen. The coach had been specially made in Italy and Mary soon passed it on to Mrs Clarencius.[25] Susan's presence, always hovering in the background and often at the queen's right hand, could not be ignored by those who sought private audience. It is not surprising that she was one of only a handful of people who had keys to the privy apartments. But her judgement was not always good, and though she fussed over Mary, the evidence of her behaviour in 1555, when she was chief among those who raised false hopes of pregnancy in the queen, points to the fact that she was not the best choice of confidante. She was an overprotective servant rather than a trustworthy and objective adviser.

The best known of Mary's women was the young Jane Dormer, a girl of good looks and charm from a Buckinghamshire Catholic family that had long been close to the crown. As a child, Jane played with Edward VI, who was tutored by her grandfather, Sir William Sidney. She probably joined Mary in 1548, when Mary's East Anglian household was in the process of being established. Before that time, she had been brought up by her grandparents, her mother having died when she was only four. Jane's father, Sir William Dormer, remarried, but she did not stay with him. She would have been ten years old when she entered Mary's service, and this girl who had been a courtier from an early age grew up in the favoured environment of the princess's staunchly Catholic household. Jane was intelligent and accomplished as well as devoted to Mary. Contemporaries saw her as the jewel among Mary's gentlewomen and composed verses in her honour: 'Dormer is a darling and of such lively hue that who so feeds his eye on her may soon her beauty view.'[26] This, and her age and unmarried status, turned Jane Dormer into the star of Mary's court. Shortly after Mary's death, she made a splendid marriage to the Spanish count Feria, who acted as Philip's representative in England during the last months of Mary's life.

She was not, though, the only attractive woman in Mary's service. Anne Bacon was said to be comely as well as learned, and another of Mary's ladies, Frances Neville, was rather too familiarly addressed by the louche William Howard with the hearty greeting 'Come hither, thou pretty whore', which shows that Mary's court was not a strait-laced enclave of old crones who spent all their time attending mass and telling their rosaries.

Below the gentlewomen came the chamberers and the six maids of honour, the debutantes of their time, with a Mother of the Maids to chaperone them. There were only twelve males in this private environment, five gentlemen and seven grooms, but two of the important offices, that of chief usher and keeper of the privy purse, were deemed inappropriate for women. Mary did not consider that her women should act as doorkeepers or manage financial matters.

The extent of the influence of this group of 30 or so women is not easy to gauge. Their presence was the constant in Mary's life and, in many cases, they had been close to her for years. They were there with her when she rose for her first mass of the day at six in the morning and they prepared her for bed, very seldom before midnight, at the end of the day. Her dress, her toilette, her daily health, her preoccupations – all

were within their area of responsibility. It seems probable that she talked
to them freely on matters that touched her most deeply as an individual,
such as marriage, sex, religion and her relationship with her sister. The
lighter aspects of court life – culture, entertainment, her wardrobe, for
example – would also have been regular topics of conversation. We can
do no more than speculate about the ladies' role in policy-making or
whether the queen sought their views on weightier matters of government. Mary was good at keeping things to herself when she chose and
she could be imperious. She was never in any doubt that she was queen
and they were her servants, however much she cherished them, so it
would be unwise to read too much into their role.

And there were other ladies, not members of the household, but
equally close to Mary now she was queen, whose influence was regarded
as being of equal significance. One was Gertrude Courtenay,
marchioness of Exeter, who had seen her family all but wiped out
because of its support for Mary Tudor and her mother. At first, she
seemed to be rebuilding her prominent position rapidly. A plea directed
through Gertrude, so the duchess of Northumberland and others
thought, might incline the queen to mercy. Lady Exeter could not save
Northumberland himself, though it appears that she was instrumental in
the decision to spare his ally, the marquess of Northampton. But her
relations with the queen became strained after the coronation. The
reason was her son, Edward, whose suitability as a husband for Mary was,
by October 1553, being pushed much more openly. Gertrude naturally
supported his candidacy and Simon Renard believed that her influence
might sway Mary. The queen, however, had other ideas, and seems to
have resented Gertrude's stance on the matter. The resulting friction
made for a difficult atmosphere between the two women.

Another companion from long ago was much more fortunate.
Margaret Douglas, countess of Lennox, whom the queen had seen only
rarely since the end of her father's reign, became the most prominent
beneficiary of the queen's generosity. She was delighted to be able to
renew her patronage of her cousin, whom she had always loved and
whose religious beliefs she shared. Mary could scarcely contain her
desire to show favour to this still handsome woman, who had shared part
of her girlhood and whose companionship she could now enjoy again.
Margaret returned to court in magnificence. She was given apartments
at Westminster, provided with food and drink for her household and
attended the queen clad in splendid dresses and jewels, most of which

were recent presents from Mary. There was considerably more to come. Margaret was also granted revenues from the wool trade which made her a rich woman and, most tellingly of all, she was given precedence over Elizabeth at court, though only after the coronation had taken place. Her behaviour indicates that she considered this to be only right and proper. No question hovered over her legitimacy. She was a Tudor queen's daughter and it began to look as though she would be officially named as heiress presumptive. Elizabeth, already anxious about her place in Mary's affections, did not enjoy Margaret's elevation and the favours showered on her but she could not afford to be uncivil to her. Renard reported that he had attended a banquet with his fellow imperial ambassadors shortly before the other three returned to Brussels. The queen 'supped in hall' with them, while 'the music of hautboys, cornets, flutes, harps and dulcimers ceased not to play'. But the Lady Elizabeth and Margaret Douglas sat at a window, reduced, perhaps, to small talk.[27] Under the queen's eye but not allowed to share her regal repast, both the once flighty Margaret and the ambitious, discontented Elizabeth must have wondered about Mary's intentions.

So women played a major part in Mary's daily life as queen and she presided over this female world with a mixture of dependence and majesty. She could be almost embarrassing with her generosity but she expected loyalty and she defined what that loyalty meant. Views that ran counter to her own were not welcome. This was equally true of the wider household and the ceremonial posts, where men still dominated. Mary rewarded those who had put her on the throne, but her relationship with them was now on a different footing. Sir Edward Hastings, whose part in raising the Thames Valley to support her was so vital to her success, was made master-of-horse and the post was effectively upgraded, being answerable now directly to the queen herself. The earl of Arundel became great master and lord steward of the household, posts previously held by his arch-enemy, Northumberland. But despite his work in pushing the remnants of the council of Lady Jane Grey towards Mary, he was never close to the queen and soon became suspected of angling to marry his son to Elizabeth, which did not endear him. The earl of Oxford was given the revived, purely ceremonial post of Lord Great Chamberlain in recognition of his crucial conversion to Mary's claim. The posts of Lord Chamberlain and Vice Chamberlain, which carried more clout, went to Sir John Gage and Henry Jerningham respectively. Gage was nearly 80 years old and a long-standing servant of the crown. Jerningham, of course, was part of the East Anglian affinity. Sir Thomas Cheyney, the treasurer, was the only Edwardian household officer at this senior level to survive, and he was a Catholic.

The faithful, resourceful Robert Rochester was named comptroller of the queen's household, a post he had filled in the much more confined sphere of her establishment during Edward VI's reign. He was appointed Knight of the Bath just before her coronation. His rewards seem only just in view of what he had done for Mary, but his star was already beginning to wane and his relationship with the queen would become one of the most notable, and sad, casualties of the arguments already beginning about her marriage.

The two other members of the trio who had suffered confinement in the Tower for their mistress shared Rochester's devotion to her and his yearning for an English marriage. Waldegrave joined his wife in the royal household, as Keeper of the Great Wardrobe. Sir Francis Englefield had to wait longer, until the spring of 1554, before he received the office of Master of the Court of Wards and Liveries. He served Mary in Parliament, as a privy councillor and on various commissions, but, like Rochester and Waldegrave, his standing with her was never the same as it had been before she came to the throne. Mary expected unquestioning support in her household staff and when their opinions did not align with hers, a coolness developed that could not be overcome. This did not necessarily mean that their influence was gone altogether and, as personal conduits to the queen, Rochester and others were the recipients of many letters from people seeking favours, such as better treatment for prisoners. They did not, however, retain a significant role in policy-making at national level. Mary was, with the notable exception of her dealings with Archbishop Cranmer, less vengeful than her father, but she was the daughter of Henry VIII.

The establishment of a household was a pressing consideration before the coronation, but Mary had many other concerns. Her interests in education and culture and their wider impact on English life were very evident. One of her concerns was declining standards at the universities of Oxford and Cambridge, where Edward VI's visitations had imposed the new religious statutes but bitterly divided the academic community. Mary wanted an end to the subversion of the ancient statutes and ordinances of the university, which had, she wrote, led to 'youth loosely and insolently brought up'. Order was to be restored as quickly as possible and Stephen Gardiner, as chancellor of Cambridge, was instructed to implement her wish that 'the example may begin in our universities where young men and students joining godly conversation with their studies, may by their doings and preachings instruct the rest of our subjects in the knowledge and fear of God, in their obedience to our laws and all their other superiors and in their charitable demeanour'.[28]

The situation at Oxford was equally bad, and Mary provided financial support that had dried up during her brother's time. By the summer of 1554, it had borne good fruit, as Sir John Mason, the chancellor of Oxford, acknowledged:

> Many are supported by your help and gifts. We do not ask that you bestow anything on us, but that you accept the thanks we owe. Lately, when the study of letters was neglected, virtually extinct … some were compelled to forsake their studies, others were seized by the moment and no order was evident for a long time. With matters restored and prosperity, ancient learning and our forefathers' virtue recovered. You alone deemed it worthy to look after your Oxonians, and in hopeless times strove to preserve and increase our fortunes.

He went on to make the direct correlation between Renaissance humanist Catholicism and good learning: 'You direct your gifts that the worship of God and the authority of letters be increased. This is not commonplace; men were accustomed to look to religion, and only those educated in the arts encouraged learning – your majesty does both. While letters exist and these seats remain, your praises will be celebrated.'[29]

While Mary encouraged a healthier climate for learning, she also looked, in these early days, to bring culture and entertainment into her court. At the end of September, orders were given to the master of the revels for new costumes and props for the Gentlemen of the Chapel Royal, who were to give a play at the coronation. This was not actually performed, perhaps because time ran out, thought it does seem to have been given later, at Christmas. Apart from this slight hitch, all the other elements of Mary's coronation were in place by the time she left the Tower of London on 30 September, to make her state entry into London for the crowning, the high point of the first year of her rule, when she would pledge herself to God and to her people.

By mid-September 1553, preparations were well under way in London and at court for the greatest public spectacle of Mary's reign. The queen and Elizabeth arrived together by river at the Tower of London on 27 September, in preparation for the official entry into London on the last day of the month. They were attended by 'the Lord Mayor and Aldermen, and all the companies in their barges, with streamers and trumpets, and waits, shawmes and regals, together with great volley shots of guns, until her Grace came into the Tower, and some time after'.[30]

The coronation marked the high point of the sisters' relationship during the reign, as Mary give Elizabeth a prominent role in the proceedings. Whatever doubts she felt were put aside over this period in a display of dynastic unity, as Mary chose to show the world that her sister, too, was the daughter of a king. On 30 September they left the Tower to go to the palace of Westminster, riding in procession through the City of London. These kinds of events were superbly handled in Tudor England and were considered the visible signs of the monarch's magnificence and power, as well as providing the ordinary citizens with colour and excitement. There are several contemporary accounts, from English and foreign observers, describing the procession and the festivities that accompanied the occasion, which perfectly capture the richness and texture of the clothes and decorations worn: 'First went at the head many gentlemen of the court and kingdom, all arrayed with suits of silk with beautiful linings … then barons and princes, some wearing gold, others silver and many with horses decked in the same metal … some with embroidery which caused great admiration, not more by the richness of the substance than by the novelty and elegance of the device.'

The foreign merchants had also made sure that they were dressed for the occasion. The Italians wore 'suits of black velvet lined, beautifully trimmed with many points of gold and garnished all around with embroidery of more than a palm in width'. Not to be outdone, four Spanish cavaliers followed, 'attired in cloaks of mulberry coloured velvet lined with cloth of silver, with a very fine fringe of gold all about'.[31]

Amid all these gleaming textures, which were themselves a testament to the skill of London's tailors, who had been working overtime for weeks to meet the demands of those who needed to make a public statement of their wealth and style, the queen herself stood out as the one figure to whom all eyes turned. She sat in a chariot 'open on all sides save for the canopy, entirely covered with gold and horses trapped with gold'. She was a small but unmistakably superb figure, wearing 'a gown of purple velvet, furred with powdered ermines, having on her head a caul of cloth of tinsel, beset with pearl and stone, and above the same upon her head a round circlet of gold, beset so richly with precious stone that the value thereof was inestimable'.[32] Mary had tried to look every inch a queen, but there was one drawback. The sheer weight of the jewel-encrusted diadem caused her head to droop. She was compelled, it was reported, to hold her head up with her hands. So the impact of her otherwise queenly demeanour was considerably lessened.

Before her rode the old duke of Norfolk and the earl of Oxford, carrying the royal sword, while the Lord Mayor of London 'bore the sceptre of gold'. One of the four ladies, all clad in crimson velvet, who rode around the chariot was Norfolk's long-estranged duchess, Elizabeth Howard. She was 56 and he was over 80, but age had in no way taken the bitterness out of their relationship. It seems doubtful that they exchanged many words with each other on this occasion, and when the duke died the following year he left her nothing in his will.[33] The other ladies who shared Elizabeth Howard's honour in supporting the queen during the state entry were the marchioness of Exeter, the countess of Arundel and the marchioness of Winchester.

Immediately following were Elizabeth and Anne of Cleves, both wearing cloth of silver to match the trappings of their chariot. The only survivor of Henry VIII's queens had lived quietly for many years but Mary kept on good terms with her and the rejected fourth wife seems to have enjoyed her return to the limelight. Elizabeth, with her graceful bearing and natural rapport with the people, no doubt savoured the moment as much as anyone, as they passed under the many triumphal arches constructed for the occasion and gazed at the entertainments along the way.

In the space of only a few weeks, the organisers of the celebrations that surrounded the ancient ceremonial produced a marvellous series of displays and pageants, delighting the large crowds. There were dragons, giants and fountains that ran with wine, as well as choirs of children at several points along the route. The companies of foreign merchants resident in London vied to outdo each other with the ingenuity and richness of their floats. These were in the City of London and, from their descriptions, they would not have been out of place in a modern Lord Mayor's show: 'At Fenchurch was one pageant made by the Genovese, and there a child dressed in a girl's apparel was borne up by two men sitting in a chair, and gave the queen a salutation.' The Florentines, however, were determined to go one better. Their stand at Gracechurch Street was a magnificent edifice: '... very high, on the top whereof there stood three pictures, and on the side of them, on the highest top, there stood an angel clothed in green, with trumpet in his hand, and he was made with such a device that when the trumpeter, who stood secretly in the pageant, did blow his trumpet, the angel did put his trumpet to his mouth, as though it should be he that blew the same, to the marvelling of many ignorant persons'.[34]

Most impressive of all were the acrobatics of one Peter, a Dutchman, who stood on the weathercock of St Paul's 'holding a streamer in his hand five yards long, and waving thereof stood for some time on one foot shaking the other and then kneeled on his knees, to the great marvel of the people. He had two scaffolds under him, one above the cross, having torches and streamers set on it, and another over the ball of the cross, likewise set with streamers and torches which could not burn, the wind was so great.' Peter was well recompensed for these daredevil stunts atop St Paul's, being paid £16 13s 6d (nearly £4,000) by the City.[35]

As Mary passed, the conduits in Cornhill and in Cheapside ran with wine, and in St Paul's churchyard John Heywood, who had praised the beauty of the young princess Mary, sat under a vine and delivered an oration in Latin and English to mark the occasion. There was plenty to celebrate, despite the strong winds, and when the queen reached Whitehall she thanked the Lord Mayor for his pains and the City for the costs they had incurred.

The state entry had been impressively stage-managed and was undoubtedly joyous, but Mary did not do herself justice on formal occasions, appearing to be rather stiff and detached. She seems to have regarded appearing in public as a duty rather than a pleasure, and her natural shyness meant that she lacked her sister's easier manner. There had also been fears for her safety, perhaps overly dramatic, but she did not enjoy the same popularity in her capital as she did in East Anglia and other parts of the country. And there were other preoccupations as she considered the testing day that lay before her on 1 October. She had been exercised by a number of factors, great and small, in respect of the coronation, but the most fundamental of these was what it meant to rule.

While still at the Tower, she had summoned her council and involved them in an unprecedented outpouring of emotion, which shows how deeply she felt about her role and also throws light on her relationship with the councillors and what she expected of them.

> Sinking on her knees before them, [she] spoke at length of her coming to the throne, of the duties of kings and queens, her intention to acquit herself of the task God had been pleased to lay on her to His greater glory and service, to the public good and all her subjects' benefit. She had entrusted her affairs and person, she said, to them, and wished to adjure them to do their duty as they were bound by their oaths; and she appealed especially to her Lord High Chancellor [Gardiner], reminding him that he had the right of administration of justice on his conscience. Her councillors were so deeply moved that not a single one refrained from tears. No one knew how to answer, amazed as they were by this humble and lowly discourse, so unlike anything ever heard before in England, and by the queen's great goodness and integrity.

The cynical Renard, reporting this episode, wondered how some of these hardened political survivors, who were more accustomed to being physically assaulted by Henry VIII and tongue-lashed by Somerset and Northumberland during their conciliar service, would take Mary's behaviour. Would they interpret it as a sign of weakness and feminine insecurity? But he did not doubt that 'it had softened several hearts'.[36]

The queen's speech, though highly revealing of her deep and impassioned commitment, was also intended to dispel doubts and heal rifts at a sacred moment. She realised the need to bind her council to her and to each other just before the symbolic marriage with her country that she was about to make at Westminster Abbey. She may have hoped, rather than expected, that it would have a lasting effect, but her sincerity was obvious. The still-repeated view that Mary did not want to work with her councillors is not upheld by this heartfelt and very personal appeal.

But there were other things, both great and small, that troubled her. Of these, perhaps the most awkward was her illegitimacy, which could be overturned only by Parliament. Mary was distressed at the thought that by statute law she would still be a bastard when she became an anointed queen. There had been discussions about calling Parliament before the coronation, to remove this embarrassment, but the consensus was that Parliament should not be seen to be endorsing the queen's right to the throne, which was no proper part of its role. She was also very concerned about the morality of being crowned at a time when England was in schism, an anxiety that found its expression in a request for absolution to be given by Cardinal Pole for herself and all supporters of the old religion. Even the oil to be used for her anointing presented problems; that which had been used for her brother's coronation was tainted by its association with the Anglican rites and the queen wanted it replaced with holy oil that was pure and uncontaminated. So she sent to the bishop of Arras in Brussels for oil from the Low Countries, but it arrived only just in time.

Mary's quiet introspection as the colourful procession of her state entry progressed through London reflects the behaviour of a woman who did not see the need for elaborate gestures designed to please the crowd. In small groups, or at times of crisis, she could be supremely effective, but on show she was remote. She was at once the focus of attention and yet removed from it; this separate status was how she believed monarchy should be. God had chosen her to rule and do his will. This was the gift she would offer her subjects, and she was convinced that she would earn their gratitude and love by fulfilling God's command. Calm and certain, Mary arrived by barge next morning at the old palace of Westminster, where the robing for the coronation would take place. It was a Sunday, the holiest day of the week.

The crowning of a queen who would rule in her own right was a completely new event in England, but the religious ceremonial of the coronation itself was five hundred years old and Mary was determined to be crowned 'according to the olde custome', though some of the order of the service reflected changes introduced in 1547, for Edward VI's coronation, and the same ornaments were carried. There was a blurring of distinction between the traditions for the coronations of kings regnant and queen consorts, with some reports claiming that Mary went into Westminster Abbey with her hair down, as was normal for the wives of kings.[37] But she went on foot and did not ride in a litter, as her grandmother, Elizabeth of York, had done. The queen, it was reported, 'in parliament robes of crimson velvet under a rich canopy borne by the five barons of the cinque ports', walked in procession from Westminster Hall to the abbey.

Blue cloth had been laid from the marble porch of Westminster Hall to the pulpit in the abbey, railed on either side. Along this passed the queen's procession, beginning with the gentlemen, by twos, and then the knights, aldermen, the French and Latin secretaries, the privy council, the knights of the Garter and three naked swords, representing Justice (one for the Spirituality and one for the Temporality) and Mercy. The sword of state was carried by Edward Courtenay, newly ennobled as earl of Devonshire. The duke of Norfolk carried the crown and the marquess of Winchester the orb, while the earl of Arundel bore the sceptre. The queen's train was carried by the duchess of Norfolk, assisted by Sir John Gage. According to Noailles, Elizabeth and Anne of Cleves immediately followed the queen into the abbey, but there is no other corroboration of this.

The ancient abbey of Westminster was richly decorated for Mary Tudor's coronation. The pulpit was covered with red worsted and the stage royal from the choir to the high altar covered with cloth of gold and strewn with cushions of the same material. When the queen reached the mounting scaffold she went up seven stairs to sit on a great royal chair, covered with damasked cloth of gold. The chair was backed with pillars, 'whereon stood two lions of gold and in the midst of a turret with a fleur-de-lys of gold'.[38]

Once the queen was seated, the bishop of Winchester turned to the assembled grandees of England, with the words: 'Sirs, here present is Mary, rightful and undoubted inheritrix by the laws of God and man to the crown and royal dignity of this realm of England, France and Ireland, whereupon you shall understand that this day is appointed by the peers of this land for the consecration, inunction and coronation of said most excellent Princess Mary; will you serve at this time, and give your wills and assent to the same'. The people answered, 'Yea, yea, yea. God save Queen Mary.' After the acclamation, Mary gave her offering to God (20 shillings) and later lay prostrate on cushions while prayers were said over her. She then rose to listen to the sermon from the bishop of Chichester. It was on the obedience due to kings, an apposite topic, but the bishop was not, by some accounts, the most lively or concise of speakers, and his audience's powers of concentration may have been taxed by his delivery.[39]

By now the ceremony was entering its most sacred phase. Mary swore her oaths lying before the altar and was then anointed by Gardiner, on the forehead, temples, shoulders and breasts, using the holy oil so lately arrived from Flanders. Lord Paget, Sir Thomas Cheyney, Sir John Gage and Sir Anthony St Leger held a canopy over the queen, allowing her some privacy, and she had facilitated the anointing by changing into a sleeveless corset of purple velvet and a robe of white taffeta. When Gardiner had dried her with a linen cloth, Frances Walde-grave stepped forward to lace up her mistress's apparel, put on her hands a pair of linen gloves and drape her in a crimson velvet mantle. On Mary's feet were slippers of crimson cloth of gold lined with crimson satin, decorated with ribbons of Venice gold. Thus gorgeously attired, she was crowned by Gardiner with the three crowns, while trumpets sounded between each crowning. When the gold coronation ring, famil-iarly known as the wedding ring of England, was put on her finger, the Te Deum was sung by the abbey choir. Then, as would have been done for a male monarch, she was accoutred with the sword and the spurs, and received the homage of her bishops and peers, who knelt and kissed her on the left cheek. As proceedings drew to a close, she made further offer-ings of bread, a cruet of wine and a pound of gold.

It was a long and arduous ceremony, demanding much of the woman at its centre. At about four o'clock Mary emerged, exalted, as sovereign queen of England. She carried the orb and the two sceptres, as both king and queen, the time-honoured symbols of her spiritual and worldly power. Still overcome with emotion as the reality of the ceremony sank in, she played absent-mindedly with the orb as she returned for the coronation dinner. Here, while more than three hundred dishes were offered to the normally abstemious Mary, who presumably tasted only a fraction of them, the ancient practices were enjoyed by the other diners. Gardiner, Elizabeth and Anne of Cleves, who all sat at the queen's table, watched as her champion, Sir Edward Dymoke, rode up and down the hall challenging anyone who questioned her right. She drank to him and gave him the cup and his horse's splendid trappings as his fee.

Her subjects, with the customary unruliness of the London crowd on such occasions, were determined to celebrate in their own way. Their priority was to take anything of value that remained from the street decorations and to scramble for the leftover meats from the meal, which were traditionally thrown out to anyone prepared to struggle for them. On this occasion, there was a near-riot. It was a far from dignified end to an otherwise solemn day.

When Mary retired to bed at Westminster that night, after further feasting, music and dancing, she had good cause to be satisfied with what had been achieved in the first two and a half months of her reign. But there was also uneasiness in her mind, and uncertainty. When Parliament met on 5 October, she intended to introduce a programme of political and religious change which she hoped would not meet with opposition.

But there was one other, fundamentally important issue that could no longer be avoided now she was crowned, and that was to find a suitable husband. It was not a quest for which she felt the slightest enthusiasm.

Chapter Nine

Wyatt's Rebellion

'Lo now, even at hand, Spaniards be already arrived at Dover.'

Proclamation of Sir Thomas Wyatt the younger at Maidstone, 25 January 1554

The question of marriage had first been raised more than two months earlier, before Mary even entered London. It was not instigated by the queen herself, or even by her privy councillors, who were otherwise preoccupied in late July. Renard took the credit for introducing the idea at his initial audience with the queen at New Hall, on 29 July. To the English and their new monarch it was only one among many topics for consideration, and not the most pressing. But to the imperialists, it was the key to their policy, an unforeseen and God-given opportunity to swing the balance of power in their long-standing quarrels with France. There was one obvious solution that the emperor sought and it must be pursued carefully, but inexorably.

As soon as the coronation was over, Mary knew she could not put off any longer dealing with the marriage issue, distasteful as it was. The pressure from her councillors was mounting. She must come to a decision, first as to whether she should marry at all and, if she decided she must, who her husband was to be. The queen reluctantly reached the conclusion that she could not remain single, and the process caused her a great deal of emotional turmoil, but once her mind was made up she proceeded with a ruthless determination to get her way. The major difficulty she encountered was in the manner that this was publicly presented. She felt that, as the queen, she should not have to justify her decision to her country. Her coronation oath was sufficient proof of her responsibility. She would neither be denied nor contradicted, and she most certainly would not let anyone in England presume to tell her what she should do.

Initially, she was just as concerned by the insistence of the emperor's representatives that she must consider her situation without loss of time, telling them: 'She felt confident you would remember that she was 37 years of age and would not urge her to come to a decision before having seen the person and heard him speak, for as she was marrying against her private inclination she trusted your majesty would give her a suitable match.' Her first letter as queen to Charles V, written several days later, was full of expressions of humble thanks for his congratulations on her accession, but it did not mention marriage at all.[1]

So this first comment on her marital status and prospects reveals a great deal about Mary's frame of mind and her anxieties about becoming a wife when she was no longer a young woman. It was unthinkable that she could discuss her fears or reveal her embarrassment to a privy council composed of men. If she had to submit herself to the marriage bed, then she understandably wanted to be sure that she felt comfortable in her choice of spouse. She was realistic enough to accept that her personal attractions were fading and that the prospect of motherhood could not be the same as if she were ten years younger. Unmentioned, but accepted by everyone, Mary included, was the more serious prospect of death in childbirth, supposing that she did conceive. Nevertheless, she believed that God, who had shown her such favour in this momentous year of 1553, would extend his blessing and give her offspring, safeguarding her throne, her religion and her succession. But her first thought was that the best chance of contentment lay with with a husband near to her in age and interests, whom she might have the opportunity to meet before finally making up her mind. He must, of course, be Catholic, but that now went without saying. There were plenty of prospects who shared her faith. Yet some of the names being put forward, she told the imperial ambassador, were totally inappropriate. She was 'old enough to be their mother'. It was a revealing comment.

Charles V, however, was dismayed by her insistence that she wanted to inspect potential husbands beforehand. The emperor did not think that any European prince would be willing to submit himself to the possible indignity of being rejected. He may have been wrong about this, since there was no shortage of candidates for Mary's hand. The illegitimate ex-princess with the vague title of 'The Lady Mary' was suddenly a queen, and she might make her husband a king. Her suitors were a motley bunch, every bit as eccentric as some of those who would court her sister in years to come, and often just as unsuitable.

They split into two broad groups, the English and the foreign, and there was keen rivalry within, as well as between, the groups. Even Habsburg unity broke down in the face of fraternal squabbles. The emperor knew what he wanted but reaching a satisfactory outcome would not necessarily be straightforward. Affairs needed to be handled delicately, and he instructed Renard to conduct the negotiations without taking Scheyfve and the other ambassadors, who did not leave England till mid-October, into his confidence. This caused friction within the imperial embassy in London. Charles could live with this, but he was furious when he discovered that his brother, Ferdinand, King of the Romans, was energetically pushing the claims of his own second son as a rival to Philip and had written personally to Mary. He gave clear instructions to his sibling to desist that were not well received. Meanwhile, his brother-in-law, the long-unmarried Dom Luis of Portugal, resurfaced with a new-found devotion to Mary's person as well as her money. He, too, had to be deterred from pursuing his interest, since in age and outlook he was by far the closest to Mary's criteria for an ideal husband.

There were also three English contenders, one serious and the other two improbable. The main prospect was thought to be Edward Courtenay, recently ennobled as earl of Devon, but Cardinal Pole and the son of the earl of Arundel were also mentioned as possibilities. Pole was six years older than Mary and an unlikely choice, whatever ties she felt to him as distant kin and to his mother, her executed lady governess. Though he was a cardinal, he had never been ordained as a priest and could still, in theory, marry. But he wanted to govern a revitalised Catholic Church in England rather than share his cousin Mary's throne. Arundel's son, Lord Maltravers, was sometimes spoken of as a suitor for Elizabeth, rather than Mary, and his name may have been put in the frame by those who wished to represent his father as being over-ambitious. Courtenay, though, was a much more serious prospect and the choice of many in government and the royal household who wanted an Englishman, not a foreigner, as Mary's spouse.

Mary herself desired, above all, someone with whom she could live in harmony and who would be a constant presence in her life. She does not seem to have accepted that this latter requirement could only realistically be met by marriage to one of her own countrymen. Though she acknowledged that marrying was a duty she owed to England, she was also adamant that the selection of a husband was a personal and intensely private process. She would be mindful of the advantages that her choice could offer her country, but she always intended for her English advisers to follow her lead, not express opinions of their own. Charles V might make suggestions, she told Renard, and she would be happy to follow them, provided she could accommodate her own concerns about marriage. The problem with this approach was its major element of self-deception, since the emperor was not a disinterested party. He already knew how he was going to handle the question, and Mary must at least have guessed what he would propose. At one and the same time, she wanted complete freedom to make her decision and yet to have it come from someone else. To the queen, the process was disturbingly stressful, and she was genuinely anguished, as her behaviour in October revealed.

Nor was there anyone else apart from the emperor to whom she could turn for advice. 'She would never dare raise the subject with her council,' she claimed, somewhat disingenuously, and she declared that 'she had never felt that which was called love, nor harboured any thoughts of voluptuousness … wherefore her own marriage would be against her inclinations'. But she went on to reveal that, in the privacy of her chamber, 'the ladies who surrounded her talked of nothing else but marriage'.[2] This female chattering and encouragement were evidently a great influence on the queen, who could have put a stop to them if she wished but did nothing to discourage them. Many of her women were married, or had been, and they were her main source of information on just what it meant to be a wife. When she told Renard that she had never felt sexual desire she did not mean that she was completely ignorant about sex. Mary refrained from saying so directly, of course, but sex was obviously her main area of concern. She would not be marrying for love, but reproduction was a wifely duty and she was reliant on her ladies to explain the essentials. Her comments indicate that they tried to bolster her resolution by romantic gossip and speculation about the bridegroom's identity. They were concerned about the queen's happiness and well aware that she was uneasy about what lay ahead. Yet even within Mary's chamber, there were disagreements about whom their lady should marry. Without saying so publicly, the queen already accepted in her heart that she could not marry a subject. Whatever others might want for her, no matter how strong the case they put for her to marry within the realm, she would not wed an Englishman.

Though Mary was encouraged towards a foreign match by Charles V and his ambassador, she reached her conclusion independently. She told Renard in September that 'she knew no one in England with whom she would wish to ally herself'. He could not have been surprised, as he had earlier described her to the bishop of Arras, to whom he wrote more frankly than the emperor, as 'great-hearted, proud and magnanimous. If she married an Englishman, her posterity would not have as much renown as if her husband were a foreign prince.'[3] In making this observation, Renard displayed a greater grasp of the queen's character and outlook than many of those who had been around her for years. But he did not comprehend the full picture. As Mary tried to cope with her emotions, only superficially distracted by her ladies and their ceaseless talk of weddings, she came to believe that what was right for her was right for England. A well-chosen, carefully negotiated marriage would raise her country's stock in Europe, putting it at the centre, rather than the periphery, of European politics. No longer a pariah state, it would be a godly, Catholic country with voice and influence, prosperous and well governed. This was her vision for her country and she was committed to its achievement. Her own happiness would flow naturally from the realisation of this goal. History, temperament and a consciousness that hers was a unique situation, an unequalled opportunity, propelled Mary towards an inevitable choice. She would marry the emperor's son, Philip of Spain.

Once the queen persuaded herself that she must accept God's intention for her to marry – and it was an age when everyone expected monarchs to marry and produce children, bachelor kings being virtually unknown – the dynastic choice was an obvious one. The most difficult part for Mary, as she had already made clear, was facing up to the fact that marriage was her duty, just as much as government and religion.

The reaction to her choice has been misunderstood. Strong feelings were aroused but much of the passion evaporated by the time the queen finally went to the altar in the summer of 1554. Political rivalries, religious differences, self-interest and uncertainties about the role of a female ruler were more potent than the simplistic hatred of all things Spanish that has so often been asserted as the sole cause of opposition to

Mary's determination to marry Philip of Spain. But this was still one of the most divisive decisions of her reign. Mary's determination to pursue the matter in its early stages with only the minimum of consultation has been depicted as a sign of uncertainty and weakness. In fact, it shows an almost arrogant confidence in her role as a monarch. Yet there is no denying the impact, not just of the choice but the way in which it was handled. Mary wanted to make up her mind alone. Pestered by Renard to make a foreign match and her household staff to make an English one, it is hardly surprising that the queen grew overwrought. No matter what she decided, she knew that many people would disapprove.

She was quite right. The issue of Mary's marriage led to rifts in the council and destroyed the influence of some of the foremost members of her household, who had served her faithfully for years. Another casualty was the Lady Elizabeth, whose fragile relationship with Mary went downhill rapidly in October 1553, as the queen struggled to retain her composure. In thinking of her future, Mary was unable to avoid the past. Elizabeth could not escape the fact that her mother was Anne Boleyn. The fact that the divorce was overturned by Mary's first parliament, in November, gave the queen great satisfaction, but the scars remained.

The wrangling over the Spanish marriage caused Mary great distress and brought out her fighting qualities. She rejected the notion that it would harm English interests and she had history on her side. It was a union that would have been well regarded in early Tudor England. Her grandfather's foreign policy had hinged on the match between her mother and Prince Arthur. Charles V, himself half Spanish, had been briefly Mary's fiancé in the 1520s, when the wider Habsburg alliance was considered not just reasonable but desirable. But times had changed. The map of Europe was complicated by religious revolt and the emperor's unrealistic commitment to dynastic unity. Then there was the contrary nature of the English themselves. Over and over, Renard repeated that the English did not like foreigners, but they were not the only European people with this negative outlook. The truth was that the issue of the queen's marriage raised questions for which there were no convenient answers. As the implications of this became more obvious, Mary's concern to keep things to herself, to avoid becoming the object of an experiment that might deprive her of power, was perhaps a tacit acknowledgement that this was uncharted territory.

If the ruler of England had been a king seeking to marry a Spanish princess, voices of disapprobation would have been far more muted, even in 1553. But Mary was a sovereign lady, a queen ruling in her own right. This fundamentally changed the way her marriage was viewed, and there is no reason to suppose that a French suitor, for example, would have been more acceptable. He would have been just as foreign, Catholic and male as any Habsburg candidate for Mary's hand. Part of the problem was that there was no clear view of precisely what the husband of a queen regnant should do. What would be the extent of his powers? Would he be an equal, but with as yet undefined executive powers of his own? Or would the queen be turned into no more than a consort if she married, deferring all things to her spouse while she tried to produce heirs? No one knew the answers to these questions because the situation was unprecedented – at least, in England – though there was guidance to be gained from looking at the way Isabella of Castile had ruled. Her husband had no say in the internal politics of his wife's domains and did not inherit them when she predeceased him. This example was not directly invoked, but Mary, encouraged by Katherine of Aragon long ago to think of herself as a prospective queen, seems to have followed a similar approach.

Charles V could not, however, be entirely sure of how Mary's thoughts were developing, and he did not want to proceed with a haste that might be counterproductive. He was dealing with a woman he did not really know, and though she spoke of him as her father, his parental role had been a long-distance one. He felt it unlikely that Mary would marry an Englishman, but it was not a foregone conclusion. Achieving the desired result required proper groundwork. The day after his ambassadors were ushered into Mary's presence at New Hall, at the end of July, Charles V set his campaign in motion. To his son Philip, far away in Spain, he wrote a masterly letter: 'I am glad to see our cousin in the place that is hers by right and I hope that her prudence will enable her to restore religious matters.' To facilitate matters and help reinforce Mary's success, he was considering, he said, marrying her himself. 'Her discretion and tact may render it possible', he mused, 'to propose once more a match which was talked of many years ago … I am sure that if the English made up their minds to accept a foreigner they would more readily accept me than any other, for they have always shown a liking for me.'[4]

But this was merely the emperor's cunning. He had no intention of

marrying Mary himself. Tired and ill as he was, a new marriage, even to
a woman of mature years, was the last thing he wanted. Apparently
thinking aloud, he went on to wonder whether Philip might not be a
better choice, though he was 'to consider it privately and keep the matter
a close secret'. Then he waited for the prince's response to this carefully
phrased instruction.

With his customary languor, for he was never a man to rush things,
the emperor's son did not reply until the end of August. When he did
write, his lack of enthusiasm was very apparent:

> I very well see the advantages which might accrue from the successful
> conclusion of this affair ... All I have to say about the English affair is
> that I am rejoiced to hear that my aunt [he was evidently somewhat
> hazy about his actual relationship to Mary] has come to the throne ...
> as well as out of natural feeling as because of the advantages mentioned
> by your majesty where France and the Low Countries are concerned.
> It is certain that if she suggested a match between herself and your
> majesty, and your majesty were disposed, it would be the very best
> thing possible.

But he already, very reluctantly, accepted his father's real purpose: 'As
your majesty feels as you say about the match for me, you know that I
am so obedient a son that I have no will other than yours, especially in
a matter of such high import.'[5]

In fact, Philip was anticipating marrying again. But his thoughts were
not of Mary. Negotiations, admittedly at an early stage, were under way
for a possible match with the Infanta Maria of Portugal. He had already
been married, very briefly and very young, to another Portuguese
cousin, who died shortly after giving birth to his son, Don Carlos. There
were rumours at the time that Philip and his teenage bride were not
close and that he did not regret her early death. As he was only 18 at the
time, and they were married less than two years, they were scarcely given
time to form much of a relationship. Eight years on, the widower prince
was the most eligible prize in Europe.

At 26, Philip was an elegant, fashionable man who clearly enjoyed his
freedom but had a well-developed sense of duty. In appearance he
resembled his Portuguese mother more than his Habsburg father, with
his unmistakable Iberian bearing. Unfortunately, the overall effect was
spoiled by the large jaw and thick lips of his Burgundian ancestors, but

if he was not exactly handsome, he certainly had presence and very considerable charm and social skills. He also had an eye for the ladies, a love of music and court revels, tournaments and Titian paintings. This highly educated Renaissance prince was not the grim Spanish Catholic bogeyman and foe of fearless Elizabethan England that is so often represented. The burden of ruling creased and changed him in later life, but the Philip of the 1550s was another man.

But he was already, in language and outlook, very much a product of Spain, the country in which he had been educated and trained to rule. It was claimed that he understood French, Latin and Italian, but it is not certain that he spoke any language except Spanish proficiently. England and its middle-aged queen held no attractions for him, though he was well aware of the importance of the Low Countries, spent time in Brussels and enjoyed the court there. Yet he concurred with his father's view that the English marriage would be highly advantageous. Already experienced in government (he ruled Spain on his father's behalf), he could see it clearly enough for himself. Above all else, he was a Habsburg and a dutiful son. So he waited with patience to see how matters would develop, and continued his affair with one of the ladies of the Valladolid court, Isabel Osorio, his mistress of several years. She never married and he made careful provision for her financial welfare.

Charles V could command his son, but he needed to rely on his representatives in England to handle the detail and to proceed with real diplomatic skill. He knew there would be other names proposed and sensed early on that the idea of Mary's marrying a foreigner would have to be carefully handled. Edward Courtenay was likely to attract vocal support among Mary's advisers, both in the royal household and the privy council.

At first, it seemed that Courtenay, 'the last sprig of the White Rose', was the firm favourite to succeed. Stephen Gardiner supported him, and so did Robert Rochester, Edward Waldegrave and Francis Englefield. As they had all been prisoners together in the Tower they had a shared experience and a strong bond. None of them thought Courtenay's age or long period of confinement disqualified him as a serious contender. Though their sponsorship of him probably had an element of self-interest, and Rochester, in particular, had demonstrated his desire to moderate imperial influence on Mary, they seem to have felt genuine affection for someone whose life had been blighted by the accident of his birth. But being high born, even without the other, more serious, effects of prolonged loss of liberty and the threat of execution, was no guarantee of suitability for an unprecedented role. Gardiner and the East Anglians could not admit this, or perhaps thought that time and training would overcome any flaws in their protégé. And there were other reasons to suppose that Mary might be persuaded to accept Courtenay. His mother, the marchioness of Exeter, was daily in the queen's company and she was superbly placed to use her influence in his favour. Unhappily, family ties and maternal love for her only surviving son also blinded Gertrude Courtenay, who could not admit that he was permanently damaged by almost 15 years in the Tower. Persuading the queen to accept him became her mission.

He was a charming and good-looking young man of 27 when Mary released him from his long incarceration on 3 August. His education had continued during his imprisonment and his literary and musical accomplishments were admirable, but he lacked any experience of real life. It had been his misfortune to suffer for who he was, but the fact that both he and Mary were great-grandchildren of Edward IV was much more dangerous to him than it was advantageous. The earl found himself suddenly the centre of attention, spoken of openly as the future king of England, courted by everyone who opposed a Habsburg marriage for the queen. The sudden freedom and celebrity deprived him of any care for his reputation, as he threw himself into a dissipated lifestyle of drink, 'loose women' and, much more sinister in the eyes of the imperialists, socialising with the French and Venetian diplomats. The queen gave him lands, but she could not endow him with common sense. She did not seek out his company because she never truly wanted to get to know him. Edward Courtenay took a surprisingly long time to realise that he was being used by others and that his future was no more secure now than it had ever been. Towards the end of the year, when Mary made it very clear that she was not going to be browbeaten into accepting him as a husband, his thoughts began to turn to Elizabeth as an alternative. This ill-advised development did neither of them any good.

Mary never seriously considered Courtenay, but she had not yet been presented with a formal proposal by Charles V, so her reticence to discuss marriage with her council is perfectly understandable. At the beginning of September she told Renard that the topic had not even been raised, 'either in general terms or otherwise'. But this polite avoidance of so crucial a question did not last. Mary, with no name yet forthcoming from Brussels, later revealed that she had been obliged to cut short any speculation, saying 'she had always rebuffed those who had brought up the subject in such fashion that they had never mentioned it again'.[6] It was a phrase worthy of her father.

This evasion bothered the council considerably. They were surprised by the silence from the emperor, fully expecting Mary to be in consultation with him. Behind the scenes, they began to take sides, with the majority favouring an English husband. The Spaniards had acquired an ill reputation for their government of the Low Countries and particularly for the way they dealt with religious dissent there. Commercial links furnished plenty of information about what was going on across the North Sea. This flow of information provided the French, as well as the literate and well-organised opponents of Catholicism, with emotive ammunition. There were also fears among those in government and at court that they would lose their positions and influence to a wave of Spanish incomers. Nor were these anxieties entirely selfish. Some, including Rochester and the other Catholic gentlemen of Mary's household, were concerned that a Spanish husband would endanger the restoration of their religion if he became a focus for widespread discontent. An English Catholic, like Courtenay, presented no such drawback. If Mary was to succeed in undoing the pernicious developments of her brother's reign she must not be compromised by playing into her opponents' hands.

And no one could ignore the inevitable reaction of the French. Every attempt must be made to avoid a war for which England had little stomach and fewer resources. Only four months previously, France had been England's main ally in Europe. Now their ambassador feared the worse. Noailles felt he had been treated with courtesy by the council, but, like Renard, he did not really trust any of them and he had not been persuaded by Mary's assurances about her wish to maintain peaceful relations. Courtenay was obviously the preferred choice for France, and Noailles had the financial means to buy him support, if necessary. He also had, in Sir Edward Leigh, a member of Mary's household, an informer who was a valuable source of information on the queen's sentiments. It was unfortunate for Noailles that domestic politics in France left him without clear instructions as to what he should do. Montmorency was ill for much of the autumn and Henry II came increasingly under the influence of the Guise brothers, the uncles of Mary Queen of Scots. They had their own family's agenda to pursue.

The French king himself most certainly wished to stop the queen of England's marriage with the son of Charles V. When Mary eventually wrote to him, just before the end of the year, with the assurance that her marriage did not alter her desire for friendly relations with France, Henry II was withering in his response. He told Wooton, the English ambassador, 'that he clearly saw that she was allying herself with the greatest enemy he had in the world, and he knew marital authority to be very strong with ladies. He had not thought she would choose a match so odious to him.'[7] His hatred of the emperor went much deeper than the prolonged struggle for European dominance between the two countries. Henry never forgot the years he spent as a child in imperial custody, when he and his brother were hostages for their father after the defeat at Pavia. But Mary was a fellow-monarch and anointed queen and he did not want his ambassador directly identified with treasonable activities.

Whatever the queen's personal inclinations, her marriage was becoming the first major test of her authority, and one that threatened to isolate her from council and household. Parliament, too, was disen-chanted by the idea of the queen marrying a foreigner, and expected to have its say on the matter. It is unlikely that Mary would have been daunted or given way, even to this weighty combination of male influ-ence. She knew her own mind, and the ladies of her chamber believed she must be allowed to get what she wanted. From Brussels, Arras asked Renard whether he had heard rumours that Susan Clarencius had spoken to a Spanish grandee passing through London in mid-September. His information was not substantiated, but, if true, it indi-cates that the queen felt comfortable using her personal servants to sound others out about the emperor's intentions.[8] Yet the situation remained one of rumour and counter-rumour, talk without substance and general indecision, until Mary was crowned. Then, two things happened that greatly strengthened both Mary and the frenetic imperial ambassador. Lord Paget stepped out of the shadows to emerge as the major English champion of a Habsburg alliance and Charles V officially proposed Philip as Mary's husband.

Paget brought with him all his years of diplomatic experience and genuine commitment to a course that he believed was right for England. This was his supreme moment. The queen's marriage restored him to the centre of political activity. He seized the opportunity thankfully, despite the burden of work involved and recurring problems with his health. His portrait emphasises his power and wealth, but the face betrays some insecurity. He is resplendent in so many furs that he looks more like a bear than a man, an impression accentuated by his long double-pointed beard. Here was a man who favoured moderation, who did not act in heat or haste. These may have been admirable qualities, but they were not the norm in mid-Tudor England.

The contribution Paget made at this juncture was important for other reasons. His influence enabled him to act as an antidote to the constant drip of venom against Elizabeth. Paget's pragmatic view of the succession irritated the imperial ambassador and his master. It was also unwelcome to Mary's ears. But the minister realised the disadvantages of cutting Elizabeth out before Mary produced heirs. It was vital to avoid another succession crisis.

Renard, always wanting to depict himself as firmly in the lead, was still greatly relieved to be able to work with someone of Paget's ability, who knew how matters could be taken forward effectively. The ambassador had made it clear to the bishop of Arras exactly what he thought of Mary as a ruler, belittling her judgement and intimating that she would be lucky to survive many months. She was, he wrote, 'easily influenced, inexpert in worldly matters and a novice all round ... To tell you between ourselves what I think of her, I believe that if God does not preserve her she will be deceived and lost, either by the machinations of the French, the conspiracies of the English, by poison or otherwise.'[9] But this patronising assessment he concealed from the queen herself. It has always been thought that she was entirely in thrall to his undoubted energy, seeing him as the visible link with her cousin and bowing to his every whim. But Mary was more hard-headed than he realised. She knew how to press him for information and she told him what she wanted him to hear. And now she could talk things through with her minister before she gave audience to Renard. The ambassador was aware of this but assumed that she was merely Paget's mouthpiece, a woman who could not think for herself in matters of state. It reassured him that the marriage discussions could now proceed on a man-to-man basis. Paget, who had sat in council meetings with the queen, knew differently. Mary possessed a very strong mind of her own. She would want things done thoroughly and through the proper channels. There was never any question of her sacrificing her power or handing over her realm to become a Habsburg satellite. Mary, who did not much care for Paget as a person, appreciated his skill. She was willing to hand over the detail of negotiation to him now that she had a formal offer to consider and his expertise at her disposal.

Paget decided to take a decisive role almost as soon as the decorations from the coronation were removed from London's streets. There was too much to be risked by waiting longer. There were great burdens resting on the queen, but the country was not in a good condition, he divulged to Renard. The succession was a tricky area that could not be left up in the air because of lack of a true heir in the direct line, and 'the stain of bastardy on the Lady Elizabeth' could not be overlooked. There was no alternative for Mary but to marry. 'So as to restore the succession and continue the line, they [the council] considered it necessary for the good of the kingdom that the queen should enter into an alliance and marry, and the sooner the better because of the state of her affairs and her years.'[10] What was urgently needed was for the emperor to write to Mary in the same vein, and a week later the emperor followed Paget's advice, using almost identical wording. 'The sooner you make up your mind the better,' he told her, 'for many reasons.' The same day he thanked the Englishman in a separate letter, for his devotion to Mary, to England and to Charles himself. He was careful to add a sweetener at the end, assuring Paget 'we will show recognition of your goodwill and devotion as occasion shall offer'.[11] This does not mean that Paget acted only out of the desire for reward; like most politicians of the period, he probably expected no more. His main aim was to move things forward for the benefit of England. If he succeeded, then, of course, it would enhance his political stature. First and last, he was a servant of the Crown.

Less than two weeks after the coronation, Mary received the offer for which she had been waiting. She was fully ready with questions and comments when, on 10 October, the ambassador knelt before her and offered the hand of his highness Prince Philip in marriage. This was by no means the first time the emperor's son had been mentioned and Mary had dealt very cleverly with Renard in the past by telling him that she knew Philip was already promised elsewhere. 'She said straight out that his highness was married to the princess of Portugal, daughter of the queen dowager of France.'[12] Caught on the back foot at that time,

Renard told her that he did not think the marriage was concluded. Now, he could assure her that Charles V wanted her, not Dona Maria, as Philip's wife. Ever conscious of the place he occupied in Mary's affections, the emperor offered Philip as a substitute for himself: Renard told her that he was commanded to say that, 'if age and health had permitted, you would have desired no other match, but as years and infirmity rendered your person a poor thing to be offered to her, you could think of no one dearer to you or better suited than my lord the prince, your son, who was of middle age, of distinguished qualities and of honourable and Catholic upbringing'. But, of course, the decision was entirely Mary's – Charles had 'no private object in this'.

She responded graciously, saying it was a 'greater match than she deserved'. If she was thrilled, however, she kept herself well in check, beginning immediately to address the wider implications. There were difficulties that must be faced and she sounded more lukewarm than elated. She could not say whether the people of England or her councillors would be supportive. Was it realistic to suppose that Philip, the heir to 'many realms and provinces', would come to live in England, as her countrymen would expect? An absentee consort was not acceptable. And she did not know the young man at all, though she had heard that 'he was not as wise as your majesty and was very young, being only twenty-six years of age'. There were aspects of the relationship that needed to be made clear from the start: 'If he were disposed to be amorous, such was not her desire, for she was of the age your majesty knew of and had never harboured thoughts of love.' She would pledge herself to be a good wife and 'love and obey him to whom she had given herself', as God's law required, but secular aspects of the marriage were a different consideration. The limits of her husband's role were made clear from the outset. 'If he wished to encroach in the government of the kingdom she would be unable to permit it, nor if he attempted to fill posts and offices with strangers, for the country itself would never stand such interference. It was difficult, indeed almost impossible, for her to make up her mind so quickly and without the assistance of some of her council, for the step was of great importance, and for all her life.' Almost as an afterthought, she added defiantly that 'she was as free as on the day of her birth, and had never taken a fancy to anyone'. The best way to handle the proposal, she concluded, would be for the emperor to write directly to half a dozen or so of her councillors, whom she named, and she would then sound out their response.

Paget had already discussed the need to smooth things by adopting this course, so Renard was not surprised by it. He dealt with each of the other objections raised by Mary briskly. The people of England and the council would surely be aware of the benefits to the realm of such a marriage, promising as it did 'peace, repose, prosperity and liberty'. Councillors would not oppose if the matter were raised with them appropriately and, anyhow, 'means should be contrived to bring them to a favourable view'. They surely could not be blind to the advantages of Philip 'because he was a prince so puissant that the kingdom would be able to look to him for succour and aid, and vassals for advancement out of his own patrimony, not England's'. And as for his being an absentee, he would have 'no dearer wish than to stay with her'.

He then catalogued the prince's virtues in the most glowing of terms: 'His highness' nature was so admirable, so virtuous, prudent and modest as to appear too wonderful to be human, and though the queen might believe me to be speaking the language of a subject or servant I was in reality minimising his qualities.' A husband of 50 was a totally unrealistic option. He would be too old to have children and, besides, 'men grew old at fifty or sixty, which age very few passed'. Experience had matured the prince; indeed, it had aged him: 'His highness had already been married, had a son of eight and was a prince of so stable and settled a character that he was no longer young, for nowadays a man nearly thirty was considered as old as men formerly were at forty.' Renard did not enlarge on what had happened to mid-16th-century European males to bring about this effect, which many might have found unfortunate rather than encouraging. He managed to refrain from any further extrapolation about what the world thought of ladies who were close to 40 in age. Mary listened but made no comment. She reiterated her conviction that the council must be involved and she reassured him, in response to his repeated warnings about the intentions of her enemies, 'the heretics and schismatics, the rebels and partisans of the late Duke of Northumberland, the French and Scots, and the Lady Elizabeth', that she was better informed than even he was, because she had her own channels of information: 'She well knew what the French were doing and saying, and put no trust in their words … but they should not approach Courtenay or Elizabeth without her knowledge, for Courtenay's mother had promised to inform her.' Renard remained unconvinced by this, telling Mary 'she had better not believe all that was said to her'.[13] But he knew he could go no further without the letters for her councillors that the queen required.

· ❖ ·

The next three weeks must have seemed very slow to the imperial ambassador. The queen asked for a memo in writing from him, covering the main points of their meeting. She was still unconvinced that Philip was not pre-contracted to his Portuguese cousin. Then she requested draft marriage articles that she could discuss with the council. The ambassador could oblige with assurances of the former but not the latter, and Charles V baulked at being required at very short notice to produce the terms of a treaty for a marriage that neither Mary nor her council had yet accepted. But he did provide letters for individual councillors in which he explained that he was proposing Philip as Mary's husband. Renard was, though, reluctant to present them until his three colleagues, who were being very slow to depart, actually left England. As Scheyfve did not go till 27 October, his hands were tied until he was finally left alone.

Mary herself did not reach a decision until the very end of the month, and in between she had been put under further pressure by all and sundry to consider alternatives to Philip. Even Anne of Cleves intervened, favouring the other Habsburg wing, in the person of Archduke Ferdinand. But the greatest pressure came from her household staff and the Lord Chancellor. Gardiner, Rochester, Englefield and Waldegrave would not easily abandon the idea of an English marriage. Conscious that the initiative was passing from them, they made a determined attempt to state the case for Courtenay. The bishop was forthright, as he had always been. 'The country never would abide a foreigner, Courtenay was the only possible match for her.' Englefield also did not mince words, saying 'that his highness had a kingdom of his own he would not wish to leave to come to England and that his own subjects spoke ill of him'. Waldegrave kept up the attack by invoking the spectre of war with France, if Mary wedded Philip.

Faced with this onslaught, Mary held her ground and, apparently, kept her temper. She 'begged them all to lay aside private considerations [a shrewd dig] and think of the present condition of affairs, the French plottings, the marriage of the French dauphin with the queen of Scotland, what benefit the country could look for were she to marry Courtenay, and what profit might accrue to it if she chose a foreigner'.

And there the matter rested, for the time being, but Mary felt sure they would try again. When she related all this to Renard, he reassured

her that he had the letters for the council that she wanted. But why was
she so deferent to her council, who were urging her 'to marry a vassal
for whom she had no liking'? Mary was piqued. 'She retorted that they
had no authority in matters that touched her so nearly.' Yet she still
insisted, as she inched her way to a decision, that a core of councillors
more favourably disposed to a foreign marriage meet with Renard on
27 October so that they could be informed personally of what
Charles V was proposing. The emotional toll on her was, by this time,
rising alarmingly. 'She had wept over two hours that very day, praying
God to inspire her in her decision.' There was more to be told, about
what she had said to Courtenay on this topic, but 'she could not say
more without bursting into tears'. As Gardiner, Paget, Arundel and
Secretary Petre awaited her, she found the strength to pull herself
together. She commanded them to give close attention to Renard and
left him to put the case for Philip of Spain. But she had already intimated
to the ambassador that her mind was made up for the emperor's son.

Renard found the small group of councillors to whom the emperor
had written suitably receptive:

> Your majesty had never laid the queen and her country under so great
> an obligation, and in the name of the queen, her realm and themselves
> they most humbly thanked you for this holy, good, profitable and
> necessary reminder. Though some of their number had already
> thought of it, yet the matter was so important and personal to the
> queen that they had not dared to make so bold as to mention it to her
> ... they repeated that they could not tell me how agreeable my
> message had been.[14]

He then tried to soothe the fears of known opponents to the Spanish
marriage in the queen's household by calling on Sir Robert Rochester
'in his room' and presenting the controller with a personal letter from
Charles V. Affecting to sound out Rochester on 'his opinion as to what
alliance would be best for her [the queen] and the country', he even
went so far as to say that he intended to guide the negotiation by following Rochester's advice, something which they both knew was a lie. Sir
Robert gave little away, beyond saying that he 'felt wonderfully obliged
to your majesty ... for having written letters on the subject yourself'. He
offered no opinion as to the identity of a suitable husband, but he did
warn Renard that 'the queen had some dangerous men in her council,

persons who felt no devotion to her but only feigned it for the time being because they could not do otherwise'. He wanted the ambassador to be careful to whom he spoke, pointing out that in Waldegrave and Englefield the queen had 'councillors old as well as new', and that they were true, good men. This glimpse of ill feeling among the privy councillors did not surprise Renard, and he realised that he would have to proceed with caution, 'to keep in with some and confide in others. This problem is so difficult as to pass my capacity.' Nevertheless, he was confident that Mary had already made the right decision: 'I believe that when she summons me to speak privately to her she will give me a plain affirmation.'

In this he proved to be entirely correct. At about midnight of the same day on which he penned his dispatch to the emperor, Mary sent him a short note. She told him that 'Paget knows what is happening', but that she would like to speak to Renard in private before doing so in the council's presence. He came full of expectation and was not disappointed. Mary had made up her mind.

The queen wanted the agonising over her marriage to be over, but she had not pushed ahead without speaking to her advisers. Perhaps she was not always entirely frank with them, but then neither were they with her, or with each other. Her past made her long for emotional certainties that her rational intelligence knew would be difficult, if not impossible, to attain. Still, she hoped at least for consideration and cordial relations with a husband who was a member of her family. And she wanted a prestigious match. However much her household staff loved her, they could not make out a convincing case for Edward Courtenay.

We have only Renard's word for what actually took place on the evening of Sunday, 29 October, but, even given his penchant for representing Mary as skittish and suggestible, there is no reason to suppose that he greatly exaggerated what passed between them. Only two other decisions in her life – the acknowledgement of her own illegitimacy in 1536 and the determination to fight for her throne – were of equal importance to her. 'She told me', reported Renard,

> that since I had presented your majesty's letters to her she had not slept, but had continually wept and prayed God to inspire her with an answer to the question of marriage that I had first raised at Beaulieu [New Hall]. As the Holy Sacrament had been in her room, she had invoked it as her protector, guide and counsellor, and still prayed with

all her heart that it would come to her help. She then knelt and said
Veni, creator spiritus. There was no one else in the room except Mrs
Clarencius and myself and we did the same.

Did Susan Clarencius, he wondered, follow all this? Mary and the
ambassador spoke in French but presumably Mrs Clarencius knew very
well her mistress's mind by this time. Mary then explained her decision
and how she had reached it.

> She had considered all things, thought over what I had said to her, and
> had also spoken with Arundel [who by now had also received his letter
> from the emperor], Paget and Petre. She believed what I had told her
> of his highness' qualities and that your majesty would ever show her
> kindness, observe the conditions that were to safeguard the welfare of
> the country, be a good father to her as you had been in the past and
> more, now that you would be doubly her father, and cause his high-
> ness to be a good husband to her.

She spoke as Mary the queen and Mary the woman, confident still in
divine guidance: 'She felt herself inspired by God, who had performed
so many miracles in her favour, to give me her promise to his highness
there before the Holy Sacrament and her mind, once made up, would
never change, but she would love him perfectly and never give him cause
to be jealous.'[15] At peace with herself after a long struggle, she meant
every word she said.

Simon Renard was relieved and delighted. 'If she had invoked the
Holy Ghost, I had invoked the Trinity to inspire her with the desired
answer,' he told Charles V. But he also knew that it would be difficult to
progress things until the queen made her decision public, something
which she did not seem inclined to rush, and that opponents would not
suddenly abandon their efforts to get her to marry Courtenay. In fact,
the approach from Charles V galvanised the party that supported an
English marriage into action, to the point that a fracture in relations
between the queen and her 'old advisers' could not be evaded. Both
Rochester and Gardiner avoided seeing Renard, while attempts were
made to get Englefield, who was ill and unhappy at the break-up of his
marriage, back to court. Rumours that the queen had made up her mind
for Philip antagonised the French and the Venetians (who had no love
for the emperor) equally. Feelings in London ran high, and though Paget

assured the imperialists that Mary would never change her mind, the entire question seemed to be still up in the air. By mid-November, when the House of Commons sent a deputation to see the queen, a confrontation could not be avoided.

They were an impressive gathering of lords, temporal and spiritual, and members of the House of Commons. Having very recently, and not without some acrimony, repealed all of Edward VI's religious legislation, perhaps they thought that the queen would now heed their concerns. Mary, for her part, was fully aware that this was a public occasion, and even though it touched on matters that were very private and personal to her, there would be no tears or prayers. She had a role to play in such circumstances, and it called for dignity and majesty. There was a need to demonstrate the full extent of her queenship while exhibiting restraint. And restraint was certainly needed, as the Speaker of the Commons, Sir John Pollard, set forth the concerns of her parliament.

Pollard, a trained lawyer and judge, was elected Speaker in Mary's first parliament, and he brought to bear all his legal training in the presentation of the case for an English marriage to the queen. He gave 'a long and carefully composed discourse, full of art and rhetoric and illustrated by historic examples, in order to arrive at two objects: to induce her to marry, and to choose a husband in England'. Mary, who rose to greet the deputation, was obliged to sit down as Pollard droned on about the present state of the succession, what would happen if she died childless, the danger posed by Scotland under such circumstances and the desirability of her having children of her own. So far, she found him long-winded but would not have taken exception to his overall drift. But then he launched into the most delicate part of his brief, 'all the disadvantages, dangers and difficulties that could be imagined or dreamt of in the case of her choosing a foreign husband'. Aside from displeasing the entire population of England, both people and nobles, such a choice conjured up a vision of disaster, with a wicked foreigner lording it over the English, depleting the country of money and arms and finally removing Mary physically from the kingdom, 'out of husbandly tyranny'. He was, in other words, going to be the husband from hell.

Mary had already grown restive when Pollard, warming to his theme, unwisely committed his greatest faux pas. He asserted that 'it would be better for the queen to marry a subject of hers'. In so doing, he completely lost the queen's fast-disappearing patience. Without waiting for the chancellor to answer on her behalf, as protocol dictated in such circumstances, she replied herself. Given the presumption, the evident carelessness of her own feelings and the insult to her position as queen, she showed remarkable forbearance.

> She ... thanked parliament for their good offices in persuading her to marry, and said that although it was contrary to her own inclination, she would conquer her own feelings as the welfare and tranquillity of her kingdom were in question. She would marry, but she found the second point very strange. Parliament was not accustomed to use such language to the kings of England, nor was it suitable or respectful that they should do so. Histories and chronicles would show that such words had never been spoken, for even when the kings had been in childhood they had been given liberty in questions of marriage.

Thereafter, the effort of remaining measured in what she said nearly proved too much, as she stated dramatically that 'if she were married against her will she would not live three months and would have no children'. She soon recovered her equilibrium, however, assuring them that she was mindful of her coronation oath and that she always thought of the welfare of her kingdom, 'as a good princess and mistress should'. It was impossible to challenge her further, and the deputation retired without achieving its underlying aim. Almost everyone present seems to have found the outcome uncomfortable, and Arundel could not refrain from the opportunity of scoring points at Gardiner's expense by scornfully noting that he was essentially redundant, since the queen had usurped his role by answering herself.[16]

This, though, was nothing to the stinging rebuke the bishop subsequently received direct from Mary, when she told him she suspected him of having inspired the Speaker. 'She did not wish him to make any mistake and would tell him openly ... that she would never marry Courtenay. She never practised hypocrisy or deceit, and had preferred to speak her mind, and she had come near to being angry on hearing such disrespectful words.' The bishop, an emotional man himself, was in tears as he denied her accusation.[17] Mary, though affronted by what had taken place, was not shaken in her determination one iota. Like Renard and Paget, she wanted to press ahead with the details of the marriage, the treaty and its terms (which the emperor accepted must be as favourable to England as possible) and preparing the ground in England, since this was an aspect stress and pride had caused her to neglect. She knew very well now the kind of opposition she faced and the dangers that might ensue. In order to tackle these effectively, she must also make another decision, very close to home. Her marriage did not automatically solve the question mark that hung over the succession. What was to be done about her sister?

Elizabeth was still at court, in a thoroughly unenviable situation. She was often with the queen, who insisted that they attend mass and vespers together, but was not in Mary's confidence. Her entire future was under review without her participation and she had acquired, through no fault of her own, an influential enemy in the imperial ambassador. Perhaps even more alarming in the short term was that her name came up so often in tandem with Courtenay's, as an alternative wife if Mary would not have him. Mary never said whether she and Elizabeth discussed Courtenay, but it is highly unlikely that Elizabeth viewed him any more favourably than did the queen. She was not keen on the idea of marriage at all, and she had plenty of opportunity to observe Courtenay's increasingly ill-judged and petulant behaviour as he realised that his star was waning. And though she was socially isolated, she was not without her backers. Paget believed that constantly thinking of her as an enemy was unwise because it risked creating a danger that was not really there. Nor, he argued, could she be removed from the succession without repealing the very same act of parliament that Mary had used to justify her own accession. He thought it was 'better to keep in with Elizabeth than to antagonise her', and he 'entirely disapproved of those who wish to put her in the Tower' and counselled that the best course was 'to reduce her with kindness'.[18] But he was a firm adherent of the view that Elizabeth could best be contained by marrying her off to Courtenay. Renard did not concur. He believed, probably with justification, that Paget was looking to his own future if Mary should die without direct heirs.

Mary was torn. Renard had not entirely persuaded her that Elizabeth was plotting treason but she knew she did not want her sister to succeed. Neither did she want the question to overshadow the negotiations for her marriage to Philip. On 25 November, she saw Renard, with Paget present, and outlined to him her view of the succession and the various claimants. The extent of her doubts about her sister was made crystal clear: 'the queen would scruple to allow her to succeed because of her heretical opinions, illegitimacy and characteristics in which she resembled her mother; and as her mother had caused great trouble in the kingdom, the queen feared that Elizabeth might do the same, and particularly that she would imitate her mother in being a French partisan'.[19] Even without Simon Renard's constant reminders that the main threat to Mary's throne, and perhaps her life, was kneeling beside her at the altar in an entirely hypocritical display of religious conformity, Mary could not accept that Elizabeth might succeed her. It was not merely the young woman herself, with her irritating prevarication about making a public pronouncement of her support for Catholicism, who so tormented the queen. She was still oppressed by what she had endured 20 years earlier. Mary never saw their father in the adult Elizabeth; it was all Anne Boleyn.

Small wonder, then, that Elizabeth asked for permission to spend Christmas on her own estate at Ashridge, away from the unpleasantness that had built up at court. What is rather more surprising is that Mary, given her suspicions of the younger woman, agreed. Elizabeth was the most likely figurehead for any rebellion against Mary, whether she had direct involvement or not. Why let her go back to a place where she could not easily be watched, where she had men at her command and could organise an entire private army from her other properties?

The answer to this question probably lies in the central contradiction of Mary's view of Elizabeth, one that was to last for her entire reign. Her head may have told her to require Elizabeth's permanent presence at court, where she could be observed closely, but her heart could not bear the thought, any longer, of her sister's constant company. The relationship was just too fraught and it had a bad effect on both of them. Yet Mary was never entirely consistent in her treatment of her sister, and sometimes her residual generosity of spirit overcame her frustrated anger. She may well have been more relieved than anything else when Elizabeth left court in early December. As they parted, outwardly on more affectionate terms, the queen gave her sister a handsome sable hood and two ropes of beautiful pearls. It was a very feminine gift from a woman who loved such fine things herself. Evidently anxious to play her part in healing the breach, Elizabeth wrote to Mary while travelling back to Hertfordshire, asking for the correct Catholic ornaments and priestly garments to be provided for her chapel at Ashridge. It was the right gesture, but Mary remained unconvinced that the conviction was there.

Meanwhile, the queen was planning her own Christmas, which was to be spent at Richmond. There, as well as the normal Tudor festivities that marked the period between Christmas and Twelfth Night, she enjoyed a performance of the masque originally written for her coronation, though it had not actually figured in the celebrations at the time. Like many such entertainments in those days, it had a distinctly moral tone, in the tradition of medieval theatre. The fluid dialogue and complex characterisation of Shakespearean plays had not yet come to Mary's England. The piece's main theme was the suffering of mankind and the various purveyors of that suffering: deceit, self-love, scarcity, sickness, feebleness and deformity were all portrayed in different, colour-coded costumes. Then there were good and bad angels fighting for the destiny of man, until reason, verity and plenty triumphed. Mary had never known scarcity or deformity, but she had plenty of experience of the other allegories being portrayed.

Mary loved Richmond and welcomed the break from government business, despite the bitter winter weather that set in at the end of December. The stress of the last few months was taking its toll and she was dismayed by popular reaction to her decision to marry Philip. 'She told me that she had for some days past been ill from melancholy caused by the rumours that were going the rounds among her subjects,' wrote Renard. 'Several people had warned her that attacks, verbal and written were being made against the Spaniards and the alliance in terms that rang with revolt. The very ladies of her chamber, alarmed by the talk they had heard from certain gentlemen, had spoken to her in such a tone of fear that she had fallen a prey to melancholy and sadness to the point of illness.'[20] She had also heard from Wooton, her ambassador in France, that the French would not put up with this alliance, and at home religion, as well, was becoming a difficult issue: 'every day that passed was revealing signs of a rebellious spirit in the country against the acts of parliament on religion; and, what was worse, her own council were at variance about the alliance, wherefore, what with one thing and another, there was plenty to be disturbed about'. So the queen was not in the most festive frame of mind when she departed from Westminster Palace, and the notion that she was blissfully ignorant of the trouble that lay ahead is completely wrong. She was, however, defiant in her determination to marry Philip. No one would sway her and she would sooner die than back down.

· ❖ ·

'So be it' would have been the verdict of some of those already plotting her deposition. Following Mary's firm rejection of the House of Commons delegation, there were, as Mary feared, moves afoot to impose by force another solution. On 26 November, a group of gentlemen met in London to discuss what action should now be taken to ensure that England did not fall under foreign domination. Their mutterings of discontent turned into a rebellion that seemed to threaten Mary's throne but, in reality, brought far more peril to Elizabeth.

No one knows for sure who the guiding force behind the conspiracy was. William Thomas – the same man for whom, as his political tutor, the late King Edward had written his *Devise for the Succession* – was certainly an active participant. But the French ambassador, Noailles, did not cast Thomas in the leading role in his dispatches to Henry II. He believed that the driving organisational force was Sir James Croft, a former governor of Ireland and a Protestant who had only belatedly defected from Northumberland back in the summer. For all the conspirators, the queen's restoration of Catholicism, as well as her marriage intentions, appears to have been an additional concern.

They were a well-connected group. Several of them knew members of Elizabeth's household and probably Elizabeth herself. Two, the Devonian Sir Peter Carew and Sir Edward Rogers, were members of parliament. Carew was a soldier and adventurer who had been a wayward youth. Refusing to submit himself to the restrictions of a formal education, he was packed off to France in his early teens, and enjoyed an exciting career as a European soldier of fortune. His fluent French, military experience and local knowledge of Devonshire made him a key member of the plot.

Sir Thomas Wyatt, whose name stuck to the rebellion but who claimed that he was 'only the fourth or fifth man', was a Kentish landowner with good diplomatic links through his friend, Sir William Pickering, ambassador to France in the previous reign. Wyatt was also a soldier. He served for seven years in France and the Low Countries under Henry VIII, alongside the Spaniards fighting the French. This experience seems to have given him a dislike of Philip of Spain's countrymen that he took with him into his retirement. But though he had hoped to live quietly at his home, Allington Castle in Kent, following the pursuits of a country gentleman, his view of Mary was ambivalent. Like many others, he waited to see what her reign might offer and increasingly

did not like what he was witnessing. He definitely had Protestant leanings, though he claimed to be a Catholic still. Precisely how he became
embroiled is not known.

The first idea was for a rising in Devon, led by Carew and Courtenay, who at some point was unwisely taken into the conspirators' confidence. He was too febrile a character to be entrusted with such
knowledge and the burden of it eventually proved unbearable for him.
But for almost a month be managed to keep his secret, despite growing
suspicion by the government that he could not be trusted. By Christmas, Croft and his group could claim another, impressive (or so it must
have seemed) recruit. This was the duke of Suffolk, father of Lady Jane
Grey. He had good reason to share his daughter's view that Mary was 'a
merciful prince' but his political judgement was non-existent. He does
not seem to have given the slightest thought to what might happen to
his daughter if the enterprise he was now caught up in were to fail. But,
then, he had never given much thought to her at all, except as marriage
fodder and, briefly, as a biddable if unlikely monarch. Supported by his
two brothers, who were apparently as misguided and ungrateful as he
was, the duke became the most prominent member of the conspiracy.
With his dubious track record he was also the least reliable, despite his
large estates in the Midlands.

The overall plan was for simultaneous risings in Devon, the Welsh
Borders, where Croft's lands were situated, the Midlands, led by the duke
of Suffolk, and Kent, where Wyatt would command. The rebels would
then converge on London in an impressive show of force. Acknowledging the difficulties of fighting during the middle of winter, the plotters
decided to wait until Palm Sunday, 18 March 1554, to raise their standards. It was to be a significant date, but not for the reasons they hoped.

The plan sounded impressive, formidable even, but it had many flaws.
Too many people, spread over too wide an area, were involved. Notify-
ing Courtenay of what was afoot was a huge mistake, as was the involvement of Suffolk. The conspirators were understandably nervous about
drawing in the French, who were no more popular in England than the
Spaniards, but realised that they would need at least arms and money
from across the Channel if they were to stand any long-term chance of
success.

Noailles, disappointed that he had been unable to shipwreck the
Habsburg marriage, urged his government to ensure that support would
be forthcoming. By now, there was enthusiastic backing from the Guise

brothers, who saw an opening for their niece, the Queen of Scots. But the king remained very cautious. He opposed the Spanish marriage but feared the English were better at starting rebellions than finishing them. 'If you see that the queen is resolved to marry the Prince of Spain,' wrote Henry II on 23 November 1553, 'and also that there is a likelihood that Courtenay has the will and the means to upset the apple-cart, you may say still more confidently that you are sure that for such a great benefit to the realm of England I would not deny my favour either to him or to the other gentlemen who know the evil which the marriage could bring to the realm and would like to oppose it.' Noailles was not to make any move or reveal France's intentions, however, until he was absolutely sure that there was 'a real chance of stopping the queen's marriage'. Of course, the French king did not want to see any opportunity slip in the possible prevention of an alliance that he saw as 'so pernicious and destructive to my interests', but a wait-and-see policy was the best approach. After Northumberland's fall, there were real doubts about the ability of Mary's opponents to carry things through to a successful conclusion. 'Our chief aim must be to see that Courtenay and those who have the power, if they see things going badly, take example from the recent tragedies over there and do not let themselves be anticipated and arrested.' And Henry went on to add the following dismissive comments about Mary herself: 'They [the conspirators] have only to do with a woman who is badly provided with good counsel and men of ability, so it should be easy for them to guard against discovery if they are prudent enough and have enough blood in their nails.'[21]

This assessment of Mary's political predicament was by no means accurate and it completely failed to take account of her own personal courage and determination. Otherwise, the shrewd analysis of the French went to the heart of the conspirators' problems. Undertaking rebellion was a deadly game, even with a clear idea of objectives. Croft, Wyatt and their friends knew that they wanted to prevent the Spanish marriage and that this would most probably mean dethroning Mary. But even on this fundamental point, there is evidence that some of them, at least, were undecided. Carew was later quoted as saying: 'If the queen would forbear this marriage with the Spaniard, and use moderation in matters of religion, I would die at her foot.'[22] The plotters never had a clear strategy for what they would do if they succeeded. They probably thought there was time enough to decide before March.

At this stage, their hopes were pinned on establishing Courtenay and

Elizabeth on the throne, as husband and wife. None of the plotters considered that Elizabeth or her sister could rule without a husband. The commonsense solution, that Mary should not marry at all, was alien to the men who sought to impose their view of the queenship of England's first woman ruler. It was the choice which mattered above all. The idea of the union of Elizabeth and Edward Courtenay perhaps sounded impressive to zealously patriotic ears but was always a non-starter, since it took for granted the princess's acquiescence and the young lord's reliability. Even Courtenay's supporters on the council, such as Gardiner, viewed him as a ditherer. Noailles thought he was also a coward. If she knew anything at all of this aspect of the plotters' intentions, Elizabeth's Christmas must have been an anxious one.

Meanwhile, the final stages in the negotiations of the marriage treaty were scheduled to begin as soon as the New Year had passed. Paget and Renard, overseen by Charles V and with input from Mary, had already hammered out a draft. It stated unequivocally the limitations of Philip's role. 'Prince Philip shall ... enjoy jointly with the queen her style and kingly name, and shall aid her in her administration. The prince shall leave to the queen the disposition of all offices, land and revenues of their dominions; they shall be disposed to those born there. All matters shall be treated in English ... Lest controversy over the succession arises, it is ordered: in England males and females of the marriage shall succeed according to law and custom.' In Spain and Italy, Don Carlos would become ruler, but if he died without children, any male heir of Mary and Philip would succeed in those lands as well as the emperor's in Burgundy and the Low Countries. If there was only a daughter of the marriage, she would rule both England and the Low Countries, but not elsewhere.

As well as this potentially vast patrimony, which would greatly have increased the power of any English monarch, whether male or female, there were stringent safeguards for the country's ruling class: 'the prince shall swear he will not promote to any office in England any foreigner ... He shall make no innovation in the laws and customs of England.' The queen could not be removed from the country unless she desired it and any children of the marriage must remain in England unless the nobility permitted their departure overseas. Further restrictions forbade Philip from removing jewels, ships and arms and required that 'England shall not be entangled with the war between the emperor and the French king. Philip, as much as he can, shall see peace observed between France and England, and give no cause of breach, but may assist his father in defence of his lands and revenge of his injuries.'[23]

Philip, who played no part in the marriage negotiations, was understandably furious when he learned, in January 1554, of the restrictions placed on him. He was reduced to the role of second-class companion to a woman 11 years his senior, with whom he was supposed to beget heirs. This was the price his father was willing to make him pay for the union of England with the Low Countries. On paper, it was the most advantageous marriage treaty that England had ever seen. But it still remained for the final details to be hammered out with a distinguished group of special ambassadors sent by Charles V to close the deal.

The imperial party of five commissioners, headed by one of the emperor's most trusted advisers, the count of Egmont, landed at Tower Wharf on 2 January, under leaden, freezing skies. The party (none of whom was Spanish, in deference to continuing English sensibilities) was met by a deputation of English lords led, improbably, by Edward Courtenay. At least at this point he managed to conceal his awareness of what Wyatt and the others were planning, but he surely felt uncomfortable. Still, Egmont's reception was more courteous than that given to his servants the next day. The retinue was pelted with snowballs by disgruntled London urchins.

But this hostile reception by the populace was easily dismissed as a typical show of how unwelcoming the English normally were to foreigners. For Mary, the arrival of Egmont was thrilling; tangible proof that the marriage was really going to go ahead. The anguished conversations with Susan Clarencius and her other ladies about the embarrassing intimacies of marriage, about whether an old maid like herself could ever hope to please a suave, worldly young prince, were now firmly in the past. Less than two weeks should suffice for the necessary refinements to be agreed between the English and the imperial negotiators.

Mary did not yet know that some of her advisers were as uneasy as she was about the mood of the country. Talk of rebellion had already reached the council. The catalyst for their suspicions was the precipitate disappearance from London between Christmas and New Year of Sir Peter Carew, who had gone back down to Devon to assess his strength there and wait out the winter till Palm Sunday. At this stage nothing was said to the queen, but it was felt prudent to summon Carew to attend the council personally so he could be interrogated on his motives. So, on the same day that Egmont's party came to London, Carew was ordered back to the capital to explain himself. His predictable failure to obey merely reinforced suspicions, reported by Renard to the emperor a few days later, that he was part of a heretical plot 'to induce Courtenay or the Lady Elizabeth to act as their leader'. Renard would have loved to pounce on Elizabeth at this early stage, but there was absolutely no evidence to connect her with Carew beyond these unsubstantiated rumours.

The council's concern was well founded but the problem for the conspirators was that the cat was now well and truly out of the bag. During the second week of January the queen was made aware of the potential for serious opposition, something that could not have come as a surprise given the source of her depression before Christmas. But her resolve was still there, and she began to work with the council, as Noailles reported on 12 January, 'to break up the plot of those who are conspiring against the marriage'.[24] Mary had, at this stage, no idea of the extent of the plot or how much popular support her opponents could really count on if it came to an actual fight. The government has been criticised for its inadequate response to the threat but, in mid-January, it was hard to quantify just what that threat was. In fact, queen and council embarked on a staged propaganda campaign two days later when they issued a proclamation giving the text of the marriage treaty. There was nothing wrong with this – indeed, as a tactic, it seems surprisingly modern in approach – and it was perhaps the best that could have been done in the absence of firm information on the plotters' plans and even their identities. But for the conspirators themselves, even the vague revelations of early January meant that, unless they were willing to hold off and risk almost certain discovery, they would have to take up arms much sooner than expected. And a successful campaign in the foul winter weather of 1554, with snow giving way to torrential rain and flooding, looked like a very dubious prospect.

Meanwhile, Mary was putting her own public relations plan into action. The finishing touches on the marriage treaty now complete, Gardiner, who had consistently opposed the Spanish alliance, was given the unenviable task of selling it to the court and council in the Presence Chamber at Westminster Palace. It was apparently a compelling performance: 'an oration very eloquently [delivered], wherein he declared that the queen's majesty, partly for the wealth and enriching of the realm, and partly for friendship and other weighty considerations, hath, after much suite on his [the prince of Spain's] behalf made, determined, by the consent of her council and nobility, to match herself with him in most godly and lawful matrimony'.

Warming to his task, Gardiner pointed out the advantages to England – a generous income of 30,000 ducats a year, all of the Low Countries and Flanders, any son of the marriage to be heir as well to the kingdom of Spain – and he expressed the view that 'we were much bounden to thank God that so noble, worthy and famous a prince would vouchsafe so to humble himself, as in this marriage to take upon him rather as a subject than otherwise; and that the queen should rule all things as she doth now'. Furthermore, there would be no Spaniards on the council, in positions of military command or in the queen's household. In conclusion, Gardiner asked that Philip be received, for Mary's sake, 'with reverence, joy and honour'.[25] This was a heartfelt plea, with an underlying hint of acknowledgement of the emotional cost to Mary in marrying at all.

Unfortunately for Mary, her Lord Chancellor's exhortations fell on the ears of a hardened group of men, many of whom shared the queen's religion but not her vision. In theory, the package as described by Gardiner sounded good, but no one believed that Philip and his Spanish advisers would keep out of English politics. The fear was that, once married to Mary, he would do whatever he liked. As Lord Windsor remarked at the end of Gardiner's speech: 'You tell us many fine words on the part of the queen and many large promises on the part of the emperor and his son; but if it happens that they choose not to carry out what they promise, what pledges and assurances will you have of them to compel them to hold by their agreement?' At this, murmurs of assent arose. Even if Philip kept a low profile in England's domestic policy, where did this leave the country's foreign relations? The handing over to England of one of the Flemish towns (perhaps Gravelines) as a token of imperial commitment might, had it happened, have changed a few minds. But Gardiner's listeners did not all share Mary's view of an England made greater by being part of Europe. Some saw only diminishing independence and the speedy reduction of England's role to one of junior partner, a useful source of men and money to the Spaniard, but nothing more. Paget's fine-sounding clauses and Mary's personal concerns left them unmoved.

The conclusion of the treaty and its sour reception in Westminster gave the rebels cause for hope, but also meant that they needed to move fast. On 18 January Renard, with his normal blend of self-importance and drama, took it upon himself to inform the queen authoritatively about the conspiracy that was afoot. Up till now, he told the emperor, he had not wanted to alarm her, afraid that Mary might go to pieces if she thought there was a serious plot against her. The emperor upbraided him for his misguided (and wholly unjustified) attempt to spare the queen's feelings. In any case, Mary already knew that the conclusion of the treaty might inspire some men to treason. Carew's refusal to come to London was a very big clue, though on 19 January he and his uncle, the romantically named Sir Gawain, were still professing their loyalty: 'we are faithful to the queen', they wrote to the sheriff of Devon, 'and intend to follow her religion'. They had no idea why there were moves to apprehend them, they claimed, but unless proper cause was shown 'you will drive us to stand to the best of our powers for our liberty'. On 21 January the outline of the plot was finally discovered when Gardiner sent for Courtenay and got him to reveal everything that he knew.

The Lord Chancellor seems to have suspected for some time that Courtenay might be implicated but he had delayed confronting the young man, whose candidature for Mary's hand he had so fervently supported. Nobody likes to admit that they have picked a rotten apple. Renard's tête-à-tête with Mary left Gardiner little choice but to hold an uncomfortable interview with Courtenay. If there was going to be bad news, as he strongly suspected, he wanted to make sure the queen heard it directly from him and not from his political rival, Paget, or the ubiquitous imperial ambassador. It was not difficult to get the tearful and confused Courtenay to confess. Probably he told Gardiner more than the bishop was willing to reveal initially, while he was desperate to find some way to salvage his reputation. Thus more time was lost and the danger to the queen grew. She, however, decided to seize as much of the initiative as she could by a pre-emptive strike intended to galvanise support in the counties. On 22 January she wrote informing her subjects that the treaty was concluded, 'with covenants for the preservation of the laws and surety of our realm, as appears by the articles herewith sent'. But she acknowledged that all was not well: 'Certain ill-disposed persons, meaning under pretence of misliking this marriage to rebel against the Catholic religion and divine service restored in this realm, and to take from us that liberty which is not denied to the meanest woman in the choice of husband, spread false reports of our cousin ...

stirring up our subjects by those and other devilish ways to rebel.'[26] The same day Croft, the last of the conspirators still in London, left to go back to his estates on the Welsh Borders. On 25 January, with all the participants now apparently in place, Sir Thomas Wyatt raised his standard at Maidstone. The rebellion had finally begun. But when it came to raising Devon, Carew had found himself stoutly opposed by local militias. He could not deliver his county, so he fled to France, dangerously exposing the others in the plot and providing ammunition for all those who said that the conspirators were in the pay of the French.

Mary and the council were informed at once but still seem to have been unclear as to the ultimate aims of the rebels. The duke of Suffolk was at first thought to be the ringleader and it was assumed that he intended to 'advance Lady Jane and Guildford Dudley, attainted traitors, to the crown'. Why else would he be taking up arms against the queen, who had pardoned him for his part in Northumberland's attempted coup only two months earlier? No mention was made publicly of an altogether different aim, that of replacing Mary with Courtenay and Elizabeth.

The queen wrote to her sister from the palace of St James as soon as the news was confirmed that Wyatt was at the head of a substantial force in Kent. The letter described the danger of rebellion and also revealed that the queen knew something of Elizabeth's plans, which Mary was ordering her to change. It described how

> certain ill-disposed persons, minding more the satisfaction of their own malicious and seditious minds than their duty of allegiance towards us, have of late falsely spread lewd and untrue rumours and … do travail to induce our good and loving subjects to an unnatural rebellion … we, tendering the surety of your person, which might be in some peril if any sudden tumult should arise, either where you be now or at Donnington, whither (as we understand) you are bound shortly to remove, do therefore think it expedient you should put yourself in good readiness with all convenient speed to make your repair hither to us, which, we pray you, fail not to do …[27]

Elizabeth, pleading ill health and the great difficulties of travelling given the poor condition of the roads, declined. Besides, the news could not have come as a great surprise to her, since she had known about the timing of the uprising before Mary. Sir James Croft had made a detour to Ashridge on his way home to Wales and had taken Elizabeth into his confidence. It was he who advised her to move out of harm's way, to her house at Donnington in Berkshire. Enigmatic as ever, Elizabeth stayed put, but she did not send post-haste to advise her sister of what she knew, nor did she make any public profession of loyalty at this stage. The decision to allow Elizabeth to leave court now seemed a dangerous mistake, especially when events took a still more serious turn. On the same day that Mary wrote to her sister, a French spy was intercepted near Rochester carrying Noailles' dispatches. He was found to have in his possession a French translation of a letter written by Elizabeth to Mary some days earlier.

How did it get there and what, if anything, did it prove? The case of Elizabeth's letter is one of the great diplomatic intrigues of the 16th century, and there has never been a wholly compelling explanation of how it came to be in the Frenchman's pouch. The letter itself was unremarkable. It referred to Elizabeth's continued ill health and gave the impression that she had not enjoyed the festive season: 'I have been troubled, since my arrival at my house, with such a cold and headache that I have never felt their like, and especially during the last three weeks I have had no respite because of the pain in my head and also in my arms.' Then there was a reference to the fact that Mary had written, in her own hand, to her sister: 'To tell me the conclusion of your marriage and of the articles to accompany it.' She was circumspect in what she said about this, noting only that 'this is a deep and weighty matter, but I have no doubt that it will redound to the glory of God'.[28] Despite what some writers have said, this was not a copy of Elizabeth's refusal to come to court in response to Wyatt's uprising in Kent. Mary did not write to Ashridge until the day the French courier was detained, and Elizabeth's letter, though undated, is clearly earlier.

But the implications for the queen of this unexpected find were disturbing. Either there were traitors on the council, passing on her correspondence to the French, or her sister had established a secret line of communication with the French ambassador. The first possibility left Mary isolated, with only the increasingly hysterical Renard as someone she could trust. The second explanation intensified her suspicions of her absent sister. She could not discount either theory.

The truth will never be known for sure, but the deviousness of those involved, an atmosphere laden with false trails, half-lies and a complex system of espionage, suggests one possible interpretation that Mary

never considered. Renard was often given copies of Mary's correspondence by the queen herself. He could have translated it personally and
ensured that it got to Noailles through the shadowy network of agents
that both men used. Its discovery would be a further indictment against
Elizabeth, the kind of proof that Mary's advisers were demanding if
action were to be taken against the queen's sister. Yet the timing of the
'discovery' meant that Renard, if he was, indeed, responsible, had played
his hand too soon. The prospect of a major attack on London by Wyatt's
men was far more serious. Elizabeth could wait.

Once Wyatt moved, he did not do things by half-measures. His
campaigning instincts and leadership qualities quickly brought 3,000
men flocking to his standard. Kent was fertile ground for any attack on
the government, with its history of rebelliousness and dislike of
London's authority. But in London, at the hastily convened meetings and
crisis talks of the court and council, there was fear and uncertainty mixed
with an air of unreality. Paget and Gardiner blamed each other for the
threat that the queen now faced, while concurring that as much should
be kept from her as possible. Their withholding of information disadvantaged them as much as it infuriated Mary. The only person willing,
almost eager, to tell her what he thought was going on was, of course,
Renard. The council resented his intimacy with the queen, his self-
appointed role as chief adviser, which gave the entirely false impression
that the defence of Mary Tudor's throne was being orchestrated by an
agent of the emperor.

   And Mary had dire need of men that she could trust and who would
treat her as the monarch she was, rather than as a feeble woman. For
although the intended uprisings in Devon, the Midlands and Wales failed
to materialise through lack of local support, Wyatt's insurrection looked
daily more menacing. It needed to be met with organised military
strength. The force sent to confront Wyatt at Rochester was commanded
by the duke of Norfolk, still the senior peer of the realm, and despite his
age it was felt that he had the authority to handle the situation. But even
Norfolk himself, when he wrote to the council on 29 January, did not
sound optimistic about his chances: 'they have fortified the bridge at
Rochester, so it will be hard passing them. We shall do the best we can
… Think no ill of such lords and gentlemen as were appointed to come

with me, for they have honest excuse, the weather being so terrible that no man can stir by water or well by land.'[29] The duke was compelled to retire the next day when most of his men, who may have received financial inducements from Noailles, went over to Wyatt. In this ignominious way, the council's attempt to defeat the rebels by direct military engagement was snuffed out and Wyatt moved towards London unimpeded.

Contrasting emotions now beset those around the queen. Panicked by rumours that their lives were in danger, the imperial commissioners decided to hotfoot it back to the Low Countries before the approaching rebels could muster an attack on the capital. Gardiner advised the queen to flee for her own safety, but Renard and Paget told her she must not leave. The lords in charge of the military defence of the capital, the earl of Pembroke and Lord Edward Clinton, thought the physical danger exaggerated. But both had been strong supporters of Northumberland and had joined him on his ill-fated military foray against Mary in July. They received the queen's clemency, but how far their loyalty to her went was unproven. Both claimed they did not rate Wyatt's supporters, despite Wyatt's own undoubted military prowess. Instead, they contented themselves with raising a crack force of 500 foot and 200 horse, of whose loyalty to the queen they could be more certain than they could of that of the normal defence, the London-trained bands, who opposed the Spanish marriage.

The one person who showed consistent calm determination and a great deal of personal courage, amid all this uncertainty and foreboding, was Mary. She knew instinctively the importance of the defiant gesture and the sheer power of majesty. In resolve and eloquence she was every bit the equal of her father and sister. And she also knew that she would fail if she could not turn public opinion in London to her cause. She must intervene personally, or the situation could slip away from her. On 1 February, she rode with her councillors to the Guildhall to make an impassioned speech to the government of London.

Mary told her listeners that Wyatt had rejected an attempt at compromise and that he proposed to hold her hostage. Her speech to the wary audience of aldermen and City of London worthies was a masterclass in Tudor oratory. At her coronation, she said, she had been 'wedded to the realm', and she showed her audience her coronation ring: 'I have on my finger, which hitherto never was, nor hereafter never shall be, left off.' She reminded them that she was Henry VIII's daughter and that she loved her people: 'On the word of a prince, I cannot tell how naturally the mother loveth the child, for I was never mother of any. But certainly, if a prince and a governor may as naturally and earnestly love her subjects as the mother doth love the child, then assure yourselves that I, being your lady and mistress, do as earnestly and tenderly love and favour you.' This was clever stuff with just the right note of underlying feminine vulnerability. It alluded to the long years of disappointment when she was young and naturally hoped for motherhood, yet it also subtly suggested that Mary's marriage, the underlying cause of the current unrest and her direct appeal to London, would always come second to her commitment to England. She went on to speak of the reasons that had led her make the decision to marry, against her personal volition. Then she made an extraordinary statement, not previously discussed with any adviser, even Simon Renard: 'On the word of a queen I promise you that if it shall not probably appear to all the nobility and commons in the high court of parliament that this marriage shall be for the benefit and commodity of the whole realm, then I will abstain from marriage while I live.'[30]

Mary's audience, swept up in her emotion and the stirring manner of her delivery (her deep, strong voice was a powerful weapon, filling the Guildhall), did not raise the obvious question; she had already roundly dismissed the deputation from the House of Commons in November when it pleaded with her not to proceed with the Spanish marriage. So what had changed her mind and was the change genuine? Perhaps those present believed that the danger she faced had caused her to think again.

The only problem was that it had not. At another moment of extreme crisis, in 1536, when her father's psychological abuse had become too much to bear, Mary was compelled to lie. Now she even lied to Renard about what she had actually said, claiming that she told the people of London 'that if they had not understood the causes and occasions [of her marriage], she would repeat them to a Parliament'. And she certainly intended, as did her advisers, for a bill confirming her marriage and detailing the treaty to go before Parliament, as it eventually did in April 1554. But she was not truly prepared to alter her decision. Clearly, she did not care how her credibility would be damaged if the lie were exposed. Such considerations were not for princes.

The speech worked. When Wyatt arrived with his force at London Bridge two days later, on 3 February, he found it well guarded by forces loyal to the queen. The imperial commissioners might have fled for their lives but the prospects of London going over to the rebels did not seem good. Nevertheless, he persisted and on 6 February he managed to evade Mary's soldiers and cross the River Thames by night at Kingston. He would attack the city from the west.

The news that Wyatt had not faded away, that attack was imminent, caused pandemonium when it reached the palace of Westminster in the small hours of the morning. Wyatt's forces launched a half-hearted attack on the palace, shooting arrows at the windows, but made no attempt to breach its outer defences. Mary was woken at 3 a.m. and informed of the likelihood of a direct assault. She rose, to find her presence chamber full of armed men and her ladies wild with fright. Edward Underhill, one of the queen's pensioners, described the scene vividly: 'After supper I put on my armour as the rest did, for we were appointed to watch all the night. So being all armed, we came up into the chamber of presence with our poleaxes in our hands, wherewith the ladies were very fearful; some lamenting, crying, and wringing their hands, said, "Alas, there is some great mischief toward; we shall all be destroyed this night! What a sight is this, to see the queen's chamber full of armed men".'[31] Their understandable alarm was not helped when there were further calls for the queen to flee, this time by boat: 'All is lost; away, away; a barge, a barge!' Reluctant to follow such advice, Mary resisted courageously:

> ... her grace never changed her cheer, nor would remove one foot out of the house, but asked for the lord of Pembroke, in whom her grace had worthily reposed great confidence. Answer being made that he was in the field, 'Well then,' quod her grace, 'fall to prayer, and I warrant you we shall hear better news anon; for my lord will not deceive me, I know well; if he would, God will not, in whom my chief trust is, who will not deceive me.'[32]

None of the agitated inhabitants of the palace could have anticipated what happened next. After a few brief skirmishes along Fleet Street and the Strand, in which the guard supposedly defending Mary behaved with almost comical cowardice, and would probably have been put to flight if Wyatt's supporters were not already deserting, the rebellion suddenly fizzled out without warning. Finding he could not advance beyond Ludgate, which was well fortified, Wyatt was suddenly overwhelmed by despondency. He alone of the plotters had honoured his commitments and he knew, as he sat outside a tavern near Ludgate Bar and gathered his thoughts, that he could not prevail. The enormity of his offence against the Crown was stark. He seems to have believed that a pardon might be offered if he surrendered and so he gave himself up without resistance. But only the Tower and the scaffold awaited him.

The aftermath of the rebellion was not pretty. The queen's mercy was exhausted and retribution came quickly, to the innocent as well as the guilty. The Carew brothers had already reached safety in France before Wyatt fired a shot, but the other conspirators were soon hunted down and about a hundred participants in the uprising were executed between mid-February and mid-March. Edward Courtenay found himself back in the Tower within a week of the end of the rebellion, despite having commanded some of the queen's guard during the fighting in London. In disgrace, his mother left court, never to recover her position of influence with Mary.[33] But the first and most famous victim was Lady Jane Grey, who died on 12 February. The decision to execute her troubled the queen greatly, but Mary bowed to her councillors' advice that her cousin would always be a focus for rebellion. The duke of Suffolk's almost whimsical involvement sealed his daughter's fate. Her life and that of Guildford Dudley were forfeit. It could not have been unexpected.

Jane made herself watch as her young husband's headless body returned in a cart filled with bloodied straw from the block on Tower Green. She had not seen him during their detention, yet the sight moved her more than any intimacy between the couple in their brief marriage. When she went to meet her own death only 30 minutes later, wearing a mourning dress edged with black velvet and clutching a prayer-book, she was well prepared for the address to the people that was expected. Born of the blood royal, a Tudor like Mary, she asked the small crowd gathered to observe her end 'to bear me witness that I die a good Christian woman, and that I looked to be saved by no other means, but only by the mercy of God in the merits of the blood of his only son Jesus Christ: and I confess when I did know the word of God I neglected the same, loved myself and the world, and therefore this plague or punishment is happily and worthily happened unto me for my sins; and yet I thank God of his goodness that he hath given me a time and respite to repent'. Then she added: 'and now, good people, while I am alive, I pray you to assist me with your prayers'.[34] She had resisted all Mary's attempts to get her to die in the Catholic religion, strong in her Protestant faith and convinced that, as she wrote to her father, 'to me there is nothing that can be more welcome than from this vale of misery to aspire to that heavenly throne of all joy and pleasure with Christ my Saviour'.[35]

Yet right at the end, when she was blindfolded and had just moments to live, her composure deserted her. She could not find the block. 'What shall I do? Where is it?' she cried out, until a bystander guided her and she recovered from her terror. Then the axe fell swiftly and cleanly and this hideously manipulated, unloved slip of a girl was gone.

In the flyleaf of her prayer-book she had written to the lieutenant of the Tower, John Brydges, who showed her much kindness and thoughtful consideration while she lodged as a prisoner with him: 'Forasmuch as you have desired so simple a woman to write in so worthy a book … therefore shall I as a good friend desire you … live still to die, that by death you may purchase eternal life … for as the preacher sayeth, there is a time to be born and a time to die; and the day of death is better than the day of our birth. Yours, as the Lord knoweth, as a friend, Jane Dudley.'[36]

The axe had fallen on Lady Jane and its shadow now hung over Elizabeth herself. But despite repeated questioning, some of it probably under torture, Wyatt never admitted that Elizabeth was involved in the rebellion and no solid evidence could be found against her, much to Renard's irritation. She could not, however, be allowed to remain free while the trials of Wyatt and his accomplices were taking place and now that the imperial commissioners had returned.[37] It may also have been hoped that her servants, some of whom were not known for their discretion, would give the game away once separated from her. Elizabeth's health was poor and she was, in her different way, as highly strung as her sister. The prospect of prolonged interrogation and imprisonment might break her spirit.

It has been suggested that, in the difficult relationship between Elizabeth and Mary, Elizabeth held all the cards and Mary was actually the victim. But while it is true that Elizabeth's lands and men, as well as her natural rapport with the populace, gave her a great deal of power, there can be no doubt that Mary, as queen, could have destroyed her if she had ever fully hardened her heart. And Elizabeth was quite clearly terrified of sharing her mother's fate, despite being aware that Paget and his clique on the council would do everything they could to prevent her being sacrificed.

When another, more imperious summons to court arrived as soon as Wyatt's rebellion failed, Elizabeth was in a quandary. She did not want to leave, partly because she was genuinely unwell, but she was desperate to seek a personal interview with Mary. In order to assess whether her sister was really ill or just malingering, Mary sent her own physicians to examine Elizabeth. When three of Mary's councillors, led by the lord admiral, William Howard, arrived to inform Elizabeth that Mary's summons was not negotiable, they reported to the queen: 'Your physicians told us she might without danger repair to you with all speed. We found her comfortable, save that she desired longer to recover her strength; but on the persuasion of us and her own council and servants (whom we found ready to accomplish your pleasure) she is resolved to move tomorrow – the journey is enclosed. She desires lodging further from the water than she had last at court, which your physicians think meet.'[38] This short missive reveals that Elizabeth was still very clear-headed, despite being stressed and feeling weak, and it also suggests that those around her may well have persuaded her that she could hold out no longer at Ashridge.

She left on 12 February, the day that Lady Jane was beheaded. But having been taken ill again en route, she did not arrive in London until nearly two weeks later. It was a curiously regal entry for someone whose position was at best uncertain and at worst approaching disgrace. Accompanied by two hundred scarlet-clad horsemen, the invalid sat in her litter dressed entirely in white and with the curtains open so that people could see her – and also to give the lie to rumours put about by Renard that she was pregnant.

The entry may have been impressive but the reality of Elizabeth's position was much more desperate. She was taken to Whitehall and kept in a secure lodging. Despite impassioned pleas, Mary refused to see her. The queen evidently feared that there was still sufficient residual affection and family feeling for her judgement to be swayed at a critical time. Mary's coldness was Elizabeth's worst nightmare.

Isolated and sick with worry, the queen's sister languished in Whitehall until mid-March. Then, at his trial, Wyatt, in attempting to defend her, actually made matters worse. He acknowledged that he had sent her a letter about the rebellion and she had replied verbally, via her servant, William St Loe, 'that she did thank him much for his goodwill and she would do as she should see cause'.[39] This was just the kind of vague sentiment, notably lacking in declarations of personal loyalty to Mary herself, that the queen so detested about her sister. The situation looked bad and even Paget could not prevent the fall-out. The day after Wyatt made his remarks, the entire council came to Whitehall and charged her with involvement in the Carew and Wyatt conspiracies. Though she denied the charges absolutely, the next move was predictable and much dreaded by the 20-year-old Elizabeth. Like Lady Jane, and her own mother before her, she would be made a prisoner in the Tower. And there were clearly those, including perhaps her own sister, who would try to ensure that she met the same fate.

On Saturday, 17 March 1554, the marquess of Winchester and the earl of Sussex, two of Mary's most faithful supporters, came to escort the daughter of Anne Boleyn to the Tower by water. Deprived of her servants and under armed guard, Elizabeth tried desperately to delay, convinced that if she were allowed to see the queen in person, she could plead her case much more effectively. She begged, and was granted, time to write a letter. Winchester had been inclined not to humour her, but Sussex prevailed on him to relent. She was, the old earl pointed out, a king's daughter.

At about noon she composed herself sufficiently to write a brief, heartfelt but still elegant note to her estranged sister and sovereign lady. It is one of the most poignant of all her correspondence, redolent of fear and past suffering:

> If any ever did try this old saying, that a king's word was more than another man's oath, I beseech your majesty to verify it to me and to remember your last promise and my last demand that I be not condemned without answer and proof; which now it seems I am, for without cause proved I am by your council from you commanded to the Tower. I know I deserve it not, yet it appears proved. I profess before God I never practised, counselled or consented to anything prejudicial to you or dangerous to the state. Let me answer before you, before I go to the Tower (if possible) – if not, before I am further condemned. Pardon my boldness. I have heard of many cast away for want of coming to their prince.

Here old nightmares surfaced as she saw again Tom Seymour and the ghosts of her girlhood: 'I have heard Somerset say that if his brother had been allowed to speak with him, he would never have suffered ... I pray evil persuades not one sister against the other. Wyatt might write me a

letter, but I never received any from him. As for the copy of my letter to
the french king, God confound me if I ever sent him word, token, or
letter by any means.' She added as postscript:'I crave but one word of
answer.'The rest of the parchment was heavily scored in ink by Elizabeth
to prevent additions or forgeries.[40]

The letter had one immediate, advantageous effect. While she was
writing the tide turned and it was necessary to wait until Palm Sunday,
18 March, to convey her to the Tower. This had been the day originally
set for Wyatt and the others to begin their revolt. But whether Elizabeth
had bought herself more than one extra day of life remained to be seen.

Chapter Ten

King Philip

'Philip is the spouse of Mary, but treats her so
deferentially as to appear her son.'

Cardinal Pole's revealing analysis of Mary's marital relationship in
late 1554

At the moment that Elizabeth landed as a prisoner at Tower Wharf on
a rainy spring morning, her future brother-in-law was a thousand
miles away to the south in the sunnier climes of Valladolid. He had
passed the winter here, in regular correspondence with his father and
aunt in the Netherlands but with no word or gift to his intended wife.

The outbreak of rebellion in England inevitably delayed the final
stages of the marriage negotiations, and though Simon Renard made
sure the prince got a rather watered-down version of events, Philip was
well informed about what had happened in his prospective kingdom. In
Brussels there was, for a while, sufficient gloom for doubts to be raised
about whether the marriage could actually go ahead, but these were
soon dispelled by the firm action taken by Mary and her government
against the rebels. Egmont and his deputation returned in mid-February
and the finishing touches were soon put to the marriage treaty. Mary had
already made it clear that she would not marry in Lent, an idea that
offended her religious sensibilities, but she hoped that she would be a
wife soon after.

On 6 March, she was formally betrothed. A positive development,
certainly, but Mary had first been betrothed at the age of two and a half,
and well knew that the condition was only an expression of intent. And

the happiness of the occasion was somewhat marred by the realisation that the magnificent ring placed on her finger came from Charles V, not his son. Yet more than three months earlier Philip had written to his father with apparent enthusiasm: 'As for what you say of the English match and the great progress that is being made, I kiss your majesty's hands many times, for it is clear that you are conducting the matter with great love and care. I lay great value on the queen's professions of good-will … My own happiness and dearest hopes hang on the result … If the queen wishes me to go soon I will start without loss of time.'[1] In fact, eight months would elapse between the date of this letter and his setting foot on English soil. He was a very dilatory bridegroom.

And perhaps, it might be added, a dishonest one. Yet this would not be entirely fair. He was never an easy man to read, even to those who knew him well, and he was still young enough to wish that duty did not always have to be so irksome. Besides, things had changed in the three months since he wrote so positively to Charles V, and, from Philip's perspective, the developments were all unwelcome. The main cause of his dissatisfaction was not the rebellion in England; it was the marriage treaty negotiated without his input which eviscerated his power. His optimism of late November gave way to fury by early January, when the detail of the treaty was finally revealed to him. He did not say so, but he clearly felt that he had been deceived by his own father. The emperor had gone too far in accommodating the wishes of the English. Although there were still obvious advantages in the arrangement from the perspective of governing the Low Countries, in England he would be nothing. His wife-to-be was 11 years his senior and already showing signs of a desire to be with him that he could not reciprocate. Nor did he know how many years he would have to play second fiddle to her, constantly striving to be nice to her treacherous nobility and her charm-less, uncivilised subjects. When he came, he wanted to be sure that he had the trappings of a king, even if the small print of his marriage arrangements said otherwise. He needed time to prepare a fleet, to arrange his household and to make preparations for the administration of Castile in his absence. Entreated from all sides to move with dispatch, he dug his heels in. He would go only when all was ready. Betrothed he might be. Eager he was not.

Philip did not tell the emperor of his reservations but he was suffi-ciently angry to commit them to paper, in front of witnesses. His secre-tary, Juan Vásquez de Molina, took down his statement. There were no

The Tudor lady in this miniature by Flemish painter Lavinia Teerlinc has recently been identified by Dr David Starkey as Lady Jane Grey, the cousin chosen by Edward VI in 1553 to inherit his throne.

ABOVE John Dudley, duke of Northumberland, chief minister of Edward VI in 1553. One of the period's most enigmatic figures, he and Mary had known each other for many years and their antipathy was palpable. He made a fatal misjudgement when he discounted Mary's determination to fight for the throne.

LEFT A medallion portrait of Sir Thomas Wyatt the younger. Wyatt was a former soldier who became embroiled in an ill-fated attempt to prevent Mary's marriage to Philip of Spain. The failed rebellion dangerously compromised Elizabeth, who was imprisoned in the Tower of London for two months.

Mary and her husband, King Philip, son of Charles V. After Mary's death, he recalled with distaste his time as king of England. In this portrait, Mary appears regal and content while Philip looks awkward and rather absurd with his spindly legs.

This superb replica of Queen Mary's elegant purple and white wedding gown, set with pearls, was made by costume expert Tanya Elliott.

A portrait of Queen Elizabeth dating from around 1560. This is the closest depiction we have of what Elizabeth must have looked like during Mary's reign. As queen, Mary came to detest Anne Boleyn's daughter, viewing her as devious and disloyal. Despite being belatedly acknowledged as Mary's heir, Elizabeth always resented her treatment during her half-sister's reign.

Simon Renard, Charles V's ambassador to England during the first three years of Mary's reign. An energetic man of considerable ability, he did not really understand English politics and his judgement of Mary was often condescending. This portrait captures his charm, intensity and cunning.

A page from the *Queen Mary Atlas*, commissioned by Mary for her husband Philip, by Portuguese cartographer Diego Homen. This map shows the British Isles. The arms of Philip II, on the left, were partially removed during Elizabeth's reign.

Framlingham Castle in Suffolk, where Mary raised her standard and gathered an army in July 1553. Her triumph was one of the very few successful revolts of the provinces against central authority in English history.

BELOW Winchester Cathedral, where Mary married Philip in the wet July of 1554.

ABOVE RIGHT The burning of Cranmer. Thomas Cranmer, archbishop of Canterbury from 1533 to 1556, was hated by Mary for his role in her mother's divorce and his reforming ideas on religion. This woodcut from John Foxe's *Book of Martyrs* shows his death at the stake in Oxford in March 1556.

tactful words here. In his name, the ambassadors to England were about to ratify the articles of the marriage treaty negotiated by 'the emperor and king, his father'. This process could not be stopped but it was being done against his will. 'Until the articles had been drawn up,' he protested,

> he had not known of them, and he intended to grant the said power and swear to observe the articles in order that his marriage with the queen of England might take place, but by no means in order to bind himself or his heirs to observe the articles, especially any that might burden his conscience. And because by his own free will he had never agreed and never would agree to the articles ... he protested before me, the secretary and other witnesses ... against the articles and everything contained therein ... desiring that it should forever be recorded, as a plain, clear and certain fact to stand as long as the world should last, that his highness had given the above-mentioned oath in order, as he had said, that his marriage should take place, and not of his own free will ... This he swore by Our Lord, by Saint Mary and by the sign of the Cross ... and by the words of the Holy Gospel ... that he would not be bound by the said ratification to be made in his name, nor by his own promise to observe or keep anything contained in the said articles ...[2]

Two days later, having vented his spleen in private, he wrote a polite note to his father in which he confined himself to bland comments about the marriage negotiations being 'a source of satisfaction to me and I trust that the result will contribute to the welfare of Christendom'.[3] He knew that he could not say anything else. It was supremely ironic that on the same day the emperor's ambassador to the papal court, Don Juan Manrique de Lara, wrote to the prince with the sort of unwanted advice that must have jarred painfully: 'I remind your highness that, as they say in Castile, you must be so yielding towards them [the English] that it may seem that the husband is of the same country as his wife. So gladden that kingdom and he happy there in the company of its sons, employing them in all offices and posts. Thus your highness shall win the goodwill of the English as well as that of the Flemings. For the love of God, appear to be pleased ...'[4]

Mary knew nothing of Philip's sense of betrayal, but it must have been obvious to her that he was not rushing to her side. The period between her decision to marry him and his actual arrival was a difficult one. All she had of him was a portrait painted by Titian three years earlier, which Mary of Hungary sent her in November 1553. It was, the dowager queen told Renard, 'considered a good likeness by everybody at the time. It is true that the portrait has suffered a little from time and its journey from Augsburg hither; but it will serve to tell her what he is like, if she will put it in a proper light and look at it from a distance, as all Titian's paintings have to be looked at.' She went on to add, rather ruefully, 'So you will present the portrait to her under one condition; that I shall have it again, as it is only a dead thing, when she has the living model in her presence.'[5] This request suggests that Mary of Hungary was fond of her nephew. Perhaps she was, but her affection had its limits. She was not willing to serve him in the Low Countries as she had served her brother. He was an absentee king of England by the time she made this clear, when Mary of England would have given much to have him stay with her and her Habsburg cousin wanted only to be allowed to retire.

The prolonged engagement, if it can be called that, cannot have done much for Mary's confidence. There had been rumours that this virtuous prince was not the paragon that Renard had claimed. Mary could dismiss as malicious the gossip that he was the father of a growing brood of illegitimate children, but a letter from him would have greatly raised her spirits. She pointed out his dereliction in this respect by instructing Renard in his next dispatch to the prince to 'commend her most affectionately to you and inform you that she would have liked to have written to you in her own hand an account of the troubles caused in her realm … but as he had not yet received any letters from you it was not for a lady to begin'. Instead, she asked the ambassador to assure Philip of her constant goodwill and her anxiety to please him in his every wish. 'She herself', Renard wrote, 'will leave nothing undone in order to welcome you in all gladness and obedience. She finds the time long and asks continually when you will come'.[6] Philip did not take the hint. He persisted in using others as intermediaries, assuring the increasingly exasperated Renard that 'he would gladly affront any peril in order to free her from anxiety and show my sense of duty towards her'. But Mary wanted more than this, and by April she had grown tired of waiting, and of observing the ladylike proprieties. She was, after all, a queen and he was still a prince. She would write if she chose. Her letter was in French and rather formal: '*Je vous advertis que le Parlement, qui represente les états de mon Royaume, a apprené les articles de notre Mariage sans contradiction.*'[7] (I inform you that Parliament, which represents the states of my kingdom, has approved the articles of our marriage without contradiction.) It might be 'our' marriage, but it was still 'my' kingdom. This time Philip responded, though not with any great alacrity. On 11 May he sent the marquis de las Navas to England with a letter written in his own hand and a jewel for Mary. It was a very belated gesture, but a welcome one. As the warmer weather beckoned, the queen believed that she would, finally, be a summer bride.

Mary had much to occupy her during the long months of waiting. The business of government was a constant pressure and her council remained quarrelsome and on edge, though by no means ineffective. A parliament was summoned for early April and initial thoughts that it might go more smoothly if it met in Oxford were soon replaced by the acknowledgement that this would cause too much resentment in London. Parliament needed to ratify the marriage treaty and embark on the next step of religious legislation; moving the session outside the capital was to invite unwanted friction at an important time. And there was still the dilemma of what to do with Elizabeth.

Many legends have grown up about Elizabeth's time in the Tower of London. They are based on a colourful retelling of her story that was appended to John Foxe's *Acts and Monuments*. These tales are affecting and dramatic, but largely untrue. The princess entered the Tower not by the Traitors Gate – an impossibility, given the low tide at the time she arrived – but over the drawbridge. She passed along a route lined with armed men, disconcerting in itself, and below the Bloody Tower. In the distance, Lady Jane Grey's scaffold was still there, a grim reminder of the fate of another young woman who had entered the Tower as the queen's prisoner and never left it. And somewhere in her consciousness, though she never alluded to it, must have been the knowledge that her own mother, desperate and bewildered, had made this journey 18 years before. 'Oh Lord!' she said to Winchester and Sussex and the others accompanying her. 'I never thought to come here as prisoner; and I pray you all, good friends and fellows, bear me witness, that I come in no traitor but as true a woman to the queen's majesty as any is now living; and thereon will I take my death.' Brave as the declaration was, much as she hoped to live, death must have seemed a hideous possibility.

Though confined, she was treated honourably, lodged in a suite of four rooms in part of the royal palace in the Tower and not in some iron-grilled dungeon. A retinue of servants attended her.[8] It was more than her sister had been granted when Henry VIII confined Mary in Elizabeth's household in 1533. But the threat was more immediate than the loss of status her sister faced when Elizabeth was a baby. On Good Friday, the council came to interrogate her, armed with some very awkward questions about her foreknowledge of Wyatt's uprising. To add to her discomfort, they sprang a surprise. They demanded to know 'what conference she had with Sir James Acroffts, being then a prisoner in the Tower, and brought into her presence on set purpose to confront her, alleging that the speech, which they had privately, was about her removal … to Donnington Castle.'

Caught off guard, Elizabeth struggled to find the right answer. She said she could not remember that she owned such a house. But then, sensing that this prevarication was unhelpful to her situation, she 'recollected herself'. Gathering her wits, the princess fell back on her standard defence against such accusations, which was to deny them while actually evading the specifics. 'My officers and you, Sir James Crofts,' she said, addressing her fellow-prisoner directly, 'can well testify, whether any rash or unbeseeming word did at that time pass my lips, which might not have well become a faithful and loyal subject.' Croft obligingly played his part, kneeling before her and 'taking God to witness that he never knew anything by her worthy of the least suspicion'.[9] If the council had hoped that they would incriminate each other, or provide further avenues of enquiry, they would have been disappointed. But not all of them wished for such an outcome. Gardiner, who led the examination, probably did, but Paget and others who took the longer view were relieved that nothing more substantial could be raised against Elizabeth.

With the execution of Sir Thomas Wyatt on 11 April, the danger to Elizabeth was effectively over. There was still hope that he would incriminate her and Courtenay, even on the scaffold, but he would not be drawn. In fact, he took pains to exonerate Elizabeth, beginning his final speech with an unequivocal denial: 'And whereas it is said and whistled abroad that I should accuse my Lady Elizabeth's grace and my lord Courtenay; it is not so good people.'[10] His statement was certainly unhelpful to the government, but his refusal to implicate either of the principal figures imprisoned in the Tower was, in the end, a relief to Gardiner as well as Paget. The chancellor did not want anything more to come out about his connection with Courtenay. Wyatt died the death of a gentleman, though his corpse was not spared the traditional horrors of quartering reserved for traitors. But Mary took pity on his wife and children, ruined by his attainder. She granted Jane Wyatt an annuity of 200 marks and made a small restitution of the income from their confiscated lands at the end of 1555.

Wyatt had not obliged the regime, which was swiftly to suffer another reverse. Just a few days after his execution, the trial of Sir Nicholas Throckmorton, who was accused of supporting the rebels but had not himself taken up arms, came to a swift end when a jury of Londoners acquitted him. His transition from versifying supporter of the queen to palpable traitor was impossible to prove. If he had been found guilty, Throckmorton's case could have been used as a template to bring charges of treason against Elizabeth. As it was, the attempt collapsed ignominiously for the government. It seemed time to draw a line under events, to move on to more positive ground. Nothing would be gained by drawing further attention to Elizabeth. She was allowed greater freedom to take exercise and move about in the Tower until, on 19 May, she was allowed to leave. 'We have appointed our sister the Lady Elizabeth, for divers good considerations,' wrote Mary on 21 May, 'to be removed from the Tower of London unto our manor of Woodstock, there to remain until we shall otherwise determine'.

In her further instructions to Sir Henry Bedingfeld, the lieutenant of the Tower and now appointed Elizabeth's custodian, Mary made clear that Elizabeth's release did not mean that she was exonerated. 'Although she be not thoroughly cleared, yet have we, for her better quiet and to the end she may be more honourably used, thought meet to appoint her to remain at our said manor of Woodstock until such time as certain matters touching her case which be not yet cleared may be thoroughly tried and examined.' If this was less than crystal clear, so were the rest of Bedingfeld's instructions. Elizabeth was 'to be safely looked after for the safeguard of her person, having nevertheless regarded to use her in such good and honourable sort as may be agreeable to our honour and her estate and degree'. The princess would have some liberty of movement, but could walk in the grounds only accompanied by Bedingfeld, and he was 'to give good heed to our said sister's behaviour, for seeing that neither she be suffered to have conference with any suspected person out of his hearing, nor that she by any means either receive or send any message, letter or token to or from any manner of person'.[11]

Elizabeth, in other words, was not to be trusted or indulged. She had

no idea when, or indeed if, she would see Mary again. Her departure
from the Tower was much less dramatic than her arrival, but she was not
a free woman. Relieved to be alive, but aggrieved at the restrictive,
insulting regime to which she was now subjected, Elizabeth set out to
make the life of the unfortunate Sir Henry Bedingfeld every bit as
unpleasant as her own.

Mary could now look forward to Philip's arrival with her sister firmly in
the background. During April, Parliament had considered several important pieces of legislation, not all of which passed easily or to the queen's
satisfaction. The main business was to ratify the marriage treaty, as Mary
had promised in her Guildhall speech. This took place quickly, passing
both houses of Parliament by 12 April. Mary, as she wrote to Charles V
on the following day, viewed this as good progress. Her overall optimism
was, however, misplaced. Other legislation on which she set much store
fared far less well. She was angry when a bill to extend the treason laws
to cover anyone plotting against her husband was passed only in a
diluted version and absolutely furious when a bill against heresy, introduced with her full support by Gardiner, failed altogether.[12]

The loss of the heresy bill, whose precise details have not survived,
was probably brought about by the intensifying of the feud between
Gardiner and Paget. Paget feared that Gardiner would introduce a bill to
disinherit Elizabeth and he struck back instinctively, determined to hurt
the chancellor where he could. Because he was also a moderate man
who favoured a cautious approach to the imposition of Catholicism and
the return to Rome, he looked askance at the methods being employed
by Mary and Gardiner. And his doubts were shared by many others. At
first sight it seems strange that a piece of legislation 'for the avoiding of
erroneous opinions and books containing heresies' should have attracted
much opposition at all in an overwhelmingly Catholic House of Lords.
No peer claimed to support heresy. But the bill was seen as the thin end
of the wedge. The nobility feared that it was the first step in a wholesale
return of Church lands. Catholics, much more than Protestants, had
grown rich on the proceeds of the dismantling of the wealth of the
English Church, a fact not lost on the imperial ambassador. Mobilising
his considerable support in the House of Lords, Paget scuppered the
heresy bill of 1554. Ten months would pass before new legislation was

introduced and Mary could move against the Protestants she had despised for so long. Nor could she rid herself of the supreme headship of the Church, a title that she hated. Her lords were happy for the ritual of the Catholic religion to be restored but they would not part with their wealth, nor were they keen to rush back to the jurisdiction of the papacy.

Paget had won, but at great personal cost. Mary never forgave him. He wrote afterwards that 'Queen Mary hated me'. He attended the privy council less frequently and, as his health deteriorated, spent less time at court. His partial restoration to royal favour he owed to the man Mary awaited as her husband. None of the queen's other advisers seemed to Philip to have the faintest understanding of Europe.

Despite these significant losses, the parliament of April 1554 passed other notable pieces of legislation, including 14 statutes dealing with economic problems which benefited English commerce and industry. But the most interesting piece of legislation concerned Mary herself. This was the act concerning the regal power, defined in the case of this first queen regnant of England as being identical to her male predecessors:

> ... the regal power of this realm is in the queen's majesty as fully and absolutely as ever it was in any of her most noble progenitors, kings of this realm ... be it declared and enacted by the authority of this present parliament that the law of this realm is and ever hath been ... that the kingly or regal office of the realm ... being invested in either male or female, are and ought to be as fully, wholly absolutely and entirely deemed, judged, accepted, invested and taken in the one as the other.[13]

Wyatt's rebellion had not been a direct challenge to Mary's position as queen but its underlying uncertainties about her role and the effect of her marriage evidently did have an impact. Mary and her advisers wanted statute clarification of the queen's position before her husband arrived. There is no evidence that Philip knew anything about this move.

The queen might be displeased with the truculence of her parliament and some of her ministers, but her wedding day was edging closer, and as monarch and future wife, she was well prepared for it. A substantial English household of 350 people was put in place to await Philip's arrival, headed by the earl of Arundel, who would act as lord steward for both Mary and her husband. Several of the men who gave Mary early support in July 1553 were rewarded with posts in the household, including John Huddleston, who had sheltered her as she journeyed into East Anglia. The plum roles of gentlemen of the privy chamber were given to the sons of seven leading peers and interpreters were appointed in recognition of language problems that would inevitably arise. The entire household, perhaps inspired by the arrival of the marquis de las Navas, was in place by mid-June, awaiting Philip's arrival at Southampton. Such optimism was understandable, but the move was a premature and costly one. Worse still, there had been a complete failure of communication between London and Valladolid about the royal household, and the English establishment was unaware that Philip was bringing a duplicate Spanish organisation with him. June turned into July and, to the despair of Renard, there was still no sign of the prince himself.

He was, though, on the move. It had taken several months to mobilise the very large fleet and military force he wanted to accompany him: 6,000 sailors and soldiers as a military escort, some intended to reinforce the garrisons in the Low Countries but most required as a safeguard against the threat of interception by the French, as well as a personal retinue of between 3,000 and 5,000. Philip apparently did not think that support of this order was excessive, or that it might send the wrong signals to a country where there had recently been an uprising based on the fear that the Spanish were more interested in invasion rather than alliance.[14] Naturally, the sheer amount of time it took to assemble all the people, including many of the leading nobility of Castile who accompanied him, slowed down his departure. A fleet also had to be gathered and readied. Seventy ships were prepared to carry the prince, his nobles, his religious advisers, his horses and his men. It was a grand gesture but not a speedy operation.

Before he could think about a precise date for his embarkation, Philip needed to settle the government of Spain, the country he was leaving behind. It was entrusted to his 19-year-old sister, Juana, for whom 1554 was an eventful year. Married to a Portuguese prince, she had been widowed on the second day of January, just three weeks after giving birth to a son. Like all of Charles V's family, this good-looking but very serious young woman did not flinch from her duty. The regency of Spain was to be her responsibility and her brother, who was fond of her, never doubted her ability and commitment to the role. Having spent a few weeks with Juana and the regency council appointed to assist her in Valladolid, Philip left the capital on 16 May. He travelled north to Santiago de Compostela, where he met the English ambassadors specially appointed by Mary to escort him to England, who were led by the earl of Bedford. Here the prince finally signed the marriage treaty, attending high mass with the English nobles in the cathedral of St James in this ancient town of pilgrimage, on 24 June. Then he moved on to Coruña, where, nearly three weeks later, confident that everything was in place and aware that he must follow his sister's example of Habsburg duty, he at last went on board the *Espiritu Santo* and set sail for England. Closely shadowed by 30 heavily armed vessels, ready to see off any threat from French men-of-war, the prince's flagship slipped out of port on the afternoon tide. It was 13 July, the height of summer, and the Spanish lords and ladies who accompanied Philip had persuaded themselves that they were going to a land of chivalry and Arthurian romance, where the meadows would be filled with flowers and birdsong. There, they expected to be well rewarded for their service to Philip. It would be a benign conquest, but they never doubted their superiority over the English.

Alas, they were cruelly deceived. The voyage itself was dreadful. The Bay of Biscay fully lived up to its reputation for stormy seas and Philip, like everyone else, was ill for most of the crossing. Ruy Gomez, Philip's confidant and chamberlain, suffered from such terrible sea-sickness that he thought he would die. When the ships finally dropped anchor in Southampton Water on 20 July, the rain was falling in torrents. It hardly stopped in three days. But Mary, already in Winchester, cared nothing for the weather, or the pretensions of Philip's entourage. At last, her husband was here.

Protocol, rather more than the desire to recover from the rigours of the voyage, meant that Philip could not rush to Mary's side; he was no Philip of Bavaria, anxious to claim his prize at the earliest opportunity. The prince made a gradual acclimatisation to the wet English summer, while all the while receiving honours and exchanging gifts with his bride. Mary had granted him the Order of the Garter, and this was presented to him on board ship by the earl of Arundel, before he even came ashore. He accepted it graciously and sent off Egmont 'to inform the queen of his arrival, visit her, tell her of his health and assure her of his affection'. The next day Gardiner came with the gift of a large diamond from Mary. Philip reciprocated with a diamond of his own, though it was noted that it was 'considerably smaller'. This unfortunate discrepancy might be viewed as a metaphor for the different degree of feeling that the two parties brought to their marriage.

There were further presents from Mary. She sent 'a very richly wrought poignard, studded with gems, and two robes, one of them as rich and beautiful as could be imagined'.[15] Equally fine was the white horse, trapped with crimson velvet and embroidered with gold, that Philip found waiting for him when he came ashore. He mounted it and rode off to hear mass and give thanks for his landing. Then he returned to the lodgings prepared for him, to learn more about when he would first meet the queen and to be briefed about arrangements for the wedding ceremony.

The first impressions he made on the English were all favourable. The prince went out of his way to be affable, to learn about the customs of these strange people, such as removing his hat during audiences with leading politicians and quaffing beer with his meals. He made sure that he was visible to the people, since he had been told that it would be necessary to court public favour. There can be no doubt that he was making an effort, or that he was playing a part, but he played it well. On 23 July, he set off for Winchester and his first meeting with Mary, in the unrelenting rain. By the time he got there his 'rich coat embroidered with gold, his doublet hosen and hat suite-like' were drenched, and the fair white feather in his cap had lost its jauntiness.[16] Despite this, Philip went straight to the cathedral, 'a fine building where there was such a crowd that they were all in danger of stifling', to hear the Te Deum sung. Perhaps he also wanted the opportunity to familiarise himself with the cathedral's interior before his marriage. Certainly, he would have found the fact that so many people wanted to see their new king gratifying, aware as he must have been that the marriage was taking place in Winchester rather than London because the mood of the citizens in the capital was deemed too unreliable for comfort.

When the service was concluded, 'he was brought with torch-light to the dean's house, the lords going before him and the queen's guard in their rich coats standing all the way'. The house 'was very gorgeously prepared for him', but he was probably more concerned to get out of his wet clothes and take some sustenance. The prince ate a quiet supper with his closest Spanish confidants until, at about ten in the evening, he made the short journey across the gardens to the bishop's palace, for his first meeting with Mary Tudor.

As he came up the private stairs, she was waiting at the top to greet him, supported by her leading councillors and ladies-in-waiting. As was the English custom, she kissed her own hand first and then took his. Then Philip kissed her on the mouth, something he would not have done in Spain but which was expected here, and 'hand in hand they sat down and remained for a time in present conversation'. Mary probably spoke in French, Philip in Spanish. No one present eavesdropped on what they had to say, but though Mary evidently still understood Spanish, she must not have heard it spoken for many years. At times they may both have conversed in Latin, the one common language they had.

This exchange of pleasantries provided both of them with the opportunity to take stock of each other. Mary saw a slim, fair-haired man, not much taller than she was. He was considered to have a soldier's bearing and good legs, yet to modern eyes they seem spindly. But there is no point in judging by the standards of a different age. He looked suitably regal to his bride, and it was her response which mattered. He was only the second of her Habsburg relatives she had ever met, and she was disposed to love him, not find fault. Although the age difference was not so extreme, it was still marked. Philip was a different generation, the great-grandson of Isabella of Castile, whereas she was the granddaughter. Searching his face for any immediate sign of misgiving or doubt, she would have found nothing to unsettle her. He was charming and easy-mannered. Perhaps the age difference was less important than she had feared. Their common heritage was, to her, a great advantage. It would not be hard to be his wife.

But Philip's politeness, his determination to do the right thing, belied his true feelings. There she was before him, in her black velvet dress, flamboyant with heavy jewels but not elegant: deep-voiced, white-faced and thin. Philip was far too discreet to commit to writing any views on Mary's appearance, but others in his entourage were not. They dismissed her as 'a perfect saint who dresses badly', and thought that if she dressed in a more restrained fashion, she might look younger. The queen appeared to Philip's courtiers as mutton dressed as lamb. They found her love of rich fabrics, her devotion to the French style of dress, unflattering. Spanish ladies, they were sure, looked better.[17] To them she seemed flabby and sagging, as if the firmness of her youth was gone, as, indeed, it was. He skin did not fit her any more. She still had a fine, clear complexion but it was very pale, probably as the result of anaemia caused by too many bleedings. The difficulties of her life, the stress and ill health, were only too visible in her face. She looked older even than Philip had expected. They might have family ties, interests in common, dynastic ambitions they hoped to realise through each other, but he knew he could not love her.

Ruy Gomez made plain that what Philip felt was more than absence of attraction; it was closer to distaste. He told a colleague in Brussels four days after the wedding: 'to speak frankly with you, it will take a great God to drink this cup [but] … the king realises that the marriage was concluded for no fleshly consideration, but in order to remedy the disorders of this kingdom and to preserve the Low Countries'.[18] The physical side of marriage would be a trial, but perhaps not one to be endured for very long. In the small talk of that July night, Philip did not tell Mary that his father, concerned about the deteriorating situation in the Netherlands, had given him instructions to stay in England for no more than five or six days after the wedding. He knew that it would be unwise to suggest that the interminable delay of his arrival would be followed by an immediate departure. But the Low Countries did offer the possibility of escape and that knowledge alone may have soothed him.

When he took his leave, he greatly endeared himself to the company by demonstrating that he was already learning English. During their exchanges, Mary had taught him to say 'Goodnight, my lords all', and this he managed to repeat. It was a clever move, but there is no indication that he ever mastered much more of the language. Yet he had already completely won Mary's heart.

The pleasant conversation of their first meeting increased the queen's confidence about her marriage. If Philip was not exactly a fairy-tale prince, he still seemed romantic to Mary. He was her equal in birth, an experienced ruler, and it was apparent that he knew how to behave. But the meeting evidently took something of a toll on Philip. 'On Tuesday, 24 July, his highness rose very late,' a Spanish commentator reported. When he did get up, he realised that he must have made a good first impression. There was still no end to Mary's generosity. 'The queen sent to him her tailor with two suits, one of rich brocade adorned with gold thread, pearls and diamond buttons, the other of crimson brocade.' Since the Spaniards did not share Mary's tastes in women's clothes, it is hard to know whether they found her choice of men's apparel more acceptable. In any event, he did not don one of the new outfits, preferring instead 'a coat of purple brocade with silver fringes and a friese cloak with similar trimmings, white breeches and doublet'.[19] Thus attired, he heard mass, took his midday meal and then went off to attend his first public engagement with Mary. She met him accompanied by her ladies, who, it was noted, were 'not beautiful but very numerous'. They were all dressed in purple velvet, a fortunate match with Philip's brocade.

Philip and Mary kissed and 'then stood talking for a long time. His highness talked with the ladies according to his custom [he was known for his gallantry in this respect], while we all kissed the queen's hands in Spanish fashion.' Then they parted for a while, making their religious devotions separately. Philip heard vespers in Winchester Cathedral while Mary stayed in her private chapel. He did not dine with her that night, but met her again in the late evening. This time, he brought good news with him. Charles V had conferred on him the kingdom of Naples. Tomorrow he would marry Mary not as a mere prince, but as a fellow-monarch. Mary was delighted by the appropriateness of this gesture by the emperor. All was now ready for the great ceremony the next day.

The wedding of Mary and Philip took place on 25 July, the feast day of St James, the patron saint of Spain. This compliment to the groom was not matched by an improvement in the weather. Mary was married in the rain. But in all other respects the wedding was one of the most magnificent in English history. Its setting, in the beautiful cathedral begun in 1079, was partly dictated by security fears and the danger of summer epidemics in central London. Winchester was also chosen because it was the bishopric of Stephen Gardiner, who performed the ceremony in the continued absence of a Catholic archbishop of Canterbury. His status as chancellor also reinforced the double nature of the act, a spiritual union of two people and a secular union of two earthly powers. This was a ceremony full of symbolism and spectacle, to match that of Mary's coronation. It had been carefully prepared, and no doubt both Mary and Philip studied the order of proceedings, making sure they knew the various elements, where they would walk and stand, how they must respond. This was an important occasion of state, not the private, even secretive plighting of troths that characterised all of Henry VIII's marriages.

There are several sources of information about the wedding and the celebrations following it, from Spanish, English and Italian sources, as well as from the Scot, John Elder. Elder was appointed, about this time, as tutor to the countess of Lennox's son, Lord Darnley. He may have been present because of this connection. Since Elder was, untypically for the time, a supporter of union between England and Scotland, he viewed the alliance between an English queen and a Habsburg prince with especial interest.

Philip arrived first at the cathedral, at ten in the morning, going 'forth with a brave following of grandees and gentlemen of his court, so magnificently attired that neither his majesty's nor his highness's court ever saw the like, such was the display of rich garments and chains, each one finer than the last'.[20] He himself was superbly dressed: 'His breeches and doublet were white, the collar of the doublet exceeding rich, and over all a mantle of rich cloth of gold, a present from the queen ... this robe was ornamented with pearls and precious stones; and wearing the collar of the Garter.'[21] The mantle was 'adorned with crimson velvet and thistles of curled gold, lined in crimson satin, with twelve buttons made of four pearls on each sleeve'. Philip referred to his wedding outfit in the inventory of his jewels and clothing that was drawn up after Mary's death.[22] He did not comment, at that or any other time, that his apparel was specially designed to match Mary's and that its style was French rather than Spanish, because the French style was what was worn in England at the time. This was, naturally, a point of some sensitivity for Philip's Spanish entourage.[23]

In the half-hour before the queen arrived, he had time to take in the sumptuous decorations, to reflect, perhaps, that his bride might be a worse disappointment than he had feared, but that the English had not stinted in their preparations for his nuptials. The cathedral itself 'was richly hanged with arras and cloth of gold, and in the midst of the church, from the west door unto the rood, was a scaffold erected of timber, at the end whereof was raised a mount, covered all with red say, and underneath the roode-loft were erected two traverses, one for the queen on the right hand, and the other for the prince on the left, which places served very well for the purpose'. They must also have served to remind Philip, as he contemplated the scene, that his bride's place on his right emphasised the honour she was bestowing in marrying him.

Mary, 'with all her council and nobility before her', arrived at half past ten. The sword of state was carried before her by the earl of Derby and she was attended by 'a great company of ladies and gentlewomen very richly apparelled'. Yet none of the male reporters of the scene bothered to describe her wedding dress, referring only to the fact that it had a train, 'borne up by the marchioness of Winchester, assisted by Sir John Gage her lord chamberlain'.[24] Fortunately, the wardrobe records supply the missing information, and they tell us that Mary had chosen a dress that was rich and queenly with pleasing lines. It was in the French style that Mary favoured, made of 'rich tissue with a border and wide sleeves, embroidered upon purple satin, set with pearls of our store, lined with purple taffeta'. It had a partlet, the sleeveless jacket covering just the chest, which had been a feature of women's clothing for some years, and a high collar. The kirtle was of white satin enriched with silver and there was, indeed, a train. The overall effect, as can be seen in the replica made for the exhibition that accompanied the 450th anniversary of the wedding in Winchester, was superb.[25] But it does not seem fussy. Mary may have deliberately opted for restraint, conscious of the fact that her wedding was a solemn occasion as well as a state function. This would have been in keeping with the wedding ring she chose, 'a plain hoop of gold without any stone in it: for that was as it is said her pleasure, because maidens were so married in old times'.

Entering the cathedral by the west door, Mary ascended the steps to the dais where her bridegroom was waiting. Gardiner and the five leading bishops of the realm, all coped and mitred, stood ready. Standing beside Philip, she prepared to take the vows that would make her, a 38-year-old woman who had abandoned any thought of marriage years ago, a wife.

Before he began the marriage ceremony proper, Gardiner made a speech about the marriage treaty and its ratification in both England and Spain. He then announced to the congregation that Charles V had bestowed on his son the kingdom of Naples, before moving on to the espousal itself. The official record shows that some aspects of the marriage service are as familiar now as they were in 1554. 'With a loud voice [Gardiner] said that, if there be any man that knoweth any lawful impediment between these two parties, that they should not go together according to the contract concluded between both realms, that they should come forth, and they should be heard.' But whatever doubts had been raised earlier that year, in Winchester Cathedral on 25 July no dissenting voice was heard. So the bishop continued with the ceremony. It 'was pronounced in English and Latin; and when it came to the gift of the queen it was asked who should give her. Then the marquess of Winchester, the earls of Derby, Bedford and Pembroke, gave her highness, in the name of the whole realm.' Mary might be lacking close male relatives, but she had four peers and all her subjects to offer her in marriage.

'Then all the people', it was recorded, 'gave a great shout, praying God to send them joy.' The ring was laid upon the Bible to be blessed and Philip, in accordance with custom, added three handfuls of fine gold. Lady Margaret Clifford, the queen's 14-year-old cousin and chief attendant, opened Mary's purse, 'and the queen smilingly put up in the same purse. And when they had enclosed their hands, immediately the sword was advanced before the king, by the earl of Pembroke'.[26] Now joined as man and wife, Philip and Mary returned hand in hand to their places on the raised dais as trumpets sounded, Mary still on the right, to hear high mass. During the hour-long service, the queen's eyes remained fixed on the sacrament, her source of succour throughout her life. Once mass was finished, the Garter King of Arms and the heralds announced the new style of their majesties: 'Philip and Mary, by the grace of God king and queen of England, France, Naples, Jerusalem and Ireland, defenders of the faith, princes of Spain and Sicily, archdukes of Austria, dukes of Milan, Burgundy and Brabant, counts of Habsburg, Flanders and Tyrol.'[27] So Mary and her realm became suddenly part of a much wider, European empire, and Philip heard himself take precedence over her for the first time. In proclamations, at least, there was no possibility of a queen being placed before a king. A king was a king, and that was that. But he knew, as he walked down the long nave of Winchester Cathedral, out into the rain and the waiting crowds, all the while holding Mary's hand in his, that to be proclaimed a king was one thing. To be allowed to rule was quite another.

The couple proceeded on foot to the bishop's palace, where the finest of wedding receptions was prepared for them. There they 'dined most sumptuously together' under the cloth of state, just the two of them at their table, while music played. The privy councillors and ambassadors sat separately and there were two further tables for all the rest of the Spanish and English gentlemen, about 140 people in total. The ladies occupied their own table and all 'were admirably served, in perfect order and silence'. An indication of the kind of fare offered to this large company was given by the same Edward Underhill who had reported on the alarm in the queen's quarters during Wyatt's attack on London. 'We were the chief servitors, to carry the meat,' he recorded. 'The second course at the marriage of a king is given unto the bearers' (a custom that must have helped those with less than gargantuan appetites).

'I mean', he continued, 'the meat, but not the dishes, for they were of gold. It was my chance to carry a great pasty of red deer in a great charger, very delicately baked; which for the weight thereof, divers refused; the which pasty I sent unto London to my wife and her brother, who cheered therewith many of their friends.'[28]

After the meal was finished, everyone went to another hall, where there was dancing. Philip danced with Mary and 'the dukes and noble-men of Spain ... with the fair ladies and the most beautiful nymphs of England'. Here, John Elder seems to have allowed himself some poetic leeway. The Spaniards were far from impressed by the English ladies, whom they regarded as unappealing in their self-confidence and not at all attractive. They were shockingly bold and unrestrained: 'they wear black stockings and show their legs up to the knee when walking. As their skirts are not long they are passably immodest when walking, and even when seated. They are neither beautiful nor graceful when dancing and their dances only consist in strutting or trotting about. Not a single Spanish gentleman has fallen in love with one of them ... and their feel-ings for us are the same.' And things were even more trying for the Spanish ladies, who could hardly be expected to go to court 'because they would have no one to talk with, as the English ladies are of evil conversation'.[29] But Underhill thought there was another reason for all this aggravation. The Iberian guests 'were greatly out of countenance' because the English lords were better dancers, even showing up King Philip. Seldom can the pastime of dancing have provoked so much controversy over what constituted propriety and grace.

The dancing on Mary's wedding night did not go on late into the evening; the English habitually retired early, even in summer. After a while, the king and queen departed and took supper separately. Each needed to be readied for the final act of the day. No one knows what passed in private conversation between Mary and her ladies, or whether she was anxious as the time to retire for the night approached. When all was ready, Gardiner blessed the marriage bed and they were left alone together, like any couple. 'What happened that night only they know,' was the comment of one of Philip's Spanish retinue. The English, perhaps conscious of their queen's sensibilities, refrained from any such speculation.

· ❖ ·

It seems probable that they did not spend the entire night together, as Philip got up at seven o'clock the next morning and heard mass. Mary, in time-honoured fashion, remained quietly in private with her women for the next couple of days. Her husband had plenty of business to occupy him as he constantly reviewed the situation in the Low Countries and supervised the arrangements for sending the soldiers who had accompanied him from Spain to buttress the garrisons across the North Sea. Mary also emerged to meet the duchess of Alva, the highest ranked of the Spanish ladies, and to see ambassadors. The couple dined together in public again on 29 July, in the company of the earls of Pembroke and Arundel, and, while Mary's ladies passed their time in dancing and entertainment, the Spanish did what tourists do and visited the local sights. They went to see what was reputed to be King Arthur's famous Round Table at the castle, noting that 'the names of his twelve knights are written where they used to sit round the table'. In general, however, they found that the age of chivalry was long dead. The roads were full of robbers, even in daylight, and some of Philip's belongings had already gone missing.

On the last day of the month, the royal party left Winchester in the early afternoon to begin the leisurely journey back to London. Philip already knew that the situation in Flanders was improving, so he could not have been entirely surprised when he received a letter from his father countermanding the earlier order for his speedy departure. Charles was not filled with optimism but the rainy season was coming on and he did not think there would be any more fighting for a while. It was important, he felt, for Philip to establish a good reputation in England. 'On the whole, therefore, we think you had better stay where you are and be with the queen, my daughter, busying yourself with the government of England, settling affairs there and making yourself familiar with the people, which it is most important for you to do for present and future considerations'.[30] At that point, he was probably not counting Mary's contentment among these, but two days later, after hearing accounts of the marriage, he acknowledged that this too was a consideration, writing to his son: 'I am sure you are doing your best to make the queen happy, showing her all the love and devotion she deserves.'

In this respect, in the early days of their relationship, Philip could not be faulted. He was an admirably attentive husband, so much so that he even fooled the same Spanish gentlemen who were so appalled by the sight of an Englishwoman's legs. 'Their majesties are the happiest couple in the world, and more in love than words can say. His highness never leaves her, and when they are on the road he is ever by her side, helping her to mount and dismount.' Mary, who rode well, must have found this degree of attention touching. Her affectionate nature was completely beguiled and she wanted her father-in-law to know how pleased she was. In the emperor's consideration for her, she told him,

> I see a proof of your majesty's watchful care for the realm's and my own interests, for which, and above all for having so far spared the person of the king, my husband, I most humbly thank you. I own that you are thereby imposing on me an obligation so far surpassing all other bene-fits that I shall never be able to acquit myself; so I will only offer to your majesty all that my small powers enable me to give, always praying God so as to inspire my subjects that they may realise the affection you bear this kingdom and the honour and advantages you have conferred upon it by this marriage and alliance, which renders me happier than I can say, as I daily discover in the king, my husband and your son, so many virtues and perfections that I constantly pray God to grant me grace to please him and behave in all things as befits one who is so deeply embounden to him …[31]

Her own inclinations, the encouragement of her ladies and Philip's exemplary behaviour combined to heady effect. She, certainly, was in love, and in the surge of unexpected emotion she did not stop to think that she was confusing pretty manners with genuine feeling. Philip's servants knew differently. It was a constant effort for him, but one that would reap benefits politically. Ruy Gomez was impressed by his master: 'He treats the queen very kindly and well knows how to pass over the fact that she is no good from the point of view of fleshly sensuality. He makes her so happy that the other day when they were alone she almost talked love-talk to him, and he replied in the same vein. And his way with the English lords is so winning that they themselves say they have never had a king to whom they so quickly grew attached.'[32]

The royal couple arrived at Richmond on 11 August and, one week later, they made a triumphal entry into London itself. The pageants and displays this time, almost a year after the celebrations of Mary's state entry before her coronation, were very much focused on the new king. He was greeted as a mighty prince: 'sole hope of Caesar's side, By God appointed all the world to guide, Right heartily welcome art thou to our land', read the banners over the Tower. Further along, Philip saw himself compared to four noble Philips of the past, the king of ancient Macedonia, two dukes of Burgundy named Philip and a Roman emperor: 'In birth, in fortune, boldness, vertuous name, thou Philip passest these Philips four, alone,' it was claimed. The parade went on as far as Whitehall, all the while echoing similar sentiments. It was gratifying, but no more than show. When the king and queen reached the palace, reality struck home for Philip. Mary took the lodgings on what was commonly called the king's side, and he was housed in the apartments of the queen consorts. After a few days, he and the queen left for Hampton Court, there to remain through the autumn until the opening of Mary's third parliament on 12 November.

His honeymoon was over, and now Philip needed to take stock of what role he could actually play in English politics. Simon Renard believed things would go well, and informed the emperor. But his analysis shrewdly put the impression Philip was making before the effectiveness of his position. The English thought of him 'as a handsome prince of benign and humane countenance, and likely to turn out to be a good ruler'. It was thought that he would attend privy council meetings regularly, at least twice a week. There, he could learn the detail of government business and his presence might do much to bring about unanimity. Mary duly gave orders that notes were to be translated into Spanish. If this happened, such notes have not survived, nor is there any record of his attendance at meetings being frequent. Perhaps the language problem was just too great for him and he preferred to deal with the councillors, many of whom had already been amply rewarded by the emperor, on an individual basis, rather than waste his time in meetings where he could not follow what was being said. It is impossible to know whether he picked up much English during his time in the country, though he must have heard it spoken often enough. But there is no indication that he ever uttered more words in it than his goodnight wishes to the assembled throng when he first met Mary. Perhaps he did acquire some understanding but wished to keep it hidden, an effective tactic in getting people to speak openly. At conversational level, he could communicate adequately in Latin with English politicians. Still smarting under the restrictions placed on him by the marriage treaty and preoccupied by the problems of the Netherlands, all of his concentration initially was directed towards successfully developing a public image of charm and affability. For a reserved and proud man, this was no mean achievement.

His first priority was to try to sort out the difficulties posed by having two households. These did not, though, last long, because he realised he would have to accept the arrangements that Mary had made for him. In November he told Eraso, his father's secretary, that he was embarrassed by the duplication of servants, 'not so much on account of the expense as of the troubles it gave me'. Some of the English officers would be retained to serve permanently at table but he was not so keen on the bedchamber servants: 'they are accustomed to serve here in a very different manner from that observed at his majesty's court, and as you know I am not satisfied that they are good enough Catholics to be constantly about my person'. But in general he was satisfied with the way things were going and the fact that the Spanish and English were getting on well together. There had been a few 'unavoidable incidents' and he had punished those involved firmly; there was, in his view, nothing brewing now.[33] A good many Spanish gentlemen, and some of the Spanish artisans whose arrival threatened the livelihoods of their English counterparts, were also leaving or had left. It would all settle down.

His optimism hid his own discontent. He had been furious to discover that he had no English patrimony and would have to reward his supporters out of his Spanish income. Nor would the English agree to his coronation, saying that they already had a crowned queen. If this were not enough, he conceived, probably at the instigation of Ruy Gomez, an unhelpful dislike and distrust of Simon Renard.

The ambassador was rendered largely superfluous by the arrival of the Castilian entourage and he wanted to leave. His work was done. But, although allowed back briefly to Brussels, he was required to stay on in England until September 1555, growing ever more embittered at the way he was treated. His position had not, in fact, been easy since the early part of 1554. There was acrimony within the imperial embassy before Philip left Spain, when Dubois, still second-in-command, accused Renard of taking bribes in the aftermath of Wyatt's rebellion. No firm evidence was found, but the suspicion stuck. Ruy Gomez raised it again in late August. 'I do not want to injure anyone,' he wrote, in the damning fashion of a man who knew just what effect his words would have, 'but I fear our ambassador's attitude has not always been wise, for from what we have been able to make out, he has taken sides for one of the parties here, and as his influence with the queen is great he has been able to be of use to some and do serious harm to others. The result is that those who are out of favour are resentful, and one of them is Paget, who, as the ambassador himself confesses, helped him more than anyone else during the marriage negotiations.' He went on to criticise Renard for getting 'everything into a muddle'. But then he took a swipe at a greater adversary than the ambassador. 'I do not blame him but rather the person [the bishop of Arras] who sent a man of his small attainments to conduct so capital an affair as this match, instead of entrusting it to a Spaniard.'[34] Ruy Gomez was actually Portuguese, not Spanish, but he was Iberian by birth and that made him an insider, in his own eyes and those of Philip.

So it was basically prejudice which damaged Simon Renard. What was to be expected, Ruy Gomez was saying, from someone like him? He was not one of them, and neither, for that matter, was Arras. The French-speakers who served Charles V so ably were looked down on by Philip and his staff. And there was probably also a psychological dimension to their reservations. Philip had to face the fact that Renard knew Mary better than he did, and was fully aware of the limitations on his power in England. Who better, since Renard had helped enshrine them in the terms of the treaty? There was truth in the assertion that the ambassador was a schemer, but so were all 16th-century diplomats. It was part of the job. Paget would have fallen out with Mary without Renard's encouragement, but Philip did not know this. The one thing that he and the ambassador did agree on, however, was the state of religion in England. Although many Protestants had left in self-imposed exile, it was feared that some were returning. While England remained in schism, the benefits of Mary's accession were in doubt. Philip himself had expressed doubts that his English servants were good Catholics. The queen's religious programme had stalled and she very much wanted it taken forward, now that her marriage was concluded. The breach with Rome must be healed and Philip, the titular king of England, seemed ideally placed to handle the delicate manoeuvring required to reach a satisfactory outcome for both sides. It was to be one of the most significant achievements of his time as Mary's husband.

Aware that the major stumbling block was always going to be the question of the return of Church lands, Philip concentrated on working with the privy council to ensure that their fears were addressed. The English ruling class was perfectly happy to hear mass but they would not contemplate giving up their wealth. The queen had tried leading by example, waiving Crown revenues from some former Church lands, but all she did was cause alarm and inflict some damage on her own finances. Philip knew that this approach would not gain the result Mary desired, which was to rid herself of the supremacy as established by her father and gain papal absolution for England's 20 years of religious disobedience.

By November 1554, he had made good progress with his task. Despite his reservations about the imperial ambassador, he sent Renard off to Brussels to gain the agreement of Cardinal Pole, still stranded at the emperor's court, and set about gaining the confidence of the privy council in England. Distribution of pensions from his own funds probably helped this process, but there was also general support, once it was clear that the Cromwellian redistribution of Church property would remain untouched. Satisfied at last, the council finally issued, on 3 November, an invitation to the long-absent Pole to return to his native land. Mary's third parliament, summoned for 12 November, reversed the act of attainder against Pole and prepared to draft the bill for reunification with Rome.

Paget and Sir Edward Hastings were sent to escort the cardinal from Brussels but he set out before they arrived, meeting them at Ghent on 16 November. His eagerness is understandable, since as recently as late September he had written to Philip indirectly accusing the emperor of obstructing his return. 'A year has passed', he complained, 'since I began to knock at the door of this royal house, and none has opened unto me.'[35] He had suffered banishment and 20 years of exile to ensure that Mary would not be barred from the throne. As crowds came to see him on his journey from Dover to London, he knew that the prolonged ordeal was over. The archbishopric of Canterbury, the prize he always dreamed of, would now be his.

Still, it was thought prudent for him to arrive in London quietly, by river, rather than make a great entry. He came in the royal barge from Gravesend, landing at Whitehall steps on 22 November. Here Philip was waiting to take him to the queen, his kinswoman. Pole had not seen her since she was a young princess in full bloom. It was an emotional moment, as Mary 'made a deep reverence to the king and cardinal, who were walking side by side'. Pole knelt and Mary raised him up. She and her husband, it was reported, 'received him with great signs of respect and affection; both shed tears'.[36] Then the three of them went together into the queen's presence chamber, where they spent half an hour talking in English and Italian.

Just over a week later Parliament was summoned to court to hear Pole give assurances, in the presence of the king and queen, that 'my commission is not of prejudice to any person. I come not to destroy but to build. I come to reconcile, not to condemn. I come not to compel, but to call again.' On the last day of November, he pronounced the words Mary had longed to hear, absolving her country of its years of sin and schism: 'Our Lord Jesus Christ, which with his precious blood has redeemed us, and purified all our sins and pollutions, in order to make himself a glorious bride without stains and without wrinkle, whom the Father made chief over the church, he through his mercy absolves you.'[37] Pole was a considerable orator and his words made a great impression on those who heard them. And Mary at last could be confident that the sins of her father and brother were wiped clean. She wrote to Charles V to inform him of the return of her people to 'the obedience of the Holy Church and the Catholic faith', an outcome due in large part to her husband. And though this was a very solemn moment, she wanted to mark it with rejoicing as well as prayer. Renard reported that 'the queen gave a banquet to the king and his gentlemen, and after supper there were dancing and masks. The king had that day shown liberality to the ladies of the court, who were dressed in the gowns he had given them.'[38]

But points of difference about Church property remained, and the bill to restore England to Roman jurisdiction was not passed by Parliament until 3 January 1555, after some very hard talking. Philip found it necessary to speak to Pole himself, and Mary also joined a meeting with the privy council and lawyers just before Christmas when, provoked by references to statutes in her brother's reign, she threatened to abdicate if her subjects decided to use the example of the Edwardian regime as guidance.

She had, though, played little direct part in the orchestration of the return to Rome, preferring, as she acknowledged to the emperor, to leave its management to Philip. As she never shirked responsibility, her reasons for following this course can only be conjectured. Although it meant a great deal to her personally, there were elements that may have embarrassed her. She loathed the supreme headship, with its unhappy associations of the persecution she had suffered in the 1530s, but she seems to have wanted someone else to rid her of it. Perhaps she also felt that matters of Church government were, as Pole himself had so bluntly told her, best left to men. Then there was also the international dimension of dealing with the papacy, which Philip's Habsburg connections made him well equipped to handle. But there was probably also another, much more immediate and personal reason which explains why the queen was content to let her husband handle the delicate papal relationship. Mary believed that she was pregnant.

It was on 18 September, barely two months after the wedding, that Simon Renard first reported the news that everyone at the imperial court – and the majority of Englishmen – wanted to hear. 'One of the queen's physicians has told me that she is probably with child.' Never one to miss an opportunity, the ambassador made sure that this piece of information was spread around. He was sure that the news, if true, would prove the panacea for all the ills with which England was still afflicted. It would silence malcontents in an outpouring of national joy, negate any threat posed by Elizabeth and dampen anti-Spanish sentiment. The next day his information was confirmed by Count Stroppiana, the duke of Savoy's envoy to the emperor, who was visiting London. The count added an interesting piece of information based on his own observation; he had seen Mary being sick. Greatly heartened by the rumours coming from England, Charles V wrote to his son that he hoped the news of the queen's pregnancy would be confirmed. And very soon it was. Ruy Gomez reported on 2 October that it was now definite that Mary was expecting a child. It 'will put a stop to every difficulty', he wrote.[39]

Mary herself was overcome with joy. Her doctors and her delighted attendants concurred with what she herself wanted so much to believe. The boundless extent of God's benevolence towards her was something in which she now had absolute faith. The Almighty had given her a husband so much more wonderful than she had any right to expect, and it was perfectly natural that this blessing would be followed by the miracle of conception.

There was no public rejoicing at the news until, as was customary, the queen believed she had felt the child move. This came at the end of November, coinciding with the emotion of Reginald Pole's return. The privy council instructed Edmund Bonner, bishop of London, that the time had come for official acknowledgement of Mary's condition: 'Whereas it hath pleased Almighty God ... to extend his Benediction upon the Queen's Majesty in such sort as she is conceived and quick with child, [we] ... do pray and require you ... give order that thanks may be openly given by singing of the Te Deum in all the churches in your diocese.'[40] Dr Weston, the dean of Westminster and Mary's chaplain, composed a prayer for the queen which, in its sombre tone, is highly revealing of the Church's attitude to women and childbirth:

> Oh most righteous Lord God, which for the offence of the first woman, hath threatened unto all women a common, sharp and inevitable malediction; and hath enjoined them that they should conceive in sin, and being conceived, should be subject to many and grievous torments, and finally be delivered with the danger and jeopardy of their lives; we beseech thee for thine extending great goodness and bottomless mercy, to mitigate the strictness of that law; assuage thine anger for a while and cherish … our most gracious Queen Mary … so help her that in due season [she may] bring forth a child, in body beautiful and comely, in mind noble and valiant …[41]

As a woman of her time, Mary would not have been surprised by this reminder of her sex's sinfulness and the dangers of childbirth. Her mood, however, remained resolute and positive. Just before Christmas, she wrote to Charles V, in a rare reference to her condition: 'As for that which I carry in my belly, I declare it to be alive and with great humility thank God for His great goodness shown to me'. She had suffered morning sickness, her belly was growing, and she had felt the child move. Her medical advisers were monitoring her; Susan Clarencius and all (save one) of her women assured her she was expecting a child. Everybody, including Philip, wanted to believe it. She was absolutely convinced and no one around her wanted to cause her pain – or risk her anger – by suggesting otherwise. She must be pregnant. It was God's will.

Mary passionately wanted a child and her reasons were dynastic as much as personal. The birth of an heir would resolve all doubts over the succession and help her attain her vision of England's role in Europe. Elizabeth, Courtenay, even Mary Queen of Scots and other, more distant claimants would not matter any more. As a monarch, Mary needed security as much as she may have welcomed maternity. There is no evidence that she had always longed for a baby, or that she was more sentimental about motherhood than other 16th-century women of high birth. She had numerous godchildren, but that went with her rank. She may certainly have enjoyed this role, but it proves nothing about her own maternal inclinations. The only baby she had known at close quarters was Elizabeth, whose household she so unwillingly shared for three years. That period had been the nadir of her existence. As a queen she would not have understood modern concepts like bonding between a newborn and its mother. The same sort of household that had looked after her as a baby princess would take care of all the needs of her child. There would be a wet-nurse, rockers to soothe the child in its splendid cradle, laundresses and attendants. Mary was an affectionate person and she expected to love her baby dearly. But it would not get in the way of her being a queen.

In general, Mary's health seemed good, even better than before. She filled out and observers noted that her stomach was growing. But there were those who, right from the outset, had their doubts. Could a woman of her age, with a history of poor health, really have conceived? What if it was not true? Certainly, the French and Mary's Protestant opponents were quick to raise doubts and they maintained them throughout the winter. At the end of March, Renard reported to Charles V that seditious broadsheets were circulating in London claiming that the queen was not expecting a child and that there was a plot to pass off a substitute as her own.[42]

Everyone watched with great interest as the period of her withdrawal from public life drew near. The delivery was expected some time in the early spring, and in mid-April, around Easter, Mary withdrew to Hampton Court for her lying-in. 'The queen has withdrawn,' the ambassador noted, 'and no one else enters her apartments except the women who serve her.' But Philip was already growing embarrassed, writing to his brother-in-law: 'The queen's pregnancy turns out not to have been as certain as we thought. Your highness and my sister manage it better than the queen and I do.'[43] Whether he meant that the date or the pregnancy itself was uncertain is not clear. He could not have been much comforted when, on 30 April, London went wild as word circulated that the queen had been delivered of a son during the night. The Venetian ambassador reported that church bells were rung, bonfires lit and feasting began in the streets. But the rumour, though it reached as far as Brussels, was false. There was no bonny prince yet, and the authorities found it necessary to issue explicit denials. Whatever the queen might desire or her subjects want to hear, the birth was not imminent.

Medical advisers then revised the due date. There had been some miscalculation, it was said, but the queen was definitely pregnant. They would not, in any case, have ventured to contradict a queen who was so steadfast in her belief. And the ladies of Mary's household continued to tell their mistress exactly what she wanted to hear, with no apparent thought for their credibility or her own if, as some of them already knew, they were utterly wrong.

By the end of May, it was not just the king who was concerned. Ruy Gomez made his own disquiet plain:

> I would have written to you as you asked me to do about the queen's giving birth if I had seen in her any sign of heaviness. These last days she has been walking all about the garden on foot, and she steps so well that it seems to me that there is no hope at all for this month. I asked Dr Caligala what he thought about her highness's condition, and when she would be delivered. He said it might happen any day now, for she had entered the month. But according to her count it would not be strange if the delivery were to be delayed until 6 June.[44]

At some point in May, letters were prepared announcing the queen's safe delivery. They were, naturally, undated, and the sex of the child was left blank. Among the intended recipients was Henry II of France, whose ambassador had heard from paid sources that there was no possibility that Mary was pregnant – those around her were merely giving her false hope by saying that she had got the dates wrong.

Although Mary had not been seen in public since moving to Hampton Court, she continued to conduct affairs of state. In early July, she gave audience to the Noailles brothers and roundly chastised them for the failure of the French to participate constructively in the abortive peace negotiations with the emperor. It thoroughly undermined her position as mediator, she complained. The two diplomats were dismayed by her 'sour reply': 'She would never have thought that, as she had been asked to take a hand in this matter, she would be treated with so little deference. She had been a Christian and Catholic princess all her life and she had felt the inroads of the Turks in Christendom as if it had been her own kingdom, having deep compassion for the victims of this war.'[45] Later in the month she wrote to Charles V and Mary of Hungary about trade in the Low Countries and told Sir John Mason, her ambassador to the imperial court, that he was to issue explicit denials that she was not with child.

It was her last, weary gesture of belief. Everyone else knew the truth. Precisely when Mary herself acknowledged it is not known but the mere fact that she met Antoine and François de Noailles when the official line was still that she might give birth at any time is strongly indicative of an earlier acceptance of reality than has previously been thought. On 4 August she left Hampton Court for the nearby residence of Oatlands. Hampton Court itself was in dire need of cleaning and fast becoming unsanitary. Throughout the summer it had heaved with freeloading ladies hoping to do well from the birth. When she finally faced the truth, Mary could not wait to get away from it. Her state of mind can only be imagined, but the stress and disappointment had made her paler than ever. She was embittered and despairing, for she knew now that there was nothing to keep her husband in England. She had failed him and she had failed her country. Once more, the intentions of the God she worshipped so devoutly seemed inscrutable. In a lifetime of bitter blows, of loss and fear and uncertainty, there can have been no greater misery.

It is impossible to say with any confidence what had actually happened to Mary. Given her history of menstrual problems and the general medical ignorance of the age, her belief that she was pregnant is perfectly understandable. She was an anointed queen and there would have been no question of an internal examination. Even to mention the possibility might have been regarded as treason. Phantom pregnancies are a recognised medical condition and they were not uncommon in Mary's time. Lady Lisle, the wife of the governor of Calais, experienced one in the 1530s. She, too, had a cradle and baby clothes prepared and received many congratulatory letters. In June 1537 she took to her chamber, but, by August, her doubts were growing. Her devoted servant, John Husee, wrote before all hope was abandoned: '... your ladyship is not the first woman of honour that hath overshot or mistaken your time and reckoning ... therefore, good madam, in the name of God, be not so faint-hearted, nor mistrust not yourself. For I assuredly hope that all is for the best; but I admit that it might chance otherwise (which God forbid), yet should not your ladyship take is so earnestly, but refer all unto God.'[46] But Honor Lisle, like Mary Tudor, took it very earnestly indeed.

There is, of course, the possibility that Mary had become pregnant and miscarried. Her own mother, though many years younger, had just that experience with her first pregnancy. Through a combination of ignorance and wishful thinking, Katherine of Aragon also went some months before she accepted that the pregnancy was over. We can probably discount the lurid and malicious stories put about by the Venetians that Mary had evacuated a 'mole', a shapeless lump of flesh, which is a rare occurrence but can happen. Nor is it likely that she had ovarian cancer. She lived a further three years in delicate health, but was not seriously ill until the summer of 1558, when the great epidemic of influenza hit England. Some of her symptoms might be explained by a tumour of the pituitary gland, but this cannot be proved conclusively without an autopsy on her remains. The most likely explanation remains a phantom pregnancy, and that is sad enough it itself.

Mary's devastation was revealed in reported exchanges with Frideswide Strelly, the only one of her women who had told the queen from the outset that she did not think she was pregnant. 'But ... when the rockers and cradle and all such things were provided for the queen's delivery,' said one source, 'that her time should be nigh, as it was supposed, and those parasites had had all the spoil of such things amongst them, and no such matter in the end ... when the uttermost time was come, and the queen thus deluded, she sent for Strelly, her woman, again, to whom she said, "Ah, Strelly, Strelly, I see they be all flatterers, and none true to me but thou" '.[47]

So it was not just the loss of the child who had never been, but the loss of confidence in those she relied upon most. They had cost her dearly. She had known since the spring that only the prospect of fatherhood was keeping Philip in England. He was needed in the Low Countries and the whole debacle spurred his eagerness to get away. Humiliated almost as much as Mary, Philip was nonetheless nervous about how to break to her the news that he was going. 'Let me know what line I am to take with the queen about leaving her and about religion,' he pleaded in a rough draft probably intended for Ruy Gomez, on 2 August. 'I see I must say something, but God help me!'[48] He did not want a terrible scene when his wife learned that her worst fears were to be realised. Not that she would be left entirely alone. Since the spring, her sister had been with her, as well.

On 17 April 1555, Mary issued the order for Elizabeth 'to repair nearer to us'. She was to come to Hampton Court, there to await the queen's delivery and, presumably, to participate in the christening ceremonies that would follow. It would be apparent to all, including the princess herself, that the royal infant negated her hopes of succession. The man with whom her name was often coupled, Edward Courtenay, was allowed to leave the Tower of London ten days before Elizabeth's

summons. By the time she arrived at court, he was already in Brussels, under the watchful eye of the emperor and English secret agents. The regime did not discount the threat the pair could still pose, but believed it to be diminishing.

Elizabeth's confinement at Woodstock had lasted 11 months. During that time, she tried the patience of her guardian (or her jailer, as she preferred to think of Sir Henry Bedingfeld) to the utmost. Her constant, and increasing, demands, her complaints, her episodes of ill health, led to a very fractious atmosphere. Performing his duty, to the letter, if possible, mattered a great deal to Bedingfeld, and he did not understand how his conscientiousness could be used against him by a resentful, clever young woman and her devious staff.

The problems started almost as soon as Elizabeth, accompanied by three waiting women, two grooms and a yeoman of the robes, arrived at Woodstock. Elizabeth Sands, one of the female attendants, was a known Protestant and had to be replaced. Then there was the palace itself. As Bedingfeld soon discovered, the buildings were in a state of disrepair. It was damp, draughty, had only three rooms that could actually be locked with a key and was, he feared, a fire-trap. Despite the fact that he had soldiers with him, it was scarcely a high-security prison. His concerns were increased by Elizabeth's attitude. She took issue with him immediately on her freedom of movement, saying the council had guaranteed that she could have the use of the entire park. Bedingfeld had visions of his charge just disappearing on one of her perambulations. Then she demanded more reading material, including an English Bible, a request that seemed deliberately calculated to rouse the suspicions of the devoutly Catholic Sir Henry. But it was not just her questionable religious faith which bothered him. Unless he vetted every single page of her books, he could not be sure that messages were not passed in and out by her supporters, especially as her cofferer, the fat Welshman Thomas Parry, had established himself at the nearby Bull Inn.

If that were not enough, Elizabeth demanded to be allowed to write to the queen. She wanted to plead her case directly. Bedingfeld duly approached the council on her behalf with this request, which was granted. But it did not help. The queen wrote from Farnham Castle, while she was awaiting Philip's arrival, to say she had received her sister's letters. Mary was unimpressed. She could not forget the letter found in the French messenger's pouch at the time of Wyatt's rebellion and still believed her sister was involved. She had, she said, used more clemency 'than in like matters hath been accustomed, yet cannot these fair words [in Elizabeth's justifications to Mary] so much abuse us, but we do well understand how things have been wrought'. In other words, the queen would no longer let her sister pull the wool over her eyes. Conspiracies could easily be secretly practised 'where the plain direct proof may chance to fail ... wherefore our pleasure is not [to] be hereafter any more molested with such her disguise and colourable letters'.[49] Elizabeth, Mary said, needed to make her peace with God before she could expect a change of heart from the queen.

This was a setback, and, combined with stress, the princess became very unwell. Sir Henry was even more bothered. No royal physician was available to come to Oxford and Elizabeth rejected with absolute contempt the notion of seeing local doctors. 'I am not minded', she said, 'to make any stranger privy to the estate of my body.' She continued to protest her innocence and to ask to be able to see the queen in person. By mid-autumn 1554 Bedingfeld was nearly in despair, and Elizabeth still persisted in vexing him and fussing to be moved. On 19 November, she was requesting to be allowed to live nearer to London, or even to go to one of her own properties.

This audacious demand was ignored and Elizabeth passed the winter under the leaky roof of Woodstock, in flagrant communication with the outside world, but still confined. Mary, caught up in her own private happiness with Philip, would not have been encouraged if she had known of the lines Elizabeth is supposed to have etched on a window during this time: 'Much suspected of me. Nothing proved can be, quoth Elizabeth, prisoner.' It is not the most convincing assertion of innocence.

Elizabeth arrived at Hampton Court between 25 and 29 April 1555. But if she expected an immediate rapprochement with Mary, she must have been disappointed. Released she might be. Restored to favour she most definitely was not. Two weeks, during which Elizabeth was ignored completely, went by, and then she grew restive and asked to see the council. When a deputation, led by Gardiner, came, she continued to refuse to admit any guilt, although it was pointed out to her that this was tantamount to accusing the queen of false imprisonment. Finally, after a further week in isolation, she was summoned late in the evening to see Mary.

Elizabeth's overactive imagination came into full play. Were there, she feared, assassins waiting for her in the dark garden that she must cross to go up the private stairs? But instead Sir Henry Bedingfeld himself accompanied her, leaving her at the foot of the staircase, where Susan Clarencius awaited. Not a friendly presence by any means, for Mrs Clarencius loved the queen devotedly and had probably convinced herself as well as Mary that there would shortly be a royal birth. She had no reason to be welcoming to Elizabeth, who had caused her mistress so much trouble. And this meeting was unlikely to have the satisfactory outcome of that earlier, highly charged exchange which Susan witnessed, when Mary told Renard of her decision to marry Philip.

It was, though, an emotional confrontation. The sisters had not seen each other since the winter's day at the end of 1553 when Elizabeth left court under a cloud to go to Ashridge for Christmas. Now she knelt and 'desired God to preserve her majesty, not mistrusting but that she should try herself as true a subject her majesty as ever did any; and desired her majesty even so to judge of her; and said that she could not find her to the contrary, whatsoever report otherwise had gone of her'. Mary was tetchy. If she had hoped to hear a confession of guilt, or even an apology for being associated with rebellion, none was forthcoming. 'You will not confess your offence, but stand stoutly in your truth,' she noted. 'I pray God it may so fall out.' Sensing that she had gained the higher ground, Elizabeth persisted. 'If it doth not, I request neither favour nor pardon at your majesty's hands.' Mary realised that the younger woman would not give way. 'You stiffly persevere in your truth,' she repeated. 'Belike you will not confess but that you have been wrongfully punished.' Elizabeth would not give a straight answer: 'I must not say so, if it please your majesty, to you.' Mary acidly pointed out that she might well give a different account to others, but this was denied: 'No, if it please your majesty, I have borne the burden and must bear it. I humbly beseech your majesty to have a good opinion of me, and to think me to be your true subject, not only from the beginning hitherto, but for ever, as long as life lasteth.'[50]

It is an intimate account of a tortured exchange. Mary's bluntness and Elizabeth's laboured denials, or half-truths, sound convincing. Yet the story, with its precise dialogue, originates with John Foxe, who is not a reliable source. In his animosity to the entire Marian regime, he had good reason to want to depict Elizabeth as the injured party, scolded by a narrow-minded, suspicious older sister. Foxe also claimed that Philip had been there throughout the interview, concealed behind a hanging on the wall, and that Mary had made asides to him in Spanish. If so, it would have been his first glimpse of the difficult sister-in-law who was to cause him so much trouble in later life. Certainly, Philip never confided details of any such meeting between the Tudor sisters to Simon Renard, but the ambassador was not in his confidence. If there was a contemporary source, it was likely to have been Elizabeth herself, who had the most to gain from making it appear that she had bested her sister. Since Foxe does not say from whom he obtained the story, it is impossible to be sure of its veracity.

In the end, Mary's defeat, if such it was, was self-inflicted. Elizabeth must have scrutinised her sister for signs of pregnancy but she was too discreet to be drawn into the public doubt about its reality. She stayed with Mary throughout the queen's ordeal and was still with her when Philip left for the Netherlands, on 29 August.

At the end, he was anxious to get away. He had done all he could in England and now his duty was to Charles V, who was in the process of abdicating. Philip had played the role of considerate consort to perfection, but there never was any guarantee he would stay, even if the queen had produced a healthy son. His presence was urgently required in Brussels and his wife, though deeply unhappy, understood this. Mary came with him through London, to the evident relief of the crowds, who feared that her prolonged withdrawal from public life meant that she was dead. She wanted to go with him all the way to Dover, but he persuaded her that this would cause him too much delay.

Philip departed by water from Greenwich, where the queen watched from a window. The Venetian ambassador reported that she retained her composure when they said their farewells, but that she had broken down when she went back into the palace:

> The queen really, on this occasion showed proper grief for a woman, and a woman clothed as she was with royal state and dignity. There was no external manifestation of agitation, although it was evident she was in great trouble, and she chose to accompany the king through all the chambers and halls, as far as the head of the staircase: all the way she had a struggle to command herself and prevent any exhibition inconsistent with her high position from being perceptible to so many persons. But she was much affected by the kissing of hands by the Spanish lords and especially at seeing the ladies taking leave of the king

in tears, when he kissed them one by one as is customary. But when she returned to her own rooms, she lent on her elbows at a window overlooking the river, and there, thinking she was not observed, she gave scope to her grief in floods of tears. She did not stir from the spot until she had seen the king embark and depart; not till the last sight of him; he mounted on a raised and open part of the barge, so as to be better visible as long as he was in sight of the window, kept on raising his hat and making salutes with the most affectionate gestures.[51]

Even if these reports were exaggerated – Mary was extremely short-sighted and probably could not see her husband on the boat clearly, if at all – the distress she felt was acute. Philip was the only person of her own rank she had been close to since Katherine Parr, and that was a relationship based on friendship and respect between women. When she became a wife, she committed herself wholeheartedly to loving her husband. As she watched him go downriver towards Gravesend and Dover, she did not know when they would meet again. Suddenly, in a series of overwhelming blows, God seemed to have withdrawn His favour from her. But her faith was not shaken. She was still queen of England, and life must go on.

PART FIVE

The Neglected Wife
1554–1558

Chapter Eleven

Mary Alone

'Cranmer is burned, standing obstinately in his opinions.'

Sir John Mason to Edward Courtenay, earl of Devon, Brussels, 29 March 1556

Whatever her personal grief, the queen knew that matters of state always came first. She acknowledged this fully when she wrote to Charles V about her husband's imminent departure: 'My lord and good father, I have learned by what the king, my lord and good husband, has told me and also by the letter which you were pleased to send me that for a long time past the state of your affairs has demanded that your majesty and he should meet in order to be able to confer together and reach the appropriate decisions. However, you have been pleased to put off the moment of separating me from him until now, for which I humbly thank your majesty.' Here was no mention of the travesty of her pregnancy, of course. Instead, she went on: 'I assure you, sire, that there is nothing in this world that I set so much store by as the king's presence. But as I have more concern for your majesty's welfare than for my own desires, I submit to what you regard as necessary. I firmly hope that the king's absence will be brief, for I assure your majesty, his presence in this kingdom has done much good and is of great importance for the good governance of this country. For the rest, I am content with whatever may be your majesty's pleasure.'[1] It was a plaintive but dignified summation of her feelings.

Delayed by high winds at Dover, Philip did not cross to Calais until

4 September. On his arrival in Brussels he spent three days in consultation with his father, as the emperor reviewed with him the situation of
the Low Countries. Charles was determined to abdicate, to invest his son
with these strategically vital but troublesome lands. On 25 October, in
an emotional ceremony, he addressed a large gathering in the great hall
of the palace in Brussels. Worn by the responsibilities of a lifetime and
the illnesses that plagued his body and spirit, Charles V was a far cry from
the energetic young prince that his daughter-in-law, Mary Tudor, had
met in her childhood. His had been a life constantly on the move, from
one country to another, from palace to palace, frequently in the saddle,
on the field of battle, long periods apart from his wife and children; he
had known little rest. And now he yearned for the quiet contemplation
of the religious retreat, to return to Spain, the country of his mother,
Juana the Mad, who had died only six months earlier. He knew that if
he did not stop now, he would swiftly follow her to the grave. 'I have
been nine times to Germany,' he told his audience, 'six times to Spain,
and seven to Italy; I have come here to Flanders ten times, and have been
four times to France in war and peace, twice to England, and twice to
Africa … without mentioning other lesser journeys. I have made eight
voyages in the Mediterranean and three in the seas of Spain, and soon I
shall make the fourth voyage when I return there to be buried.'[2] Then,
overcome with weeping, he signalled Philip to kneel before him and,
placing his hands on the head of his son, he invested him with the
Netherlands. They would be a constant source of friction, rebellion and
bloodshed for much of Philip's long life.

Perhaps Charles took some comfort from the knowledge that his son
was also king of England. If so, that point was not reinforced by Mary's
presence. There is no indication that consideration was ever given to the
possibility of her accompanying Philip to this important family event.
The privy council would not have been enthusiastic about her leaving
the country, even for a brief period, yet her father had travelled during
his reign, for both diplomacy and war. Like her sister Elizabeth, Mary
never left England, though she thought about it often enough. Her
failure to produce a child, as well as the reservations of her councillors,
probably explains her absence. Philip was already thinking about the
future of England and the succession. The attendance of his haggard,
disappointed and sterile wife would have done nothing but raise doubts
in Brussels, at a time when the family needed a show of unity. She was
better left by herself in England.

And it was not just the emperor who was bidding the Netherlands farewell. After years as her brother's lieutenant in a country she disliked, surrounded by people she detested, Mary of Hungary had been given permission to retire, as well. It was a favour that was hard won and given only with reluctance. In a letter to the emperor written in August 1555, this severe woman, who had known little love or happiness, stated with absolute clarity the demands she had faced over the years and the difficulty of being a woman ruler in 16th-century Europe. She felt that her brother had vindicated her wish to step down by his own abdication: 'If he, with all his wisdom, experience and knowledge, feels that he must lay down the burdens of state, how much more she must feel the same, given her inferiority to him in every respect and the fact that she is a woman, for which reason alone her ability, compared to a man's, is as black compared with white!' Even in times of peace, which had been few and far between, the complexity of governing the Low Countries was challenging. 'A woman is never feared or respected as a man, whatever her rank.' No doubt she felt this sincerely, but her political acumen was as good as any man's. 'In time of war,' she continued, 'in which these countries are more often engaged than is necessary, it is entirely impossible for a woman to govern them satisfactorily. All she can do is shoulder responsibility for mistakes committed by others and bear the odium for the crushing taxation then imposed on the people. She would have been unable to face the position at all, during this war, if the emperor had not been present. The Low Countries would have been lost, and she would have been blamed for it.' As regent, she had managed to hold things together. But she would not stay under the new order. 'However much she may love King Philip, the writer believes she need not stress how hard it would be for her, having served the emperor for 25 years, to start learning her ABC again now she is past 50. There is much youth about, with whose ways she is not in sympathy. Many people are corrupt, and the upright are few.'[3] Her day was done. Like Charles himself, she wanted to go back to Spain, to live quietly there in the company of her sister Eleanor, the dowager queen of France. Her emotions, as she sat beside her brother that October day in Brussels, were more of relief than regret.

Mary Tudor might have recognised some of the assertions in her cousin's letter, but there was one crucial difference. She was a queen regnant, not a substitute for a male ruler. She felt lonely and bereft by her husband's departure, but she could not opt out of her role. In the physical sense, she was never alone, however isolated she might feel emotionally. Her household and political advisers were always there. And throughout the blisteringly hot summer of 1555, Elizabeth had been with her. Now she stayed on, 'more in favour than she used to be', reported Noailles, 'going every day to mass with the queen and often in her company'.[4] This might be, he believed, because Philip favoured better treatment for Elizabeth, and had written to his wife on the subject.

How much of a genuine rapprochement there had been between the sisters at this point is hard to say. Mary needed comfort from somewhere and perhaps Elizabeth felt sorry for her. She had not participated in any subterfuge about the queen's pregnancy and had never been called upon to express an opinion on the subject. She was there merely as an observer, albeit one who would have been seriously disadvantaged by the dubious privilege of becoming an aunt. But she also knew, once it was clear that there would be no occupant of the royal nursery, that her own position was definitely strengthened. There is no reason to be swayed by the imaginings of historical novelists that Philip had any *tendresse* for his sister-in-law; it would have been as obvious to him as to anyone else that Elizabeth was younger and more attractive than Mary. Philip's interest was surely more political than personal. There was no point in demonising Elizabeth and creating even more ill feeling. She was the heiress presumptive by act of parliament and by her father's will. And she was unmarried, which left scope for a match that would be advantageous to the Habsburg interests. Above all, she was not Mary Queen of Scots, a good Catholic, certainly, but a tool of the French.

Elizabeth stayed with Mary until mid-October 1555, when she obtained permission to take up residence again at Hatfield House. There, her faithful household staff awaited her, the imprudent but fiercely loyal Katherine Ashley, the only mother she had ever really known, Thomas Parry, Francis Verney, William St Loe and others whose loyalty to Mary was suspect. Freed from the tiresome restrictions of Sir Henry Bedingfeld, the princess resumed her linguistic studies, polishing her Greek with Roger Ascham, who had guided much of her education, and her Italian with Battista Castiglione. It was a far more agreeable existence than she had known since the first days of Mary's reign. Yet there was no sense of gratitude. Elizabeth and those around her considered she had been grievously ill treated, but they were quite ready to go down the same perilous path of intrigue again if an opportunity presented itself.

Also taking his leave of Mary that autumn was Simon Renard, who, with Paget, had been the architect of her marriage. She knew, despite the fact that her husband did not share her view of the imperial ambassador, that she would miss him. In recommending him to Charles V, she wrote: 'He was here with me through very dangerous times and … he showed himself during the marriage negotiations to be a most indispensable minister, inspired by the greatest desire to serve us and the greatest zeal for my affairs.'[5] Now, she knew, she would need some of that zeal herself.

She had always been a devout woman. Each day she began with the same prayer: 'Oh Lord my maker and redeemer, I thank thy goodness most humbly that thou hast preserved me all this night'.[6] It is for her religious policy that she is now chiefly remembered, yet she was no theologian. Her own views she summed up in December 1554. Although she committed them to paper, in a document intended for her council, they read more like the ideas of someone thinking aloud. They begin with a reference to her cousin, Cardinal Pole, the visible face of the authority of the Church in Rome, and end with her own conscience. They are a revealing insight into the extent – and limits – of her spiritual preoccupations:

> First, that such as had commission to talk with my Lord Cardinal at his first coming touching the goods of the Church should have recourse to him at the least once in a week, not only for putting those matters in execution as may be before Parliament but also to understand of him which ways might be best to bring to good effect those matters that have been begun concerning Religion, both touching good preachings. I wish that [they] may supply and overcome the evil preaching in time past and also to make a sure provision that none evil books shall either be printed, bought or sold, without just punishment.

> I think it should be well done that the universities and churches of this Realm should be visited by such persons as my Lord Cardinal, with the rest of you, may be well assured to be worthy and sufficient persons to make a true and just account thereof, remitting the choice of them to him, and you.

Touching punishment of heretics, we thinketh it ought to be done without rashness, not leaving in the meanwhile to do justice to such as by learning would seem to deceive the simple. And the rest so to be used that the people might well perceive them not to be condemned without just oration, whereby they shall both understand the truth and beware to do the like. And especially within London I would wish none to be burnt without some of the Council's presence and – both there and everywhere – good sermons at the same.

I verily believe that many benefices should not be in one man's hands, but after such sort as every priest might look to his own charge and remain resident there, whereby they should have but one bond to discharge toward God, whereas now they have many: which I take to be the cause that in most parts of this Realm there is over much want of good preachers, and such as should with their doctrine overcome the evil diligence of the abused preachers in the time of the schisms, not only by their preaching, but also by their good example, without which, in my opinion, their sermons shall not so much profit as I wish. And like as their good example on their behalf shall undoubtedly do much good, so I accept my self bound on my behalf also to show such example in encouraging and maintaining those persons well doing their duty, not forgetting in the mean while to correct and punish them which do the contrary, [so] that it may be evident to all in this realm how I discharge my conscience therein, and minister true justice in the doing.[7]

Mary's confidence that the word of God, in the mouth of good Catholic priests, would overcome the misleading interpretations of Protestant reformers was great. She was also well aware of the damage that could be done by the printing press among the literate sections of English society. Her ideas do not sound like those of a zealot with a programme for mass extermination of religious opponents. Yet they take for granted the assumption that heretics will burn, as had always been their fate throughout the centuries. It is unlikely that the queen's thoughts struck any particular note of alarm, or repugnance, in her councillors when they read them.

Almost a year later, when the parliament of 1555 met in the autumn, the first burnings had already taken place in London. John Rogers in February 1555 was the first of the Protestant martyrs whose deaths were

dwelt on with almost loving horror by John Foxe decades later. When
Rogers died, Sir Robert Rochester, a council member, was present as
Mary had decreed. Foxe described Rogers' end in detail: 'When it [the
fire] had taken hold upon his legs and shoulders, he, as one feeling no
smart, washed his hands in the flames, as though it had been cold water.
After lifting up his hands unto heaven, not removing the same until such
time as the devouring fire had consumed them, most mildly this happy
martyr yielded up his spirit'.[8]

There were several other high-profile victims in the ensuing months,
and Bishops Latimer and Ridley went to the stake at Oxford on 16
October, just five days before Parliament met. But it was not their
agonising deaths which made the 1555 parliament the most querulous of
Mary's reign. The parliament had a higher number of representatives
from the wealthy and titled classes than its predecessors, and they were
still nervous about the security of their property. The queen's determination to pay back monies from her ecclesiastical lands to Rome caused
a great deal of concern. Where would things stop? Was it just a matter of
time before Cardinal Pole came asking for their revenues, too? And why
should they vote a subsidy to a woman who seemed bent on giving away
her money to the pope? Things got so bad that William Cecil was
cajoled out of his self-imposed retirement to ensure the passage of a bill
for the payment of first fruits and tenths, taxation on clerical lands that
had come to the English Crown since 1534, back to Rome. The bill
eventually passed, but only after the House of Commons had been
locked in their chamber all day on 3 December 1555. There was also
opposition to a bill intended to allow the Crown to confiscate the property of Englishmen who had gone abroad, though it has been pointed
out that by no means all these people were religious exiles. The queen
realised, when she dissolved Parliament, that Philip would never achieve
his aim of being crowned. The constitutional implications, that he might
continue to rule after her death, were too serious. By now, she had lost
Bishop Gardiner, as well. He had managed to make his last address as
chancellor when Parliament opened, but he was very ill, and he died on
12 November. Philip proposed Paget for Gardiner's role, but Mary
would not agree. She had accepted the idea of a 'select council', or inner
council composed of a smaller number of advisers who had Philip's
confidence, but making Paget Lord Chancellor was a step too far. Her
thoughts turned back to her religious opponents, and the one man,
above all, who epitomised everything she hated about the changes

wrought during the reign of Henry VIII. That man was Thomas Cranmer, and he was to be the most famous of her victims.

It might seem, given the gap of more than two and a half years between Mary's accession and Cranmer's death, that she was unsure of what to do with him. But she always had him in her sights. The archbishop, over 60 and an elderly man by 16th-century standards, certainly hoped for mercy. Seeing the way in which Mary treated her political opponents there was, on the face of it, some grounds for optimism. The reality was different. It was not his secular opposition, the fact that he had signed Edward VI's Letters Patent disinheriting her, nor that he had held out almost to the end on 19 July 1553 against Mary's proclamation as queen, which was his downfall. He had sinned against the religious belief and order she held dear all her life, encouraged her father to break with Rome and pronounced her mother's divorce on his own authority. Much of the misery she endured as a young woman she could lay at his door. She was determined to break him, in body and spirit. It would not be a swift act of vengeance. There was no hurry and at times affairs of state got in the way, prolonging his ordeal.

Although allowed to officiate at the funeral of Edward VI, Cranmer knew it was only a matter of time before he lost his liberty. Mary steadfastly refused to see him, as if the mere fact of being in his presence would pollute her.

Infuriated by the reintroduction of the mass, Cranmer issued a public declaration of his opposition at the beginning of September, which was printed and widely distributed in London. Such recalcitrance could not be permitted. On 14 September 1553, he was summoned to appear before the privy council in the Star Chamber and then, 'after long and ferocious debating of his offence by the whole board, it was thought convenient that, as well for the treason committed by him against the queen's highness, as for the aggravating of the same his offence, by spreading abroad seditious bills, moving tumults to the disquietness of the present state, he should be committed to the Tower, there to remain and to be referred to justice, or further ordered as shall stand with the queen's pleasure'.[9] Mary's pleasure, though she did not make it apparent at the time, was that he should die the death of a heretic.

But first he had to be dealt with by the secular arm. On 13 November he, three of Northumberland's sons and Lady Jane Grey were tried for treason at the Guildhall. Initially, he pleaded not guilty, but then changed his mind. The inevitable verdict meant that he was deprived of his see under English common law and the ensuing act of attainder against him by Parliament deprived him of his property. In the eyes of the law, he was now a dead man, and Simon Renard expected his imminent execution.

Yet it did not come. Mary wanted him tried for heresy, and this raised legal problems, since he was already convicted for secular offences. She took very ill a letter he wrote her asking for mercy. In it, he made clear that he would accept the political reality of her role as sovereign lady but that he would not budge on matters of religion. The archbishop began in obsequious terms, asking her mercy:

> Most lamentably mourning and moaning himself unto your highness, Thomas Cranmer, though unworthy either to speak or write unto your highness, yet having no person that I know to be mediator for me and knowing your pitiful ears being ready to hear all pitiful complaints, and seeing so many before to have felt your abundant clemency in like cause, am now constrained … to ask mercy and pardon for my heinous folly and offence, in consenting and following the testament and last will of our late sovereign lord King Edward VI …

He went on to claim that he had never liked the will 'nor never anything grieved me so much that your grace's brother did'. But he was adamant that he never conspired with Northumberland to deprive Mary of the throne. After all, the duke hated him: '… his heart was not such towards me (seeking long time my destruction) that he would either trust me in such matter, or think that I would be persuaded by him'.[10] Whether truthful or not, his version of the events of the summer of 1553 hardly mattered.

Yet it was not easy to proceed against him with the absolute propriety on which the queen insisted. The return of the English Church to Rome must come before action against Cranmer, who had, after all, been appointed archbishop of Canterbury by the pope. A priority for both Mary and her government was to get Cranmer to recant publicly. This would be a tremendous propaganda coup and would go a long way to silencing the Protestant opposition in London and abroad.

Through much of 1554 Cranmer was under house arrest in Oxford, whose university was thought to be sounder theologically than

Cambridge. He engaged in long and fruitless disputations with Catholic divines, but it was not until September 1555 that his trial for heresy began, at the university church. By that time, the ashes of Mary's first Protestant martyr at Smithfield were seven months cold. The outcome of Cranmer's heresy trial, like that of his secular one, was never in doubt, and when the charges against him were proved, he had 80 days to obey a summons to present himself in Rome, for final judgement.

Did he seriously think that the queen would sanction such a journey? Perhaps, since he wrote to her appealing for writing and research materials to help him present his case there. But he continued to under-estimate the extent of Mary's hatred of him and to increase her anger by identifying the pope with the Antichrist and making an unremitting attack on transubstantiation, the Catholic belief in the real presence of the body and blood of Christ in the bread and wine of the mass. The Catholic mass was, to him, grounded in fundamental disobedience to the intention of Christ himself: '... the pope keepeth from all lay-persons the sacrament of their redemption by Christ's blood, which Christ commanded to be given unto them'.[11] And he further reproached Mary for failing in her duty as queen of England by suborning the country to papal jurisdiction. Her coronation oath required her to maintain the laws, liberties and customs of England; Mary's oath of obedience to the pope was in direct conflict.

With him at Oxford were Bishops Latimer and Ridley, whose moral support helped keep up Cranmer's spirits. By October 1555 Mary and Pole began to fear that the trio represented a considerable threat to law and order, as they were inspiring Protestant dissent. After a failed attempt by the Spanish Dominican friar de Soto to change their minds, the deci-sion was taken to send Latimer and Ridley to the stake. Such high-profile deaths, it was believed, would act as a stern deterrent. It was also hoped that they would weaken Cranmer's resolve. The old man was taken to the tower of the gatehouse where he lodged, to witness their deaths in the flames. He was appalled by what he saw, as was intended. Cranmer, like Mary, had never seen anyone die this terrible death, and the horror of it engulfed his spirit. He was too far away to hear the famous last words attributed to Latimer by John Foxe: 'Be of good courage, Master Ridley, and play the man: we shall this day light such a candle by God's grace in England as [I trust] shall never be put out.' Latimer died quickly but Ridley suffered appallingly 'from the ill-making of the fire, the faggots being green and piled too high, so that the flames, which burned fiercely beneath, could not well get to him, was put to such exquisite pain that he desired them for God's sake to let the fire come unto him'.[12] Latimer's words must have haunted his companion's prolonged agony. But Cranmer, faint with horror, could not – yet – play the man himself.

Mary now handed over to Pole the task of dealing with Cranmer, but, like the queen, the cardinal was not willing to meet his foe face to face. Instead, he pleaded with Cranmer in writing to save himself: 'I say if you be not plucked out by the ear, you be utterly undone in body and soul.'[13] For a while, it seemed that he might prevail. Isolated and despairing, terrified of being burned alive, ceaselessly pressured by attempts to convert him, Cranmer suffered a complete collapse on 28 January 1556. Two of his sisters, one Catholic, the other Protestant, had been fighting a war for his soul, and he could not bear the strain any more. He signed a recantation, hoping to the last for clemency from Mary. As with the duke of Northumberland, the man Mary hated as much as Cranmer, none came. When the news was brought to him on 17 March, he collapsed again. Ghastly dreams, in which he saw himself rejected by both God and man, left alone to face the abyss of hell, tormented him. He wrote (or had written for him) an abject acknowledgement of his crimes: the divorce, the betrayal of the spiritual welfare of Henry VIII, the injury done to Katherine of Aragon, the introduction of heresies, denial of the real presence and abolition of the requiem mass – all were imputed to his evil influence. The original author of this list could have been Mary herself, so close to her own experience does it read.

On the drizzly morning of 21 March, a much calmer man prepared for death. Those around him were convinced he would die a good Catholic. But he had one last scene to play. As he stood to speak in the university church, expected to uphold what he had written, he began to diverge from the script. At first, some of those present did not even notice. But it was, he said, 'contrary to the truth I had in my heart, and written for fear of death'. But now, that fear had gone and he disavowed 'all such bills and papers which I have written or signed with my hand since my degradation'.[14] It was a devastating volte-face, depriving the government of the moral and public relations victory they had fully expected. Commotion raged in the church, and Cranmer kept on shouting, refusing the pope 'with all his false doctrine'. He was about to reiterate his views on the sacrament when he was bodily pulled from the pulpit and bundled through the damp streets to the stake, in the ditch for rubbish which surrounded the town of Oxford.

There, in a historic gesture that has lost none of its power and pathos over the centuries, he thrust his right hand, the hand that had signed the recantation, into the flames and asked, as Anne Boleyn and Jane Grey had done before him, 'Lord Jesus, receive my spirit.' An observer described him as 'very soon dead'.

In the end, this very private, learned, emotional man of 67 had won a great public victory. The government hastily sought to negate the damage done by Cranmer's sensational abjuration of Catholicism. It rushed into print his recantations, of course omitting the fact that he had withdrawn them in his final minutes of life. The day after his death, Reginald Pole was finally ordained a priest and consecrated as arch-bishop of Canterbury. Mary was rid of the man she seems to have regarded as the epitome of the snares and wickedness of the new reli-gion. She could not, however, stamp out the beliefs he embodied. Today his sublime liturgy, one of the glories of the English language, is seldom heard more than once a month in English churches, having given way to a more 'accessible' modern version. Perhaps Cranmer, who believed in bringing the word of God in comprehensible form to all men, would not have disapproved.

Whether Cranmer's death became an immediate inspiration to others to stand firm is not so easy to discern. The 'Marian persecution', the burning of nearly three hundred people condemned as heretics in the three years between 1555 and 1558, is the best-known, but by no means the best-understood, aspect of Mary Tudor's life. While this most famously negative aspect of Marian religious policy has, for centuries, stolen all the headlines, more recent attempts to put it in perspective risk being classed as evasion. As Eamon Duffy has said in his monumental work about traditional religion in England between 1400 and 1680, 'England had never experienced the hounding down of so many reli-gious deviants over so wide an area in so short a period of time.'[15] Chill-ingly, in our own time, the idea of religious terrorism has, once again, become familiar. The belief that those who hold a different faith should suffer a horrible death sits deep in the human psyche. It is nothing new.

The basic facts of the drive to destroy heresy in Mary's reign can be given in terms of numbers, geography and social background. Nearly three hundred people died at the stake. The majority were in south-east England (Kent especially) and London, though some of those who died at Smithfield were brought in from neighbouring areas like Essex. Most were not grandees of the Edwardian Church, like Cranmer, but ordinary people – pewterers, housewives, millers. Many were young and had grown up with the new ideas, with no memory of papal authority over England. In Kent, one in three were women, but overall female victims were a minority, no more than 17 per cent nationally. The majority of them died with great bravery, having fortified themselves by reciting scriptures and psalms, but their beliefs were far from uniform. For it should be remembered that there was little that could be called a Protestant orthodoxy in England at this point; the Edwardian regime had legislated religious change but it had not taken root. Among those who died were upholders of ideas that Cranmer and his bishops found extreme and unacceptable: Anabaptists, Freewillers and those who denied the Holy Trinity. These people were anathema to Mary and her government, to supporters of the Edwardian Church settlement and often to their neighbours and families as well.

But the question remains, why institute a policy of religious terror at all? What was to be gained from it, and could it have succeeded without popular support? Mary came to the throne with the determination to free her country from the grave errors of practice and doctrine that had characterised her brother's reign and to repair the schism with Rome that was her father's doing. But this does not mean she wanted to turn the clock back to 1529 or wage a limitless campaign against religious opponents; neither was the inevitable corollary of her ascending the throne. It might be tempting to depict her as an embittered woman whose soul was shrunken and her personality changed by the loss of her hopes of a child and departure of her husband. But this would not be true. The decision to begin the burnings was made while Philip was still in England, at a time when Mary believed that she was carrying an heir to the throne. Philip's political advisers, and especially Simon Renard, took the view that encouraging martyrdom was likely to be a mistake. So did some of the Spanish friars who had come with Philip to England. Alfonso de Castro, preaching in front of Mary and Philip shortly after the burning of John Rogers in February 1555, issued what seemed to constitute a rebuke: he 'did earnestly inveigh against the bishops for burning of men, saying plainly that they learned it not in scripture to burn any for conscience sake; but the contrary, that they should live and be converted'.[16] Philip's own thoughts on the subject, at this time, were kept to himself. His main concern was to keep England tranquil, but that does not mean that he personally disapproved of the moral aspects of his wife's policy. If he ever made a serious attempt to dissuade her, he was unsuccessful.

Castro's belief was based on scripture, but the politicians' reservations were more pragmatic – the public spectacle that was part of the ritual of death by burning would foster unrest, they feared, not suppress it. And here was the rub for Mary's council. Where did the balance of advantage in this approach to a serious problem lie? Opposition to the queen's religious policy was, by definition, seditious. Those who opposed the restoration of Catholicism were challenging the state and royal authority. Their boldness was fed by a stream of material from the printing presses of Protestant exiles in Strasbourg and Germany, exhorting them to stand firm and defy the crown. 'Popish prelates' practices', wrote John Ponet in 1556, 'are no warrant to discharge a Christian man's conscience. He must seek what God will have him do'.[17] For a regime already threatened by rebellion, this was alarming stuff. Mary knew that something must be done to make an example of heretics who threatened the rule of law. They must be dealt with promptly, 'so as … both God's glory may be better advanced and the commonwealth more quietly governed'.[18] There was no fixed intention to burn hundreds of people, but there was a conviction that only this extreme form of punishment would send a powerful message concerning the dreadful implications of religious dissent.

As a deterrent, it was ineffective. Feelings on both sides were hardened, and so what had long been regarded as an exemplary punishment for a few became more widespread. The responsibility for the continuance of such a policy has been widely debated. John Foxe, writing in Elizabeth's time, tended to exonerate Mary herself. He laid the blame for the inception of the idea with Gardiner and believed that its continuance, after Gardiner's death, was the work of Pole and Bishop Edmund Bonner of London. In this reading of events, the queen is sincere but ill advised; terrible things are being done in her name, but she is not directly involved. Yet though the business of government placed many demands on Mary's time and attention, the fact remains that she could have stopped the burnings with a simple order to desist. She did not do so because of the nature of the crime. Mary could never condone heresy. It was an affront to her conscience and that conscience had guided her actions since she was 17 years old. For her, extending any kind of mercy to these deluded sinners was unthinkable. Many of them wanted her dead, or, at least, dethroned. The queen understood well the power of the written and spoken word, but not the even greater propaganda victory that came with martyrdom. There could be no middle course, no bargaining with such error. She would have seen this as negotiating with the devil. In mid-16th-century Europe the idea of respecting another person's beliefs would have provoked incredulity. Such certainties bred oppressors and those who were willing to be sacrificed. Mary herself had said she would die for her faith during Edward VI's reign. There is no reason to doubt her.

How, then, did contemporaries regard the burnings? Policy-making lay with the queen and her lay and religious advisers, but its implementation was the responsibility of local authorities. With the exception of the early and well-known victims, the Crown did not single out individuals for prosecution. The executions had a very local face, and it is not a pleasant one at all. Here was an opportunity to settle many old scores in the name of religion. Neighbours accused each other of a range of derelictions: of non-attendance at church, of missing processions, or of insufficient attention to the sacrament during services. In Canterbury, Thomasine Asshendon began a civil suit for slander against one Richard Baker, who had claimed: 'Well, Asshendon's wife, thou wast an heretic before that thou camest hither, and will be an heretic still ... You would have been burnt for your heresy seven years ago.'[19] The implication of this threat was very plain – Mrs Asshendon might not escape this time.

The persecution split families and divided communities. The earl of Oxford, whose last-minute military support for Mary was crucial in the accession crisis, handed over one of his own servants to the authorities. In Suffolk, many local people gathered to lament the burning of Dr Rowland Taylor were enraged at his cruel treatment by the sheriff's escort who accompanied him to the stake. Alice Benden of Staplehurst in Kent was reported to the authorities by her own husband and disowned by her father. She had refused to attend church, because, she said, much idolatry was practised there. This does not tell us much about the detail of her beliefs, but she must have known the almost certain outcome of her absence from regular worship. She was burned at Canterbury with six others in June 1557. And at Maidstone, well into the 1570s, parishioners did not allow their priest to forget that he had preached against heretics the same year that Alice Benden died.

Some local administrators and justices were as zealous as individuals in pursuing heretics. Most notable, again in Kent, was Sir John Baker, a member of Mary's privy council, who indefatigably rounded up offenders, keeping them in a jail he set up above the parish porch in Cranbrook. This former speaker of the House of Commons under Henry VIII was already in his mid-sixties and otherwise regarded as serious and learned. Age had evidently not made him merciful. Foxe called him 'Butcher Baker' and regarded him as one of the worst of all of those who had hunted down Protestants during Mary's reign.

Kent, however, was not typical of Mary's England. It had a long tradition of opposition to the Crown and the capital, witnessed in different form in Wyatt's rebellion, and a considerable number of those who were put to the flames there were of extreme opinions. And they were still a minority in the county itself, as they were nationally. Their deaths, often regarded as an excuse for a day out by the crowds of friends and foes who came to witness, acquired the same entertainment value as hangings at Tyburn in the 18th century. This may seem obscene to us but death was more visible then and executions were part of a ritual that everyone – including the victims – expected.

The Marian burnings did not give rise to a wave of revulsion in England. In fact, they might have become a mere footnote to history were it not for the Protestant reformer and historian John Foxe. There is no indication that Mary knew anything about this man who was to contribute so much to the blackening of her reputation. But if she ever spoke to the old duke of Norfolk about his grandchildren, the offspring of the ill-fated earl of Surrey, she may have been told that their education was in the hands of Master Foxe. It was, on the face of it, an unlikely combination, a reformer instructing the heir of a conservative Catholic duke, but Surrey's children seem to have greatly respected Foxe.

Their tutor left them in early 1554; he could not live with the restoration of Catholicism. So he journeyed, as did many others, to the Continent, living in Strasbourg and Frankfurt before settling in Basle. In Europe he inhabited the alternative world of Protestant dissent that was to feed the commitment of like-minded believers at home, those who were unable or unwilling to follow in his footsteps and leave England altogether. He had begun work on a general book of Christian martyrs before his departure, but the Marian regime's methods of extirpating heresy provided him with a sharper focus for his study. It was Foxe's determination to gather information about those who died which created a national martyrology. For over twenty years, through several editions of his *Acts and Monuments*, he collected and revised material. Much of what had happened in the 1550s was fading in popular memory; the details of the martyrs' passing, their last words and deportment had gone largely unrecorded. But memories, especially of the young who had witnessed these events in Kent and East Anglia, were still there 30 years later, as was a residual resentment for the regime that had inflicted such awful punishment. Those who were haunted by what they had seen poured out their descriptions. Their recollections brought forth an astonishing eight-volume work (not all of it on the Marian martyrs, admittedly), which became a kind of bible for the Protestant Church, and a powerful tool in the hands of those who wished to attack Catholicism and discredit Mary. The positive aspects of her religious programme, not to mention the achievements of the reign, all but disappeared from public view. Foxe's publications, however, have been continuously in print since the year 1563.

Yet there was a positive programme of religious reconstruction, in all aspects of the word. Mary and her bishops knew that there was a great task ahead. It went far beyond the restoration of damaged, deserted churches and religious institutions. The reintroduction of the mass was straightforward, on one level; it had been, since time out of mind, the centrepiece of life for everyone, rich and poor, educated or ignorant. Daily mass was probably not observed by the majority, but the Sunday service was the focal point of the week. It is easy to assume that the sudden reversion to the Latin mass left people adrift in incomprehension. This was not so. Parts of the service, prayers both public and private, for the monarch, for the pope, even for pregnant women, had been spoken in English since its widespread adoption as the language of the ruling classes in the mid-14th century. Primers, such as *The Lay Folks Mass Book*, a rhyming work in Chaucerian English, were long-established sources for guiding the faithful as they worshipped. Most of the population shared with Mary the view that the mass was not something alien and distant, arbitrarily imposed on them. Rather, it was easily accepted because of its familiarity.

For many, the silent majority, perhaps, this was so. But by no means all. Mary accepted that a battle needed to be waged for the hearts and

minds of those deluded or bewildered by the changes of the preceding
20 years. As reprehensible as the content of Protestant literature was, its
potential for further damage was never underestimated. Cranmer had
demurred on matters of belief, but acknowledged Mary's earthly authority. The exiles in Europe were not afraid to challenge her throne and to
condone attacks on her life. This threat must be addressed. A complete
programme of education, both of people and priesthood, was needed.
And it was not to be a rarefied, academic exercise. The populace needed
to engage with Catholicism – and their queen – in ways that ordinary
people, in a pre-literate age, could understand. Only recently has the
effectiveness of Mary's policy in this respect re-emerged.

The truth was that the return of Catholicism enjoyed widespread
popular support, even in London. John Foxe's lurid accounts of a
country suffering religious repression find no echo in the account of the
Marian period given by London cloth merchant Henry Machyn. This is
generally referred to as a 'diary' but it is, more accurately, a chronicle of
events written by a London businessman. As such, it provides fascinating insights into the religious culture of Mary's reign. There is nothing
here that fits with preconceptions of a dismayed, cowed populace ruled
by a dour monarch unfit (as many historians have claimed) to bear the
name of Tudor. Machyn did, indeed, chronicle, in his succinct and
matter-of-fact way, a number of burnings in London, but he also listed
many other judgements against criminals. On his pages are catalogued
the full range of miscreants: murderers, pirates, young ladies who have
committed 'shameful deeds'. Hangings and nailings to the pillory are
frequently mentioned, the witness of a violent age where summary
justice was the norm.

Machyn was a devout Catholic with great reverence for Tudor
monarchy. The thing he seems to have appreciated most about Mary's
religious policy is the way that it included him and other citizens in
communal activities which allowed them to demonstrate their devotion
to their sovereign. He loved the religious celebrations and processions,
which embraced everyone. There were about sixty of these in Mary's
reign, though they petered out in the last year of her rule, perhaps
because of the widespread outbreak of viral illness that year.

The use of ritual and spectacle allowed Mary to establish a bond
between herself and her subjects which was a strong force for unity of
purpose. Although Mary was not really comfortable with public appearances, she realised that the message she wished to get across would be

strengthened by her personal participation in some of these ceremonies. Machyn records that for Rogation Week in the spring of 1554 (before her marriage), when the court was at St James's Palace, 'the queen's grace went in procession … with heralds and serjeants of arms and four bishops'. The procession went round the queen's chapel and moved on the next day to St Giles, 'and there sung mass … and the next day, Tuesday, to Saint Martin's in the Fields … and the third day to West-minster, and there a sermon and then mass and made good cheer and after about the park and so to St James court there'.[20] Earlier in the same year, Mary used public spectacle to reinforce her victory over Wyatt's rebels and to ensure that the people saw their ritual humiliation when they were released: '… all the Kent men went to the court with halters about their necks and bound with cords two and two together through London to Westminster … and the poor prisoners knelt down in the mire and the queen's grace looked out over the gate and gave them all pardon and they cried out God save the queen'.[21]

No doubt the men of Kent did not enjoy this treatment, but it reminded the onlookers of the queen's power and majesty, as well as her capacity to forgive political opponents. Machyn also recorded the cele-brations surrounding Mary's supposed quickening with child in November 1554 and the enraptured response to rumours of her delivery the following spring. The disappointment of her false pregnancy he does not mention, but the joyful reaction to the victory of Philip's combined Anglo-Imperial force against the French after the battle of St Quentin in 1557 is chronicled. The Te Deum was sung in all the parishes, bells rung, bonfires lit, and there was much drinking in the streets. This hardly suggests a virulent hatred of the queen and her Spanish husband, even if the response was encouraged by the authorities.

The views of ordinary people on Mary's religious programme and their judgements on the queen herself at the time have seldom been scrutinised. It is not easy to do so, given the vociferousness of her oppo-nents and the general silence of the majority. Yet Machyn's account indi-cates that she did touch a chord. Respect for monarchy and the rule of law was deeply embedded in Mary's subjects, both great and small. It is impossible to say whether Mary consciously applied what today would be called a communications strategy or not. But her approach reflected not just her own priorities, which had nothing to do with doctrinal niceties, but also her own experiences. She had seen for herself how the faithful yearned for the mass during her brother's time, when her house was a magnet for those who opposed the Edwardian religious legislation. She also knew the political power of symbolism when she entered London in March 1551 with all her retinue provocatively wearing rosaries. And she was keen to maintain the mysterious practice of touching victims of scrofula, the skin disease known as 'the king's evil', which emphasised the sovereign's mysterious and divine powers of healing. *Queen Mary's Manual for the blessing of cramp rings and touching for the evil*, beautifully illuminated, is one of the loveliest artefacts to survive from her reign.[22]

Machyn approved of his queen, but he had acquiesced quietly in the changes of her brother's reign and adapted readily under Elizabeth. He was a devout man, but no extremist. Already in his fifties when Mary came to the throne, he had seen most of his children die before him, but he did not question the ways of God, any more than Mary did. He himself seems to have been a victim of the plague when he died in 1563, the same year that John Foxe published the first edition of his *Acts and Monuments*.

Machyn's picture of the public face of Catholic culture during Mary's reign tells only one part of the story of the Marian Church. Its agenda was not to turn the clock back, but to adapt the best of reforming Catholicism to the situation of England. Pole and Mary's bishops recognised the need for education, and they shared the queen's belief in the benefits that would come from good preaching. Instructing the young would be key. As bishop of London, Bonner produced 'An honest godlye instruction and information for the ... bringinge up of Children'. It was intended for use by all the schoolmasters in the diocese who had responsibility for the first instruction of children. 'All the youth', according to Bonner, 'must have some honest introduction and entry in things convenient for them to learn, that is to say, both to know the letters, with joining of them together, and thereby the sooner made apt to go further, both in reading and also in writing.' And they should also learn how to bless themselves morning and evening and 'to say also the Paternoster, the Ave Maria, the Creed, the Confiteor [the confession], with the rest to answer the priest at mass, to say grace at dinner and supper'. In his little book was printed the alphabet, in both lower and upper case, and the main prayers and devotions the child must learn. These were given in both English and Latin, and the English versions of the Lord's Prayer and the Creed are almost word for word the same as in the 1552 Book of Common Prayer.[23] Marian Catholicism did not seek to obliterate the changes under Edward VI. Rather, it used what was thought acceptable and proper to underpin its own messages.

One of the difficulties was how to get these messages across. It was one thing for Mary to demand a step-change in the quality and output of pulpit utterances, another to bring it about. And the written word would also be needed to overcome the onslaught of material from the exiles in Europe. Pole was well aware of the power of preaching and of books, though also wary of them as tools in the hands of Protestants. The misuse of the spoken word to seduce the gullible troubled him, as did exposure to unguided reliance on the scriptures. Here were all sorts of pitfalls, whatever the merits of the underlying intention: 'The which only desire of itself being good, yet not taking the right way to the accomplishing of the same, maketh many to fall into heresies, thinking no better nor speedier way ... for to come to the knowledge of God and his law, than by reading of books, wherein they be sore deceived. And yet, so it be done in his place, and with right order and circumstance, it helpeth much.'[24] He was not hostile to the idea of giving preaching and Bible study a prominence they never enjoyed in the earlier part of the Tudor century, so long as there was no indiscriminate recourse to them. What was sorely needed was appropriate material. It was easier to produce primers for the laity in fairly short order than it was to produce guidance to the priesthood on the topics that were to be encouraged for sermons.

Here, the diligent Bonner was of help again. In 1555, a very busy year for him, he produced a book called *A profitable and necessary doctrine, with certain homilies adjoined*. It drew on the King's Book of the 1540s, a stalwart of the last years of Henry VIII, and, much more remarkably, on Cranmer's homilies, to provide an invaluable source for propounding the major elements of Christian belief. Lively and full of useful examples for the clergy to draw upon, the *Profitable and necessary doctrine* was the work of an able and active mind. It showed that there was nothing sterile about the direction of the Marian Church. At the beginning of 1558, Thomas Watson, the bishop of Lincoln, published a further contribution, in a series of 30 sermons, which could be used directly by priests too busy (or ill educated) to prepare their own. This 'wholesome Catholic doctrine concerning the seven sacraments of Christ's church' was described as 'expedient to be known of all men, set forth in manner of short sermons to be made to the people'.[25]

So the Catholic hierarchy and its printers took very much to heart the queen's exhortations to support better preaching and counter

Protestant literature. But this was only part of the drive necessary to make Catholicism healthy. The universities, particularly Cambridge, were purged of suspect academics, after visitations carried out on the orders of Cardinal Pole. Many scholars who supported new religious ideas fled abroad, as the authorities began to reintroduce the ideas of Christian humanism that had been flourishing on the Continent for years. Both institutions received the support of new benefactors. St John's College, Oxford, was established in 1555 by Sir Thomas White, a former Lord Mayor of London, and in 1557, Dr John Caius refounded Gonville Hall, Cambridge, as Gonville and Caius College.

Another, very visible beneficiary of the positive religious changes under Mary was Westminster Abbey, refounded as a Benedictine house in 1555 and restored to its independence outside the diocese of London. The shrine of Edward the Confessor, so central to the identity of English monarchy, had escaped the worst depredations of Henry VIII and his son, but it needed attention. Its present form we owe to the man who was to be the last abbot of Westminster, John Feckenham, Mary's own confessor when she first ascended the throne.

Westminster Abbey may have been something of a showpiece but Mary and Pole knew that real progress needed to be made at parish level. Here the amount of work to be done was daunting. The state of the churches themselves was often pitiful and it could not suddenly be rectified. Edward VI had reigned for only six years, but the removal of the trappings of the old religion had been comprehensive. Their loss was by no means welcome. The images that were taken away had literally been part of the fabric of church life for hundreds of years. They were familiar to parishioners and were a source of local pride, as well as local employment. Ironically, the beginning of the 16th century had seen an upsurge in work on churches and their decorations, the money for all of this coming from individual bequests and donations. Half a century later, the results were ruthlessly despoiled. The Edwardian religious leaders would have none of this dangerously misleading frippery. They considered images of jewel-bedecked saints, the gleam of chalice and cup, the splendour of the priest's vestments, the depiction of saints on the rood-screen that separated the nave from the altar, as idolatrous and divisive. These trappings hindered religious devotion and distracted the faithful from the simple beauty of God's word. The commissioners who visited churches in the early 1550s were under instructions to leave behind only the bare essentials: a cup, a bell, a covering for the table and a surplice for the priest.

Mary's bishops were realistic enough to appreciate the extent of the problem they faced. It would not be easy to reinvigorate Catholic worship while the churches remained bare. Their austerity was uninspiring, but, while it had been swiftly achieved, it could not so quickly be reinstated. Many of the items confiscated remained in private hands, and though some were recovered, most of the plate taken from churches was not. Nevertheless, by the end of 1554 Mary could take some satisfaction in the progress that had been made, which provided a basis for moving forward. High altars were rebuilt and vestments and copes for the clergy provided. This was a sound start, and many parishes set about the task of building side altars and providing themselves with the many other accoutrements of Catholicism as best they could. But the various books describing the different services, the altar cloths for different seasons, the decoration of the rood-screen and the acquisition of religious ornaments all came more slowly. Bequests were encouraged, but in Marian England, with its growing problems of poverty and want, the faithful were often more concerned to provide for the living, in alms and charity, than to make generous provision for the local church on their deathbeds. When Archdeacon Nicholas Harpsfield conducted his visitation of Kent in 1557, he found that neglect of the churches was still considerable. At Goudhurst, for example, he was met by a sorry sight. There was no register book for births, marriages and deaths and no fair record of the church's accounts; the glass windows of the church and the vicarage house both needed repair; the churchyard was overgrown. He also noted that 'the window in the belfry be glassed before Midsummer, and to be closed otherwise decently (so that no pigeons may come into the church) before All Saints'.[26] It is a picture of general neglect, a lapse of standards and, perhaps more profoundly, of a malaise brought about by the conflicting demands of mid-Tudor religious legislation. Most parishes did their best. They were not ill intentioned, only wearied by the demands of government.

Whatever might have been desired in terms of decoration, repair and observance, the Marian Church did not want to restore medieval Catholicism to England. Reviving the mass was central to its programme, as it was to the daily life of Queen Mary herself. Despite the fact that it was a profoundly personal experience, appreciated in varying ways by people of differing social classes and education, the mass was a focus for social cohesion and national unity. It mattered much more to the average Englishman than the distant authority of the pope. Progress was being made on what the queen viewed as spiritual reconstruction for England, and it seems that she had much of the country on her side. The lurid woodcuts of Protestant victims in Foxe's publications are only part of the story of the religious experience under Mary.

In other areas, too, Mary's reign saw achievements that have long gone unacknowledged. Hers was a cultured court, with a strong emphasis on music and drama. Thomas Tallis, one of the greatest of English 16th-century composers, was a Gentleman of Mary's Chapel Royal, as he had been in the reigns of Henry VIII and Edward VI. As a lay singer, she would have heard his voice often. His works from this period cannot be dated with accuracy, but he may have written his great seven-part mass, *Puer natus est nobis*, in 1554 as a celebration of Mary's supposed pregnancy.

John Heywood, who had so charmingly celebrated the beauty of the young Princess Mary 20 years earlier, thrived while she was queen. He wrote a ballad to celebrate her marriage to Philip, 'The eagle's bird hath spread his wings', and his allegorical poem, *The Spider and the Flie*, was completed and published in 1556. The year before, the queen had awarded him a pension of £50 per annum. There were also two editions of his ongoing magnum opus on English proverbs and epigrams, in 1555 and 1556. It eventually ran to over 1,260 entries.

Mary was fond of masques and plays, as she reminded the Master of the Revels in December 1554. Requiring him to provide the costumes and props for a play by Nicholas Udall, she noted: 'Whereas our well-beloved Nicholas Udall hath at sundry seasons convenient ... shewed and mindeth thereafter to show his diligence in setting forth of dialogues and interludes before us for our regal disport and recreation'.[27] Udall and Heywood were not the only people who wrote for her. Baldwyn's play, *Love and Life*, was 'set down' on Christmas Eve, 1556. This was described as a comedy, but its touch was very heavy. All the characters had names beginning with the letter 'L'. They included Leonard Lustyguts, an epicure, and Sir Lewis Lewdlife, a chaplain. Whether Mary would have been amused by this reference to the continued failings of the clergy is a moot point. She did, though, like to enjoy herself and be entertained. Apparently she could even hold her own in the cut and thrust of witty exchanges with John Heywood.

Mary's love of music and drama was an essential part of her

character. These interests provided an important outlet for relaxation. They were a necessary antidote for the sheer grind of government, and though the court was quieter when Philip was not there, Mary did not go completely into her shell. Once she had recovered from the trauma of her phantom pregnancy, the queen accepted that there was much still to be done if she was to improve the state of her country. With Philip gone, she must assume full responsibility and work with her advisers to encourage commerce, improve fiscal management and tackle the question of social and municipal reform. A number of the improvements she set in motion were developed by the Elizabethan government. But her sister never acknowledged the debt she owed to Mary.

Helping commerce to thrive was a priority. Initially, relations with the queen's overseas merchants were prickly and rather contradictory. The stranglehold of the Hanseatic merchants of northern Europe and their privileged position in England was deeply unpopular with their English competitors in European trade, the Merchant Adventurers. The Hanse paid only 1 per cent duty on its merchandise and had complete control of prices. Mary's first parliament passed a bill of tonnage and poundage requiring them to pay the same duties as other merchants, but the quid pro quo was a lifting of the ban on Hanseatic purchases of cloth in England. This may have been partly the result of imperial pressure but it also reflected the uncomfortable truth that the merchants of the Hanse had provided loans to the English monarchy for a long time. The Merchant Adventurers were furious and by 1555 Mary and the government were rethinking their Hanseatic strategy. Two years later the ban was reimposed and the Hanse's charter revoked.

Tensions in traditional markets encouraged the search for new ones. The great age of exploration is associated with Elizabeth, but Mary had her own adventurers. When it became clear that there would be no immediate opening of South America to English merchants, whatever hopes may have been raised by the marriage to Philip of Spain, attention turned east. The first expedition looking for a north-eastern passage to the wealth of the Orient set out as Edward VI lay dying, in June 1553. It was led by Sir Hugh Willoughby and consisted of three ships. The little fleet was scattered by a violent storm off Norway, and though Willoughby eventually reached the Russian coast, he was to die there, trapped by the extreme cold of the winter.

His second-in-command, Richard Chancellor, was more fortunate. He found his way into the White Sea as far as Archangel, and from there

he travelled through Russia to Moscow, where he was received by the
tsar known to history as Ivan the Terrible. Chancellor found life in
Russia very different from England. 'Moscow itself is great: I take the
whole town to be greater than London with the suburbs: but it is very
rude and standeth without all order.' He thought the timber houses a fire
risk and those inhabited by ordinary citizens were crude, made of 'beams
of fir-trees'. The Russian religion he correctly described as a variant of
the Greek Church, with no graven images of saints but many icons and
paintings. Both Old and New Testaments were available in the vernacular, but no one seemed to understand them and neither the Lord's Prayer
nor the Ten Commandments was widely known. To Chancellor, Russia
seemed to have the building blocks of civilisation, but to be a society
very much on the edge of the world.

The unexpected visitor was, though, favourably impressed by the
welcome he received from Ivan. The informality of proceedings was
congenial – Ivan knew all his nobles by name and he made legal judgements himself, without recourse to lawyers. This might be seen as an
indication of autocracy rather than directness, but Chancellor, who
evidently did not like lawyers as a class, found it refreshing. 'This duke',
Chancellor wrote, 'is lord and emperor of many countries and his power
is marvellous great … he is able to bring into the field two or three
hundred thousand men.'[28] No doubt this was an impression of might
that Ivan wanted to make, but he had no hostile intentions against his
visitor's country. In fact, he was keen to reach a trade agreement. So was
Mary, and on 5 April 1555 she and Philip signed a letter thanking the tsar
for his hospitality and confirming their desire to trade. Chancellor's
colourful depiction of life in Russia provoked huge interest and excitement. The Muscovy Company was issued a royal charter in 1555 for
northern, north-eastern and north-western discoveries and was allowed
to raise the flag of England over new territories, in the name of the king
and queen. Sebastian Cabot was nominated first governor of the
company, empowered to trade with any part of the world, 'before the late
said adventure or enterprise unknown, and by our merchants and
subjects not commonly frequented',[29] a suitably broad undertaking to be
headed by someone who, like his father before him, had committed his
life to exploration and cartography.

Mary's councillors were eager to invest in the new venture. Its initial
capital of £6,000 is said to have been raised by 240 men subscribing £25
each. Seven peers were members, including the marquis of Winchester,

Lord Paget, the earl of Arundel and the earl of Bedford. So were Mary's household staff, Sir Robert Rochester, William Waldegrave and Henry Jerningham, as well as a selection of aldermen of the City of London and other knights, esquires and gentlemen. Two of the company's members were women, widows who were merchants in their own right.

But Richard Chancellor did not live to reap the rewards of his discovery. He went back to Moscow to negotiate a commercial treaty and set off for home accompanied by a newly appointed Russian ambassador to the English court. When their ship was wrecked off the coast of Scotland, Chancellor drowned. The ambassador survived this ordeal, though he had to be 'rescued' from the Scots and brought down to London, with due honours. The treaty was eventually concluded on very advantageous terms for the English, allowing for imports of much-needed naval supplies in return for selling to the Russians herbs, woollens and metalwork. It gave a great boost to English trade.

Chancellor had gone north and been killed by the very risky nature of exploration. His fate did not deter Mary's other adventurers, though they turned south. Voyages by William Winter, John Lok and William Towerson along the west coast of Africa established a foothold in Guinea. Here there were rich sources of gold, ivory and pepper. Unfortunately, the Portuguese were already active in this part of Africa and Philip felt obliged to defend their interests against those of his wife's merchants. Mary agreed, but Elizabeth reacted differently when she came to the throne. Here, as in other commercial areas, she was able to build on the closer ties between the mercantile community and the government begun in her sister's reign.

Interest in foreign lands is exemplified by what is perhaps the most beautiful piece of work to survive from Mary's reign. The Queen Mary Atlas was commissioned around 1555 as a gift for Philip from his wife. She could not have chosen anything he would have liked more. Maps were the closest thing that Philip had to a hobby. He consulted them for all his military campaigns and commissioned them whenever he felt it necessary. Mary must have known this, but she probably also wanted the atlas to remind him of their joint inheritance. No record of her actual commission survives but the careful attention paid to the heraldry that decorates the pages gives us a clue; this was a statement of grandeur and power, as well as a record of the known world.

It was also fitting that the atlas should be commissioned by an English monarch, in keeping with the country's long tradition of map-making.

Under Edward VI, Sebastian Cabot had himself created a world map which was printed and hung on the walls of the Privy Chamber in Whitehall. Perhaps Philip had seen it there and Mary, alert to his interest, decided to go one better by employing one of the greatest of all 16th-century cartographers to produce an atlas specially for him. That man was the Portuguese map-maker and pilot Diogo Homem.

Born in 1520, Homem had a colourful past. He had been imprisoned in a Moroccan fortress in 1544, on suspicion of implication in a murder in Lisbon. But he escaped and made his way to England, where he joined as many as 60 other cartographers working for Henry VIII. Their work was important but not always glamorous, since it frequently involved mapping harbours and fortifications as Henry prepared to fight the French and the Scots. Homem must have been unusually skilful. After only three years in England he was a chart-maker with a European reputation, supporting himself as a freelance working for an international clientele. Most of his commissions were for private libraries. The atlas ordered by the queen of England was, though, of a different order of magnificence.

The atlas is dated 1558, which is probably the year of its completion. Not all of it survives – nine maps out of a likely 14 or 15 – but what remains is breathtaking. The maps are surprisingly accurate for Europe, Africa and Asia, and they also show the coast of north-eastern America as well as all of South America. Originally, there may have been a decorative circular diagram of the zodiac as well as the surviving calendar, tables of solar declination, a lunar chart and the zonal world map. Most striking of all is the ethnographical and wildlife decoration, which would have been undertaken in Venice. Here are camels and vivid tents in North Africa and great fishes swimming in the oceans. Diogo Homem's world teems with life and colour and the spirit of discovery. The Queen Mary Atlas, overlooked for many years, as so much else to do with Mary, is no dry document from the past. It is a work of art.[30]

While Mary encouraged the search for exotic new markets, she also knew that domestic commerce and industry must be supported. Guilds, towns and boroughs were seen as potential sources of wealth, and it was recognised that a more coherent structure for local government would be of benefit to the country as a whole. Guilds were strengthened, apprenticeship laws enforced and the mobility of workers restricted. This would appal 21st-century advocates of market forces, but free enterprise was not a concept appreciated by Mary and her government. They thought English domestic prosperity could best be achieved by protecting traditional institutions and industries, and Parliament agreed with them. A conservative approach was typified by the legislation passed by the parliament of 1555; it was cantankerous on matters of religion but its achievements in social and economic legislation were considerable. Local authorities were able to issue licences to beggars, in an attempt to handle vagrancy more successfully, and, for those who were in work, there was legislation to ensure that they stayed employed, where they were, so that they did not add to the problem. The right to weave was confined to those living in corporate towns, and the number of looms operated by any one individual was restricted. Two years later, the Woollen Cloth Act reinforced this determination to manage the manufacture of what was still the country's main industrial staple, by placing heavy fines on manufacturers who tried to set up independently.

To make local government and industry more efficient, and civic dignitaries more amenable, the Crown encouraged incorporation of towns and boroughs. They were the front line in administering law and order in England and in dealing with burgeoning social problems. Mary granted more than twice the number of charters per year compared to her predecessors and was working towards a uniform standard for the structure and power of municipal governments. Towns could act as corporate entities before the law, enabling them to hold lands that might be sold or let as a source of income for education, poor relief and public works. They were also able to issue by-laws, providing them with a local framework for justice. Incorporation was a matter of local pride and many of these charters were still being used as instruments of government right up till 1835. The charter incorporating the borough of Wycombe in Buckinghamshire is typical of the privileges granted to many others. In this case, the loyalty of the town during the succession crisis of 1553 and Wyatt's rebellion was noted. The mayor, two bailiffs and burgesses would be a 'body corporate and politic ... able to plead and be impleaded in all courts and places both spiritual and temporal'. They were empowered to hold a court at least once every three weeks, 'with full power to hear and determine all pleas of debt, account, covenant, contract, force and arms'.[31] And to facilitate local trade and industry, a market was granted weekly, with major fairs twice a year.

Mary could take comfort from the fact that the conduct of local government was mainly in the hands of people she trusted. Here the queen's supporters played a large part. Her marriage to Philip of Spain was of international significance, but Mary ruled the shires of England through the relatives and friends of those with whom she had long-standing ties. Lords lieutenant in the counties and justices of the peace were frequently appointed as the result of their kinship to someone in this network. All were good Catholics in the queen's eyes. Marriage to Philip may have reduced the influence of Mary's wider affinity on matters of state, but in terms of English daily life, they remained an important force.

Certainly a level of centralisation was required to tackle the severe problems of famine and disease that beset Mary's reign. Measures of social welfare were needed on a nationwide scale, and the Marian regime did not throw up its hands and leave the outcome to God. In London, five charities were brought together to provide a city-wide system of poor relief. Failed harvests meant that proclamations had to be used to provide for the distribution of grain where the situation was most desperate. Laws against grain-hoarders were vigorously enforced and systematic surveys of stocks undertaken. In Yorkshire in 1557, justices of the peace were appointed with specific responsibility for overseeing this process.

Throughout Mary's reign there was another trend that had considerable impact on English prosperity. This was a sustained effort to overhaul financial management and provide a better underpinning for the economy as a whole. Financing the cost of government itself was a constant difficulty, as Mary's predecessors well knew. The crux of the problem was that the financial structure was medieval and had not remotely kept pace with the requirements of an early-modern monarchy. Ireland alone cost Mary nearly £40,000 a year and household charges had spiralled, with no overhaul since 1519, when Mary was only three years old. But worse still were areas that should have brought in revenue, such as the exchequer and various of the other ancient departments originally set up to provide income, but now little more than the preserve of placemen. And an absolute priority was to restore the currency, the foundation on which everything else depended. Henry

VIII and Edward VI had both debased the coinage. Minting continued through most of Mary's reign and plans were put in place between 1556 and 1558 for a major recoinage, but these had to be shelved in the face of the mounting pressures of war, dearth and disease. The plans formed the basis for the great Elizabethan recoinage carried out in 1560–61, however.

Reform of the exchequer had long been anticipated, but Mary was able to put it into practice. The project was handed to the aged marquess of Winchester, a long-time servant of the Crown but, as someone who had carried out her father's orders for the treatment of Mary and her mother in the 1530s, scarcely a confidant. Winchester duly amalgamated the courts of Augmentation and First Fruits and Tenths into the exchequer, but his attempts to stamp out corruption, rife as it probably was, involved reverting to accountancy methods so ancient that Mary would have none of them. She wanted the more advanced methods of accounting and auditing developed in the King's Chamber, which demonstrates that she had a far better financial grasp than her critics have claimed. Mary was not fascinated by figures, but as someone who had signed off her accounts since she was in her early twenties and a woman of property on a large scale, she appreciated the importance of a well-run fiscal organisation. But she may have suspected that Winchester was as interested in his own aggrandisement as he was in good practice at the exchequer, and in 1557 she moved him across to a different but nonetheless important area of responsibility, the financial administration of the navy.

The main achievement of these years in bringing revenues to the Crown was the extensive overhaul of customs and excise. This was a corollary of the drive to increase trade, but it also tapped unused sources of income. Hundreds of commodities remained untaxed, and those that were were taxed on the basis of valuations going back as far as 1507. Rampant inflation of 350 per cent made them completely useless. A new Book of Rates was introduced, surviving almost unchanged until 1604. Most of the revisions and additions were on non-essential imported goods, a move intended to help English industry. Customs collection was centralised, thus ensuring that money came directly to the Crown instead of being creamed off by the multitude of professional collectors who were awarded receivership rights for political support. Sir Francis Englefield, a Mary loyalist, was awarded the post of Surveyor General of the Customs for the Port of London. This role was extended nationwide under Elizabeth, until she reverted to the old system of individual collectors in the 1570s. As a means of rewarding service it was too tempting, but decentralisation was a retrograde step.

Sound financial management meant leading by example. The royal household itself was subject to scrutiny. A report of 1555 looked in detail at possible reductions in costs and wages. It made uncomfortable reading. Wages were far too high and the requirement to feed, clothe, house and educate members of the household and their families was proving an unacceptable burden. The report suggested strongly that liberties were being taken with royal generosity and that this must stop, no matter how much offence was caused: '£396 [per annum] is paid for clothing 21 ladies and gentlemen under warrant dormant. There is no precedent for such largesse.' But even more tricky was the amount that the monarch spent on herself: 'I place in this category', wrote the unsparing auditor, 'clothing for adorning the royal person, bed coverlets, material for horsecloths and litters, with other equipment for horses and mules. In his tenth year, Henry VIII spent £1631 and in his eleventh only £911, on the wardrobe of the robes, the wardrobe of the beds, on the stable and on saddles and harnesses.' And what had his daughter done? 'In her first year, the queen spent £5100 on the same ... Henry VIII, who had two minstrels, gave £29 annually to both. Since she has 38 minstrels [a comment revealing just how much Mary loved music], the queen gives £572 annually for clothing.' Then came the crunch. 'In summary: the largesse of Henry VIII amounted to £4300 in 1518/19. The largesse of the queen [in 1553/4] amounted to £9600. If warrants dormant, or grants of the same certain kind, were reduced to an annual £1000 and those uncertain could be contained to £3000, the expense of the wardrobe would diminish to £4300, and so a great decrease from the present charge would ensue.'[32] Although this summation was written 450 years ago, it would surely meet the approval of a modern financial adviser. Basically, Madam was too kind-hearted to those around her and utterly self-indulgent when it came to clothes and entertainment. Mary Tudor was human, after all. In the queen's defence, it should be pointed out that the very high expenses of the first two years of her reign were caused by her coronation and marriage. But, so far as we can tell, she never did cut back her spending on her wardrobe.

Nevertheless, as the reign progressed, Mary was presiding over a series of laudable initiatives that were beginning to improve life in England. Stability and tranquillity, however, remained elusive goals. The threat of intrigue and the prospect of war were ever present. For wherever Elizabeth was, there also lurked deceit. And wherever Philip, Mary's husband, might be, in England or in Brussels, there was another inescapable reality: sooner or later, his troubles would be England's, too.

Chapter Twelve

Triumph and Disaster

> 'And I do humbly beseech my said most dearest lord
> and husband to accept of my bequest and to keep for
> a memory of me one jewel, being a table diamond
> which the emperor's majesty, his and my most
> honourable father, sent unto me ...'
>
> Queen Mary's will, 30 March 1558

Mary kept up a regular correspondence with Philip while he was in Brussels, providing him with information and seeking his views. The king replied with advice, comments and sometimes instructions; it was not just a one-way flow. In other respects he was less dutiful. Freed from his wife's smothering attentions, he apparently embarked on a couple of liaisons with attractive ladies of the Flemish court. There was gossip about his infidelities in London, though it may not have reached Mary's ears. But she missed him terribly and it took her almost a year to adapt to his absence. During that period, she sent Charles V a series of imploring and increasingly bitter letters, pleading for her husband's return. The rational part of her realised the difficulties, yet 'I cannot', she told the emperor, 'but deeply feel the solitude in which the king's absence leaves me. As your majesty well knows, he is the chief joy and comfort I have in this world'.[1] No doubt Charles felt the same. He needed Philip, too. He could not yet leave the Low Countries for the retreat he so desperately desired; the European situation was too uncertain. The coffers of the Netherlands were empty and, despite a truce with France negotiated by Philip in February 1556, war did not seem far away. Charles V and his son might be good Catholics, but they were still hated by the aggressive and anti-Spanish Gianpietro Caraffa, an Italian who had become pope in 1555 as Paul IV. Caraffa was 80 years old but age had not calmed his spleen. He wanted the Habsburgs out of Italy. It could only be a matter of time before he allied with the French in a renewed military campaign, with serious implications for Philip and potentially embarrassing ones for Mary and her country, not long returned to papal authority.

The queen was aware of all this, but still found it impossible to contain her emotions. In her eyes, the emperor was not a monarch besieged by a multitude of problems but a parent withholding the support that she, his daughter-in-law, desperately needed. She was filled with anxiety and dread. In September 1556 she wrote to Charles again, overwhelmed by depression and trying to justify her argument for Philip's presence in terms of God's will. She asked the emperor

to consider the miserable plight into which this country has now fallen. I have written to the king my husband in detail on the subject and I assure your majesty that I am not moved by my personal desire for his presence, although I confess I do unspeakably long to have him here, but by my care for this kingdom. Unless he comes to remedy matters, not I only but also wiser persons than I fear that great danger will ensue for lack of a firm hand, and indeed we see it before our eyes … My desire is that his highness should be in the place where he may best serve God, and his conscience and mine be at rest.[2]

But the queen was projecting her own feelings on others. The council continued to govern England effectively in Philip's absence and did not themselves petition the king for his immediate return. As it happened, Charles V almost certainly never saw Mary's letter. He had finally set sail, for the last time, to Spain, with his sisters Mary and Eleanor.

It was understandable that Mary felt concern about the state of her country, even if she had dramatised her personal feelings. The winter of 1555/6 saw the genesis of another conspiracy against her throne. It dissolved with the coming of spring and never got close to being the armed uprising of Wyatt's rebellion, but the nervousness of the government was palpable. Again, dissident gentlemen were found to be in cahoots with the French ambassador. Again, there was talk of invasion from France. And, most grievously of all for Mary, again there was the involvement of Elizabeth and her household. Only this time their complicity was wider and deeper. It seemed almost brazen. But virtually nothing was done about it, because Philip counselled restraint. Some of the effort this cost Mary comes across in her letter to his father.

The Dudley conspiracy, as it is generally known, had its origins among the disaffected members of the 1555 parliament. The name of Sir Henry Dudley stuck to the intrigue, but he was only one of several gentlemen who were plotting against Mary. A cousin of the duke of Northumberland, he had been vice-admiral of the English Channel and captain of the English enclave at Guisnes during his relative's rule. All that came to an end with Mary's accession. Dudley was briefly in the Tower of London but, though his incarceration lasted no more than three months, he was never going to be a favourite of the queen's. Like his fellow-conspirators, Dudley was concerned about the exiles bill and its implication that lands gained from the dissolution of the monasteries might still be at risk from Mary's desire to return Church lands to Rome. The conspirators hoped for security and further, though unspecified, rewards if they could get Elizabeth on the throne. Dudley's father-in-law, Christopher Ashton, had gained much of his wealth in Berkshire from former monastic lands, as well as what had come to him as the last husband of Mary's former lady-in-waiting, Lady Katherine Gordon. Ashton was a bully, much hated by his neighbours. But he thought Elizabeth a 'jolly liberal dame'. Just what moved him to this belief in the generosity of a young woman not long out of disgrace and whose position was still perilous is unknown. Ashton himself does not seem to have been over-liberal with Dudley, who was constantly in debt. In fact, this financial embarrassment was probably a compelling motive for the younger man to seek to recoup his fortune through a treasonable venture funded by the king of France.

Like the other major figures in this far-reaching but disorganised affair, Dudley was a gentleman-soldier who had fallen on hard times. Peace was not profitable for men who lived by the sword. A considerable number of the English self-exiled in France had gone there to find work in Henry II's army. They were not the earnest, committed refugees who attacked Mary through the medium of the printing press in Switzerland and Germany. Dudley's motives, and those of his colleagues, were far from high-minded, even if he tried to dress them up that way: 'I am going to France and mind to serve the French king for a while, to get a band of men, most of them English, 2,000–3,000 at least. When I see my time, I will come with them and land at Portsmouth and either

banish this vile nation of Spaniards, or die for it.'³ This was hardly the
most ringing of confident declarations. It had about it something more
of hope than expectation. But Dudley and Ashton had spread their net
wide, including in their schemes the Cornish Killigrew brothers, who
commanded a small fleet of privateers in the Channel and were basically
no more than pirates. They had also planned for a substantial rising in
the West Country, amounting to perhaps 6,000 men, to be organised by
Sir Anthony Kingston; it would be supported by Richard Uvedale, who
commanded the key coastal garrison for the Solent, at Yarmouth on the
Isle of Wight. Uvedale was to betray his charge and let an invading
French force into England. Both he and Kingston were middle-aged
men of political and military experience, who succumbed to Dudley's
assurances of French support.

But, as with Wyatt's rebellion, most of that support was in the ever-
scheming mind of ambassador Noailles. Henry II and Montmorency
were still very, very cautious, and particularly so after the Truce of
Vaucelles was signed with the Habsburgs in February 1556. Temporarily,
at least, Philip and his English wife were less of a concern to the king of
France. Montmorency, though, was anxious for other reasons. The main
beneficiary of the planned uprising and invasion needed to be fore-
warned to keep her head down while matters were in abeyance. 'And
above all,' Noailles was told, 'make sure that Madame Elizabeth does not
begin, for anything in the world, to undertake what you have written to
me. For that would spoil everything and lose the benefit which they [the
conspirators] can hope from their schemes, which must be played out in
the long game, waiting meanwhile until time gives them the opportunity.'⁴ He omitted to mention the other name, always so closely associated with Elizabeth's, but Christopher Ashton was more frank when he
described the plotters' main aims: 'A great many of the western gentlemen [are] in a confederacy to send the queen's highness over to the king
and to make the lady Elizabeth queen and to marry the earl of Devonshire to the said lady'.⁵ This was not direct proof that either the princess
or Edward Courtenay supported what was happening, but the circumstantial evidence for their both being aware of Dudley's intentions is
very strong.

Yet by the beginning of March, well before Dudley himself crossed
to France, the government was already starting to unravel his intentions.
There were far too many people involved, and not all were trustworthy.
Even so, it was a complex undertaking and the various elements were

not uncovered at once. The first firm evidence was provided in connection with a separate but connected exercise to rob the exchequer of £50,000 in Spanish silver. This sounds, on the face of it, impossibly romantic and far-fetched, but several of the treasury officials were apparently quite willing to be bribed, helpfully providing impressions of keys. Unfortunately for Dudley and the circle of his supporters left in England, one of them was equally willing to tell all he knew to Cardinal Pole. On 18 March 1556, two years to the day since Elizabeth had entered the Tower of London as her sister's prisoner, around twenty men were arrested for involvement in this new treason. Among them were John Throckmorton, the leader of the conspirators left behind in England, and Richard Uvedale. In time-honoured fashion, those arrested blamed each other. Uvedale, who was unwell, could not get things off his chest fast enough. Kingston was ordered back to London but died on the way, perhaps as the result of suicide. And, as the interrogations continued, under the supervision of a special commission led by Robert Rochester and Mary's trusted personal staff, they began to delve deeper and to point the finger of suspicion strongly at the household of Elizabeth herself.

Richard Uvedale's head had been adorning London Bridge for a month when, at the end of May, Sir Henry Jerningham, Mary's vice-chamberlain and a member of the privy council, arrived at Hatfield and put an armed guard on Elizabeth's house. He arrested the accident-prone Katherine Ashley, three of the princess's ladies and her Italian teacher. Sang-froid was one of Elizabeth's great strengths in times of crisis and she retained her composure throughout this episode. Back in London, a search was made of Katherine Ashley's apartments at Somerset Place and incriminating literature was found, some of it anti-Catholic, some of it rude about Mary and Philip. Elizabeth's servants, under questioning, confessed that they had known about Dudley's intentions. Their acknowledgement of Elizabeth's complicity was no comfort to Mary, even if it did confirm her deep-seated suspicions about her sister's good faith. But Elizabeth had not confessed herself, or even been directly accused of anything. She was left at Hatfield when her servants were removed.

It is hard to know who was most uncomfortable over the next two weeks – Elizabeth, waiting on events in the capital, or Mary, wondering what to do with this troublesome sibling. Anxious about the repercussions of making the wrong decision, Mary, according to the Venetian ambassador, consulted her husband. Philip's reply arrived quickly. Its precise contents are unknown, but its drift can be discerned from what happened. Philip believed that Habsburg interest could best be served by dealing gently with Elizabeth. Neither imprisonment nor exile in dishonour was the answer. The priority, now the conspiracy was unmasked, was to avoid any situation in which the French could push the claims to the English succession of their dauphiness, Mary Queen of Scots. Personal animosity between the Tudor sisters was inevitable but also irrelevant, as far as Philip was concerned. His wife did not demur from his advice. Elizabeth was even sent a diamond as proof of the queen's belief in the princess's innocence. The diamond was a symbol of purity. Yet it could not remove the taint of disloyalty that hung over Elizabeth in 1556.

Eventually, she wrote to the queen, having audaciously refused an invitation to come to court because that might have been construed as an act of contrition. Instead she waited until her newly appointed guardian, Sir Thomas Pope, a Catholic loyalist more congenial than Sir Henry Bedingfeld, received a letter from the council clearing her of all involvement in the Dudley conspiracy. Elizabeth's response is a heady melange of cynicism and flowery writing:

> When I revolve in mind (most noble queen) the old love of pagans to their prince and the reverent fear of Romans to their Senate, I can but muse for my part and blush for theirs, to see the rebellious hearts and devilish intents of Christian in names, but Jew in deed, toward their anointed king. Which, methinks, if they had feared God though they could have loved the state, they should for dread of their plague have refrained that wickedness which their bounded duty to your majesty hath not restrained. But when I call to remembrance that the devil *tanquam leo rugiens circumit querens quem devorare potest*[6] I do the less marvel though he hath gotten such novices into his professed house, as vessels (without God's grace) more apt to serve his palace than meet to inhabit English land … Of this I assure your majesty, though it be my part above the rest to bewail such things though my name had not been in them, yet it vexeth me too much that the devil owes me such a hate as to put me in any part of his mischievous instigations.

In the second half of her letter she spared her sister this mix of classical and religious references and indulged in a more personal ramble through the psychology of loyalty, highly revealing of the tensions that had existed between the sisters almost from the moment of Mary's accession:

> And among earthly things, I chiefly wish this one: that there were as good surgeons for making anatomies of hearts that might show my thoughts to your majesty as there are expert physicians of the bodies, able to express the inward griefs of their maladies to their patient. For then I doubt not but know well that whatsoever other should suggest by malice, yet your majesty should be sure by knowledge, so that the more such misty clouds obfuscate the clear light of my truth, the more my tried thoughts should glister to the dimming of the hidden malice. But since wishes are vain and desires oft fail, I must crave that my deeds may supply that my thoughts cannot declare, and they be not misdeemed there as the facts have been so well tried. And like as I have been your faithful subject from the beginning of your reign, so shall no wicked persons cause me to change to the end of my life. And thus I commit your majesty to God's tuition, whom I beseech long time to preserve ...[7]

This belaboured declaration was Elizabeth's way of saying that she had been true to Mary in her fashion, and if the queen could not accept that others had taken her name in vain, then there was little to be done about it. Mary had agreed with Philip that it would be better for England if a policy of public reconciliation was followed, and she stuck to her resolution to play this distasteful game for reasons of state. Elizabeth did agree to come to court for Christmas 1556, making an impressive entry into London on 28 November 1556: 'The Lady Elizabeth came riding through Smithfield, the Old Bailey and Fleet Street unto Somerset Place, with a great company of velvet coats and chains, being her grace's gentlemen'. It was a scene reminiscent of Mary's visits to Edward VI, with an identical, unspoken message − 'I am your heir, even if not publicly acknowledged, and I have my own wealth and power. There is, in truth, nothing you can do to touch me that will not cause more damage than it would be worth'. Mary received her sister with every outward sign of pleasure. But five days later Elizabeth was on her way back again to Hatfield, her plans evidently gone awry, her discomfiture remarked by observers. She had learned that Philip's support came with a high price.

He was not a man to give something for nothing, and that price was marriage. There was a suitable candidate in Duke Emanuel Philibert of Savoy, a man with a grandiose name to match Elizabeth's high-flown written style. He was 28, Catholic, Philip's first cousin and a keen Habsburg ally, determined to rid his duchy of the French force that occupied it. The 19th-century Spanish historian Luis Cabrera described him as 'all sinew, little flesh … born to command'. Emanuel Philibert was a good catch for the illegitimate daughter of a king, and he and Elizabeth would have been a powerful couple on the European scene. But Elizabeth evidently refused to have him. She did not share her sister's view of England's place in Europe. It could be argued that her sights were, at this time, actually set rather low. They were dictated by an overwhelming desire for independence and to gain the throne of England, in due course, on her own terms, beholden to nobody. She saw the duke of Savoy as an infringement of the power she anticipated, not as a means of extending it. Philip had implicitly recognised her as Mary's successor, but he needed her contained.

His solution was a form of exile as far as Elizabeth was concerned. Her refusal meant that she was sent back to Hatfield to contemplate her ungratefulness and to ponder what would happen next. She was still holding out when Philip came back to England three months later, bringing with him his illegitimate sister, Margaret of Parma, and the merry widow who had refused Henry VIII, Christina of Denmark. Nothing these two ladies could say would persuade Elizabeth to agree to become duchess of Savoy. Mary, though, was probably relieved. She did not want to see Elizabeth married. Sometimes she even questioned that they shared the same father, so great was her long-standing hatred of Anne Boleyn. Any marriage, but particularly one that produced children, would put pressure on Mary to recognise Elizabeth as her successor. For the time being, she was spared that most difficult of decisions. Elizabeth's intractability bought the queen some breathing space. She had done what Philip wanted but the blame for failure could not be laid at her door. The year 1556 ended quietly. Christmas was spent at Greenwich, the palace of her childhood, surrounded by her courtiers. After more than a year of melancholy, Mary's spirits were beginning to improve.

There were other reasons to hope that the constant fear of uprisings and treachery might now diminish. One of the chief fomenters of disaffection had gone. Antoine de Noailles left England when the Dudley conspiracy collapsed, afraid that if he stayed he would be arrested. He had pushed his luck as far as it could go. And Edward Courtenay died in Italy in September at the age of 30. There were rumours that he had been poisoned. But, though his death removed someone who had attracted trouble throughout Mary's reign, it seems to have been the result of illness rather than assassination. He had been out hawking, got soaked in a thunderstorm and contracted a fever that killed him in a fortnight. His loss was a terrible blow to his mother, who entertained such hopes for him as Mary's consort. But Gertrude Courtenay remembered her queen, as duty required her to do, at the beginning of 1557, when she gave her £10 in a purse as a New Year's gift.

The presents Mary received for that year are among the most fully recorded of the period. Perhaps the most striking thing about the list is that there is no mention of any exchange of gifts between Mary and Philip. It was certainly the custom for an English monarch to recognise relatives and those who had served them; in 1557 the queen gave nearly three hundred separate items of plate, mostly in the form of cups, bowls and jugs. The recipients ranged from Cardinal Pole and Elizabeth, through all the bishops, the council and the nobility (including their wives), the household staff and well beyond. They encompassed her launderer, Beatrice ap Rice, who had been in her service since Mary was three years old, and Sybil Penne (the nurse of Edward VI), her fruiterer, hosier and fishmonger and the sergeant of the pastry. Appropriately, he presented the queen with a quince pie. Many others gave the queen cash, but there was evidently a fair amount of ingenuity exercised by people like Sir John Mason, who gave 'a map of England, stained upon cloth of silver in a wooden frame, drawn with the King's and Queen's arms, and a Spanish book covered with black velvet'. Elizabeth, well aware of the queen's love of clothes, gave 'the fore part of a kirtell and a pair of sleeves of cloth of silver, richly embroidered'.[8] It was a well-considered choice, for Mary was in the process of updating her wardrobe, in eager anticipation of her husband's return.

This time, she was not disappointed. He left Calais with a fair wind on 18 March 1557 and was reunited with his wife at Greenwich two days later. The favourable weather had speeded him along, but there was a more practical reason for his celerity; he needed English troops to help him in the renewed war with France. He had been engaged in hostilities with the pope since the autumn of the previous year, and the vengeful Paul IV, determined to requite him in kind, managed, over the winter, to draw in the French. In a two-pronged attack, the duke of Guise invaded Italy and Coligny, the admiral of France, moved against the Low Countries. Philip may have seen it coming, but it was still the most serious crisis that he had yet encountered. His resources were stretched wafer-thin and he was in urgent need of English support, on land and by sea.

From Philip's perspective, the Dudley conspiracy had one very positive side effect. Before the king left for Flanders in 1555, he had been disturbed by the state of disrepair of Mary's navy. Less than ten years after Henry VIII lavished attention on the English fleet, much of it was rotting in the dockyards. Only three of Henry's great ships were left, the result of neglect during peacetime and the strapped condition of the English treasury. Philip discovered the extent of the problem only when he requested a fleet of 12 to 14 ships to accompany his father and his aunts on their voyage back to Spain. The council told him then that it would be impossible to fit out a fleet of this size in the short timescale he required. His response was searing: 'England's chief defence', he reminded Mary's squirming ministers, 'depends upon the navy being always ready to defend the realm against invasion, so that it is right that the ships should not only be fit for sea, but instantly available.'[9] He refrained from adding that he also needed English ships to protect the galleons carrying Spanish silver from being attacked in the Channel. The last part of the long voyage from South America was often the most dangerous. His financial extremities made him the unlikely saviour of the English fleet.

This lecture on their maritime weakness from a Spaniard embarrassed the council into action, though it is possible that they had exaggerated the condition of the ships in the first place, to avoid unwanted expense. By mid-October 1555, 15 ships were ready. At the end of the year, the royal fleet comprised 30 vessels. The prospect of invasion from France, raised by Dudley's intrigues, provided a further spur to action. A squadron of eight royal ships was sent to patrol the English Channel and it captured most of a small fleet of French privateers off Plymouth. Two new warships, the *Mary Rose* and the *Philip and Mary*, were constructed during 1556, so that by the time Philip joined Mary at the palace where he had left her 17 months earlier, England once more had a respectable navy. In fact, on 7 June, the day war between England and France was declared, Mary had 24 royal ships at sea and 13 others ready to sail, a better record than either her father or brother. Habsburg priorities lay behind these improvements, but the credit for effecting such a comprehensive turnaround lay with the Lord High Admiral, William Howard, he of the bluff character and ribald jokes, and his subordinates, above all William Winter (whose experience outweighed concerns about his involvement in 1554 with Sir Thomas Wyatt), and the royal shipwright, Richard Bull.

So Philip did not have to concern himself about naval preparedness in England. The major difficulty he faced, and the primary reason for his return, was the lack of political will. The council was reluctant to commit to war and so was Cardinal Pole, often used by Mary as a sounding board in her husband's absence. Pole was concerned about the war with Paul IV; the council had more general fears: cost, the effect of famine, social unrest – all these considerations worried them. The marriage treaty, they claimed, disallowed their involvement, though it was actually ambiguous on the subject of new aggression by France. The king was banking on his hold over Mary, but her obvious pleasure in his reappearance did not mean that she would agree to browbeat her council. They all knew why he had come, though only Paget had been informally told in advance. In the face of so many obstacles, Philip resorted to the only tactic that might bring about their acquiescence. He saw them individually, rather than as a group. A direct appeal, a reminder of the personal gains, in profit and in glory, that could be expected in his service, these were more relevant incentives than national interest. The nobility knew where the source of their power lay. As the earl of Westmorland told a Scottish earl in 1557, during a discussion of identity and national loyalty: 'As long as God shall preserve my master and mistress together, I am and shall be a Spaniard to the uttermost of my power.'[10]

Philip's persuasiveness may have helped, but the French eventually brought England into the war through their persistent support of traitors. The final straw was an ill-conceived expedition, led not by Henry Dudley or Christopher Ashton, who had wisely gone to ground in France, but by Sir Thomas Stafford, whose father had petitioned Mary for financial support when she came to the throne. Provided with a warship by the French, Stafford landed in the north of England at the end of April 1557, hoping to stir up rebellion there. In a dramatic but empty gesture, he managed to capture Scarborough Castle before tamely submitting to a force led by the earl of Westmorland, a man who clearly believed in backing up his words of loyalty to Philip and Mary with appropriate deeds.

Stafford's foray marked the end of the threat to Mary from her own nobility. The war had, as Philip hoped, a unifying effect on the English aristocracy. They were delighted at the opportunity to perform stirring deeds (and to gain booty, if they could) against their long-standing enemy. When the Anglo-Imperial forces laid siege to St Quentin in northern France, three of the duke of Northumberland's sons (Henry, Robert and Ambrose) fought for their queen. Sir James Croft and Sir Peter Carew were also there and the buccaneer Peter Killigrew was rehabilitated and given a naval command a few months later.

The English military contingent of nearly 18,000 men, commanded by the earl of Pembroke, landed in July in France. They managed to miss the decisive battle on 10 August, when Montmorency tried to relieve St Quentin. His force was scattered by troops commanded by the man who might have been Elizabeth's husband, the duke of Savoy. Montmorency was captured, along with many others, but the town held out. When Philip arrived, tactfully placed at the head of the English force, he found that St Quentin had still not fallen. Coligny put up desperate resistance for more than two weeks. On 27 August a massive assault was made by Philip's troops, who won a famous victory. Mary was gratified to learn that 2,000 of her Englishmen were among the first through the breach. The news was received as a triumph in London, with more street parties and rejoicing than had been seen for a good while. The self-esteem of Henry II suffered a blow, but Philip had not the men or money to follow up his victory by advancing on Paris. Henry was left to sulk and to plot his revenge.

During the course of the autumn, the pope made peace with Philip, though the Holy Father nearly lost England all over again when he announced his intention to remove Pole as papal legate. He also proposed to try the cardinal for heresy. Mary wanted to be a good daughter of the Church but she was infuriated by this display of papal interference in her domestic affairs. For a while, it seemed that the woman who had so desired to heal the breach with Rome might be moving towards her own schism. It did not come to that, but Mary's uncompromising tone to Paul IV shows her willingness to consider such a possibility: 'she again prays and supplicates the Pope to restore the legation of Cardinal Pole, and to pardon her if she professes to know the men who are good for the government of her kingdom better than His Holiness'.[11]

But elsewhere, the queen's position seemed strong. Any fears that the war would draw in Scotland, France's traditional ally, were allayed when the Scottish lords refused to fight. Mary of Guise, the regent, was humiliated but there was nothing she could do. Mary Tudor, however, ended the year 1557 on a positive note.

During that year, Philip had been with her for barely four months. Once England committed to fight the French, there was no reason for him to stay. Mary was, by this time, realistic enough to accept it with, apparently, none of the distress of their parting in 1555. As king, Philip must command his troops. She knew he could not fight a war at her side in London. But she was in much better health and spirits than two years earlier, and so she accompanied him as far as Dover. They parted in the darkness of the small hours of 3 July, in the expectation that, if the war went to their advantage, they would certainly see each other again.

Perhaps during their brief reunion Mary found occasion to wear some of the dresses she had ordered back in the winter. One of these was the most extravagant gown in the French style Mary ever ordered. It was of white tissue with a round kirtle and sleeves also of tissue. Her husband might, though, have been more pleased with the Spanish-style gown of black velvet described in the April 1557 wardrobe accounts. It was furred with 23 sables, rather warm, one would have thought, for spring.[12]

Philip was not the only one to take his farewell of Mary in 1557. Two people she had been close to in difficult times, Anne of Cleves and Robert Rochester, died in that year. Henry VIII's fourth wife was buried in Westminster Abbey on 4 August. She had lived quietly except for her appearance at Mary's coronation. Anne, who had been comfortable rather than wealthy over the past 20 years, left small bequests of items of jewellery to her stepdaughters. Her relationship with them was one of the pleasanter aspects of the long twilight of her years as an ex-queen in England.

In Robert Rochester, Mary had been fortunate to have a dedicated servant with great organising ability, who was faithful to her from the moment he entered her employment. In his will, he left her £100, with the poignant comment that it was 'a poor witness of my humble heart, duty and service'. Though he had benefited financially from Mary's continued generosity to those who helped make her queen, there is, in his last words to her, a trace of the wistfulness of a man who knew that, in opposing her choice of husband, something intangible in their own relationship was lost permanently. Most of his estate he left to the

Carthusian order, in memory, no doubt, of his brother martyred by Henry VIII 22 years earlier.

The successes of the summer campaign in northern France were very expensive for England, even if they did inflict on Henry II the most humiliating military defeat suffered by France in the 16th century. Mary's government knew that the French king would strike back when he could. Yet no one in London wanted to think too much about the implications. The English contingent returned home and Philip's force, reduced for the season, retired across the border into Artois (a region that later became part of northern France). Philip was desperately short of cash to pay his soldiers and could not afford to maintain a large army. There would, in any case, be a breathing space. Winter was not a time for warfare.

The French believed otherwise. Throughout the autumn of 1557, they prepared their revenge. Then, on the morning of New Year's Day 1558, Nicholas Alexander, commanding a tiny force of 13 men at Newnham Bridge, awoke to find a force of more than twenty thousand Frenchmen approaching him across the frozen marshes. His fort was situated on a causeway, the main defence on the land side of Calais. It was well stocked with arms, but Alexander knew it could not be defended without reinforcements. He consulted Lord Wentworth, the lord deputy of Calais, and the decision was taken to abandon Newnham Bridge and to fall back into the town.

Meanwhile Duke Francis of Guise, commanding the French army, divided his force, sending one part out to the coast, with orders to proceed through the sand dunes to the fort of Rysbank, which protected Calais on the seaward side. It surrendered, again without a fight, on 2 January. The next day, a few miles to the east at Hammes, another of the forts in the Pale of Calais, Edward Dudley, brother of the man whose dreams of invading England had come to naught in 1556, wrote desperately to Wentworth: 'and surely if I had been better appointed with horsemen and footmen, I would have trusted ... to have been the deaths of many more [Frenchmen]'.[13] He, at least, had tried to put up resistance. But the tone of his dispatch makes it quite clear that he did not expect that help would arrive.

The town of Calais itself was now at the mercy of the French artillery. For five days after the fall of Rysbank, the guns bombarded the old, badly fortified castle. In the town, the English fought with more conviction, but the loss of life and overwhelming numerical superiority of the French merely delayed the inevitable. Wentworth surrendered, and on 7 January Guise wrote to the mayor of Amiens, the town responsible for supplying the French army with food, to tell him the great news. 'It has', he said, 'pleased God to favour so greatly the enterprise that the king commanded ... that He has restored to the crown that which was taken by the English'. The French then ransacked the town, house by house, and turned its inhabitants out into the countryside to fend for themselves as best they could in the dire weather. Calais had been in English hands since 1340. No wonder the French court was beside itself with joy when the news reached Henry II on 9 January. It looked as if his confidence in a bold strike at this most inauspicious time of the year had paid off, despite the initial misgivings of Duke Francis himself.

But all was not quite over yet. A third major fortress, Guisnes, was commanded by Lord Grey of Wilton, and he was determined not to surrender. He was also the only commander in the Pale of Calais to receive any help from King Philip's troops in the nearby Habsburg-held town of Gravelines. Grey defied the French until 21 January, when his troops threatened to throw him over the walls, telling him that 'for his vain glory they would not sell their lives'. Grey capitulated, and he eventually became the prisoner of the count de la Rochefoucauld, who demanded 25,000 crowns for his release. Elizabeth loaned him £8,000 in 1559 and he regained his freedom, but struggled to repay his debt. He was, however, the only commander to emerge from the debacle of the fall of Calais with his reputation intact.

The loss of Calais is one of the greatest reproaches that history has aimed at Mary. England had a presence in France for centuries; this woman, so nationalist historians have lamented, presided over nothing less than the final demise of an empire. It was also, as tradition goes, the major regret of her life. But there is no evidence that she ever spoke the words attributed to her – 'When I am dead and opened you will find Calais lying in my heart.' At the time, the loss of this last piece of English territory in France was blamed on treason and cowardice. This was a convenient explanation, and perhaps contains elements of the truth, but it is far from being the whole story. For Calais had been nothing more than a token of English territory on the European continent for many years. And it was an expensive and potentially dangerous one at that.

The Pale was a small area, 20 miles by six. The town of Calais was not well fortified but the outer forts were in reasonably good shape, though woefully undermanned. Keeping up the defences of the area and ensuring an adequate food supply for the more than four thousand people who lived there cost a great deal of money and, as the trading status of Calais declined, successive English governments were reluctant to commit the necessary funds. By 1540, the rising price of raw wool and instability in the international markets meant that there were only 150 Merchants of the Staple still operating in Calais. The town had never been totally anglicised and was, in the 1550s, home to a considerable population of French religious dissenters who did not like Mary any more than they liked Henry II. Their numbers, and their disaffection, were swelled by English Protestant exiles. After Boulogne was returned to the French by Edward VI, the restoration of Calais became a priority for Henry II. The defeat at St Quentin in 1557, far from securing the town's future, meant that its survival as an English possession was actually to be counted in mere months. The French king committed himself tirelessly in the autumn of that year to planning his campaign of recapture. General rumour and more specific information from spies warned the council in London and the garrison in Calais that it was only a matter of time before the French moved against them. Philip was also well aware of these intentions. But nobody did anything. Instead, there was a collective reliance on the impossibility of a serious campaign in winter. This proved to be a disastrous miscalculation.

Part of the blame must attach to Lord Wentworth, at 33 comparatively young and untried for what turned out to be such a demanding role as the last lord deputy of Calais. His undoubted Protestant leanings made him a dubious choice for the job and it is impossible to say how much they may have influenced his behaviour. Probably, though, he was simply lulled, like everyone else, into a false sense of security. Wishful thinking convinced him that though there were reports of large numbers of French forces in the area, Calais was not the target. It was more comforting to believe that Guise would attack the imperial enclave at Hesdin, just to the south of Boulogne. Back in London, a relieved group of privy councillors, who probably saw the Scottish campaign as a priority, rather naively accepted this view. Not till the last day of 1557 does Wentworth really seem to have embraced the threat he faced. Even then he did not use his most potent weapon, which was to open the sluice gates and flood the marshes around Calais completely. He explained his reluctance to do this in a letter to Mary on 2 January: 'I would also take in the salt water about the town, but I cannot do it, by reason I should infect our own water, wherewith we brew; and notwithstanding all I can do, our brewers be so behindhand in grinding and otherwise, as we shall find that one of our greatest lacks.'[14] Nor, despite his subsequent claims, does he seem to have requested help from Philip until the French were besieging him.

Back in England, the Christmas period saw a number of absences from the privy council, which failed to take decisive action until the meeting of 1 January, when the earl of Rutland was ordered across to France with 500 men from Kent. But the sailors, hearing that the fortress at Rysbank had fallen by the time they arrived, refused to land. On 5 January, with the leading earls, such as Arundel, Pembroke and Shrewsbury, returned to London, the council ordered mass levies of soldiers nationwide and the impressment of all shipping. This action could not have got a significant force to Calais before Wentworth surrendered, though it might have made it difficult for the French to hold the town. But the weather had one devastating trick still to play. On the night of 9/10 January one of the worst storms in recent memory howled through the Channel, scattering the English fleet. All hope of immediate re-invasion was abandoned and Henry II made a triumphant entry into the town on 24 January. There was still talk of recovering Calais a year later but the French were adamant that they would never part with it, no matter what diplomatic seductions were offered.

There was certainly embarrassment and anger in England in January 1558 when Calais was lost. Despite its difficulties and the fact that it was a drain on English resources, the symbolism of this little piece of England was potent, at least to the ruling class. Lord Grey apart, the manner of its loss was so abject that treachery was naturally suspected and morale at home severely dented. There may even have been a temporary loss of faith. When Philip's special envoy, Count Feria, arrived in England to try to put some stomach into the council to fight for the return of Calais, he said he had been told that 'not one third as many Englishmen go to mass as went before'.[15] Cardinal Pole referred to it as 'this sudden and grievous catastrophe', in a letter to Philip. But though he described the words of laboured comfort he gave the queen, invoking divine providence and 'the example of the Emperor, of King Philip and her own likewise, in bearing with fortitude and constancy any distressing and adverse casualty, not allowing herself to be depressed', his description of Mary's reaction is somewhat coyly expressed: 'Her majesty really shows that in generosity of nature and in pardoning she is very like herself, and no less connected with your majesties in this respect, than she is by ties of blood.'[16] But who was Mary 'pardoning' and why should she be exhibiting 'generosity of nature'? Was this an awkward way of saying that she held no one to blame, or does it imply quite the reverse, that she did hold her husband at least in part accountable, but was willing to forgive him for his failure to come to her aid? Mary's precise response to the news that Calais had fallen is unknown. Perhaps it did not grieve her as desperately as it outraged later commentators. She may also have derived false comfort from the belief that she might be pregnant again. Certainly, neither her council nor her parliament was willing to commit vast sums of money for the town's recovery. It had been an anomaly for a long time, and its loss was tinged with relief as well as regret.

Philip's reaction was different. He feared, quite rightly, that this would gravely compromise English support for his military ventures in Europe. 'We feel compelled to urge you', he wrote to the privy council, 'to be swayed by no private interests or passions, but only by your care for the welfare of the kingdom, lest its reputation for power and greatness, earned the world over in former times, be lost now through your own neglect and indifference.'[17] That Calais may have been lost through his own neglect and indifference was not something Philip wanted to consider. The king probably cared little for the blow to English pride, but he recognised that his own position was weakened as a result and that he needed to show his concern. Consequently, in his reply to Pole he was eager to demonstrate that he was distressed by the loss of Calais. 'That sorrow', he wrote, 'was unspeakable, for reasons which you may well imagine and because the event was an extremely grave one for these states.'[18] By which, of course, he meant the Netherlands. He saw Calais primarily as a piece of a European jigsaw. The blow to English patriotism was unfortunate but such losses were inevitable in war.

If Mary hoped that Philip would come over in person to talk her ministers into further expenditure, she was to be disappointed. That task fell to Feria, whose visit in February was one of three he made on Philip's behalf in 1558. For the English, Feria was perhaps the most well liked of the Spanish courtiers who had accompanied the king from Spain. He was betrothed to Jane Dormer and their wedding was planned for later in the year. But though personable and less openly dismissive of English ways than many of his colleagues, he still had his share of haughty superiority. He could also be horribly lacking in tact; it was

Feria who took it upon himself to inform Mary that the stories she had heard of English heroism at St Quentin were untrue. Not surprisingly, he reported that the queen was very much distressed. Like Renard before him, he never grasped the way politics was conducted in England. The council's prevarication, its lack of unanimity and, above all, its apparent spinelessness in accepting that Calais had gone exasperated him. By March, having failed to secure more troops for Philip, or produce any plan of action at all, he began to get desperate. 'I am at my wits' end with these people here, as God shall be my witness, and I do not know what to do … The queen tells me she is doing all she can. It is true she has spirit and goodwill. With the rest, it is hard labour.' Pole he referred to as a dead man (this seems to have been a reference to the cardinal's spirit, weighed down by his dispute with the pope, rather than to any bodily illness at this point) and 'as for the others, I do not know which is the worst of them from the point of view of your majesty's service; but I do know that those to whom you have shown the greatest favour are doing the least for you'. He went on to castigate in particular Pembroke, Paget, Arundel, Petre and the Lord Chancellor, Nicholas Heath, who was archbishop of York: 'They do nothing but raise difficulties, whatever one proposes, and never find any remedy.'[19] He could not even get a decision out of the council as to which of the towns in Flanders might replace Calais as a staple for the wool trade.

Mary had taken an active interest in the preparations for levying men in January, exhorting her servants in the counties to do their duty. She was working as hard as ever and her commitment was no doubt intensified by the sad delusion that she was, once again, pregnant. Her claim that she had held off making the announcement until she was certain convinced nobody. Strangely, she does not seem to have informed Philip herself; he learned the news from Pole. The king was evidently, and understandably, sceptical, but he made the right noises. There was a politely enthusiastic reference in the same letter he wrote to the cardinal about the fall of Calais: '… news of the pregnancy of the queen, my beloved wife, … has given me greater joy than I can express to you, as it is the one thing in the world I have most desired and which is of the greatest importance for the cause of religion and the welfare of our realm'. Yet though Mary was still maintaining that her condition was genuine eight months after

she had last seen Philip, there were no prayers offered for her, no elaborate lying-in planned and, apparently, no encouragement from anyone in
her household. She made her will at the end of March,

> thinking myself to be with child in lawful marriage between my said
> dearly beloved husband and lord, although I be at this present (thanks
> be unto Almighty God) otherwise in good health, yet foreseeing the
> great danger which by God's ordinance remain to all women in their
> travail of children, have thought good, both for the discharge of my
> conscience and continuance of good order within my realms and
> dominions to declare my last will and testament …[20]

Mary's assertion that she was carrying an heir was more than the defiant
refusal to accept reality. It was, above all, a statement of her determination to keep the throne away from Elizabeth.

The spring came, but no child. This time there was no major public
humiliation. The topic simply disappeared. The question of Elizabeth's
marriage, however, did not. Philip had never given up entirely on the
quest to marry his sister-in-law to the duke of Savoy. The pressure he
brought on Mary – and her resistance to it – put a further strain on their
relationship. The queen continued to find excuses to prevent any
marriage at all. Her first line of argument was that nothing could be
done without the consent of Parliament. Mary's own marriage treaty
had been approved by Parliament, though the assent of the peers and
commons was assured in 1554. Maybe she felt that protocol dictated that
a match for Elizabeth must be handled similarly. Philip saw it as an
unnecessary delaying tactic. The dispute between husband and wife
became acrimonious, with Philip urging his wife to examine her
conscience and Mary responding that she was willing to be instructed
by learned men on the matter. Those who had tried thus far, however,
had not yet convinced her: 'in so short a time it is impossible for me to
regulate my conscience'. She reminded him that she had said she would
agree to 'this marriage … if I should have the assent of the kingdom, but
without that consent I fear that neither your highness nor the kingdom
will be the better for it'.

Philip would have no truck with this kind of argument. His half of
the correspondence has not survived but he must have made it clear that
if she persisted and Parliament did not oblige, then he would hold her
responsible. Mary was immensely hurt, but still she would not give in.

This was too weighty a matter to be decided in his absence. She was probably influenced by the subtext of trying to get him back to England, assuring him that his presence would be required: 'But since your highness writes in those letters, that if Parliament set itself against this thing, you will lay the blame upon me, I beseech you in all humility to put off the business till your return, and then you shall judge if I am blameworthy or no. For otherwise your highness will be angry against me, and that will be worse than death for me, for already I have begun to taste your anger all too often, to my great sorrow.' Yet even his coming in person, she made clear, was no guarantee that she would submit to his wishes. She intended that they should both appeal to a higher authority – God. 'Wherefore, my lord,' she continued,

> in as humble a sort as I may, I, your most true and obedient wife – (which indeed I confess that I ought to be, and to my thinking more than all other wives, having such a husband as your highness – not that I am speaking of the multitude of your kingdoms, for that is not the chief thing in my eyes) I beg your majesty that we two should pray to God and put our whole trust in him, that we may live and come together again; and that the very God who has the thoughts of the hearts of princes in his hand, will, I make no doubt, so enlighten us, that the outcome shall be to his glory and your contentation. But I beg your highness nevertheless to pardon my assurance of God's mercy. For, though I have not deserved, nevertheless I have had the experience of it, and that beyond the expectation of all the world, in whom I have the same hope that I have always had. [21]

It is an extraordinary letter. For there is no doubt that though Mary was miserable at the quarrel with Philip and the tone of his reprimand to her, she was not going to do his bidding, unless she could be utterly convinced that God willed it. And her words convey her underlying belief that God would favour her interpretation.

Mary might displease Philip, but Elizabeth was quietly delighted to find her sister, for once, firmly on her side. She had no desire whatsoever to be bounced into a marriage. Her reasoning was the obverse of Mary's. The queen felt that marriage would strengthen Elizabeth's position as heiress to the throne. The princess thought that her freedom of manoeuvre would be greatly weakened by it. Their unanimity of approach had the superficial effect of bringing them closer together. Mary was cast in the role of her sister's protector and Elizabeth responded by making sure that she was punctilious in her dealings with the queen. There was no further talk of disloyalty. When an ambassador from the heir to the Swedish throne (the future Erik XIV) called on Elizabeth to seek her hand for his master, the princess was quick to point out the impropriety of such an action. She would entertain no requests for her hand unless they came through the proper channels. Mary was queen and must be consulted first. Sir Thomas Pope, who was still officially in charge of Elizabeth, reported 'how well the queen liked her prudent answer'. But he also wanted to know, on Mary's behalf, what Elizabeth thought of the proposal. The princess's reply is highly revealing of her attitude to marriage, not just at this point, but throughout her reign. 'In the king my brother's time,' she told Pope, 'there was offered me a very honourable marriage or two … whereupon I made suit to his highness, as some yet living can testify, for leave to remain in that state that I was, which best pleased me. I am at present of the same mind, and intend so to continue, with her majesty's favour. There is no life comparable to it.' Pope heard her in some amazement. Surely she would be content with an appropriate match should the queen suggest one? 'Her grace answered: What I shall do hereafter I know not, but I am not at this time otherwise minded than I have declared, though I were offered the greatest prince in Europe.' [22] But this reply was only diplomatic. When she was queen her brother-in-law, by any definition the greatest prince in Europe, proposed to her himself. She turned Philip down, too. Her mind was already decided during Mary's lifetime. Elizabeth considered that her sister's marriage was a mistake. She would not compromise her own freedom of action by repeating the error.

The daughters of Henry VIII saw each other for the last time when Elizabeth came to London at the end of February 1558. She stayed briefly, spending just over a week at Somerset House before returning to Hatfield. The reason for the visit is unclear. She may have wanted to judge for herself whether there was any possibility that the queen could be pregnant; possibly, with her debts mounting, she also hoped to persuade Mary to increase her allowance. If so, she did not succeed. A monarch who could not afford to retake Calais was never going to provide extra funds for a wayward sibling. Sir Thomas Pope's 18th-century biographer painted a picture of more harmonious relations between the sisters and an exchange of pleasant summer visits in 1558. It would be nice to think that there was a rapprochement, but there is no

evidence that the idyllic picnics described ever took place.[23] But Elizabeth did not provoke Mary again. Feria visited the princess when he
made a second trip to England in June. He found her content with her
situation and pleased with Philip's support. She might be in financial
difficulties but her confidence about her future was higher than it had
ever been, and with good reason. The long-awaited marriage of Mary
Queen of Scots and the future Francis II of France had taken place on
25 April 1558. Philip was well aware of the danger posed by the young
Scottish queen and her claim to the throne of England. He needed Elizabeth and she knew it.

Throughout the spring and summer England remained in a state of high
alert, fearful of French invasion. But none came, and Mary's navy continued to acquit itself in exemplary fashion. On 13 July, Captain John
Malen, commanding ten ships sent to protect Habsburg-held Dunkirk,
fired on French forces attempting to take the town and was instrumental in giving the victory to Philip's forces. Though some fighting continued, and an attempt by Admiral Clinton to mount a counter-attack on
Brittany failed, the war in France was essentially over, to the great relief
of Mary and her government.

For now they faced a much greater foe, one that could not be overcome by arms or diplomacy. It moved, unseen, among the people,
equally at home in town or countryside. No one – least of all the well-
to-do, whom it targeted so effectively – could be sure that they would
escape. Of all the misfortunes wreaked by forces beyond the control of
man, this was the most feared.

Disease was stalking Mary's kingdom. In 1557, Charles Wriothesley
wrote in his *Chronicle*: 'This summer reigned in England divers strange
and new sicknesses, taking men and women in their heads; as strange
agues and fevers, whereof many died.'[24] In the countryside and in the
towns people began to fall ill with unexplained fevers and a general
malaise that sapped their strength, often over a long period of time.
Death was not always sudden, but for many it was inescapable. During
the summer of 1558, the situation deteriorated, accelerating to produce
the greatest mortality crisis of the 16th century. The result was a demo-
graphic disaster of huge proportions, with nearly 40 per cent of the
country affected. In 1558/9, the number of deaths reported was 124 per

cent above the national average. Burials exceeded baptisms in parish registers almost everywhere. Among the major towns of England, only Hull and Shrewsbury were not severely affected.[25] The situation grew worse as the summer gave way to autumn. In the fields the harvest lay ungathered: 'Much corn was lost ... for lack of workmen and labourers.'

The governor of the Isle of Wight, Lord St John, reported to the queen at the beginning of September that sickness was affecting more than half the people in Portsmouth, Southampton and the island itself. A month later, it was noted in Dover that 'the people that die daily are those that come out of the ships and such poor people as come out of Calais'.[26] Certainly, the extent of the epidemic was not confined to England. Much of Europe was affected as well. Sir Thomas Gresham was alarmed to discover Sir Thomas Pickering extremely ill in Dunkirk. He told the privy council that he found his colleague (a man who was the same age as the queen) 'very sore sick of this new burning ague. He has had four sore fits and is brought very low, and in danger of his life if they continue as they have done.'[27] Pickering recovered, but only very slowly. And still the epidemic tightened its grip. When the parliament of 1558 met for its second session on 5 November 1558 there was so much absenteeism that some towns feared that their interests would go unrepresented.

The epidemic came after a year of good harvests and was particularly deadly among the well-nourished ruling class. This points to it being a new type of virus, probably related to influenza. It was certainly not the plague, whose symptoms were well known and recognised, nor does it seem to have been an outbreak of the sweating sickness, which had last visited England in 1551. The sweat, as it was known, was first seen in England in 1485, but though it was almost certainly viral, it had different characteristics to the illnesses of 1558. Death within 24 hours was quite common with the sweat. There were even cases of people who had seemed quite healthy a few minutes before literally dropping dead.[28] The 1558 sickness took longer to rob its victims of life. But it did so with impunity. Godliness was no deterrent to its onward path; so many priests died 'that a great number of parishes were unserved and no curates to be gotten'. Nor was greatness any defence. Chief among the victims of that terrible year were Cardinal Pole and the queen herself.

The first indication that something was seriously wrong came at the end of August. As the royal household prepared to remove from

Hampton Court, where it had spent the summer, Jane Dormer fell ill. Her indisposition must have been unpleasant, since Mary 'would not suffer her to go in the barge by water, but sent her by land in her own litter, and her physician to attend to her'. This kind treatment was typical of the way Mary looked after those who served her. Combined with Jane's own youth, perhaps, it facilitated her recovery. Yet when Mary arrived at the palace of St James a few days later, there was an ominous development. She asked after Jane, 'who met her at the stairfoot [and] told her that she was reasonably well. The queen answered "So am not I." She retired to her apartments "and never came abroad again".'[29]

The queen was stricken by fevers, slowly sinking into greater and greater weakness. It was not a dramatic decline, but it was remorseless. As the weeks passed, she rallied occasionally, still taking an interest in government. Her recovery was not despaired of until around the end of October, when it became apparent to everyone, Mary included, that she was not going to survive.

By then, she knew that one of the key figures in her life, Charles V, was gone. He had died peacefully on 21 September at his retreat in Extremadura, in the south-west of Spain. God granted him two tranquil years in the warmth of the sun: 'No noise of his armies, with which he had often made the world tremble, had followed him to the monastery of Yuste; he had forgotten his steel-clad battalions and his floating banners as completely as if all the days of his life had been passed in that solitude.'[30] The wars were truly in the past for him, and the brief period when he gave up public life does seem to have been a happy one. A mere month later, his sister Mary of Hungary was preparing, unwillingly but dutifully, to return to the Netherlands as regent when she, too, expired. Still with his army in Flanders, Philip received firm news of his father's death only on 1 November. By that time, reports from London indicated that his wife did not have long to live. But there was never any question that he would be there to comfort her on her deathbed. As well as attending to the arrangements for the funerals of his father and aunt, he was pursuing a diplomatic solution to the war and coping with the refusal of Emanuel Philibert to continue as regent in the Netherlands. His hands were completely full. Reeling under the strain, he found an emotional outlet in writing frequent letters to his sister Juana: 'You may imagine what a state I am in,' he told her. 'It seems to me that everything is being taken from me at once.' Yet he knew that he needed to keep England on his side. It would be important to ensure that Elizabeth succeeded to the throne smoothly and, he hoped, gratefully. So Feria was sent off once more to England, under instruction to manage the transition.

He found part of his task already done. Though Mary was prostrated and often delirious, during her more lucid moments she had gone through a journey of self-realisation – of the acceptance of death but also the acknowledgement that she must face up to the responsibility of being a queen. She knew she must nominate her successor, for England's sake. It was a difficult but courageous decision that Elizabeth herself evaded when her time came.

The first stage of this process came at the end of October, when Mary made a codicil to her will. In it, she acknowledged that she was 'presently sick and weak in body (and yet of whole and perfect remembrance, our Lord be thanked)' but that 'God hath hitherto sent me no fruit nor heir of my body'. She asked her 'next heir and successor' to honour her will, specifying her desire that the provisions she had made for religious houses and the establishment of a soldiers' hospital be realised. But Mary recognised that Philip would have no further role to play in England after her death, though she asked him 'for the ancient amity sake that hath always been between our most noble progenitors ... to show himself as a father in his care, as a brother or member of the realm in his love and favour and as a most assured and undoubted friend in his power and strength to my said heir and successor'.[31] But precisely who that successor was she could not quite yet bring herself to say.

The codicil was signed on 28 October. Ten days later, probably as the result of pressure from Parliament via the council, the queen sent for William Cordell, the speaker of the House of Commons. We do not know what passed between them but Mary had finally accepted that her sister would succeed her. On 8 November, Sir Thomas Cornwallis, controller of the queen's household, and the secretary to the privy council, John Boxall, arrived at Hatfield to tell Elizabeth that the queen had named her as the heir to the throne. Jane Dormer also claimed to have taken some of Mary's jewels to the princess, together with a request that she would pay the queen's debts and maintain the Catholic religion as the Marian Church had established it. The date of this visit is unknown, and there is no evidence that she either accompanied the two councillors or that she went with her future husband, Feria, when he arrived to see Elizabeth on 10 November. Jane was a very elderly lady when she recalled what had happened, but though her memory may have been faulty regarding details, there is no reason to suppose she made up the entire episode. She recalled that Elizabeth had assured her 'that the earth might open and swallow her up alive' if she were not a true Catholic.[32] But to others, Elizabeth gave a subtly different message: 'I promise this much, that I will not change it, provided only that it can be proved by the word of God, which shall be the only foundation and rule of my religion.'

Was Mary making a gesture of last-minute conciliation in sending Jane Dormer to her sister? Perhaps her conscience told her that she should not die full of animosity towards Elizabeth. Despite her extreme state, Mary knew that her successor would do whatever she wanted. It was an appeal to a better nature that Mary never believed that the adult Elizabeth possessed.

Feria viewed the entire situation in England as most alarming from Philip's perspective. His master's influence was gone, replaced by self-serving ingratitude among the councillors and a strongly independent outlook from the queen-in-waiting. The count was taken aback by how much Elizabeth's attitude had changed since he last saw her in June. His meeting with her started well enough: 'During the meal we laughed and enjoyed ourselves a great deal,' he wrote. Afterwards, Elizabeth invited him to speak more freely to her, saying that only two or three of her women who spoke nothing but English should remain. She began well enough, assuring Feria that she would maintain good relations with Philip: 'when she was in prison, your majesty had shown her favour and helped her to obtain her release. She felt that it was not dishonourable to admit that she had been a prisoner; on the contrary, it was those who had put her there who were dishonoured because she had never been guilty of having acted or said anything against the queen, nor would she ever confess otherwise.' Her indignation struck Feria forcibly, as did her assertion that she owed her present position to the people of England, not to Philip or to the English nobility. He could see that 'she was determined to be governed by no one'. There was a cold reaction to the news that Philip had ordered all his pensioners and servants in England to serve her 'should the need arise'. She would be the one to determine, she said, whether they should continue receiving money from Philip. Then she went on to complain bitterly that her sister had deprived her of the means of meeting her debts while sending large sums of money and jewels out of the country to her husband. This Feria parried. Elizabeth could investigate the matter, of course, but she would find out that

Philip 'had given much more to the queen than she ever gave to your majesty'.

On the question of her marriage, she was equally forthright. She believed Philip was responsible for all the pressure put on her to marry the duke of Savoy and did not accept Feria's explanation that this had been done to assure her place in the succession. Her comments were illuminating. She was sure that 'the queen had lost the affection of the people of this realm because she had married a foreigner'. The assertion that Mary was no longer loved by the majority of ordinary folk cannot be substantiated, but it shows that Elizabeth was happy to damage her sister's reputation before she was actually dead.

The Spaniard was a troubled man when he left: 'She is a very vain and clever woman. She must have been thoroughly schooled in the manner in which her father conducted his affairs and I am much afraid that she will not be well-disposed in matters of religion.'[33]

Mary was now beyond all these considerations. Drifting in and out of consciousness, she was surrounded by her anguished ladies, the only people who had truly loved her since she was a child. In their company, she always found support and diversion from the cares that beset her. They helped the queen meet death as devotedly as they served her in life. She seems to have felt no pain and her dreams, or visions, were of little children like bands of angels singing to her. Did their music take her back 40 years to that long-lost haven of parental affection, when she had run after the Venetian organist Dionysius Memo imploring him to play for her again? She knew nothing then of the vicissitudes of life, only harmony and security.

At six o'clock on the morning of 17 November, before the slow dawn of a quiet autumn day, Queen Mary heard mass, as she had always done. Through tribulation and triumph, the familiar rites of the Catholic Church were her greatest comfort. She was still able to make the responses, her deep voice stronger than the muffled tears of her attendants. Then she rested. Some time around seven, as the light filtered into her bedchamber, Mary Tudor slipped away. So peaceful was her passing that those around her did not realise, at first, that she was gone.

Mary's coronation ring was taken to Elizabeth at Hatfield, as proof that the queen was, indeed, dead. Her successor, well prepared for the moment, gave thanks to God and began at once to govern, with all the confidence that Feria had observed in her a week before. Cardinal Pole survived his cousin by only 12 hours, his death probably hastened by overhearing an unguarded comment about Mary's demise from one of his household. This gave the day a sad symmetry, but it removed someone whom the new queen disliked and feared. The task of Mary's household officers and ladies was done, but there was no wholescale change in the complexion of politics. Eleven of Mary's privy councillors continued to serve Elizabeth and the changeover of power was smooth.

Philip learned of his wife's loss with resignation. He told Juana: 'I felt a reasonable regret for her death. I shall miss her'. Mary had loved him unreservedly but would probably have expected little more from him than this restraint. Kings were not supposed to weep over the deaths of their wives and he was still a young man with only one heir. Politically and personally, he needed his freedom. But his time as king of England was at an end and he was anxious to start off on a good footing with Elizabeth, in minor as well as major matters. He ordered that a thorough inventory be made of the clothes and jewels Mary had given him, lest he be accused of purloining items that the new queen might feel were rightfully her property, not his: 'In case you have to hand over this list and have it translated,' he wrote, 'I am setting down here what I remember as to when and how the things were given to me.' The list included 'a rich garter, with two large faceted diamonds, a large pearl, five flat diamonds set in a rose pattern, twelve flat rubies around the garter, set two by two, and twenty-four pearls set two by two'.[34] The king noted that the earl of Arundel had invested him with this on board ship at Southampton. It had evidently meant something to him, after all.

Mary's body remained at St James's Palace, lying in state in her privy chamber, until 13 December. Elizabeth certainly did not stint on the funeral arrangements, which were put in the hands of the marquess of Winchester. He was determined that the honours due to Mary should be fully observed and this involved a heavy financial outlay. The final bill for the ceremonies came to a staggering £7,763 (nearly £2 million today). When everything was ready, Mary's coffin was draped in cloth of gold and removed from the palace, to begin its journey to Westminster Abbey. A life-sized effigy of the queen lay on top of the coffin, crowned and carrying the sceptre and orb, as Mary had done when she left her coronation five years earlier. A superb procession accompanied the queen on her last journey through London: her household servants and gentlemen mourners, King Philip's servants, the marquess of Winchester with the banner of the English royal arms, and the heralds carrying the paraphernalia of monarchy – the sword, the helmet and the coat of armour – male symbols which would now pass from England's first female ruler to its second. Mary's ladies, 'riding all in black trailed to the ground', and her chief mourner, Margaret Douglas, countess of Lennox, immediately followed the coffin. Behind them came the clergy.

When the coffin reached Westminster Abbey it was 'met by four bishops and the abbot, mitred in copes, censing the body; and so she lay all night under the hearse with watch. There were an hundred poor men in good black gowns, bearing long torches with hoods on their heads ... and all about her guard bearing staff-torches in black coats. And all the way chandlers having torches to supply them that had their torches burnt out.'[35] On 14 December requiem mass was heard for Queen Mary, presided over by Abbot Feckenham and his monks, following the ancient Catholic rites. The queen's regalia, the symbols of her earthly power, were offered back to God and her body was buried in a vault in the north aisle of the chapel of Henry VII, her grandfather. Mary's ministers and household staff then broke their wands of office and, as was customary, threw them into the grave with their mistress. Finally, the heralds made the long-awaited and unique ceremonial proclamation: 'The Queen is dead; long live the Queen.'

The funeral was superbly planned and carried out with great dignity, as Elizabeth and the marquess of Winchester intended. But if the new queen hoped that this careful orchestration of the handover of power would pass entirely without controversy, then she was to be disappointed. Bishop John White of Winchester gave a sermon that very nearly undermined Elizabeth's efforts. True, his remarks about Mary were appropriate and heartfelt: 'She was a king's daughter, she was a king's sister, she was a king's wife; she was a queen, and by the same title a king also ... What she suffered in each of these degrees before and since she came to the crown, I will not chronicle; only this I say, however it pleased God to will her patience to be exercised in this world, she had in all estates the fear of God in her heart.' He had chosen as his text verses from Ecclesiastes: 'I can commend the state of the dead above the state of the living; but happier than any of them both is he that was never born.' This gloomy and rather perverse sentiment was not itself the cause of controversy, but further into his oration White quoted from the book of Proverbs the very same words that Mary's arch-enemy, the duke of

Northumberland, had used in his last, desperate letter: 'a living dog is better than a dead lion'. Having asked the question, 'What beast is more vile than a dog, more worthy than a lion?' White went on to expatiate on the notion that dogs were faithful, loving beasts and that King David had compared himself to one in the Old Testament. But in spite of his assertion that a proper understanding of these words was 'better is one lively preacher in the church that dareth to bark against sin, blasphemy, heresy; better is one lively officer or magistrate in the commonweal, that dareth to speak against injuries, extortions, seditions, rebellions and other discords, than the dead lion', the damage was done.[36] White appeared to be comparing Elizabeth to a dog and Mary to a lion. His words cost him his career. Elizabeth did not like the canine reference. She confined White to his house. In June 1559 he was deprived of his bishopric for continuing to oppose religious reform and in the following year he died.

Bishop White was not the only one to run into difficulties with his eulogy to Mary. The writer of *The Epitaph upon the death of our late virtuous Quene Marie deceased* penned a glowing but very badly written poem to the late queen. In it, he remembered her gentleness, virtue, suffering and generosity:

> How many noble men restored and other states also
> Well showed her princely liberal heart, which gave both friend and
> foe.

> As princely was her birth, so princely was her life,
> Constant, courtise, modest and mild; a chaste and chosen wife.

> Oh mirror of all womanhood! Oh Queen of virtues pure! Oh
> constant Marie! filled with grace; no age can thee obscure.

Elizabeth was furious that this panegyric made no mention of her, the new monarch, and insisted that this omission be rectified in an additional stanza:

> Marie now dead, Elizabeth lives, our just and lawful Queen
> In whom her sister's virtues rare, abundantly are seen.
> Obey our Quene as we are bound, – pray God her to preserve
> And send her grace life long and fruit, and subjects truth to serve.[37]

In 1603, Elizabeth's coffin was placed above Mary's in the same vault. James I, wishing to honour his predecessor, erected a magnificent monument over the twin graves, though the only effigy is that of Elizabeth. The symbolism is powerful. In death, as in history, Elizabeth dominates her sister. Despite what was written in 1558, Mary was obscured both literally and metaphorically. But the plaque on the monument gives a different interpretation to one of the most sensitive and sad relationships in all of England's past: 'Partners both in throne and grave, here rest we, two sisters, Elizabeth and Mary, in the hope of the resurrection.'

Epilogue

Those who had been close to Mary continued to thread their way through the uncertainties of 16th-century Europe with varying degrees of success. Her household staff, in particular, found that their lives were greatly changed. There was nothing for them at Elizabeth's court. But their experiences clearly illustrate that many prominent Catholics could not compromise their consciences, preferring exile to secret observance and persecution.

Jane Dormer married Count Feria on 29 December 1558. He left England the following May, having cleared up as much of Philip's business there as he could. Jane followed him to the Low Countries in July 1559. She never returned to the country of her birth, and when she and her husband established themselves in Spain, their home became the focus for the active but increasingly fractured Catholic opposition to Elizabeth in Europe. Feria was made a duke in 1567 but died only four years later. Jane lived on until 1612, by which time her only son had predeceased her. In her final years, she remembered with sorrow and abiding affection the queen she served half a century before.

Susan Clarencius accompanied Jane Dormer and Lady Dormer, Jane's grandmother, when they left England in 1559. It was to become a permanent exile, despite further grants of lands and wardships in Essex to Mrs Clarencius in October 1559. As Susan never received formal licence to live abroad, perhaps Elizabeth viewed the Essex grants as an inducement for her not to commit to the Ferias. If so, Catholicism and the shared past of Jane Dormer and Susan Clarencius evidently proved stronger than the new queen's desire to show some generosity to her sister's faithful servant. It seems probable that Susan was protected in her old age by Lord Robert Dudley, Elizabeth's favourite, who was in touch with her up until the time she left and who was used as a channel by Feria himself when the count tried, fruitlessly, to obtain licences for Mrs Clarencius and old Lady Dormer to live abroad. In ensuring that she was not persecuted and her lands were not forfeit, Robert Dudley can be said to have requited the debt to his mother when she sought Susan's help in 1553. Elizabeth did not grant the licence to stay in Spain, but Susan did not return. She seems to have died in the Ferias' household around the spring of 1564.

Sir Francis Englefield, having been asked to resign his Crown appointments, was given permission to travel abroad. He, too, left in the spring of 1559 and went to Flanders, on the understanding that he would return when summoned. But he became concerned that he would not be well treated if he returned and stayed away. Thus he became a wanderer, his lands in England confiscated (many went to Elizabeth's favourite, the earl of Leicester) and his health affected by failing eyesight. During the 1570s and 1580s he was one of the most prominent Catholic exiles and his involvement in plots against Elizabeth eventually led to an act of attainder in 1593. Englefield died in Valladolid in 1596 and was buried in the chapel of the college of St Alban, the first English seminary in Castile.

Edward Waldegrave and his wife Frances, who had been one of Mary's ladies, refused to accept the Elizabethan religious settlement. In April 1561 they were indicted in Essex on charges of hearing mass and harbouring priests. Waldegrave died a prisoner in the Tower of London four months later. His wife remained committed to her faith and was interrogated by the authorities when two of her daughters tried to escape to Europe in 1565 so that they could get a Catholic education.

Sir Henry Jerningham lost his offices as master-of-horse and privy councillor on Elizabeth's accession. He retired to his house at Costessey in Norfolk, where he died in 1572 and was buried in the parish church. A kindly man, he left provisions in his will for almshouses and for prisoners in London. His family prospered over the years, despite their unswerving devotion to Catholicism.

Sir Henry Bedingfeld, a close friend of Jerningham's, was also excluded from government under Elizabeth. This was not revenge for his awkward period as her 'jailer' in 1554 but the inevitable outcome of his religion. He ran into trouble on several occasions for allowing

Catholic worship at his home, Oxburgh Hall, and for refusing to sign a statement of loyalty after the northern rebellion against Elizabeth in 1569. His quiet but stubborn opposition continued until his death in 1583. The Bedingfeld family still live at Oxburgh Hall and have remained Catholic to this day.

The *politiques* of Mary's council fared rather better. Elizabeth confirmed the marquess of Winchester's position as Lord Treasurer, but his continued attempts at reforming the exchequer by reviving ancient practices, which Mary had curtailed, led to a system of accounting so lacking in transparency that only death saved him from having to explain why his hand seemed to have been so often in the till. Some of this may be put down to the effects of extreme old age – Winchester was 98 when he died in 1572. Six years earlier Elizabeth had dismissed him from his post as speaker of the House of Lords, 'considering the decay of his memory and hearing, griefs accompanying hoary hairs and old age'.[1]

The earl of Arundel had a colourful if chequered career under Elizabeth. Though he was more than twenty years older than the queen, there were those who still believed that he hankered after the idea of marrying her himself soon after her accession. He certainly was vocal in his opposition to other men spoken of as potential suitors, Robert Dudley and William Pickering. Arundel continued as a privy councillor but left England for a year in 1566 to travel in Europe, where he was a troublesome guest. His involvement on the fringes of Catholic plots against Elizabeth in 1569 caused him to be placed under house arrest, but by 1573 he was back on the privy council, a gnarled political survivor. Illness and old age diminished his attendance over the rest of the 1570s and he died in early 1580.

Pembroke, an admired soldier and servant of four monarchs, became close to the earl of Leicester in the 1560s. He maintained an active interest in business speculation, supporting overseas exploration and mining companies in England, but his association with the duke of Norfolk's schemes to marry Mary Queen of Scots in the late 1560s nearly compromised the earl during the twilight of his life. Elizabeth believed his protestations of innocence and he still enjoyed her favour when he died in 1570.

William, Lord Paget, was in chronic ill health by the time of Mary's death. This and his close association with the Spanish marriage meant that he did not serve Elizabeth, despite having championed her quietly behind the scenes throughout her sister's reign. Yet he could not break the habit of a lifetime of service to the Crown and continued to give advice to Elizabeth's ministers. On 20 February 1559, he wrote a heartfelt letter to William Cecil and Thomas Parry, saying that while 'lying like a beast here, [I] am not able to come to court without danger of my health; therefore I thought good, for declaration of my duty to her majesty, to put you in remembrance of things that you have known in our days'. He thought it was only a matter of time before the country became embroiled once more in the long-standing Habsburg–Valois rivalry. 'If we take part with neither of them,' he wrote, 'they will fasten their feet both of them here, and make a Piedmont of us; if we take part with the one, we ourselves shall afterwards be made a prey by the victors. God save us from the sword, for we have been plagued of late by famine and pestilence.' Doing nothing was not an option. He urged courage on Elizabeth: 'For God's sake, move that good queen to put her sword in her hand. She shall the better make her bargain with her doubtful friends and enemies … and move her majesty to use that goodly wit, that goodly knowledge and that great and special grace of understanding and judgement of things that God hath given her'. It was a handsome tribute from one of Mary's key ministers to her successor and fully in keeping with the sense of duty he had brought to his dealings with Elizabeth's father, brother and sister. 'If I have been tedious to you,' he finished, 'in writing thus foolishly, I pray you make the best of it and think it is of a zeal to the queen's majesty and to my country and to myself also.'[2] He continued to dispense advice throughout the early years of Elizabeth's rule, dying in 1563.

Paget's old rival, Simon Renard, never recovered the influence he had enjoyed as ambassador to England. His diplomatic career faltered when he fell out with his former mentor, the bishop of Arras, in 1559, amid accusations of betraying imperial secrets while he was ambassador in England. It was not the first suggestion that he was corrupt and this time, though the charges could not be proved, the taint would not go away. He retired to Madrid, far from his homeland in eastern France, and died there in 1573.

Antoine de Noailles did not fare much better. He was appointed governor of Bordeaux and might have prospered had it not been for the wholly unexpected death of Henry II. The Guise brothers do not seem to have favoured him, and although he recovered some of his status after 1561, he did not have long to live, dying suddenly at Bordeaux in March 1563.

Henry II had been overjoyed at the recovery of Calais and the marriage of his son Francis to Mary Queen of Scots. At last, he felt that France was truly in the ascendant. His determination to celebrate the peace signed with England and France in April 1559 led, alas for him, to his untimely death. While jousting on what is now the Place des Vosges in Paris on the first day of July, the king was fatally injured when his opponent's lance pierced his visor. He survived for nine agonising days before succumbing. Behind him he left a legacy of weak boy kings, an increasingly dominant queen mother in Katherine de Medici and a country more riven by religious differences than England had ever been. For 30 years, France suffered the horrors of civil war, with great loss of life and bloody massacres that stunned Europe, such as that of St Bartholomew's Eve in 1571, when at least three thousand people (ten times more than had suffered martyrdom in Mary's reign) were murdered in Paris.

Mary's two most immediate relatives after Elizabeth were Frances Brandon, duchess of Suffolk, and Margaret Douglas, countess of Lennox. Frances, who had married her master-of-horse, Adrian Stokes, a year after the execution of her husband and eldest daughter, survived Mary only by a year. She was buried with Protestant rites in Westminster Abbey in December 1559. Frances's two surviving daughters, Lady Katherine and Lady Mary Grey, both infuriated Elizabeth by making inappropriate marriages without her permission. Despite their lack of judgement, they avoided the fate of their sister, Lady Jane.

The countess of Lennox lived on, relentless in support of the interests of her son, Lord Darnley. She was in and out of trouble with Elizabeth for supporting Catholicism in the early years of the reign but it was Darnley's marriage to Mary Queen of Scots which sent Margaret back to the Tower, a place in which she was first incarcerated by her uncle, Henry VIII, nearly thirty years earlier. The young Scottish queen, an eminently desirable widow since the death of Francis II of France after barely 18 months on the throne, effectively called Elizabeth's bluff in marrying this cousin and combining their claims to the English throne. But the marriage was a disaster and the countess of Lennox's fortune appeared to have run out when the dissolute and increasingly power-hungry Darnley was murdered, possibly with his wife's connivance, in 1567. For some time Margaret harboured thoughts of vengeance against Mary Stuart, but the two women were reconciled during Mary's long exile in England. Margaret's other son died two years before she did, but though this grieved her she was confident that her line would, one day, succeed Elizabeth. She died in 1578, leaving a grandson, James VI of Scotland and I of England, who united the two countries under his rule in 1603.

Mary's husband, Philip of Spain, gave the woman who had shared his European titles a solemn funeral in Brussels at the end November 1558. The chief mourner was Emanual Philibert of Savoy, and a riderless black horse with a crown on its saddle represented the departed queen. A requiem mass was celebrated by the bishop of Arras and mourning duly observed. Then Philip got on with the demands of government. His reign was an unremitting struggle. The trouble that his aunt, Mary of Hungary, had foreseen in the Low Countries culminated in the revolt of the Netherlands, a seminal event in 16th-century Europe, and the eventual loss of the 17 northern states, which became an independent country. The loss of these provinces, so important a part of his Habsburg heritage, was a bitter blow to Philip. His devotion to work was unstinting, but the sheer size of his domains in Europe and the New World overpowered him. He seemed more powerful than he was, though he himself was under no illusions: 'I don't think that human strength is capable of everything, least of all mine, which is very feeble,' he wrote in 1578. Ten years later, after a long decline in the once strong Anglo-Spanish relationship, he was at the losing end of a war with Elizabeth. The Turks harried him, his Italian domains proved a poisoned chalice. Yet he never wanted war. The pleasure-loving prince became, over time, an austere and world-weary man.

Philip was married twice more after Mary, first to Elisabeth of Valois, once intended as the bride of Edward VI, and then, after her death, to his own niece, Anna of Austria. His son, Don Carlos, who became increasingly mentally unstable, mercifully died in 1568, and it was Philip's only surviving son by Anna who succeeded him as Philip III. Before his death, the king had erected a memorial to his dead wives and dead children. Mary was not depicted, perhaps because she was childless, but her omission may indicate how bitter were his memories of Tudor England. He died in 1598 after a long and painful illness.

Elizabeth, meanwhile, failed to honour any of the provisions of Mary's will. She did not pay her sister's debts, move the remains of Katherine of Aragon from Peterborough Cathedral to lie beside Mary, give money as directed for the universities or set up a hospital in London for old soldiers. This neglect was unfortunate but probably not inspired by deliberate malice. The new queen had other, more pressing, concerns. At the start of her rule, she faced many difficulties; this was the time of the 'perils, many, great and imminent' that Cecil nervously described. But some things went her way without too much difficulty. At home and abroad, she was helped by the impact of events at the end of Mary's reign: peace was made with France five months after Elizabeth came to the throne, and she was able to re-establish herself as head of the Church in England when the Marian bishops, their numbers diminished by deaths in the epidemic, failed by a mere three votes to block her path. Their opposition was crucial to the development of the Anglican Church, since it forced Elizabeth down a more radical Protestant path than she had, perhaps, envisaged. Elizabeth cared much more about recovering the political power that Mary had rescinded than she did about doctrine. She had spent five years practising Catholicism, and although Mary always doubted her sincerity, it is unlikely that her observance left no mark on her at all. Yet though she shared Mary's distaste for married priests, she did not legislate against them, and the persecution of Protestants stopped the day she ascended the throne. Mass was, once again, replaced by the communion service and worshippers received both the bread and the wine, as Cranmer had wanted. Catholics became, over time, a minority much discriminated against, with their own martyrs, though they did not suffer in the flames as Mary's heretical subjects had done.

Elizabeth never forgot or forgave her treatment during her sister's reign and her rancour seems to have grown with the passing years. In her eyes, she was always entirely blameless. She could not see how the pattern of her behaviour must have looked to her sister. Elizabeth could always dance nimbly around the truth and she continued to do so as queen. Unwilling to commit, ever watchful for an opportunity, she preferred to wait and see. In an ideal world, she would have wished, no doubt, to remain on good terms with Mary. There is no real sense, however, that she regretted the rift that opened up between them, except inasmuch as it made her own life as 'second person' more uncomfortable.

Her reign was nine times longer than Mary's and it is forever associated with a golden age in the popular mind. As a national identity began to emerge more strongly in England, Elizabeth was raised almost to the status of a national saint by centuries of male historians raised in the Protestant tradition. In this respect, her reputation is perfectly understandable. She was a remarkable woman presiding over a time of great achievement in many areas of human endeavour.

Less easy to explain is why modern writers still persist in denigrating Mary. Elizabeth's reputation is not diminished by acknowledging the interest or achievements of Mary's reign, short though it was. Though Mary had not enjoyed good health since her mid-teens, there was no reason to suppose she would die five years after ascending the throne. Her Habsburg relatives lived into their mid-fifties and, had Mary survived the catastrophe of 1558, she might have looked forward to another ten years on the throne.[3] This would have been quite long enough to establish the reformed Catholicism she – and, apparently, the silent majority of her subjects – favoured. Her relationship with Philip might have become more distant as he struggled with his wider responsibilities but her very childlessness could also have maintained English independence.

The blackening of Mary's name began in Elizabeth's reign and gathered force at the end of the 17th century, when James II compounded the view that Catholic monarchs were a disaster for England. But it was really the enduring popularity of John Foxe which shaped the view of her that has persisted for 450 years. Attempts to soften her image have been made, but their tendency to depict her as a sad little woman who would have been better off as the Tudor equivalent of a housewife is almost as distasteful as the legend of Bloody Mary. To dismiss her life as nothing more than a personal tragedy is both patronising and mistaken.

One of the main themes of Mary's existence is the triumph of determination over adversity. She lived in a violent, intolerant age, surrounded by the intrigues of a time when men and women gambled their lives for advancement at court. Deceit, like ambition, was endemic among the power-seekers of mid-Tudor England who passed, in procession, through her life. Pride, stubbornness and an instinct for survival saw her through tribulations that would have destroyed a lesser woman. Her bravery put her on the throne and kept her there, so that when she died she was able to bequeath to Elizabeth a precious legacy that is often overlooked: she had demonstrated that a woman could rule in her own right.

The vilification of Mary has obscured the many areas of continuity between her rule and those of the other Tudors. Today, despite the fact that much more is known about her reign, she is still the most maligned and misunderstood of English monarchs. For Mary Tudor, the first queen of England, truth has not been the daughter of time.

Select Bibliography

MANUSCRIPT SOURCES

BRITISH LIBRARY
Additional MSS
Cottonian MSS
Harley MSS
Lansdowne MSS
Royal MSS
Sloane MSS
Stowe MSS

THE NATIONAL ARCHIVES (formerly the Public Record Office)
State Papers, Domestic
Henry VIII (SP 1)
Edward VI (SP 10)
Mary, and Philip and Mary (SP 11)
Supplementary (SP46)
State Papers, Foreign
Mary, and Philip and Mary (SP 69)
Exchequer
Exchequer Accounts various (E101)
Lord Chamberlain's Office
Robes and Special Events (LC2)
Miscellanea (LC5)

OXBURGH HALL, Norfolk
  Bedingfeld MSS

WESTMINSTER ABBEY, Library and Muniments Room
  The Queen Mary Manual (on loan from Westminster Cathedral)
  Documents relating to Queen Mary and the refounding of Westminster
  Abbey: 5305, 37414, 37457, 12750, 37419, 6484F, LXXXVI, 12792, 37418

PRIMARY SOURCES
(Place of publication for all printed works is London unless otherwise stated)

'A Discourse that it was not convenient for the Queen to marrie', in
  J. Somers, *A fourth collection of scarce tracts etc*, vol. 2, 1752
*A Short-title Catalogue of Books Printed in England, Scotland, and Ireland and of
  English Books printed abroad*, 1475–1640, Bibliographical Society, 1926
Acts of the Privy Council, ed. J. R. Dasent et al., 1890–1964
Ambassades de Messieurs de Noailles en Angleterre, ed. R. Aubert de Vertot
  d'Aubeuf, 5 vols, Leyden, 1763
An epitaphe upon the Death of the Most excellent and late vertuous Queen Marie,
  1558
Autobiography of the Emperor Charles V, transl. L. F. Simpson, 1862
Beer, B. L. and S. M. Jack (eds), *The letters of William, Lord Paget of Beaudesert*,
  1547–1563, Camden Miscellany, 25 (Camden 4th series), 1974
Bonner, Edmund, *A profitable and necessarye doctryne* ...,1555
——, *An honest godlye instruction and information for the tradynge and bringinge
  up of Children* ..., 1555
——, *Homelies sette forth by the righte reuerende father in God* ..., 1555
*Calendar of State Papers and manuscripts, relating to English affairs, existing in the
  archives and collections of Venice* ..., ed. R. Brown et al., 1864–98
Calendar of State Papers, Domestic, Edward VI, ed. C. Knighton, 1992
Calendar of State Papers, Domestic, Mary I, ed. C. Knighton, 1998
Calendar of State Papers, Foreign, of the reign of Elizabeth, 1558–59, ed.
  J. Stevenson, 1863
Calendar of State Papers, Foreign, of the reign of Mary, 1553–58, ed. W. B.
  Turnbull, 1861
*Calendar of State Papers relating to the negotiations between England and
  Spain* ..., ed. R. Tyler et al., 1862–1954
Calendar of the Patent Rolls, Edward VI, Philip and Mary, Elizabeth, 1924–39
Chronicle and Political Papers of Edward VI, ed. W. K. Jordan, 1966
Chronicle of Queen Jane and of the first two years of Queen Mary...,

ed. J. Nichols, Camden Society, 48, 1850

Clifford, Henry, *The Life of Jane Dormer, Duchess of Feria*, ed. J. Stevenson, 1887

Collection des Voyages des Souverains des Pays-Bas, ed. L. P. Gachard and C. Piot, Brussels, 1874–82

Count of Feria's despatch to Philip II of 14 November 1558, ed. M. J. Rodriguez Salgado and S. Adams, Camden Miscellany, 28, 1984

Cranmer, Thomas, *The Works of Archbishop Cranmer...*, ed. J. E. Cox, London, 1844–6

Documents relating to the Revels at Court in the time of King Edward VI and Queen Mary, ed. A. Feuillerat, 1914

Du Bellay, Jean, *Ambassades en Angleterre de Jean du Bellay ... Correspondance Diplomatique*, Paris, 1905

Ecclesiastical Memorials, ed. J. Strype, Oxford, 1822

Elder, John, *The copie of a letter sent into Scotland*, 1555

'Elizabeth and Mary Tudor', in *The Early Modern Englishwoman , Series 1, Printed writings, 1500–1640*, pt 2, vol. 5, selected and introduced by L. Prescott, Aldershot, 2001

Ellis, Henry, *Original letters, illustrative of English History*, 1824

England under the reigns of Edward VI and Mary ..., ed. P. F. Tytler, 1839

England's Boy King, The Diary of Edward VI, 1547–1553, ed. J. North, Welwyn Garden City, 2005

Fox, John, *Idem iterum: or, the history of Queen Mary's Big-belly*, 1688

——, *The acts and monuments of John Foxe*, 8 vols, 1877

French Letter concerning Lady Jane Gray and Queen Mary, published from a Bruges MS by J. A. Giles, Caxton Society, 1844

Fuller, Thomas, *The History of the Worthies of England*, 1662

Furnivall, F. J. (ed.), *Ballads on the condition of England in Henry VIII's and Edward VI's reigns*, vol. 1, 1868

Giustiniano, Sebastiano, *Four Years at the court of Henry VIII*, ed. R. Brown, 1854

Grey, Lady Jane, 'Some account of Lady Jane Grey and her remains', in L. Richmond, *Fathers of the English Church*, vol. VI, 1807

Greyfriars Chronicle, ed. J. Nichols, Camden Society, LIII, 1852

Guaras, Antonio de, *The Accession and Coronation of Queen Mary*, 1892

Gunn, S. J., 'A letter of Jane, duchess of Northumberland, in 1553', *English Historical Review*, CXIV, November 1999

Hakluyt, Richard, *The Principal Navigations, Voyages, Traffics and Discoveries of the English nation made by sea or overland*, 1598

Hall's Chronicle, ed. H. Ellis, 1809

Harleian Miscellany, 1813

Haynes, Samuel, *A collection of State Papers ... from 1542 to 1570*, 1740

Hayward, John, *The Life and Raigne of King Edward VI*, ed. B. L. Beer, Kent, OH, 1993

Hearne, Thomas (ed.), *Sylloge Epistolarum*, 1716

Holinshed, Raphael, *Chronicles of England, Ireland and Scotland*, ed. H. Ellis, 1807

Homem, Diogo, *The Queen Mary Atlas*, 2005

Inventory of King Henry VIII, ed. D. Starkey, vol. 1, Society of Antiquaries, 1998

Knox, John, *The first blast of the trumpet against the monstrous regiment of women*, Geneva, 1558

Letters and Papers, Foreign and Domestic, of the Reign of Henry VIII, ed. J. Gairdner, 1862–1932

Letters of the Queens of England, 1100–1547, ed. A. Crawford, Stroud, 1994

Lisle Letters, ed. M. St Clare Byrne, 1983

Machyn, Henry, *The Diary of Henry Machyn*, ed. J Nichols, Camden Society, XLII, 1848

Malfatti, Cesare V., *The accession, coronation and marriage of Mary Tudor*, Barcelona, 1956

Marcus, L., J. Mueller and M. B. Rose (eds), *Elizabeth I: Collected Works*, 2000

Marillac, Charles de, *Correspondance politique de MM. de Castillon et de Marillac*, ed. J. Kaulek, Paris, 1885

Martin, Thomas, *A Traictise declarying and plainly provyng, that the pretensed marriage of Priests, and professed persons, is no mariage*, 1554

More-Molyneux, J., 'Letters illustrating the reign of Queen Jane', *Archaeological Journal*, vol. xxx, 1873

Muller, J. A. (ed.), *Letters of Stephen Gardiner*, Cambridge, 1933

Ponet, John, *A short treatise of politike power ...*, Strasbourg, 1556

Privy Purse Expenses of the Princess Mary, ed. F. E. Madden, 1831

Procter, John, *The Historie of Wyates rebellion*, 1554

Relations politiques des Pays-Bas et de l'Angleterre sous le regne de Philippe II, ed. Baron Kervyn de Lettenhove, Brussels, 1882

'Respublica A.D. 1553. A drama of real life in the early days of Queen Mary', in J. S. Farmer, *Recently Recovered 'Lost' Tudor Plays*, 1907

'Ritratti del regno de Inghilterra. A description of English life and institutions in the reign of Mary Tudor', in *Two Italian Accounts of Tudor England*, Barcelona, 1953

Rymer, T., *Foedera*, 1704–32

Smith, Wentworth, *The True Chronicle Historie of the whole life and death of Thomas Cromwell*, 1613

State Papers of King Henry VIII, London, 1830–52

'State Papers relating to the custody of the Princess Elizabeth at Woodstock in 1554', ed. R. C. Manning, *Norfolk Archaeology*, vol. 4, 1855

Stow, John, *The Annales of England*, 1605

Tottel's Miscellany: Songes and Sonnettes, ed. Edward Arber, 1897

Tudor Royal Proclamations, ed. P. L. Hughes and J. F. Larkin, New Haven, CT, 1964–9

Vita Mariae Angliae Reginae of Robert Wingfield of Grantham, ed. and transl. D. MacCulloch, Camden Miscellany, 4th series, 29, 1984

Vives, Juan Luis, *The education of a Christian woman*, ed. C. Fantazzi, Chicago, IL, 2000

Watson, Thomas, *Holsome and catholyke doctryne concerninge the seuen sacramentes*, 1558

Wood, M. A. E., *Letters of Royal and Illustrious Ladies of Great Britain*, 1846

Wriothesley, Charles, *A Chronicle of England*, ed. W. D. Hamilton, Camden Society, NS 11, 1875–7

Wyatt, George, *The papers of George Wyatt Esquire, of Boxley Abbey*, ed. D. Loades, Royal Historical Society, 1968

SECONDARY WORKS

Alsop, J. D., 'The act for the queen's regal power', *Parliamentary History*, 13, pt 3, 1994

Appleby, Andrew B., *Famine in Tudor and Stuart England*, Stanford, CT, 1978

Benson, Robert, *The Death-beds of Bloody Mary and Good Queen Bess*, 1906

Bernard, G. W., *The King's Reformation*, 2005

Blockmans, Wim, *Emperor Charles V, 1500–1558*, 2002

Brigden, Susan, *New Worlds, Lost Worlds*, 2001

Carter, Alison J., 'Mary Tudor's Wardrobe', *Costume, the Journal of the Costume Society*, no. 18, 1984

Chamberlin, Frederick, *The Private Character of Henry VIII*, 1932

Childs, Jessie, *Henry VIII's Last Victim*, 2006

Coleman, C. and D. Starkey (eds), *Revolution Re-assessed*, 1986

Coward, Barry, *Social Change and Continuity in Early Modern England, 1550–1750*, 1997

Creighton, Charles, *A History of Epidemics in Britain*, 2nd edn, 1965

Davey, Richard, *Historical Women Series: Mary Tudor*, 1897

Denny, Joanna, *Anne Boleyn*, 2004

———, *Katherine Howard*, 2005

Dowling, M., 'Humanist support for Katherine of Aragon', *Bulletin of the Institute of Historical Research*, 57, 1984

Duffy, E. and D. Loades (eds), *The Church of Mary Tudor*, Ashgate, 2006

Duffy, Eamon, *The Stripping of the Altars*, 2005

Emmison, F. J., *Tudor Secretary: Sir William Petre*, 1961

Erickson, C., *Bloody Mary*, 1978

Ford, Francis, *Mary Tudor. A retrospective sketch*, 1882

Galton, Arthur, *The character and times of Thomas Cromwell*, 1887

Gammon, S., *Statesman and Schemer: William, first lord Paget*, Newton Abbot, 1973

Garrett, Christina, *The Marian Exiles*, 1938

Glasgow, Tom, Jr, 'The Navy in Philip and Mary's War, 1557–1558', *Mariner's Mirror*, vol. 53(4), 1967

Hamel, Ernest, *Marie la Sanglante*, 1862

Hannay, M. (ed.), *Silent but for the Word*, Kent, OH, 1985

Harbison, E. H., *Rival Ambassadors at the Court of Queen Mary*, Princeton, NJ, 1940

Hume, M. A. S. (ed.), *Two English Queens, Mary and Elizabeth, and Philip*, 1908

Hutchinson, R., *The Last Days of Henry VIII*, 2005

———, *Thomas Cromwell*, 2007

Iongh, Jane de, *Mary of Hungary*, 1959

Ives, Eric, 'Henry VIII's will – a forensic conundrum', *Historical Journal*, 35, 1992

———, *The Life and Death of Anne Boleyn*, Oxford, 2005

Jackson, R., Esq., *An Interesting Chronology of the Coronations of all the Kings and Queens of England*, 1838

Jordan, W. K., *Edward VI*, 2 vols, 1968–70

Kamen, H., *Philip of Spain*, 1997

Keynes, Milo, 'The aching head and increasing blindness of Queen Mary I', *Journal of Medical Biography*, vol. 8(2), 2000

Lennel, F., *Calais sous la domination Anglaise*, 1911

Leti, Gregorio, *Historia o vero Vita di Elisabetta, regina d'Inghilterra*, 1693

Levin, C. et al. (eds), *'High and mighty queens' of early modern England: realities and representations*, Basingstoke, 2003

Loach, J. and R. Tittler (eds), *The Mid-Tudor Polity, c. 1540–60*, Basingstoke, 1983

Loach, Jennifer, *Parliament and the Crown in the Reign of Mary Tudor*, Oxford, 1986

———, *Edward VI*, 1999

Loades, D., *Mary Tudor*, Oxford, 1989

———, *John Dudley, Duke of Northumberland*, Oxford, 1996

———, *The Reign of Philip and Mary*, Oxford, 2001

———, *Two Tudor Conspiracies*, 2nd edn, Bangor, 1992

———, *Intrigue and Treason*, Harlow, 2004

MacCulloch, Diarmaid, *Thomas Cranmer*, 1996

Maltby, W., *The Reign of Charles V*, Basingstoke, 2002

Marshall, Rosalind K., *Mary I*, 1993

Mattingly, Garrett, *Katherine of Aragon*, 1944

Mayer, Thomas F., *Reginald Pole, Prince and Prophet*, Cambridge, 2000

Medvei, V. C., 'The illness and death of Mary Tudor', *Journal of the Royal Society of Medicine*, 80, 1987

Nicolas, Nicholas Harris, *Memoirs and Literary Remains of Lady Jane Grey*, 1832

Parker, Geoffrey, *Philip II*, Chicago, IL, 1995

Paul, John, *Katherine of Aragon and Her Friends*, 1966

Pierce, Hazel, *Margaret Pole, 1473–1541*, Cardiff, 2003

Planché, James, *Regal Records; or, a Chronicle of the Coronation of the Queens Regnant of England*, 1838

Prescott, H. F. M., *Mary Tudor*, 1940

Redworth, G., *In Defence of the Church Catholic*, Oxford, 1990

———, 'Matters impertinent to women: male and female monarchy under Philip and Mary', *English Historical Review*, CXII, June 1997

Richards, Judith, 'Mary Tudor as "Sole Quene?": gendering Tudor monarchy', *Historical Journal*, vol. 40(4), 1997

———, 'To promote a woman to beare rule', *Sixteenth Century Journal*, 28, 1997

Robinson, W. R. B., 'Princess Mary's Itinerary in the Marches of Wales, 1525–27', *Historical Research*, vol. 71, 1998

Samson, Alexander, 'Changing places: The marriage and royal entry of Philip, prince of Austria and Mary Tudor', *Sixteenth Century Journal*, 36/3, 2005

Scarisbrick, J. J., *Henry VIII*, 1997

Schutte, Kimberly, *A Biography of Margaret Douglas, Countess of Lennox*, Lampeter, 2002

Skidmore, Chris, *Edward VI: The lost king of England*, 2007

Slack, Paul, *The Impact of Plague in Tudor and Stuart England*, Oxford, 1985

Starkey, D., *Elizabeth*, 2001

———, *Six Wives: The Queens of Henry VIII*, 2004

Starkey, D. (ed.), *Henry VIII: A European court in England*, 1991

Stephen, Alford, *Kingship and Politics in the Reign of Edward VI*, Cambridge, 2002

Stone, J. M., *The History of Mary I, Queen of England*, 1902

Strickland, Agnes, *Lives of the Queens of England*, 1840–48

———, *Lives of the Tudor Princesses*, 1868

Strong, Roy, *Coronation*, 2005

Strype, John, *Annals of the reign of Queen Mary*, 1706

Tittler, R., *The Reign of Mary Tudor*, Harlow, 1981

Tridon, Mathieu, *Simon Renard, ses ambassades, ses négociations, sa lutte avec le cardinal de Granvelle*, Besançon, 1882

Vowell, otherwise Hooker, John, *The Lyffe of Sir Peter Carew*, 1840

Vredius, Olivarius, *Historiae Comitum Flandriae pars prima, Flandria Ethnic*, 1650

Wells, Stephen, *The Tudor Queen, Mary*, 1854

White, Beatrice, *Mary Tudor*, 1935

Wiesener, Louis, *La jeunesse d'Élisabeth d'Angleterre*, Paris, 1878

Willan, Thomas, *The Muscovy Merchants of 1555*, Manchester, 1953

Williams, Gwyn A., *When Was Wales?*, 1991

Wylie, John A. H. and Leslie H. Collier, 'The English sweating sickness (Sudor Anglicus): A re-appraisal', *Journal of the History of Medicine*, vol. 36, 1981

UNPUBLISHED DISSERTATIONS

Merton, Charlotte, *The women who served Queen Mary and Queen Elizabeth*, PhD dissertation, University of Cambridge, 1991

Rowley-Wiliams, Jennifer, *Image and reality: the lives of aristocratic women in early Tudor England*, DPhil dissertation, University of Wales, Bangor, 1998

Samson, Alexander, *The marriage of Philip of Habsburg and Mary Tudor*, PhD dissertation, University of London, 1999

Notes

Abbreviations used

APC	*Acts of the Privy Council of England*, ed. J. R. Dasent et al. (London, 1890–1964)
BL	British Library
Cal SP Foreign	*Calendar of State Papers, Foreign*, ed. W. Turnbull (London, 1861)
Cal SP Spanish	*Calendar of letters, despatches and state papers relating to the negotiations between England and Spain, preserved in the archives at Vienna, Simancas, Besancon and Brussels*, ed. R. Tyler et al. (London, 1867–1954)
Cal SP Venetian	*Calendar of state papers and manuscripts relating to English affairs, existing in the archives and collections of Venice*, ed. R. Brown et al. (London, 1864–98)
Chronicle QJ&QM	*Chronicle of Queen Jane and Two Years of Queen Mary*, ed. J. G. Nichols, Camden Society, Old Series, 48 (London, 1850)
CS	Camden Society
DNB	*Dictionary of National Biography* (Oxford, 2004)
HMC	*Historical Manuscripts Commission*
L&P	*Letters and Papers, Foreign and Domestic, of the Reign of Henry VIII, 1509–47*, ed. JS Brewer et al., 21 vols and addenda, London, 1862–1932
Privy Purse Expenses	*The Privy Purse Expenses of the Princess Mary*, ed. F. Madden (London, 1831)
SPD Mary I	*Calendar of State Papers, Domestic, Mary I*, ed. C. S. Knighton (London, 1998)

Notes

Chapter 1 Daughter of England, Child of Spain

1 *Cal SP Venetian*, 2, p. 285.
2 For an evocative description of life in Tudor England, see Susan Brigden, *New Worlds, Lost Worlds* (London, 2000).
3 David Starkey, *Six Wives: The Queens of Henry VIII* (London, 2004), p. 11.
4 Frederick Madden (ed.), *Privy Purse Expenses of the Princess Mary* (London, 1831), p. xx. Many writers have described the spoon as a gift from Gertrude Blount, wife of Princess Katherine's son, Henry Courtenay. She did not, however, marry Courtenay until October 1519, so it would seem more likely that the 'lady Devonshire' referred to in the accounts is, in fact, Mary's godmother herself.
5 Ibid., p. xx.
6 Hazel M Pierce, *Margaret Pole, Countess of Salisbury* (Cardiff, 2003), p. 47.
7 Margaret claimed the Salisbury title through the Montague lands of her great-grandmother. See ibid., p. 33.
8 Ibid., p. 40.
9 Madden, *Privy Purse Expenses*, p. xxiii.
10 Ibid., pp. xxviii–xxix.
11 Rawdon Brown (ed.), *Four Years at the Court of Henry VIII*, 2 vols (London, 1854), II, pp. 163–4.
12 *L&P*, 3i, no. 896.
13 Ibid., no. 1162.
14 *Cal SP Spanish Further Supplement* (1513–42), p. 185.
15 *L&P*, 3ii, pp. 288–96.
16 Margaret Pole's first period as lady governess lasted only about a year. She was replaced by a husband-and-wife team, Sir Philip and Lady Jane Calthorp. Sir Philip was brought in to manage Mary's expanding household. His wife's qualifications for her role are unknown.

Chapter 2 The Education of a Princess

1   The virginal was a small rectangular spinet without legs. It had only one wire per note and was often played in pairs. The regal was a kind of portable organ with one row of pipes.

2   See Garrett Mattingly, *Katherine of Aragon* (London, 1944), p. 154.

3   Mary's cousin, Lady Jane Grey, gave the impression in her writings that she felt more affection for the household chaplains than she did for her parents.

4   *BL Cotton MS Vitellius*, C i, f. 23.

5   Juan Luis Vives, *The Education of a Christian Woman*, ed. Charles Fantazzi (Chicago, 2000), p. 50.

6   Italian women humanists were in the forefront of Renaissance discussions of the education of women. The combination of literacy in Latin and familiarity with both classical and Christian texts informed their views.

7   Despite recurring fears that girls would lead men into sin, the illegitimacy rate in early 16th-century England was as low as 2 per cent. See Brigden, *New Worlds*, p. 63.

8   *BL Cotton MS Vitellius*, C i, f. 24b.

9   Quoted in Mattingly, *Katherine of Aragon*, p. 189.

10 Thornbury Castle still stands, the only surviving Tudor palace in England to be used as a hotel.

11 Though Henry VII had ensured that almost every Marcher lordship had been taken over by the Crown, it had not been an entirely one-way traffic. Most of the minor offices of his court were held by Welshmen. Henry VIII does not seem to have had much interest in the principality before deciding to send Mary there and did not feel inclined to pay it a visit in person. It has been pointed out that justice in Wales was not the disaster implied in the official statement and that there had been a council functioning there up to 1522. See Gwyn A Williams, *When Was Wales?* (London, 1991), p. 117, and W. R. B. Robinson, 'Princess Mary's Itinerary in the Marches of Wales, 1525–27', *Historical Research*, vol. 71 (1998).

12 Elizabeth Blount had married Gilbert Tailboys within three months of the birth of her son. The couple lived in Lincolnshire and subsequently had three children. After Tailboys' death Elizabeth married Edward Fiennes de Clinton. There are indications in a letter of 1529 to Richmond's tutor that she had more involvement in his upbringing than has generally been thought. See *DNB* entry for Elizabeth Blount.

13 Veysey seems to have been a competent administrator and he stayed on in Wales after Mary left, until Thomas Cromwell turned his attention to reorganising the principality in 1534. Cromwell removed him because he was not viewed as sufficiently tough on law and order.

14 Mary's initial stay at Thornbury was less than three weeks. On 12 September 1525 she made a ceremonial entry into Gloucester and went from there to Tewkesbury, where she spent most of the autumn living in the abbey manor.

15 'The prayer of St Thomas of Aquinas, translated out of Latin into English by the most excellent Princess Mary … in the year of our Lord God 1527', printed in Madden, *Privy Purse Expenses*, Appendix II, pp. clxxiii–clxxiv.

16 Quoted in ibid., p. xliii.

17 *Cal SP Venetian*, 4, pp. 59–61.

18 M. A. E. Wood (ed.), *Letters of Royal and Illustrious Ladies* (London, 1846), vol. ii, p. 32–3.

19 *Cal SP Venetian*, 4, p. 682, quoted in J. M. Stone, *The History of Mary I, Queen of England* (London, 1902), p. 46.

Chapter 3 The Queen and the Concubine

1 Quoted in Eric Ives, *The Life and Death of Anne Boleyn* (Oxford, 2005), p. 87. The precise dating of the letter is uncertain.
2 In fact, Francis was about to replace Françoise with an Anne of his own, Anne d'Heilly, later duchess of Etampes.
3 Henry's role in the English Reformation remains the subject of dispute between scholars. For a major reinterpretation, see G. W. Bernard, *The King's Reformation* (London, 2005).
4 *Cal SP Venetian*, 4, p. 584.
5 It has been suggested that the origin of the antipathy between Mary Tudor and Anne Boleyn dated back to the brief period in which Anne served Mary as queen of France and in particular to the unseemly haste with which Mary married Charles Brandon. See Ives, *The Life and Death of Anne Boleyn*, p. 28.
6 *L&P*, 5, p. 238.
7 Quoted in Bernard, *The King's Reformation*, p. 89.
8 *Cal SP Spanish*, 3, ii, p. 166.
9 Ibid., 3, ii, p. 131.
10 Maria Dowling has noted that Katherine surprisingly failed to undertake a public relations campaign in English, despite her undoubted popularity. See M. Dowling, 'Humanist Support for Katherine of Aragon', *Bulletin of the Institute of Historical Research*, 57 (1984), pp. 46–55.
11 *Cal SP Spanish*, 3, ii, p. 586.
12 Ibid., 4, i, p. 352.
13 *State Papers of King Henry VIII*, I, p. 352.
14 *Cal SP Venetian*, 4, p. 600.
15 *Cal SP Spanish*, 4i, p. 548.
16 Ibid., 4ii, pp. 646–7.

Chapter 4 Mary Abased

1 *L&P Henry VIII*, 6, p. 238. It might be wondered why the father of Mary's servant, Richard Wilbraham, was being knighted at such an advanced age. This was no belated recognition of services long since rendered, but a move by the king and his advisers to try to create as many knights as possible in order to tie a large part of the gentry to the increasingly radical political and religious programme.
2 Ibid., 6, p. 432.
3 Ibid., 6, p. 500.
4 Ibid., 6, pp. 491–2.
5 *Cal SP Spanish*, 4ii, p. 795. The letter has not survived.
6 Ibid., 4ii, p. 799.
7 Ibid., 4ii, p. 820.
8 *L&P Henry VIII*, 6, p. 1126.
9 *Cal SP Spanish*, 4ii, pp. 839–41.
10 By Professor Bernard in *The King's Reformation*.
11 In fact, neither Mary nor Elizabeth was ever officially created princess of Wales.
12 *Cal SP Spanish*, 4ii, pp. 881–2, 894.
13 Ibid., 4ii, p. 894.
14 *L&P Henry VIII*, 7, p. 9.
15 This was an exaggeration, though it became an effective piece of propaganda.

Katherine's household at Buckden Palace in Cambridgeshire cost Henry VIII £3,000 a year. Mary, on the other hand, was compelled to petition her father for new clothes at this time.

16 *L&P Henry VIII*, 7, p. 296.
17 Ibid., 7, p. 21.
18 Ibid., 7, p. 83.
19 Ibid., 7, p. 296.
20 Ibid., 7, p. 393. Mary found a less dramatic way of dealing with the same problem in late August, when her sister moved to Greenwich. She was allowed to ride on ahead and so got there before Elizabeth.
21 Ibid., 7, p. 1129.
22 Ibid., 8, p. 189.
23 Castillon to Francis I, ibid., 7, Appendix, p. 13, and 8, p. 174.
24 The less attractive side of Thomas More, such as his enthusiasm for burning heretics, has been conveniently overlooked.
25 Quoted in Mattingly, *Katherine of Aragon*, pp. 344–5.
26 Chapuys heard that the child Anne lost was a boy. Other rumours said that the foetus was deformed. Neither of these hypotheses can be proved and they may have been invented by Anne's enemies.
27 The portrait is in the Kunsthistoriches Museum, Vienna.
28 *Cal SP Spanish*, 6i, pp. 84–5.
29 Ibid., 5i, p. 85.
30 Ibid., 5i, p. 101.
31 *BL Cotton MS Otho CX*, f. 230 (L&P, 10, p. 792).
32 Quoted in Ives, *The Life and Death of Anne Boleyn*, p. 358.
33 *Cal SP Spanish*, 5i, p. 137.
34 *Sylloge Epistolarum*, ed. Thomas Hearne (1716), p. 140.
35 *Cal SP Spanish*, 5i, pp. 124–8.
36 *Sylloge Epistolarum*, pp. 146–7.
37 *Cal SP Spanish*, 5i, p. 139.
38 *Sylloge Epistolarum*, pp. 124–5.
39 Ibid., pp. 125–6.
40 *BL Cotton MS Otho CX*, f. 256.
41 *Cal SP Spanish*, 5i, p. 182.
42 *Sylloge Epistolarum*, pp. 137–8.
43 The Princess Mary's Submission, 22 June 1536, *L&P Henry VIII*, 10, p. 478.
44 *Sylloge Epistolarum*, pp. 128–9.
45 *Cal SP Spanish*, 5i, pp. 195–6.
46 *Sylloge Epistolarum*, p. 131.
47 *Cal SP Spanish*, 5i, pp. 237–8.
48 Charles Wriothesley, *A Chronicle of England, 1485–1559*, ed. W. D. Hamilton, Camden Society, 2nd series, vol. 20, pp. 59–60.

Chapter 5 The Quiet Years

1 Mary to Cromwell, undated, latter half of 1536; Hearne, *Sylloge Epistolarum*, pp. 145–6.
2 *Cal SP Spanish*, 5ii, p. 509.
3 John Heywood, b. 1496/7, d. in or after 1578. The poem 'A Praise of his Ladye' is in Tottel's *Songes and Sonnettes*, 1557. The description of Mary's gauntness is in H. F. M. Prescott, *Mary Tudor* (London, 1953), p. 99.

4 Marillac to Francis I, 2 October 1541, *Correspondence politique de MM de Castillon et de Marillac, ambassadeurs de France en Angleterre* (1537–42), pp. 349–50.

5 BL Royal Manuscript, Appendix 89, f. 41.

6 See Alison J. Carter, 'Mary Tudor's Wardrobe', *Costume, the Journal of the Costume Society*, no. 18 (1984), pp. 9–28.

7 Madden, *Privy Purse Expenses*, pp. 175–99.

8 Ibid., pp. 225 and 247.

9 *L&P Henry VIII*, 11, p. 656.

10 Marillac's described her, in September 1540, as of 'mediocre' beauty but very graceful and with a sweet face. *Correspondence politique*, p. 218.

11 *L&P Henry VIII*, 16, p. 1332.

12 Ibid., 17, p. 1212.

13 Margaret quarrelled with Henry VIII shortly before his death over her strict adherence to Catholicism. Henry was so angry that he cut her out of the succession in his will.

14 The view that Mary stopped because she felt she was betraying her mother's memory seems far-fetched. See B. Travitsky and P. Cullen (eds), *The Early Modern Englishwoman, Series 1, Printed Writings, 1500–1640* (Ashgate, 2001), part 2, vol. 5, p. xii, 'Elizabeth and Mary Tudor'.

15 John Foxe, *Acts and Monuments*, ed. S. R. Cattley, 8 vols (London, 1886), vol. v, pp. 559–60.

Chapter 6 **The Defiant Sister**

1 6 February 1547, *Cal SP Spanish*, 9, p. 15.

2 E. W. Ives, 'Henry VIII's will – a forensic conundrum', *Historical Journal*, 35 (1992), pp. 779–804.

3 10 February 1547, *Cal SP Spanish*, 9, p. 20.

4 *BL Lansdowne MS, 1236*, f. 26.

5 In early July, Mary asserted to Van der Delft that 'she had never spoken to him [Seymour] in her life and had only seen him once'. *Cal SP Spanish*, 9, p. 123.

6 Gregorio Leti, *Historia o vera vita di Elisabetta* (Amsterdam, 1693), vol. 1, p. 180.

7 7 March 1547, *Cal SP Spanish*, 9, p. 47.

8 28 May 1549, ibid., 9, p. 381.

9 13 April (probably 1549), ibid., *Cal SP Spanish*, 9, p. 363 (check)

10 June 1549, ibid., 9, p. 384.

11 Paget's implication that the emperor lied was used as the occasion for his expulsion from the council in 1551. By that time Northumberland's regime was in bad odour with Charles V and Paget's demission was an indirect apology and a useful way of getting rid of a political opponent.

12 7 July 1549, *State Papers Domestic of Edward VI*, ed. C Knighton (London, 1992), pp. 121–2.

13 Quoted in D. Loades, *John Dudley, Duke of Northumberland* (London, 1996), p. 138.

14 9 October 1549, Knighton, *State Papers Domestic of Edward VI*, p. 146.

15 See Loades, *John Dudley*, p. 142.

16 14 January 1550, *Cal SP Spanish*, 10, p. 6.

17 29 August 1551, *Acts of the Privy Council*, ed. J. R. Dasent (London, 1890–1964), vol. 3, p. 351.

18 Although John Dudley is best remembered by the title of his dukedom, Northumber-

land, it was not awarded until October 1551, by which time his relations with Mary had eased.

19 Report of Jehan Dubois on the matter concerning the Lady Mary, drawn up in full and as nearly as possible in the actual words spoken, July 1550 (hereafter *Dubois' report*), *Cal SP Spanish*, 10, pp. 124–50.

20 Mary's comments reported by Van der Delft to the emperor, 2 May 1550, *Cal SP Spanish,* 10, pp. 80–81.

21 Van der Delft to the emperor, 2 May 1550, ibid., 10, p. 85.

22 28 June 1550, ibid., 10, p. 117.

23 *Dubois' report*, ibid., 10, p. 127.

24 26 August 1550, *Cal SP Foreign, Edward VI*, ed. W. Turnbull (London, 1861), p. 53.

25 3 August 1550, *Cal SP Spanish*, 10, pp. 148–9.

26 Scheyfve to the emperor, 3 August 1550, ibid., 10, p. 151.

27 Mary to the council, latter half of January 1552, ibid., 10, p. 206.

28 Ibid., 10, pp. 209–12.

29 Mary to Edward VI, late January/early February 1551, ibid., 10, pp. 212–13.

30 Scheyfve to Mary of Hungary, 1 March 1551, ibid., 10, p. 259.

31 Report of Lord Rich, 29 August, in Dasent, *Acts of the Privy Council*, vol. 2, pp. 348–52.

Chapter 7 **Mary Triumphant**

1 13 March 1553, *Cal SP Spanish*, 11, pp. 14–15.

2 28 April 1553, ibid., 11, p. 35.

3 7 May 1553, *BL Lansdowne MS*, 3, f. 23.

4 30 May 1553, *Cal SP Spanish*, 11, pp. 45–8.

5 For a full treatment of the origins of the *Devise*, see D. Loades, *Intrigue and Treason: The Tudor Court, 1547–1559* (Oxford, 2004).

6 HMC, *Report on the MSS of Lord Montagu of Beaulieu* (London, 1900), 4, quoted in Jennifer Loach, *Edward VI* (London, 1999), p. 164.

7 Letters Patent for the limitation of the Crown, quoted in the *Chronicle of Queen Jane and Two Years of Queen Mary* (hereafter Chronicle QJ&QM), ed. J. G. Nichols (Camden Society, 1850), pp. 91–100.

8 *Ambassades des Messieurs de Noailles en Angleterre,* ed. Vertot (Leyden, 1763), vol. ii, p. 49.

9 *Cal SP Spanish*, 11, pp. 60–65.

10 J. More Molyneux, 'Letters illustrating the reign of Queen Jane', *Archaeological Journal*, vol. xxx (1873), p. 276. Originals in the Loseley Correspondence, 3/3, in the Guildford Museum and Muniment Room.

11 *BL Cotton MS Galba Bxii*, f. 250.

12 The main contemporary source for Mary's East Anglian campaign is the *Vita Mariae Angliae Reginae* of Robert Wingfield of Grantham, ed. and transl. by D. MacCulloch, *Camden Miscellany*, 4th series, vol. 29 (1984), pp. 250–56.

13 7 July 1553, *Cal SP Spanish*, 11, p. 73.

14 10 July 1553, ibid., 11, p. 79.

15 11 July 1553, ibid., 11, p. 81.

16 *Vita Mariae Reginae*, p. 262.

17 *Chronicle QJ&QM*, pp. 6–7.

18 *Vita Mariae Reginae*, p. 264.

19 Oxburgh Hall: *Bedingfeld MS*, proclamation of 18 July 1553.

20 *Vita Mariae Reginae*, p. 265.

21 Advice from England, translated from the Italian, 20 July 1553, *Cal SP Spanish*, 11, p. 108.

22 The epistle of Poor Pratte, *Chronicle QJ&QM*, pp. 115–21.

23 More Molyneux, 'Letters illustrating', pp. 276–8.

24 See S. J. Gunn, 'A letter of Jane, duchess of Northumberland, in 1553', *English Historical Review*, CXIV (November 1999).

25 Her letter is reported by the imperial ambassadors, 22 July 1553, *Cal SP Spanish*, 11, p. 115.

26 6 August 1553, ibid., 11, p. 151.

27 22 July 1553, ibid., 11, pp. 109–11.

28 Dispatches in July 1553, *Ambassades des Messieurs de Noailles en Angleterre*, vol. ii, pp. 57–98.

29 Antonio de Guaras, *The Accession of Queen Mary*, ed. R. Garnett (1892), p. 102.

30 Wriothesley, *Chronicle*, 2, p. 100.

31 *BL Harley MS* 787, f. 61.

32 *Chronicle QJ&QM*, pp. 25–6.

33 Guaras, *The Accession of Queen Mary*, p. 109.

Chapter 8 **Mary's England**

1 In acts of 1536 and 1543. See Brigden, *New Worlds*, p. 169.

2 Ireland did not share in the recovery, its population remaining static.

3 John Strype, *Ecclesiastical Memorials* (Oxford, 1822), vol. 3i, p. 361.

4 In C.V. Malfatti (ed.), *The Accession, Coronation and Marriage of Mary Tudor* (Barcelona, 1956), p. 91.

5 *Cal SP Spanish*, 11, p. 215.

6 *Calendar of State Papers Domestic Mary I* (hereafter *SPD Mary I*), ed. C. S. Knighton (London, 1998), no. 597

7 The imperial ambassadors to Charles V, 9 September 1553, *Cal SP Spanish*, 11, p. 215.

8 *SPD Mary 1*, no. 21.

9 16 August 1553, *Cal SP Spanish*, 11, p. 172.

10 4 September 1553, ibid., 11, p. 201.

11 9 September 1553, ibid., 11, p. 125.

12 Proclamation of 28 July 1553, in *Tudor Royal Proclamations*, ed. P. L. Hughes and J. F. Larkin (1969), vol. 2, p. 4.

13 7 August 1553, *Cal SP Venetian*, 5, p. 764.

14 8 October 1553, ibid., 5, p. 425.

15 Quoted in Eamon Duffy and David Loades (eds), *The Church of Mary Tudor* (2006), p. 19.

16 *Cal SP Spanish*, 11, p. 169.

17 *Cal SP Foreign*, 1553–8, ed. W. Turnbull (1861), p. 4.

18 *Ambassades de Messieurs de Noailles en Angleterre*, vol. 3, dispatches of 29 and 31 July and 4 and 7 August 1553, pp. 96–106.

19 When the ambassadors presented letters from Charles V on 4 September 1553, Mary said she would need time to read them 'as she was not familiar with your Majesty's handwriting'. This may, however, have just been quick-wittedness on her part. She wanted to make sure there were no direct references to her having written personally to Charles without the knowledge of the privy council. *Cal SP Spanish*, 11, p. 200.

20 Report by Francisco Duarte to Prince Philip, 9 September 1553, ibid., 11, pp. 221–7.

21 16 August 1553, ibid., 11, p. 169.

22 Undated, late August 1553, ibid., 11, p. 196.

23 9 September 1553, ibid., 11, pp. 220–21.

24 Charles V to Renard, 23 August 1553, ibid., 11, p. 180.

25 *Cal SP Venetian*, 6ii, p. 1084.

26 *BL Cotton MS Titus A xxiv,* f. 83v.

27 19 October 1553, *Cal SP Spanish*, 11, p. 308.

28 20 August 1553, *SPD Mary I*, no. 12.

29 28 June 1554, ibid., no. 119.

30 J. R. Planché, *Regal Records, or a Chronicle of the Coronations of the Queens Regnant of England* (1838), p. 3. Waits were bands of musicians playing wind instruments; shawmes were an early type of clarinet.

31 Guaras, *The Accession of Queen Mary*, p. 118.

32 Holinshed's Chronicles of England, Scotland and Ireland, quoted in R. Tittler (ed.), *The Reign of Mary I* (1991), pp. 84–5. The caul referred to is a net cap used to keep the hair in place. There is disagreement about what Mary actually wore during the state entry. The account of French ambassador Noailles has her wearing a mantle and kirtle of cloth of gold, furred with miniver and powdered ermines. *See Regal Records*, p. 5.

33 The duchess of Norfolk herself died less than two weeks after Queen Mary, on 30 November 1558.

34 *Chronicle QJ&QM*, pp. 27–31.

35 Planché, *Regal Records*, p. 11.

36 30 September 1553, *Cal SP Spanish*, 11, pp. 259–60.

37 The last queen consort to be crowned, Anne Boleyn, had gone to the ceremony with loosened hair, but it seems unlikely that Mary would wish to have been connected with her mother's usurper by copying her.

38 Planché, *Regal Records*, p. 16.

39 Ibid., p. 17.

Chapter 9 **Wyatt's Rebellion**

1 2 and 7 August 1553, *Cal SP Spanish*, 11, pp. 132, 153.

2 8 September 1553, ibid., 11, p. 213.

3 7 August and 8 September 1553, ibid., 11, pp. 154, 212.

4 30 July 1553, ibid., 11, pp. 126–7.

5 22 August 1553, ibid., 11, pp. 177–8.

6 8 September and 10 October 1553, ibid., 11, pp. 213, 290.

7 29 December 1553, ibid., 11, p. 467.

8 13 September 1553, ibid., 11, pp. 230–31.

9 9 September 1553, ibid., 11, p. 228.

10 5 October 1553, ibid., 11, p. 266.

11 10 October 1553, ibid., 11, p. 284.

12 8 September 1553, ibid., 11, p. 213.

13 12 October 1553, ibid., 11, pp. 288–93.

14 28 October 1553, ibid., 11, p. 321.

15 31 October 1553, ibid., 11, p. 328.

16 17 November 1553, ibid., 11, pp. 363–5.

17 20 November 1553, ibid., 11, p. 372.

18 4 November 1553, ibid., 11, p. 335.

19 28 November 1553, ibid., 11 p. 393.

20 17 December 1553, ibid., 11, pp. 439–40.

21 Quoted in E. H. Harbison, *Rival Ambassadors at the Court of Queen Mary* (1940), p. 116.

22 Quoted in D. Loades, *Two Tudor Conspiracies* (1992), p. 115.

23 Draft of 7 December 1553, *Cal SPD Mary I*, pp. 13–14. It is unclear whether this was the precise text that Lord Chancellor Gardiner used when presenting the treaty at court on 14 January 1554.

24 Cited in Harbison, *Rival Ambassadors*, p. 119.

25 *Chronicle QJ&QM*, pp. 34–5.

26 *SPD Mary I*, no. 28.

27 26 January 1554, Hearne, *Sylloge Epistolarum*, pp. 154–5. It is not clear how Mary knew of the possibility that her sister might move to Donnington. Renard and his network of informers may have alerted her. Elizabeth, under interrogation in March, claimed that she did not even know she owned a house at Donnington. See Chapter 10.

28 Undated, January 1554, *Cal SP Spanish*, 12, p. 50.

29 29 January, *SPD Mary I*, no. 46.

30 Foxe, *Acts and Monuments*, vi, pp. 414–15.

31 *Chronicle QJ&QM*, p. 128.

32 Ibid., p. 133.

33 Gertrude Courtenay died less than two months before Mary in September 1558. She had been unwell over several years but it is not known whether her death was hastened by the influenza epidemic of 1558.

34 *Chronicle QJ&QM*, p. 59.

35 Quoted in Alison Plowden, *Lady Jane Grey* (Stroud, 2003), p. 145.

36 Ibid., p. 148.

37 Henry Grey, duke of Suffolk, Jane's father, was executed on 23 February. So far as is known, his wife made no plea for clemency, as she had done seven months earlier.

38 11 February 1554, *SPD Mary I*, no. 86.

39 *Chronicle QJ&QM*, pp. 69–70.

40 17 March 1554, in Leah S. Marcus et al. (eds), *Elizabeth I, Collected Works*, (Chicago, 2000).

Chapter 10 King Philip

1 29 November 1553, *Cal SP Spanish*, 11, pp. 398–9.

2 Document drawn up 'in the noble town of Valladolid' on 4 January 1554. Among the witnesses were the duke of Alba, master of Philip's household, and Ruy Gómez de Silva, his chamberlain. *Cal SP Spanish*, 12, pp. 4–5.

3 Ibid., 12, p. 6.

4 Ibid., 12, p. 8.

5 Ibid., 11, p. 367. The portrait of Philip, in armour, is now in the Prado Museum in Madrid.

6 19 February 1554, ibid., 12, p. 121.

7 Hearne, *Sylloge Epistolarum*, p. 156.

8 See D. Starkey, *Elizabeth* (London, 2001), pp. 143–4.

9 From 'Memoirs of Sir James Croft', *Retrospective Review*, series 2, vol. 1 (1827), pp. 474–9.

10 *Chronicle QJ&QM*, pp. 73–4.

11 'State Papers relating to the custody of the Princess Elizabeth at Woodstock, in 1554', ed. R. C. Manning, *Norfolk Archaeology*, 4 (1855), pp. 133–231.

12 The 1352 treason statute covered only female consorts of the monarch.

13 Act concerning the regal power (1554) in Stephenson and Marcham (eds), *Sources of English Constitutional History* (New York, 1937), p. 328.

14 Philip was advised to reduce the number of troops to 4,000 before he left.

15 Simon Renard and M. de Courrières to the emperor, 26 July 1554, *Cal SP Spanish*, 13, p. 1.

16 'John Elder's Letter describing the arrival and marriage of King Philip, his triumphal entry into London, the legation of Cardinal Pole, etc', *Chronicle QJ&QM*, p. 139.

17 It is difficult to understand this as anything other than Spanish prejudice. A contemporary portrait of Eleanor, sister of Charles V, shows her in furred sleeves much more voluminous than anything Mary ever wore.

18 29 July 1554, *Cal SP Spanish*, 13, p. 2.

19 Ibid., 13, p. 9.

20 Ibid., 13, p. 10.

21 *Chronicle QJ&QM*, p. 167.

22 Late 1558, *Cal SP Spanish*, 13, p. 442.

23 For further discussion of the significance of this and related matters of precedence in the marriage ceremony, see Alexander Samson, 'Changing Places: the marriage and royal entry of Philip, Prince of Austria and Mary Tudor', *Sixteenth Century Journal*, xxxvi(3) (2005).

24 *Chronicle QJ&QM*, p. 168.

25 I am indebted to Tanya Elliott for this description.

26 Lady Margaret Clifford was the daughter of the earl of Cumberland and his first wife, Eleanor Brandon, sister of Frances Brandon. She was herself married in February 1555 to Henry Strange, later the third earl of Derby, in a splendid ceremony in the Chapel Royal of Whitehall Palace. Mary seems to have been fond of this young relative, who had herself a claim to the throne.

27 *Chronicle QJ&QM*, p. 142.

28 Ibid., p. 170.

29 'An account of what has befallen in the realm of England since Prince Philip landed there ...', written by a Spanish gentleman, 17 August 1554, in *Cal SP Spanish*, 13, p. 31.

30 2 August 1554, *Cal SP Spanish*, 13, p. 13.

31 15 August 1554, ibid., 13, p. 28.

32 12 August 1554, ibid., 13, p. 26.

33 November 1554, ibid., 13, p. 95.

34 23 August 1554, ibid., 13, p. 35.

35 24 September, ibid., 13, p. 53.

36 Report to the bishop of Arras, 25 November, *Cal SP Spanish*, 13, p. 105.

37 Quoted in *DNB*.

38 30 November 1554, *Cal SP Spanish*, 13, pp. 108–9.

39 Various dispatches, ibid., 13, pp. 51–60.

40 In *Idem Iterum, or The History of Queen Mary's big belly, from Mr Foxe's Acts and Monuments and Dr Heylin's History of the Reformation* (1688), p. 1.

41 Ibid., pp. 3–4.

42 27 March 1555, *Cal SP Spanish*, 13, p. 148.

43 Letter of Philip to Maximilian of Austria, 25 April 1554, quoted in H. Kamen, *Philip of Spain* (1998), p. 62.

44 Ruy Gomez to Eraso, 22 May 1555, *Cal SP Spanish*, 13, p. 176.

45 Mary's views as reported by Cardinal Pole, *Cal SP Spanish*, 13, p. 230.

46 Muriel St Clare Byrne (ed.), *The Lisle Letters* (1983), p. 310.

47 Quoted in J. M. Stone, *Mary I, Queen of England* (1901), p. 351.

48 *Cal SP Spanish*, 13, p. 240.

49 Manning, 'State Papers', pp. 182–3.

50 Quoted in Stone, *Mary I*, p. 349.

51 Michieli's report to the Doge, 3 September, quoted in Paul Friedmann (ed.), *Les Dépêches de G. Michiel, Ambassadeur de Venise en Angleterre pendant les années de 1554 á 1557* (Paris, 1864), pp. 114–15.

Chapter 11 **Mary Alone**

1 Undated, July or August 1555, *Cal SP Spanish*, 13, pp. 238–9.

2 Quoted in Kamen, *Philip of Spain*, p. 63.

3 August 1555, *Cal SP Spanish*, 13, p. 249.

4 5 September 1555, *Ambassades de MM de Noailles*, vol. 5, pp. 126–7.

5 Undated, August or September 1555, *Cal SP Spanish*, 13, p. 247.

6 *BL Sloane MS* 1583.

7 Direction of Queen Mary to her council touching the reforming of the Church to the Roman religion, *BL Harley MS 444*, ff. 27–8, in Tittler, *The Reign of Mary I*, pp. 87–8.

8 Foxe's *Book of Martyrs* (Belfast, 1995), p. 220.

9 S. Haynes (ed.), *A collection of state papers relating to the affairs in the reigns of Henry VIII, Edward VI, Queen Mary and Queen Elizabeth from 1542, left by William Cecil, Lord Burghley* (London, 1740), p. 187.

10 Undated letter, 1553, in J. E. Cox (ed.), *The Works of Thomas Cranmer* (Cambridge, 1846), vol. 2, pp. 442–4.

11 Letters written in 1555, ibid., vol. 2, pp. 447 and 454.

12 Foxe's *Book of Martyrs*, p. 307.

13 Quoted in Diarmaid MacCulloch, *Thomas Cranmer* (London, 1996), p. 583.

14 Ibid., p. 603.

15 Eamon Duffy, *The Stripping of the Altars*, 2nd edn (London, 2002), p. 560.

16 Quoted in Kamen, *Philip II*, p. 62. De Castro's views were not shared by Bartolome Carranza, who had been sent to England to re-establish the Dominican order there. See John Edwards, 'Spanish religious influence in Marian England', in E. Duffy and D. Loades (eds), *The Church of Mary Tudor* (Aldershot, 2006), p. 208.

17 John Ponet (later bishop of Rochester), *A Short Treatise of politicke power and of the true obedience which subjects owe to Kings and other civill Governours* (1556, reprinted 1639).

18 Instructions of 24 May 1555 to Bishop Bonner of London, quoted in Prescott, *Mary Tudor*, p. 304.

19 Quoted in P. Collinson, 'The Persecutions in Kent', in Duffy and Loades, *The Church of Mary Tudor*, p. 322.

20 *The Diary of Henry Machyn, citizen and Merchant-Taylor of London, from A.D. 1550 to A.D. 1563*, ed. John Gough Nichols, Camden Society (London, 1848), quoted in Gary C. Gibbs, 'Marking the Days, Henry Machyn's Manuscript and the mid-Tudor Era', in Duffy and Loades, *The Church of Mary Tudor*, p. 305.

21 Ibid., p. 304.

22 *Queen Mary's Manual* is owned by Westminster Cathedral and is now kept in the library of Westminster Abbey.

23 Edmund Bonner, *An honest godlye instruction and information for the tradynge and bringinge up of Children, set forth by the bishop of London*, printed by Robert Caly (London, 1555).

24 Quoted in Duffy, *The Stripping of the Altars*, p. 530.

25 February 1558, printed by Robert Caly.

26 The injunctions of Archdeacon Nicholas Harpsfield on the condition of parish churches, 1557, in Tittler, *The Reign of Mary I*, pp. 90–91.

27 Albert Feuillerat (ed.), *Documents relating to the revels at court in the time of King Edward VI and Queen Mary* (Louvain, 1914), p. 159.

28 Chancellor's account of Russia is in Richard Hakluyt, *The Principal Navigations, Voyages, Traffics and Discoveries of the English nation made by sea or overland* (1598), vol. 1, pp. 238–53.

29 Quoted in T. S. Willan, *The Muscovy Merchants of 1555* (Manchester, 1953), p. 9.

30 The Queen Mary Atlas, with a useful commentary by Peter Barber, can be seen in the Map Room of the British Library. One hundred copies of it were printed by the Folio Society in 2005.

31 Incorporation of the borough of High Wycombe, also known as Chipping Wycombe, by the Crown, 17 August 1558, in Tittler, *The Reign of Mary I*, pp. 94–6.

32 *SPD Mary I*, no. 234.

Chapter 12 Triumph and Disaster

1 Undated, possibly May 1556, *Cal SP Spanish*, 13, p. 267.

2 10 September 1556, ibid., 13, p. 276.

3 *SPD Mary I*, p. 334, quoted in *DNB* entry for Henry (Dudley) Sutton.

4 Quoted in Starkey, *Elizabeth*, p. 196.

5 Attributed to Ashton by Henry Peckham, under interrogation. Quoted in Loades, *Two Tudor Conspiracies*, p. 213.

6 'As a roaring lion goes about, seeking whom he may devour'. This is a quotation from 1 Peter 5:8 in the Vulgate, the Catholic version of the Bible. See the footnote to this letter in Marcus et al., *Elizabeth I, Collected Works*, p. 43.

7 2 August 1556, Marcus et al., *Elizabeth I, Collected Works*, pp. 43–4.

8 For the complete 1557 New Year's Gift List, see D. Loades, *Mary Tudor* (Oxford, 1989), pp. 358–69.

9 Quoted in Tom Glasgow Jr, 'The Navy in Philip and Mary's War, 1557–1558', *Mariner's Mirror*, vol. 53(4) (November, 1967), p. 322.

10 Quoted by C. S. L. Davies, 'England and the French War', in J. Loach and R. Tittler (eds), *The mid-Tudor Polity, c. 1540–1560* (London, 1983).

11 *Cal SP Venetian*, 6ii, p. 1240.

12 See Carter, 'Mary Tudor's Wardrobe'.

13 Intercepted dispatch in the Bibliothèque Nationale, Paris, BN fr. 23191, quoted in David Potter, 'The duc de Guise and the Fall of Calais, 1557–1558', *English Historical Review*, 98 (July 1983), pp. 481–512.

14 2 January 1558 at 10 p.m., in Edward Arber (ed.), *An English Garner* (Birmingham, 1882), vol. iv, p. 193. The marshes had been partially flooded, but not sufficiently to give major problems to the French.

15 2 February 1558, *Cal SP Spanish*, 13, p. 351.

16 10 January 1558, ibid., 6iii, p. 1421.

17 31 January 1558, ibid., 13, p. 348.

18 21 January 1558, ibid., 13, pp. 340–41.

19 10 March 1558, ibid., 13, pp. 366–8.

20 The will is quoted in full as Appendix 3 to Loades, *Mary Tudor*, pp. 370–80.

21 BL MS Cotton Titus, B.2, f. 109. Quoted in Prescott, *Mary Tudor*, pp. 377–8. The original is a draft in French, with alterations, in Mary's own hand.

22 Pope's report from Hatfield of 26 April 1558, in *SPD Mary I*, no. 753.

23 The 18th-century writer, Thomas Warton, relied on papers that proved to be forgeries.

24 Wriothesley, *Chronicle*, 2, p. 139.

25 For a general discussion of the chronology of 16th-century epidemics, see Paul Slack, *The Impact of Plague in Tudor and Stuart England* (Oxford, 1985), pp. 53–78.

26 6 October 1558, *CSP Foreign*, 1553–8, no. 834.

27 Quoted in Charles Creighton, *A History of Epidemics in Britain*, 2nd edn (1965), vol. 1, p. 404.

28 John A. H. Wylie and Leslie H. Collier, 'The English sweating sickness (Sudor Anglicus): A re-appraisal', *Journal of the History of Medicine*, vol. 36 (1981), pp. 425–45.

29 Henry Clifford, *Life of Jane Dormer, Duchess of Feria*, ed. J. Stevenson (London, 1887), p. 69.

30 The poetic tribute of Juan de Vega, president of the Council of Castile, quoted in the *Autobiography of Charles V*, ed. Kervyn de Lettenhove (London, 1862), p. xxxi. In fact, Charles never lost his interest in politics and had, earlier in the year, urged his daughter Juana to act decisively against the spread of heresy in Spain.

31 Loades, *Mary Tudor*, pp. 380–83.

32 Starkey, *Elizabeth*, p. 228.

33 'The Count of Faria's despatch to Philip II of 14 November 1558', ed. and trans. M. J. Rodriguez-Salgado and Simon Adams, *Camden Miscellany*, 4th series, vol. 29, pp. 300–44.

34 'Memorandum of the jewels that lie in a coffer at Whitehall', late 1558(?), *Cal SP Spanish*, 13, pp. 441–2.

35 Strype, *Ecclesiastical Memorials*, vol. 3, pt ii, p. 142.

36 Ibid., vol. 3, pt ii, p. 548.

37 Harleian Miscellany, X (London, 1813), pp. 259–60.

Epilogue

1 Quoted in *DNB* entry for Winchester, 2004.

2 Haynes, *A collection of state papers*, pp. 208–9.

3 The exact state of Mary's health in 1558 before she fell fatally ill is not easy to discern. Certainly she was still conducting affairs of state during Feria's visits in February and June. She had been bled so much over the years that she was almost certainly suffering from anaemia.

Index